Fourth Edition

Classroom Strategies for Interactive Learning

Doug Buehl

INTERNATIONAL
Reading Association
800 BARKSDALE ROAD, PO BOX 8139
NEWARK, DE 19714-8139, USA
www.reading.org

The International Reading Association attempts, through its publications, to provide a forum for a wide spectrum of opinions on reading. This policy permits divergent viewpoints without implying the endorsement of the Association.

Executive Editor, Publications   Shannon Fortner

Acquisitions Manager   Tori Mello Bachman

Managing Editors   Susanne Viscarra and Christina M. Lambert

Editorial Associate   Wendy Logan

Creative Services/Production Manager   Anette Schuetz

Design and Composition Associate   Lisa Kochel

Cover   Lise Holliker Dykes and Shutterstock

The publisher would appreciate notification where errors occur so that they may be corrected in subsequent printings and/or editions.

Library of Congress Cataloging-in-Publication Data

Buehl, Doug.
   Classroom strategies for interactive learning / Doug Buehl. — Fourth edition.
      pages   cm
   Includes bibliographical references.
   ISBN 978-0-87207-002-8 (alk. paper)
1. Reading comprehension. 2. Content area reading. 3. Active learning. I. Title.
   LB1050.45.B84   2013
   371.3—dc23
                         2013029920

Suggested APA Reference
Buehl, D. (2014). *Classroom strategies for interactive learning* (4th ed.). Newark, DE: International Reading Association.

This edition is dedicated to Doug Vance—the other Doug—a long-time colleague, collaborator, and mentor. Thanks for setting me off on this exciting journey as a literacy educator. Ahh, we were quite a team.

Contents

About the Author

Doug Buehl is a teacher, professional development leader, and adolescent literacy consultant. During his 33 years in the Madison Metropolitan School District in Madison, Wisconsin, USA, Doug was a social studies teacher, reading teacher, and reading specialist at Madison East High School and a district literacy support teacher for 12 middle schools and four high schools. In addition to presenting literacy workshops, his experiences include collaborating with teachers as a school literacy coach, teaching struggling readers, coordinating a schoolwide content area tutoring program, teaching college-preparatory advanced reading, and teaching night school students returning for their high school diplomas.

Doug is the author of *Developing Readers in the Academic Disciplines* (International Reading Association [IRA], 2011). In recent years, he coauthored the second edition of *Reading and the High School Student: Strategies to Enhance Literacy* (Pearson, 2007) and the third edition of *Strategies to Enhance Literacy and Learning in Middle School Content Area Classrooms* (Pearson, 2007). He was the first editor of the adolescent literacy newsletter *The Exchange,* published by the IRA Secondary Reading Interest Group.

Doug has been an active literacy professional at the local, state, and national levels. He was a founding member of IRA's Commission on Adolescent Literacy and was a member of the interdisciplinary task force that drafted the national *Standards for Middle and High School Literacy Coaches* (2006), a joint collaboration between IRA, the National Council of Teachers of English, the National Council of Teachers of Mathematics, the National Science Teachers Association, and the National Council for the Social Studies. He served terms as president of the Wisconsin State Reading Association, the IRA Secondary Reading Interest Group, and the Madison Area Reading Council. Doug was the 1996 recipient of IRA's Nila Banton Smith Award and was inducted into the Wisconsin State Reading Association's Friends of Literacy Hall of Fame in 2000. Doug also served as cochair of the Wisconsin Department of Public Instruction Adolescent Literacy Task Force, which issued its policy recommendations in 2008.

Doug is currently an educational consultant and works with school districts to provide professional development for teachers. He is an instructor of undergraduate- and graduate-level courses in adolescent literacy at Edgewood College in Madison and is the parent of two sons: Jeremy, a social studies teacher at Madison East High School, and Christopher, a biochemist currently pursuing a doctorate in cell and molecular biology at Michigan State University. Doug lives in Madison with his wife, Wendy, a professional violinist and former middle and high school orchestra teacher. Their 2-year-old grandson, Thomas, relishes a read-aloud from a good book.

Doug can be contacted at drbuehl@sbcglobal.net.

Preface

The first edition of *Classroom Strategies for Interactive Learning* (Buehl, 1995), published as a teacher resource by the Wisconsin State Reading Association, was an outgrowth of an ongoing collaboration with the Wisconsin Education Association Council. From 1990 through 2008, I served as the author of the strategies column "The Reading Room" in the council's monthly publication, *WEAC News & Views*, which was circulated to all Wisconsin public school teachers. This fourth edition continues to adapt and rework many of those strategies, which were culled from a variety of sources, including professional journals, books, and teacher variations. Newer strategies have also been folded into the mix. The book is not intended to be an exhaustive compendium of classroom strategies but aims to streamline strategy presentation so teachers can readily discern benefits to their students and implement these ideas in their instruction. Teachers who want a more in-depth treatment of a strategy can consult the resources listed at the end of each strategy description.

This fourth edition, unsurprisingly, has been notably influenced by the adoption of the Common Core State Standards by most of the states. It is now not enough to describe an effective classroom strategy and detail how the strategy develops the capacity for literacy growth; we also need to relate very specifically how the strategy can help students meet these new rigorous literacy expectations. So, a major change from previous editions is the examination of how each classroom strategy intersects with the literacy development mandated by the Common Core.

As a result, Chapter 1 has been reconceptualized in a number of respects, in particular to explore how the Common Core's literacy standards relate to the rich research on embedding comprehension instruction into the teaching of content as well as how instructional practices like these strategies can nurture increasingly independent and proficient readers and learners.

Chapter 2 continues to examine what some observers have referred to as the ultimate scaffold: background knowledge. We know that strategy instruction falls flat when students lack the requisite knowledge that enables them to comprehend complex texts and to build new knowledge. It is quite intentional that so many of the strategies outlined in this book emphasize prior knowledge variables as key to effective application.

Chapter 3 introduces a major theme of this book: reading as an act of inquiry. Mentoring students on how to question a text is central to the rhythms of working a complex text to gain understanding. The chapter explains text frames and how questioning naturally follows author choices for organizing a text. In addition, it stresses teaching toward essential questions and choosing tasks that help students prioritize how to engage in a wealth of information and detail.

Chapter 4 represents exciting new territory, the burgeoning scholarship on disciplinary literacy, which also receives unprecedented emphasis in the Common Core's literacy standards. The chapter discusses reading and thinking through a disciplinary lens and the need to take a malleable approach to classroom strategies. In other words, the demands of the discipline trump any specific literacy practice. Disciplinary literacy examines the specific and sometimes unique use of language in communicating and organizing disciplinary knowledge. Chapter 4 presents a host of disciplinary-specific questioning taxonomies to be employed by students engaged in working complex texts as learners of an academic discipline. A more comprehensive consideration of disciplinary literacy can be accessed through a companion resource to this book, *Developing Readers in the Academic Disciplines* (Buehl, 2011), also published by the International Reading Association.

Section 2 comprises the heart of the book: 43 updated classroom strategies, many with variations included. As with the previous editions, each strategy features a Strategy Index that identifies the instructional focus of each strategy, pinpoints the text frames in play as students read and learn, and correlates the comprehension processes that students engage in during the phases of the strategy's implementation. In addition, each strategy is cross-referenced with the Common Core's reading, writing, speaking and listening, and language standards.

As always, it has been invigorating to continue to investigate effective ways to mentor our students as they aspire to rigorous classroom learning demands. In turn, I invite you to test-drive these literacy practices with your students. Enjoy!

Acknowledgments

A number of individuals deserve recognition for their roles in this publication. I have relished many collegial relationships with my fellow teachers during my 33 years as a reading specialist and teacher in Madison. I would like to especially thank Pat Delmore, a former social studies teacher, middle school principal, and current professor of education at Edgewood College in Madison, for his insightful comments on the manuscript. Rebecca Griffin, a literacy coach at Sun Prairie High School in Sun Prairie, Wisconsin, also provided me with helpful feedback. In addition, my professional development interactions with countless middle and high school teachers, especially throughout Wisconsin, have greatly informed my work and helped me fine-tune ideas for and continually explore exciting variations on these strategies. Both my undergraduate and graduate students in my adolescent literacy courses at Edgewood College have been valuable sounding boards for many of these strategies.

I would especially like to acknowledge the contributions of my son Jeremy, a social studies teacher at Madison East High School. His deep commitment to the literacy development of his students and his enthusiasm for implementing literacy practices into his curriculum has been a defining professional trait, and I greatly appreciate his astute observations and perceptive analyses of the rhythms and challenges of teaching in our 21st-century world. Jeremy has become my go-to voice for classroom implications of this work.

My wife, Wendy, as has been true for everything I have written, was willing once more to use her vigilant eye for ferreting out meandering prose as a reviewer of the manuscript. Over my years as an educator, I have constantly relied on Wendy, a former middle and high school orchestra teacher, as a shrewd and trusted observer, to brainstorm ideas and vet possible classroom practices. I have long admired her thoughtful instructional touches with her students and her imaginative ways of reinforcing literacy practices in her music performance classroom.

In our home, spirited discussions about pedagogy seem to unfold naturally and inevitably. As a family of teachers—Jeremy's wife, Mandi, is a high school chemistry teacher—we seem wired to talk about the ways and means of instructing children. Even my son Christopher, immersed in his doctoral work in cell and molecular biology at Michigan State University, has been able to chime in after a stint as a teaching assistant of science undergraduates. In addition, he has been invaluable in mentoring me on the literacy practices that are inherent in his work as a scientist. His explanations have been especially influential in the development of the science self-questioning taxonomies that appear in Chapter 4.

Finally, I owe a special debt of gratitude to the over three decades of students I was privileged to work with at Madison East High School. We learned together.

References

Buehl, D. (1995). *Classroom strategies for interactive learning*. Madison: Wisconsin State Reading Association.

Buehl, D. (2011). *Developing readers in the academic disciplines*. Newark, DE: International Reading Association.

Developing Strategic Readers and Learners

CHAPTER 1

Fostering Comprehension of Complex Texts

Picture yourself as a reader. Perhaps you see yourself relaxing in the evening, burrowed into a comfortable chair, relishing a good book. Or sipping your morning coffee and perusing the daily newspaper as you tune in to the outside world before you head to work. Or poised in front of a computer screen as you navigate your way through a progression of enticing websites, quickly inventorying content as you track down a needed snippet of information. It is easy to visualize yourself in a multitude of settings, interacting with a wide spectrum of texts, engaged in the act we call "reading."

Of course, we see people reading all the time, and it is easy to describe the overt indicators of reading—eyes focusing, pages turning, digital texts scrolling—but how would you describe the mental behaviors of reading? What happens in the mind of a reader, the part we cannot see? Pause for a moment and try to put it into words. How would you describe the action "to read"?

Now consider the following "reads":

- The police officer quickly *reads* the situation and decides on an appropriate response.
- The park ranger is always careful to *read* the skies when escorting hikers into the mountains.
- The coach *reads* the opponents' defense and immediately adjusts the next play.
- The child tries to *read* his mother's reaction to see if he will be permitted to play with his friends.

How well did your definition coincide with these "reads"? Very likely, you conceptualized reading as an activity that focuses on the ability to identify written words, recognize their meanings, and comprehend an author's message. Yet, if we consider *read* in its broader meaning, we realize that reading is a process that involves strategic examination of some array of information to achieve an understanding. We read to make sense of what we are observing. Making sense—of human interactions, of weather patterns, of a competitor's moves, of facial expressions, and of course, of written language—is the purpose of reading.

Students in 21st-century classrooms are expected to read from an impressive array of written texts on a daily basis. It is sometimes easy for students, and their teachers, to lose sight of why they read. Students do not read to complete assignments, they do not read to be prepared for tests, and they do not read to meet standards. They read to understand.

Meeting the Challenges of the Common Core State Standards

Of course, as teachers these days, we are buzzing with the implications of the Common Core State Standards (National Governors Association Center for Best Practices & Council of Chief State School Officers [NGACBP & CCSSO], 2010a). The literacy standards (*Common Core Standards for English Language Arts and Literacy in History/Social Studies, Science, and Technical Subjects*) have been adopted by 46 states and are predicated on the compelling evidence that reading comprehension is fundamental to learning in all the subjects we teach. Students are now expected to grow their capacities as readers, writers, and users of language as an integral component of their learning in all curricular disciplines. Unquestionably, the Common Core's literacy standards are rigorous, ambitious, and not endorsements of the status quo. Several significant shifts in expectations for our students are directly relevant to the focus in this book:

- Students will be expected to read and comprehend texts of much greater complexity.
- Students will be expected to read a higher volume of informational (expository) texts.
- Students will be expected to perceive, analyze, and develop argumentation as readers, writers, speakers, listeners, and viewers.
- Students will be expected to considerably expand their academic vocabularies.
- Students will be expected to regularly communicate their understandings as readers and learners through writing.

In examining these shifts, Fisher, Frey, and Alfaro (2013) eloquently summarized the vision of the Common Core literacy standards:

> They contain a promise—a promise that students will be adequately prepared for life after school, whether that be college or a career. But that promise requires the active involvement of every teacher. Each of us

must take to heart the role language plays in learning. We have to ensure that students have the opportunity to read, write, speak, listen, and view in every class, every day. We have to develop the best possible lessons, based on content standards for our disciplines and the Common Core State Standards for Literacy. We have to ensure that students actually learn the amazing information that schools offer. (p. xiv)

The Common Core outlines 32 literacy standards—subdivided into four strands: reading, writing, speaking and listening, and language—that are conceptualized as an integrated model of literacy. As a result, the standards are intertwined, envisioning classroom literacy experiences where students regularly engage as readers, refine their understandings as collaborators, explore their thinking through discussion and writing, integrate their insights from reading with knowledge gained from other media and interactions, and communicate their learning as writers. Although the 10 reading anchor standards are the central focus for this book, the classroom strategies highlighted in Section 2 adhere to this integrated model, and each strategy addresses multiple reading, writing, speaking and listening, and language standards. (See Table 18 in the introduction to Section 2.)

Due to the Common Core, our conversations as teachers are more likely these days to be sprinkled with references to *close reading, complex text, text-based evidence,* and *disciplinary literacy.* Each of these key terms is explored in more depth in sections of this book, but let's start with reading comprehension. How can we explain the dynamics of what happens in a reader's mind when comprehension becomes the result?

Reading Comprehension: What Do Proficient Readers Do?

Imagine the following episode in your life as a reader: You are spending enjoyable minutes immersed in a national news magazine. As you page through it, you quickly size up articles and make instant decisions about whether to continue on or linger awhile and read. Your eye catches a headline cautioning that killing germs could actually be hazardous to your health. You are intrigued and wonder, Aren't germs harmful? Isn't that why we need antibiotics? Before you realize it, you have launched into reading this article.

The authors refer to microbes, and you briefly ponder what you remember about these microscopic creatures. Bacteria, you think, and maybe viruses. You remember that your body harbors "good" bacteria, so you theorize that the authors might focus on killing the wrong germs. You also recall warnings about doctors overprescribing antibiotics. As you read on, some of your questions are answered, and new ones surface. The authors emphasize that attacks on microbes impel

them to mutate into stronger and deadlier forms. You revise your definition of *microbes* to include fungi and protozoa.

Some paragraphs are stuffed with unfamiliar scientific terminology, and these you rapidly glance over to extract the gist of the message: Serious microbe-causing ailments are on the rise. You are particularly struck by the vivid descriptions of the human body as a colony consisting of tens of trillions of microbes, which help define us as well as facilitate our abilities to function as living organisms. (I should start referring to myself as "we" rather than "I," you whimsically muse.) Images are constantly triggered by the text: bacteria in the teeth, salmonella in the digestive tract, friendly microbes inhabiting our skin.

As you finish the article, you still have questions: How dangerous might some microbes become? What will it take for people to adopt more commonsense practices with their "coinhabitants"? How should I change my behavior? As you pause for a few moments, you realize that your understanding of germs has significantly changed because you now have an image of yourself as a "considerate host" who needs these fellow travelers as much as they need you.

The description in the preceding scenario illustrates a reader thoughtfully engaged with a written text. This scenario parallels what proficient readers do as a matter of habit. Research reveals that proficient readers employ a host of comprehension processes as they read and learn. These comprehension processes provide the bedrock for learning in our classrooms, from the early grades through high school and college.

Comprehension Processes of Proficient Readers

Proficient reading abilities are integral to the literacy challenges and choices we make as adults each day of our lives. Likewise, proficient reading abilities are integral for learning. For students to achieve success in learning in social studies and science, literature and mathematics, in fact, in all curricular disciplines, they need to develop strategic comprehension processes. In their seminal work on comprehension instruction, Keene and Zimmermann (2007) frame the rich vein of research on proficient readers around seven characteristic modes of thinking that are in constant interplay when an individual is engaged in understanding (see Table 1). As you examine these essential components of comprehension, notice how each was integral to the dynamics of reading described in our "germs" example.

Making Connections to Prior Knowledge

Researchers argue that prior knowledge—what a person already knows—may be the most important

Table 1
Comprehension Processes of Proficient Readers

Comprehension Process	Description
Make connections to prior knowledge	Reading comprehension results when readers can match what they already know (their schema) with new information and ideas in a text. Proficient readers activate prior knowledge before, during, and after reading, and they constantly evaluate how a text enhances or alters their previous understandings.
Generate questions	Comprehension is, to a significant degree, a process of inquiry. Proficient readers pose questions to themselves as they read. Asking questions is the art of carrying on an inner conversation with an author, as well as an internal dialogue within one's self.
Visualize and create sensory mental images	Comprehension involves breathing life experiences into the abstract language of written texts. Proficient readers use visual, auditory, and other sensory connections to create mental images of an author's message.
Make inferences	Much of what is to be understood in a text must be inferred. Authors rely on readers to contribute to a text's meaning by linking their background knowledge to information in the text. In addition to acknowledging explicitly stated messages, proficient readers read between the lines to discern implicit meanings, make predictions, and read with a critical eye.
Determine importance	Our memories quickly overload unless we can pare down a text to its essential ideas. Texts contain key ideas and concepts amidst much background detail. Proficient readers strive to differentiate key ideas, themes, and information from details so that they are not overwhelmed by facts.
Synthesize	Proficient readers glean the essence of a text (determine importance) and organize these ideas into coherent summaries of meaning. Effective comprehension leads to new learning and the development of new schema (background knowledge). Proficient readers make evaluations, construct generalizations, and draw conclusions from a text.
Monitor reading and apply fix-up strategies	Proficient readers watch themselves as they read and expect to make adjustments in their strategies to ensure that they are able to achieve a satisfactory understanding of a text.

Note. From "A Professional Development Framework for Embedding Comprehension Instruction Into Content Classrooms" (p. 200), by D. Buehl, in *Adolescent Literacy Instruction: Policies and Promising Practices*, edited by J. Lewis and G. Moorman, 2007, Newark, DE: International Reading Association. Copyright © 2007 by the International Reading Association.

variable for reading comprehension. A mental search for meaningful connections activates previous learning and taps into past experiences, enabling a reader to understand new information and establish interest, motivation, and purpose for reading a specific text. Proficient readers constantly size up how their background knowledge might be mined to make sense of what an author is saying. Instructional practices that help students bridge their existing knowledge about a topic with the knowledge demands presented by an author, especially before they start to read, can support effective reading of even confusing or challenging material.

Generating Questions

The minds of proficient readers are literally teeming with questions. When readers wonder about something in a text—wonder why, wonder if, wonder whether, wonder what, wonder how—they are surfacing questions that direct their thinking through a text. They also use self-questioning to check their progress: Did this make sense? Do I need to clarify anything in this passage? Did I satisfactorily figure out a probable meaning of this unfamiliar term? Self-questioning, of course, is very different from answering questions prepared by someone else. Rather than relying on others to do the intellectual work of questioning a text, proficient readers raise their own questions, personally interacting with new ideas and using questions to make sense of what they are encountering. Instructional practices that elicit self-questioning are critical for sparking a highly active mind-set during reading and learning.

Creating Mental Images

Visualizing involves linking cues from the author's words with personal experiences as readers mentally craft their own versions of scenes, events, and objects. When readers are deeply engaged in imagining what a text is describing, it is as if the words disappear and instead a personal DVD is playing in their heads. Visualizing is quite idiosyncratic because no two individuals bring exactly the same set of experiences to draw on when language triggers sensory responses. Students who become bogged down in the words on the page may struggle to visualize and, as a result, have trouble "seeing" what is being portrayed by an author. Instructional practices that stimulate students' imaginations help them picture in their mind's eye what an author represents in written language.

Making Inferences

Facility with inferential thinking develops from an awareness that authors expect readers to fill in the gaps between what they are able to put into writing and what readers themselves should bring to a text. In addition, inferences are necessary to flesh out the beliefs, attitudes, and perspectives that influence an author's message. Predicting—encouraging readers to take stock of what they have read so far to think ahead and anticipate what an author might say—is a particularly critical inferential reading behavior. Instructional practices that assist students in identifying and analyzing implicit meanings in a text enable them to merge clues from an author with their prior knowledge to construct a more complete understanding of a text.

> *"Given knowledge about what good readers do when they read, researchers and educators have addressed the following question: Can we teach students to engage in these productive behaviors? The answer is a resounding yes." (Duke & Pearson, 2002, p. 206)*

Determining Importance

Comprehension depends on readers' making reflective decisions as to what is worthy of remembering over time. Proficient readers continually evaluate what to take away from their reading—the "need to know" comprehension residue that should remain after details have slipped away. They actively sort key ideas and concepts from background information, focusing on, What is the point of this? or Why is the author telling me this? Students who are not adept at getting the point of a text instead find themselves lost in a maze of factual details. Instructional practices that help students perceive the structure of a text—the relationships between ideas and information—are a prerequisite for determining importance.

Synthesizing

Synthesizing is the culmination of comprehension; to synthesize, learners must connect to their knowledge, raise questions, create mental images, make inferences, and determine importance. Synthesis represents those "Aha! I get it!" moments, when readers develop personal interpretations of an author's message and establish their take on a text's meaning. Because of the transcendent nature of synthesizing, most students find summarizing to be a difficult process. Instructional practices that engage students in summarizing what they read into personal understandings are absolutely necessary if learners are to reduce a mass of material into a manageable distillation: an explanation, a generalization, an interpretation, or a conclusion.

Monitoring Reading and Applying Fix-Up Strategies

When proficient readers encounter breakdowns in their comprehension—difficult vocabulary, unfamiliar references, confusing explanations—they hit the "pause button" to regroup. They decide whether to adjust their reading, to reread, or to use additional strategies to make sense of an unclear passage. Proficient readers do not say, "I read it, but I didn't understand it." They know that reading *means* you understood it. The classroom strategies detailed in Section 2 all model literacy practices for successfully reading challenging texts so students become comfortable with problem-solving options for working a text to achieve understanding.

Constructing Meaning From Complex Texts

An impressive depth of research underscores that readers engage in a fluid orchestration of these strategic comprehension processes to construct meaning from a text. As Duke, Pearson, Strachan, and Billman (2011) explained:

> When we read, we use our knowledge along with our perceptions of what we think the text says to literally build, or construct, mental representations of what the text means. Once those representations are constructed, we can merge, or integrate, the information in those models with the knowledge stored in our minds. When we achieve that integration, we call it learning; we literally know more than we did before the reading. (p. 53)

Comprehension is achieved when readers actively create meaning; they do not passively receive it by merely identifying the words on the page. And no two people will have exactly the same comprehension of a text because no two people will be reading a text under exactly the same conditions. According to the

RAND Reading Study Group (2002), the interactions among the following four conditions determine what meaning a reader will construct from a text:

1. What the reader brings to the reading situation
2. The characteristics of the written text
3. The activity that defines the task and purpose of the reader
4. The context within which the reading occurs

The Reader

Teachers know that every student brings certain skills as a reader to the classroom. Too often, we might attribute comprehension breakdowns to skill deficits: word identification (e.g., "This student does not apply phonics skills."), fluency (e.g., "This student is a slow, labored, or word-by-word reader."), or reading technique (e.g., "This student lacks study skills."). Although each of these is certainly a facet of what it means to be a reader, it is too simplistic to focus solely on whether students have developed specific reading skills. Because comprehension relies on a mental construction that assimilates what is on the page with what is already known, the background knowledge and experiences of the reader are primary determinants of how a text will be understood. The more students already know about a topic, the better they will be able to comprehend texts about that topic. If their background knowledge includes much of the content vocabulary that appears, for instance, in a passage on medieval cathedrals or in an article on creatures that live in arid regions, then comprehension is enhanced correspondingly. Additionally, students may have developed the facility to read materials typical of some academic disciplines but may struggle with texts in other subject areas. Finally, comprehension is influenced greatly by personal reasons for reading a particular text and the willingness or motivation to do so.

The Text

What are students expected to read in our classrooms? A textbook, a short story, a magazine article, a website, a document? Certainly, there is a wide, and growing, variety of print and electronic texts that can be accessed to learn more about the disciplines we teach. And, of course, texts vary greatly in the challenges they present to students. The Common Core, specifically Reading Anchor Standard 10, emphasizes the reading of *complex texts* as a central expectation for students, from the intermediate grades through high school. The Common Core posits that students not only need to read more as learners in our courses but also need to read texts of significantly greater complexity than is currently the norm. The Common Core identifies three categories of factors that contribute to text complexity:

1. *Qualitative factors:* Different levels of meaning, text structure, author purpose, clarity of ideas, conventionality of language, and knowledge demands. Features such as how content is presented, density of concepts, and the text's organizational structure—from the sentence level up through entire chapters or units—influence text complexity. (See Chapter 3 for a discussion of the impact of organizational text frames on reading.) Clearly, some texts are written and organized in more reader-friendly ways than others, as anyone who has struggled through a technical manual can attest. In addition, the author's use of language, particularly the more formal and impersonal academic language that is characteristic of many disciplinary texts, can challenge readers. Knowledge demands—what authors expect readers to already know—are extensively explored in Chapter 2. Furthermore, texts in one discipline, such as mathematics or science, contrast dramatically with texts in other disciplines, such as literature, history, or technology, a variable that is examined in more depth in Chapter 4. Finally, the unique nature of hypertexts presents special concerns because online texts require readers to navigate a pathway through the text according to individual needs and priorities, and such texts frequently contain a plethora of multimedia elements.

2. *Quantitative factors:* Word difficulty, sentence length, and text cohesion. Computerized evaluations of a text's vocabulary load and sophistication of sentence structure provide Lexile scores that signal possible text complexity. A higher density of less familiar vocabulary and more intricate and involved sentences are a hallmark of complex texts. Although seemingly objective measures, computerized evaluations are only one indicator of text complexity. Overreliance on these scores must be cautioned when considering the appropriateness of texts for specific students.

3. *Reader and task considerations:* Knowledge, interest, and motivation of the reader, and purpose and challenges of the task. Basically, a text may be quite complex for some readers and not terribly complex for others due to the reader variables described in the preceding segment, "The Reader." The task required of a reader might mandate an in-depth understanding or instead permit a more general comprehension. Because of its critical impact on comprehension, task is explained more extensively in the next segment, "The Activity."

The Activity

Why does a person read a specific text? Comprehension is significantly affected by the nature of the reading activity. Did students select the reading material, or did someone else? Are they reading to enhance their knowledge about a topic, to discover how to accomplish a task, to experience certain ideas, or to appreciate and enjoy an author's craft? Who determines what constitutes adequate comprehension—the reader or someone else? In the classroom, teacher expectations and instructions determine the way a student approaches reading. Does the assignment require a careful examination for mastery of details, or will a more global understanding of the major ideas suffice? Will the information be discussed the next day, tested a week later, or used to complete a project? After the reading, will students complete a worksheet, answer inferential questions, develop their interpretations, write an essay, or conduct a lab experiment? Are students expected to do independent work, or can they collaborate in their reading with others? Student comprehension of a text will vary considerably depending on the messages the teacher sends through the parameters of a reading assignment.

The Context

Reading, of course, does not occur in a vacuum. A reader's comprehension is influenced by a variety of contextual factors: physical conditions, such as noise level and comfort (e.g., on the bus, in a classroom, in bed); time elements (e.g., early morning, late in the school day, midnight); and the support, encouragement, and attitudes of others (e.g., family members, peers, teachers). In the classroom, a teacher assumes primary responsibility for creating the environment for reading. Is reading emphasized primarily as an isolated, solitary act, or are students constantly provided opportunities to converse and interact as they develop their understandings? How have students been mentored to respect and assist one another as they collaborate on classroom tasks? How are the multiple perspectives that individual readers bring to specific texts honored and encouraged? Are students comfortable with risking the interjection of their ideas and viewpoints into the classroom conversation? Are discussions of text open to a range of possible interpretations as students grapple with their understandings, or are students conditioned to supply a "correct" response?

Working Complex Texts

Let's take a closer examination of a snippet of a complex text, one by essayist Anna Quindlen (2001), targeted by the Common Core as an exemplar for grades 9 and 10:

America is an improbable idea. A mongrel nation built of ever-changing disparate parts, it is held together by a notion, the notion that all men are created equal, though everyone knows that most men consider themselves better than someone. "Of all the nations in the world, the United States was built in nobody's image," the historian Daniel Boorstin wrote. That's because it was built of bits and pieces that seem discordant, like the crazy quilts that have been one of its great folk-art forms, velvet and calico and checks and brocades. Out of many, one. That is the ideal. (para. 1)

Immediately, you are probably struck by the vocabulary demands (e.g., *improbable, mongrel, disparate, notion, discordant, brocades*) and the elaborately constructed sentences. The Lexile score for the entire essay (1290L) falls in the high end of the new text complexity range identified for ninth- and tenth-grade readers by the Common Core. The author's premise is communicated through the use of figurative language, using *crazy quilt* as a metaphor for America, and obviously the author assumes a great deal of knowledge about U.S. history and culture, as well as familiarity with folk art, particularly quilting. Readers are also expected to place important allusions ("all men are created equal," "out of many, one") as they try to grasp what she is telling them. The author tosses in a wry aside ("everyone knows that most men consider themselves better than someone") that on a second look seems to reveal a very serious undercurrent. And readers have to pick up that the author is embarking on making an argument; they will have to determine the intentions behind this message and evaluate the author's ideas as they compare them with their own thinking.

As teachers, we clearly recognize that comprehension of this complex text would present challenges for many of our students. The Common Core's 10 anchor standards for reading, presented in Table 2, expect students to effectively engage with complex texts like this one in deep and thoughtful ways. Table 2 cross-references these 10 with the comprehension processes of proficient readers. In effect, the comprehension processes define *how* a reader goes about constructing comprehension, whereas the standards determine the results of that thinking, or *what* that comprehension should accomplish. Although arguably each standard would entail application of all of the comprehension processes, some of them seem predominant for individual standards (e.g., Anchor Reading Standard 1 expressly refers to making inferences).

The term *close reading* is increasingly being used to typify these rigorous expectations for readers of complex texts. *Close reading* implies an in-depth study of a text, a careful consideration of what an author is saying, and very likely return trips for multiple looks at various

Table 2
Reading Comprehension and the Common Core State Standards' Anchor Standards for Reading

Strand	Reading Standard[a]	Focus	Comprehension Processes
Key ideas and details	1. Read closely to determine what the text says explicitly and to make logical inferences from it; cite specific textual evidence when writing or speaking to support conclusions drawn from the text.	Explicit/implicit meanings	• Make connections to prior knowledge • Make inferences • Determine importance
	2. Determine central ideas or themes of a text and analyze their development; summarize the key supporting details and ideas.	Main ideas	• Generate questions • Determine importance • Synthesize
	3. Analyze how and why individuals, events, and ideas develop and interact over the course of a text.	Text relationships	• Make connections to prior knowledge • Generate questions • Make inferences • Determine importance • Synthesize
Craft and structure	4. Interpret words and phrases as they are used in a text, including determining technical, connotative, and figurative meanings, and analyze how specific word choices shape meaning or tone.	Vocabulary	• Make connections to prior knowledge • Create mental images • Make inferences
	5. Analyze the structure of texts, including how specific sentences, paragraphs, and larger portions of the text (e.g., a section, chapter, scene, or stanza) relate to each other and the whole.	Text structure	• Generate questions • Determine importance • Synthesize
	6. Assess how point of view or purpose shapes the content and style of a text.	Author's purpose/ perspective	• Generate questions • Make inferences
Integration of knowledge and ideas	7. Integrate and evaluate content presented in diverse media and formats, including visually and quantitatively, as well as in words.	Visual literacy/ technology	• Generate questions • Create mental images • Synthesize
	8. Delineate and evaluate the argument and specific claims in a text, including the validity of the reasoning as well as the relevance and sufficiency of the evidence.	Argument and support	• Generate questions • Determine importance • Synthesize
	9. Analyze how two or more texts address similar themes or topics in order to build knowledge or to compare the approaches the authors take.	Multiple texts	• Make connections to prior knowledge • Generate questions • Determine importance • Synthesize
Range of reading and level of text complexity	10. Read and comprehend complex literary and informational texts independently and proficiently.	Text complexity	• Make connections to prior knowledge • Generate questions • Create mental images • Make inferences • Determine importance • Synthesize

Note. Adapted from *Connections to Common Core State Standards: A PD Guide for Developing Readers in the Academic Disciplines* (p. 5), by D. Buehl, 2012, Newark, DE: International Reading Association. Copyright © 2012 by the International Reading Association.

[a]From *Common Core State Standards for English Language Arts and Literacy in History/Social Studies, Science, and Technical Subjects* (p. 10), by the National Governors Association Center for Best Practices and the Council of Chief State School Officers, 2010, Washington, DC: Authors. Copyright © 2010 by the National Governors Association Center for Best Practices and the Council of Chief State School Officers.

parts of the message. A key facet of close reading is text-based evidence, that readers can support their interpretations of a text's meaning by citing specific and relevant statements or passages. Perhaps a useful summation of close reading is that the reader will need to work the text to reach a satisfactory comprehension. Working a text invariably means rereading and full engagement of all the comprehension processes described earlier.

> From the Common Core: "Being able to read complex text independently and proficiently is essential for high achievement in college and the workplace and important in numerous life tasks." (NGACBP & CCSSO, 2010b, p. 4)

To what extent do students currently demonstrate close reading of disciplinary texts? The reality in our classrooms is that many students do not regularly exhibit proficient reader behaviors with school reading tasks. Teachers often feel resigned to a presumed fate that, when it comes to reading comprehension, some students invariably get it, and others don't. Instead of working a text toward understanding, many of our students resort to the following three typical ineffective reading practices:

1. *Skimming for answers:* Much of what we call "school reading" falls into this category. Students are preoccupied with completing an assignment: If a task overemphasizes tracking literal information rather than comprehension, they can in effect bypass reading and skim for details that can be jotted down. Although such "locate and copy" homework might appear acceptable, students have only taken a superficial look at the text, and comprehension has not occurred.

2. *Surface processing:* Another common ineffective practice is reading without thinking about what an author is trying to communicate. Students may dutifully "read" the assigned text but, although their eyes are looking at the words, do not engage in an inner dialogue with the author and themselves. As a result, students essentially read to get done, and teachers hear the familiar refrain, "I read it, but I didn't understand it."

3. *Reading and forgetting:* Finally, students who do not employ proficient reader strategies are unlikely to learn from their reading. Because they have not personalized an understanding of what an author is telling them, new learning is highly vulnerable to rapid forgetting. Consequently, students are able to demonstrate little carryover from their reading to class discussions, follow-up activities, and assessments.

Teaching for Comprehension

It is perhaps easy for teachers to become discouraged with the ineffective reading behaviors they witness in their classrooms. When teachers believe their students are incapable of independently handling reading assignments, they frequently downplay the role of reading in their curriculum. Yet, when students no longer read, even average and above-average students fall behind in their development. Indeed, an extensive study by ACT (American College Testing; 2006) concluded that only 51% of today's college-bound students in the United States have developed the ability to read the complex texts that are central to college learning and the workplace. According to ACT, this alarming statistic is the result of years of teachers neglecting to provide students with sufficient practice and instruction in reading appropriately complex texts in their subject areas. Unfortunately, recent data confirms this trend: only 52% of ACT test takers met the college and career reading benchmark during 2011 assessments (ACT, 2012), and only 49% met the reading benchmark on the 2011 SAT assessments (The College Board, 2012).

The Common Core review of the research on reading achievement concluded that too many students read at too low a level and, as a result, are ill prepared for the increasingly complex texts and tasks of 21st-century life (NGACBP & CCSSO, 2010a). As a result, the literacy standards are founded on expectations that all students need to acquire high-level reading abilities throughout their years of schooling:

> Students who meet the Standards readily undertake the close, attentive reading that is at the heart of understanding and enjoying complex works of literature. They habitually perform the critical reading necessary to pick carefully through the staggering amount of information available today in print and digitally. They actively seek the wide, deep, and thoughtful engagement with high-quality literary and informational texts that builds knowledge, enlarges experience, and broadens worldviews. (p. 3)

Classroom strategies can play a significant role in developing proficient reader behaviors for all students. When teachers fully incorporate comprehension instruction into the fabric of their daily teaching, students not only learn more but also continue to develop their capacity as readers of increasingly more sophisticated texts. By integrating classroom strategies into our instruction, we foster the development of individuals who are purposeful thinkers and increasingly confident and proficient readers, capable of informing themselves in a 21st-century world. The classroom strategies presented in Section 2 of this book are each cross-referenced with the comprehension processes outlined in this chapter and with the 10 Common Core anchor standards for reading. A Strategy Index—displayed on the first page for each individual strategy—provides teachers with a guide for selecting classroom strategies that develop comprehension and meet the Common Core.

References

ACT. (2006). *Reading between the lines: What the ACT reveals about college readiness in reading.* Iowa City, IA: Author. Available at www.act.org/research/policymakers/reports/reading.html

ACT. (2012). *The condition of college and career readiness 2012.* Iowa City, IA: Author. Available at www.act.org/readiness/2012

Buehl, D. (2007). A professional development framework for embedding comprehension instruction into content classrooms. In J. Lewis & G. Moorman (Eds.), *Adolescent literacy instruction: Policies and promising practices* (pp. 192–211). Newark, DE: International Reading Association.

Buehl, D. (2012). *Connections to Common Core State Standards: A PD guide for* Developing Readers in the Academic Disciplines. Newark, DE: International Reading Association. Available at www.reading.org/General/Publications/Books/bk845.aspx

College Board, The. (2012). *The SAT® report on college and career readiness: 2012.* New York: Author. Available at media.collegeboard.com/homeOrg/content/pdf/sat-report-college-career-readiness-2012.pdf

Duke, N.K., & Pearson, P.D. (2002). Effective practices for developing reading comprehension. In A.E. Farstrup & S.J. Samuels (Eds.), *What research has to say about reading instruction* (3rd ed., pp. 205–242). Newark, DE: International Reading Association.

Duke, N.K., Pearson, P.D., Strachan, S.L., & Billman, A.K. (2011). Essential elements of fostering and teaching reading comprehension. In S.J. Samuels & A.E. Farstrup (Eds.), *What research has to say about reading instruction* (4th ed., pp. 51–93). Newark, DE: International Reading Association.

Fisher, D., Frey, N., & Alfaro, C. (2013). *The path to get there: A Common Core road map for higher student achievement across the disciplines.* New York: Teachers College Press.

Keene, E.O., & Zimmermann, S. (2007). *Mosaic of thought: The power of comprehension strategy instruction* (2nd ed.). Portsmouth, NH: Heinemann.

National Governors Association Center for Best Practices & Council of Chief State School Officers. (2010a). *Common Core State Standards for English language arts and literacy in history/social studies, science, and technical subjects.* Washington, DC: Authors. Available at www.corestandards.org/thestandards

National Governors Association Center for Best Practices & Council of Chief State School Officers. (2010b). *Common Core State Standards for English language arts and literacy in history/social studies, science, and technical subjects: Appendix A: Research supporting key elements of the standards, and glossary of key terms.* Washington, DC: Authors. Available at www.corestandards.org/assets/Appendix_A.pdf

RAND Reading Study Group. (2002). *Reading for understanding: Toward an R&D program in reading comprehension.* Santa Monica, CA: RAND.

Literature Cited

Quindlen, A. (2001, September 26). A quilt of a country. *Newsweek.* Available at www.thedailybeast.com/newsweek/2001/09/27/a-quilt-of-a-country.html

CHAPTER 2

Frontloading: Addressing Knowledge Demands of Complex Texts

*Z*oonosis—the word leaps out at you from a newspaper headline. This is a word you perhaps cannot ever remember seeing before. Your curiosity thus piqued, you decide to see what this author has to say about a possibly intriguing concept. You soon discover that Ebola, yellow fever, SARS, Lyme disease, and the West Nile virus are all examples of zoonosis. The author concedes that *zoonosis* is unfamiliar jargon to most of us, but warns that we will increasingly encounter this life-threatening phenomenon in the coming years. Of course, you do know something about this uncommon term. You recognize the prefix *zoo-*, which means having to do with animals. You know that zoology is the branch of biology concerned with animals and that zoos are where animals are gathered for exhibition. The author explains zoonosis as diseases that jump from animals to humans, and profiles scientific discoveries about these often fatal contagions, which are an ever-present reality in our lives. The author has a wealth of new insights on zoonosis to share with you.

In return, however, the author expects a great deal from you as a reader. The author assumes that you are already well versed in the impact of diseases such as rabies and smallpox, that you are geographically literate, and that you bring a degree of awareness of different cultures and conditions around the world. But in particular, the author posits readers who can access an extensive background in science. Terminology such as *pathogen*, *vectored*, *prion*, *virulence*, *pandemic*, *ecosystem*, and *host species* predominate in this article, and the author alludes extensively to standard research methods employed by scientists in their investigations of the world around us.

Your comprehension of such an article, then, is contingent on your ability to draw on your previous knowledge base to meet this author's expectations so you can obtain what the author assumes will be new knowledge to most readers. As Duke, Pearson, Strachan, and Billman (2011) cogently explained,

> *"When students do not have the knowledge necessary to comprehend a particular text, such knowledge needs to be built; one cannot activate what is not there, and one cannot strategize about things one does not know." (Learned, Stockdill, & Moje, 2011, p. 181)*

We bring knowledge to the comprehension process, and that knowledge shapes our comprehension. When we comprehend, we gain new information that changes our knowledge, which is then available for later comprehension. So, in that positive, virtuous cycle, knowledge begets comprehension, which begets knowledge, and so on. (p. 53)

In Chapter 1, we examined factors that contribute to text complexity, which included knowledge demands of a text (a qualitative factor) and reader knowledge (a reader and task consideration). This chapter explores in more depth the interplay between the knowledge demands of a complex text and comprehension.

Matching Up With Authors: The Role of Hidden Knowledge

Perhaps the most fundamental question a reader must bring to any text is, What does this author assume I already know? Proficient readers become adept at sizing up a text to determine the match. To what extent do the author's assumptions about what readers know match what they do indeed know? If the author and readers are on the same page, then readers get what the author is telling them; there was an acceptable match between author demands and reader knowledge. However, if the author assumes readers will know things that they do not know, a mismatch results. Readers are likely to be confused, frustrated, and confronted with a text that doesn't make sense. Mismatches undermine a reader's efforts to comprehend.

Daily classroom experiences with reading reveal frequent mismatches; many students who are capable of understanding fall short because an author assumes background knowledge that they lack. Indeed, in their research analysis of the variables that impact comprehension, Alexander and Jetton (2000) concluded, "Of all the factors considered in this exploration, none exerts more influence on what students understand and remember than the knowledge they possess" (p. 291).

In these computerized times, we tend to think of memory as being always at hand and practically limitless. But that's not how we access our nondigitized personal knowledge during reading comprehension. Instead, imagine a student's background knowledge as a gray file cabinet standing alone in the corner of your classroom. The file cabinet represents a memory bank of everything a student knows about the world: life experiences, prior learning, and perceptions of reality. The contents of the cabinet provide the basis for the student's development of new knowledge. Knowledge in the mental file cabinet might be conceptualized as subdivided into collections of file folders, some well organized and others more chaotic, some bulging and overfilled and others nearly bereft of contents. If a folder is already crammed with useful knowledge about a particular topic, reading about that topic will add new pieces to already well-understood material. However, if a folder is nearly empty or no folder even exists for a topic, then reading comprehension will be imprecise, incomplete, and problematic.

For example, consider your comprehension of the following sentence:

> There's a bear in a plain brown wrapper doing flip-flops on 78, taking pictures, and passing out green stamps.

What does this sentence seem to be about? How confident are you of your interpretation? Is there anything particularly complicated about this text? Do you understand the vocabulary? On one level, this appears to be a deceptively simple statement—no hard words or intricate sentence structure. These readability variables would place the sentence's difficulty at an elementary grade level. Therefore, if your comprehension falters, it is likely due to a mismatch between author assumptions and your knowledge. In fact, readers who match up with the author of this sentence could sum up their understanding as follows:

> There's a law enforcement officer in an unmarked patrol car going back and forth across the median on highway 78, using radar, and issuing speeding tickets.

Shaky initial comprehension of this sentence cannot be attributed to inadequate reading skills, difficult vocabulary, or complex writing style. Instead, the sentence will not make sense to many readers because of confusion about the author's message. You probably asked, What do I know that can help me figure out this passage? You were struggling to make a meaningful connection to the material. As readers, we are constantly evaluating the extent to which our knowledge base is a good match for what an author expects us to know. The more prior knowledge we have about what an author is telling us, the deeper and more reliable our understanding of that text is.

Many of our students do not necessarily realize that knowledge exists at two levels in written texts. One layer is the overt display of knowledge that is readily apparent: The author directly tells readers things they need to know to understand. But authors do not tell readers everything. In effect, authors establish a relationship with their readers; authors anticipate what they think their readers will already know and therefore do not need to be told. This creates a second layer of knowledge that can be explained to students as hidden knowledge. Hidden knowledge exists below the surface of a text, unstated but necessary for comprehension, and readers must assume the responsibility for filling in the rest of the message if the text is to make sense. There is much hidden knowledge in our speeding ticket example. The language is trucker talk—Citizens Band (CB) radio lingo—popularized in the 1970s by a series of movies, television programs, and popular songs. The vocabulary represents code words frequently used in CB communications. CB radios have fallen into obscurity with the general public, and this language has become antiquated. As a result, an author's message that might have been a match with most readers 40 years ago is now a mismatch with large numbers of readers.

Students have similar problems when they launch into a reading assignment cold, without an early alert on how to match their knowledge with a text. They may be unsure of what the material is about and may not have reviewed what they already might know about the topic. They glide along—reading words, noticing details, picking out pieces of information—but may be confounded in their attempts to gain meaning. The more teachers help students understand concepts prior to reading about them, the better students will comprehend. By frontloading instruction—addressing knowledge demands of a text before reading—teachers can accomplish a number of important objectives. They can discover what students already know or do not know about a topic, build relevant background for students who bring insufficient knowledge to their reading, spotlight key vocabulary, and ignite student interest in a topic.

The importance of frontloading is underscored in many of the classroom strategies outlined in this book. By using frontloading practices, teachers help students extract relevant information from the file folders in their memories and integrate new information into those folders.

> *"Having knowledge is one thing; using it another. That readers often do not relate what they are reading to what they already know has prompted research about how to encourage more extensive use of prior knowledge." (Pressley, 2002, p. 271)*

The Importance of Academic Knowledge

Because authors write for a target audience, they assume that they do not need to tell their readers everything, and they count on their readers to supply the necessary hidden knowledge to fill in the rest of the message. Therefore, frontloading activities should include frequent classroom conversations that make this assumed knowledge transparent. For example, consider how the following science passage can exemplify the concept of hidden knowledge:

> Does Pluto really have the qualifications to be considered a planet? Astronomers have long argued that its tiny size, less than one-fifth the diameter of Earth, and its strangely tilted orbit that propels it outside of Neptune every couple of hundred years, means that Pluto does not sufficiently behave like a true planet. The controversy became more pronounced in the summer of 2005 when astronomers discovered a new object larger than Pluto, also orbiting the sun in the Kuiper Belt region. Many astronomers maintained that either Pluto be demoted from its standing among the nine planets of the solar system, or this new object, named Eris, which has a tiny moon, be added as our 10th planet. As a result, the International Astronomical Union reclassified Pluto as a dwarf planet in 2006.

As students examine what they need to know but are not told by the author, they will discover much hidden knowledge. The author expects readers will have an understanding of the solar system and planets. The author expects knowledge of properties of planets, such as orbits and moons. The author expects recognition that astronomers are scientists who study the solar system and constantly discover new information about other bodies in outer space. The concept of diameter and the region of the Kuiper Belt are specific references that the author assumes readers will grasp. Finally, the author expects readers to be literate about principles of science and to be aware that scientists may disagree in their interpretations and conclusions and that varying explanations are an ongoing dynamic in science. Students will discover that the author expected a great deal from readers.

> *"The research literature supports one compelling fact: what students* already *know* about the content *is one of the strongest indicators of how well they will learn new information relative to the content."* (Marzano, 2004, p. 1)

Frontloading instruction prompts students to intentionally connect their knowledge base to written texts. Three types of prior knowledge connections are possible (Keene & Zimmerman, 2007). First, readers may consider how personal experiences—events of their lives—can help them understand a passage (text-to-self knowledge). When a student connects to a planetarium visit or remembers gazing at the skies through a telescope, this student is accessing text-to-self connections that can contribute to comprehension. Second, readers may think about other texts they have previously read that can help them understand a passage (text-to-text knowledge). When a student remembers information learned about planets from a science textbook, a newspaper article about Pluto, or a pertinent scene in a science-fictional short story, the student is employing text-to-text knowledge to understand new material. Third, readers may rely on their overall conception of, and ideas about, a topic that they have gradually gleaned from an amalgam of sources, including other media and other people's talk (text-to-world knowledge). When a reader brings to this passage a general sense of what the solar system is and how it works, or what astronomy is and how astronomers conduct their research, the reader is making a text-to-world connection.

Many of our students struggle with matching up what they know with texts they are asked to read in school. Certainly, firsthand experiences can provide readers with particularly powerful prior knowledge. When readers can relate their personal lives to a text, their connections tend to be deeper and more vivid. However, because students grow up in different circumstances, general knowledge and experiences vary widely among students. Although all students bring a personal core of general knowledge to the classroom, Marzano (2004) identified a wide disparity among students in useful academic knowledge. Academic knowledge parallels the background a person would develop when studying various academic disciplines, and it is narrower and more prescribed than general knowledge. In short, some students display a wealth of relevant academic knowledge, whereas others are seriously deficient in what authors expect them to know. Their general knowledge will not be sufficient to compensate for the academic knowledge they lack.

But isn't academic knowledge essentially a product of schooling? Marzano (2004) cited a profusion of research that concluded that those students who gain the most academic knowledge from school are those who have already developed some of this academic knowledge in their out-of-school lives. To revisit our planets example, Pluto represents academic knowledge. Some readers will be able to recall personal experiences such as visits to museums that featured exhibits of the solar system and may also recall browsing *National Geographic* articles about the planets. They may have had conversations with knowledgeable adults on this topic or listened in as adults around them engaged in discussions; perhaps they overheard their parents debating whether Pluto should rightfully be demoted from planet status. These students had access to academic knowledge outside the classroom—access to personal experiences, rich texts, and knowledgeable others—that prepared them to match up well with the materials they subsequently encountered in classroom lessons. In particular, they frequently have developed some familiarity with the insider terminology of a subject—in this case, academic vocabulary such as *planet*, *astronomer*, *orbit*, *solar system*, *Pluto*, and *Neptune*. Thus, the students who can be expected to learn the most from their first encounter with planets in the classroom will be those who already knew something about planets before the lesson.

Students who arrive in the classroom with rich reservoirs of academic knowledge tend to have grown up with a host of invaluable firsthand experiences: visits to museums, art galleries, plays, and concerts; travel opportunities outside their home area; interactions with knowledgeable adults who provide a foundation for text-to-world knowledge through conversation and mentoring; and ready access to print and other sources, including the Internet, that can pique their interest and curiosity in the various domains of academic knowledge. Students who lack such direct experiences depend on frontloading practices that broaden their academic knowledge base as they prepare for reading and learning content information.

To a significant degree, academic knowledge is vocabulary driven; in many respects, teaching science, history, music, art, math, and other disciplines is equivalent to teaching a language. Researchers refer to the language of an academic discipline as a Discourse (Gee, 2000). Insiders in an academic discourse, such as professionals in the field and teachers, are comfortable with this academic language, but outsiders, like our students, may feel overwhelmed or even alienated by all the jargon—an outsider's depiction of this specialized language—in a biology text, an algebra lesson, or a history passage. Academic language is a key component of text complexity, as examined in Chapter 1.

Readers familiar with the language of a discipline can draw on deeper and more precise academic knowledge to apply to written texts in content classrooms. Therefore, it is likely that individual students may be more successful in some disciplinary environments and less successful in others. For example, they may be more proficient readers of short stories and novels in English class and less proficient readers of science articles in biology class. Students need to become increasingly comfortable with the insider language of academic texts; they have to develop the facility to talk the talk of an academic discipline. Disciplinary literacy,

discussed at length in Chapter 4, involves developing this capacity to read and use the different disciplinary discourses that students encounter when building academic knowledge.

Teaching to the Match: Building Academic Knowledge

Teachers can have a significant impact on their students' comprehension of complex texts by frontloading instruction—providing students with opportunities to acquire missing pieces of assumed knowledge through a variety of classroom activities. Therefore, it becomes necessary to evaluate the match with texts students will be asked to read. Some complex texts will clearly be a reach; the author's expectation of the background knowledge that readers bring will prove to be out of sync with many students. In these cases, many readers do not know what they need to know to make sense of such texts. A text that is a mismatch will be too difficult unless substantial frontloading of background concepts is undertaken.

> *"The problems with activating prior knowledge without building knowledge is that it privileges the students who have knowledge already and it depends on the knowledge that students bring to school." (Cervetti, Jaynes, & Hiebert, 2009, p. 83)*

More typically, many texts will be a match for some students but a mismatch for others. A key factor in differentiating instruction is identifying potential mismatches and emphasizing proactive responses—activities that narrow the gap between what students know and what they need to know to access an author's message. Students can then be asked to read material that would have been otherwise too challenging had they been assigned to read it independently, without supporting instruction.

An important caveat regarding frontloading needs to be emphasized: The intention behind frontloading instruction is *not* to tell students what they subsequently should learn through reading; such prereading activity renders actual reading of the text unnecessary. Instead, knowledge building during frontloading should focus primarily on what the author expects readers to already know, what the author does not tell them. Coleman and Pimentel (2012), lead developers of the Common Core's literacy standards, cautioned that instruction prior to reading "should focus on words and concepts that are essential to a basic understanding and that students are not likely to know or be able to determine from context" (p. 9).

The alternatives to appropriate frontloading loom as obstacles for the reading of complex texts. Students may be sent into their reading relatively cold, which means that those who lack what the author assumes readers know will flounder during their reading. Some of these mismatched students will give up, others will plod along with only fleeting comprehension, and many will merely skim for answers that ultimately make little sense to them. This situation often plays out as a given that some students can be counted on to get it and that many others will be deemed to have poor comprehension skills.

Or instruction may veer away from the reading of texts altogether and overrely on other methods to learn content—telling (e.g., PowerPoint presentations, lectures), visual media (e.g., video), and interactive or hands-on activities. As a result, students neither meet the Common Core State Standards nor develop the capacity to learn independently as readers, a potential that could have been realized if their deficiencies in background knowledge had been remedied. Of course, telling, visual media, and interactive activities can all be integrated into frontloading instruction—not to *replace* reading but to *prepare* students to further their knowledge and delve deeper into disciplinary concepts through reading.

In particular, frontloading appears to be a "make or break" variable for the comprehension of complex informational texts. As Duke and her colleagues (2011) observed, "comprehension of the expository text, in contrast to the narrative text, was significantly related to the student's amount of world knowledge" (p. 57). Minimal knowledge building may suffice for many literary works because students will be able to gradually inform themselves about time periods, places, or related events as they interact with the story line. For example, students will learn a great deal about the Jim Crow period of segregation in U.S. history through their reading of Harper Lee's novel *To Kill a Mockingbird*. Comprehension of other literary works will be hugely dependent on appropriate frontloading because the knowledge that authors assume will be essential to unlocking meaning behind the story line. For instance, student appreciation of George Orwell's novel *Animal Farm* as an allegory will be dependent on frontloading that builds knowledge about the Russian Revolution and resultant Soviet Union. For many literary works, frontloading should focus on what Gallagher (2004) termed "framing the text" (p. 37), which engages students in some prethinking about

> *"Using discipline-based knowledge development as a context for literacy learning provides an opportunity for students to practice and apply their emerging literacy skills in the interest of developing understandings about the world that support their future learning." (Cervetti et al., 2009, p. 82)*

ideas and themes explored by an author and sets the stage for examining how their personal experiences may inform their interpretations of a story's meaning.

Frontloading activities that elicit student conversations about topics and concepts to be encountered during reading are especially valuable. Productive student interactions are essential and receive special emphasis in the Common Core, especially in Speaking and Listening Anchor Standard 1, which posits a range of conversations and collaborations with diverse partners that span one-on-one, group, and whole-class settings. Conversational frontloading activities have several advantages:

- Students are provided with a social opportunity to revisit what they currently know about a topic; as others share, students are reminded of additional things they might know.
- Students who would face a mismatch with a particular text are immersed in conversation about a topic that builds what they know before they read; some of what they will need to know emerges as they listen to comments from classmates. Students are thus able to access one another as resources for knowledge building.
- Students are cued about the aspects of their knowledge that are most relevant for the specific expectations of the author; in essence, they prime themselves to actively bring their current knowledge to construct an understanding of the author's message.
- If students display few connections to the topic, the teacher will be alerted that a mismatch exists for most students, and the teacher will need to intervene with further knowledge-building activities to ensure that comprehension will be possible.

Teachers can choose from an array of effective literacy practices, presented in Section 2, that ignite these knowledge-expanding conversations. Brainstorming strategies, which begin by asking students to jot down what they know or have heard about a topic, provide an opening for student sharing and conversation. The lesson starts with immersion in students' current knowledge base, as students who otherwise would have confronted a mismatch receive a heads-up on the topic right before they are asked to read about it in more depth (e.g., see the Brainstorming Prior Knowledge strategy in Section 2). Predictive strategies that engage students in using current knowledge to evaluate statements or arguments about a topic lead to rich and probing conversations that set up reading to confirm or revise the statements, or refine the arguments (e.g., see the Anticipation Guides strategy in Section 2). Vocabulary-intensive frontloading encourages initial consideration of key language and terminology as students converse about what they currently know about these words and speculate how an author will use them to communicate a message (e.g., see the Connect Two strategy in Section 2).

In cases where student collaborations will be insufficient (too many students exhibit mismatches), frontloading instruction needs to extend beyond activating and sharing current knowledge and focus instead on building new background knowledge. Although teachers sometimes assume students should already know these things, clearly in our classrooms today, many students do not, presenting us with a prime teachable moment. At this point, use of media such as video and teacher presentations can be an effective way to enhance missing academic knowledge. Short video clips, such as from YouTube, can be especially instrumental in mediating classroom mismatches. Often video is shown after students read, but it can be a particularly powerful frontloading technique. Judicious use of video clips, rather than showing entire works, keeps the focus on building sufficient knowledge for a successful reading experience.

Additionally, encouraging students to read broadly about a topic, in texts that are at appropriate individual difficulty levels, can reduce classroom mismatches. Much of the background knowledge we bring to texts is incidental; we read general works, such as newspapers, magazines, and books, and gradually accrue a deeper understanding of various topics, even though that is not necessarily our intention for reading. Taking the effort to incrementally grow classroom text sets (Harvey & Goudvis, 2007) can help students develop academic knowledge for disciplinary learning. A stockpile of materials on multiple reading levels related to significant curricular topics can be a resource for independent background reading. Although such materials may not specifically focus on the aspects emphasized in the curriculum, text sets can be immensely valuable in deepening academic knowledge on particular topics.

Finally, a consideration of the outreach potential of technology must be factored into a discussion on frontloading. When does googling come in? Many students (but not necessarily all) have a great deal of knowledge-building potential at their fingertips. Certainly, students can be increasingly expected to resolve some of their personal knowledge gaps as readers through quick consultations with online resources. In effect, we can expand our portable memories through technology, but clearly there is a breaking point when resorting to technology becomes unwieldy and unsatisfactory. If a reader must continually google multiple items paragraph by paragraph, reading becomes a laborious translation act that will prove to be overwhelming. Turning to technology is a highly workable option when a reader has only modest items in a text to clarify, and sharing results from

a quick online search is another excellent opportunity for student collaboration and conversation. In addition, the Common Core's Reading Anchor Standard 9 expects students to analyze how multiple texts deal with topics and ideas, a perfect setting for integrating technological assistance into the reading of complex texts.

Teaching to the match is an often overlooked but essential factor in improving student comprehension of complex disciplinary texts. Frontloading prepares students to handle challenging texts, even though they may have otherwise experienced mismatches and insufficient comprehension. Students gain the necessary daily practice they need to develop as readers because they are provided with instruction that makes them more likely to succeed. Moreover, students begin to aggressively analyze the match between their knowledge and an author's assumptions as a regular habit of mind.

References

Alexander, P.A., & Jetton, T.L. (2000). Learning from text: A multidimensional and developmental perspective. In M.L. Kamil, P.B. Mosenthal, P.D. Pearson, & R. Barr (Eds.), *Handbook of reading research* (Vol. 3, pp. 285–310). Mahwah, NJ: Erlbaum.

Cervetti, G.N., Jaynes, C.A., & Hiebert, E.H. (2009). Increasing opportunities to acquire knowledge through reading. In E.H. Hiebert (Ed.), *Reading more, reading better* (pp. 79–100). New York: Guilford.

Coleman, D., & Pimentel, S. (2012). *Revised publishers' criteria for the Common Core State Standards in English language arts and literacy, grades 3–12*. Washington, DC: National Governors Association Center for Best Practices & Council of Chief State School Officers. Available at www.corestandards.org/assets/Publishers_Criteria_for_3-12.pdf

Duke, N.K., Pearson, P.D., Strachan, S.L., & Billman, A.K. (2011). Essential elements of fostering and teaching reading comprehension. In S.J. Samuels & A.E. Farstrup (Eds.), *What research has to say about reading instruction* (4th ed., pp. 51–93). Newark, DE: International Reading Association.

Gallagher, K. (2004). *Deeper reading: Comprehending challenging texts, 4–12*. Portland, ME: Stenhouse.

Gee, J.P. (2000). Discourse and sociocultural studies in reading. In M.L. Kamil, P.B. Mosenthal, P.D. Pearson, & R. Barr (Eds.), *Handbook of reading research* (Vol. 3, pp. 195–207). Mahwah, NJ: Erlbaum.

Harvey, S., & Goudvis, A. (2007). *Strategies that work: Teaching comprehension for understanding and engagement* (2nd ed.). Portland, ME: Stenhouse.

Keene, E.O., & Zimmermann, S. (2007). *Mosaic of thought: The power of comprehension strategy instruction* (2nd ed.). Portsmouth, NH: Heinemann.

Learned, J.E., Stockdill, D., & Moje, E.B. (2011). Integrating reading strategies and knowledge building in adolescent literacy instruction. In S.J. Samuels & A.E. Farstrup (Eds.), *What research has to say about reading instruction* (4th ed., pp. 159–185). Newark, DE: International Reading Association.

Marzano, R.J. (2004). *Building background knowledge for academic achievement: Research on what works in schools*. Alexandria, VA: Association for Supervision and Curriculum Development.

Pressley, M. (2002). *Reading instruction that works: The case for balanced teaching* (2nd ed.). New York: Guilford.

CHAPTER 3

Questioning for Understanding Through Text Frames

During their daily lives in school, many of our students proceed as if they possess not one but two brains. Imagine that their minds actually were partitioned into a real-world brain and a school brain. The real-world brain can be visualized as taking up most of the storage space in a student's head. This capacious brain is the hub of what this student knows and understands about the world—all of life's experiences, all of one's personal explanations of what is, why, and how. In Chapter 2, we extensively explored this world brain as text-to-self, text-to-text, and text-to-world knowledge. The student relies on this reservoir of prior knowledge to make sense of life and the world.

Now imagine the school brain, tucked away in a remote corner of the student's mind and the destination for our classroom lessons. Ideally, learning in school should be making its way into the real-world brain. However, the school brain is apparently well insulated from the real-world brain, and very little that enters the school brain ever gets transferred into the real-world brain that makes sense of things. The school brain has a minuscule storage capacity; information does not stay there very long. The most distinctive feature of the school brain is an ever-open chute, ready to dump yesterday's lesson quickly and irrevocably into oblivion. Students use the school brain for short-term warehousing of the daily stuff of school; increasingly, brain researchers refer to this temporary destination as working memory (Sousa, 2011). As soon as the test is over or a new chapter started, students flush out the backlog of old facts and stray information and ready themselves for another cycle of short-term learning.

Obviously, this two-brain dichotomy is a fanciful depiction. Unfortunately, many students conceptualize learning in school as a short-term survival exercise. Students steel themselves each day for a steady barrage of information, and they cope by trying to remember only long enough to pass a test. Then, they move on to the next material. Teachers find it discouraging that so many students seem to retain so little of what they supposedly learned in school.

Teaching for Enduring Understandings

Certainly, some of our students are adept at perceiving the connections between what they already know and what they are learning in the classroom, of transferring classroom learning from working memory into long-term storage. They are able to synthesize their new understandings with their existing knowledge, and they find that new learning does indeed help them make more sense of their world. But for many students, school has little to do with the real world, and their failure to make connections and synthesize understandings virtually ensures that much of what they learn in school will be lost—relegated to the dead-end depot of the school brain.

Imagine the following scenario: Five years from now, as you stroll down the street, you chance upon a student you taught this year. What will this person still remember from your lessons? You realize that much of the specific information the student had encountered will be forgotten. But what learning should still be retained (lest you be bitterly disappointed)? What should this former student remember about the Cold War, or cell division, or congruent triangles, or George Orwell's *Animal Farm*? Did this former student get the point from these various units of our curricula?

It is unlikely that you would be crestfallen if your former student could not identify former Communist leader Leonid Brezhnev or list all the member countries of the Warsaw Pact, possible items on some long-ago exam. But the Cold War, a period of intense confrontation between the antagonistic ideologies of Communism and Western democracy that resulted in regional conflicts and fears of nuclear destruction, should have significant associations for this individual. Likewise, you probably would not expect your former student to name the various stages of mitosis or recite specific mathematic theorems. You would, however, expect a general understanding of the implications of cell division and the relationships regarding basic principles of triangles. You would accept that your student has forgotten most of the characters and plot details of *Animal Farm*, but you would hope that Orwell's basic premises of the oppressed becoming the oppressors and the corruption of power would be remembered.

Essentially, you would concede that most factual information will be forgotten over time but that more transcendent understandings must be remembered if one is to be regarded as a literate individual. Wiggins and McTighe (2005) term this learning that lasts "enduring understandings" (p. 17).

The Forest and Acres and Acres of Trees

The reality of school for many students is an overwhelming onslaught of factual information that is never sorted into anything useful or worth remembering. Students seem so readily disposed to quickly forget what they encounter in school, partly because of the nature of classroom texts they read. Proficient readers differentiate and prioritize as they process material; they determine what is most important and worthy of knowing over time. But textbooks in particular can make these comprehension processes a demanding task for students. In a critical analysis, Daniels and Zemelman (2004) fault textbooks for burying big ideas—those most worthy of being remembered—underneath a tremendous array of superficial details. Textbooks tend to be written to *expose* students to information rather than help them truly understand it.

The old adage that they "can't see the forest for the trees" becomes a daily occurrence for students immersed in the factual thickets of informational texts.

Figure 1 is a visual representation of the challenges facing students when they attempt to read curricular texts. Comprehension is achieved when readers can organize their learning (see the center of the diagram in Figure 1) so they are able to articulate a personal understanding (see the top of the diagram). But many students become mired in the details—isolated "factlets" of information (see the bottom of the diagram). Rather than actively connecting material to previous knowledge, raising questions, creating mental images, and drawing inferences, their minds instead are merely ticking off factlets one by one: "Here's a fact. Here's another fact. Here's a fact in bold print. (I'll have to copy something down about that one!) Here's another fact. Another one. Another fact in bold." And so on through the remainder of a passage. But what do all of these facts and details mean? At the end of a passage, students may have accumulated a mass of disorganized information for which they have little use. They have not engaged in the critical comprehension processes of determining importance and synthesizing understanding.

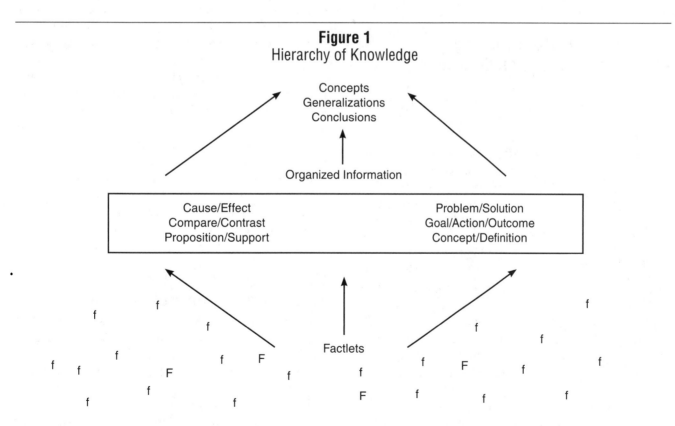

Figure 1
Hierarchy of Knowledge

Concepts
Generalizations
Conclusions

Organized Information

| Cause/Effect
Compare/Contrast
Proposition/Support | Problem/Solution
Goal/Action/Outcome
Concept/Definition |

Factlets

Note. From *Classroom Strategies for Interactive Learning* (3rd ed., p. 31), by D. Buehl, 2009, Newark, DE: International Reading Association. Copyright © 2009 by the International Reading Association.

Furthermore, the primary method of directing students through classroom materials—asking them to respond to questions—often does little to promote comprehension. A litany of concerns about classroom questioning stretches back to Durkin's (1978) landmark research, which revealed that few questions are actually designed to guide comprehension. Most questioning does not help students understand but merely assesses whether they could arrive at certain answers. Other criticisms fault questioning that predominantly targets getting the facts or that asks students to locate details. As a result, too many questions can be answered with a rote level of processing and often with only a single word or short phrase. The student response, as we discussed in Chapter 1, is "locate and copy" skimming rather than the thoughtful close reading expected by the Common Core's literacy standards.

Understanding occurs when students are able to synthesize—to interconnect facts and details to organize information into a coherent message. Classroom questions that disproportionately target isolated facts make it unlikely that readers will perceive central relationships. Students resignedly assume that anything that appears on a page of print is fair game for a question, whether it is truly important or not. In many assignments, students may answer every question correctly and yet be no closer to understanding than when they started.

Text Frames: Determining Importance Through Questioning

As detailed in Chapter 1, our minds are geared to wonder when we are immersed as readers; the questions we pose to ourselves—and to authors—set our frame of mind for reading particular texts. Proficient readers *use* reading—rather than *do* reading—and the questions they generate provide a personal blueprint for engaging with a text. Their questions establish why they are reading a particular selection and what they should look for. Of course, many students will tell us that their minds wander, not wonder, as they attempt to read materials that seemingly bombard them with details and factual information.

> *The Common Core's Reading Anchor Standard 5:*
> *"Analyze the structure of texts, including how specific sentences, paragraphs, and larger portions of the text (e.g., a section, chapter, scene, or stanza) relate to each other and the whole."*
> *(NGACBP & CCSSO, 2010, p. 10)*

The Common Core's Reading Anchor Standard 5 targets readers' abilities to discern the text structure of a written work as they analyze relationships that tie together specific textual elements and details.

Researchers use the term *text frame* to describe sets of questions inherent in these different organizational structures (Anderson & Armbruster, 1984). Text frames represent the internal structure an author chooses to weave together information to communicate ideas, concepts, themes, or conclusions. Text frame questions provide readers with a mental road map for determining what is important in texts packed with a wealth of background information.

Jones, Palincsar, Ogle, and Carr (1987) highlight six text frames typically used by authors to organize a text: problem/solution, cause/effect, compare/contrast, goal/action/outcome, concept/definition, and proposition/support. Each text frame cues a reader to a different questioning frame of mind that best correlates with an author's message. Frame questions guide readers through a maze of details toward understanding the point of a piece of writing. A world history passage about colonialism might be best analyzed through problem/solution frame questioning. A section in a chemistry textbook might be patterned around cause/effect frame questions. An essay staking a writer's position on Internet privacy would likely elicit proposition/support frame questions. A geometry chapter examining characteristics of different polygons might best correspond to compare/contrast frame questions. A culinary arts text outlining methods for preserving various fruits would invite goal/action/outcome questions. Table 3 highlights sample sets of text frame questions that help readers navigate details and information and guide their comprehension.

When students are able to perceive how background details fit together—that the point of a passage is a cause/effect relationship, for example, which binds together all of those facts—they can think about the implications of what they are reading. They can synthesize their understanding—draw conclusions, make generalizations, track explanations, construct interpretations, and develop broad conceptual insights about important content. Without this synthesis of understanding, learning does not occur, and inevitably another round of forgetting results.

Classroom Strategies That Frame Comprehension

The Common Core's Reading Anchor Standard 5 challenges students to perceive the text frame in a piece of writing so they can examine relationships and establish the point of an author's message. So, how can we mentor students to adjust to relevant questioning frames of mind when they tackle complex disciplinary texts? What frame of mind should they assume when reading a biology passage about ecosystems, or a health article about junk food, or a history chapter about the Aztec

Table 3
Determining Text Frames

What Is the Point of the Material?	Sample Questions to Ask
A problem needs solving. (problem/solution text frame)	• What is the problem? • Who has the problem? • What is causing the problem? • What are negative effects of the problem? • Who is trying to solve the problem? • What solutions are recommended or attempted? • What results from these solutions? • Is the problem solved? Do any new problems develop because of the solutions?
Certain conditions lead to certain results. (cause/effect text frame)	• What happens (or happened)? • What causes (or caused) it to happen? • What are the important elements or factors that cause this effect? • How do these factors or elements interrelate? • Will this result always happen from these causes? Why, or why not? • How would the result change if the elements or factors were different?
Certain things are similar or different. (compare/contrast text frame)	• What is being compared or contrasted? • What characteristics are being compared or contrasted? • What makes them alike or similar? • What makes them unalike or dissimilar? • What are the most important qualities that make them similar? • What are the most important qualities that make them different? • In terms of what's most important, are they more alike or more different?
Someone is doing something for a specific reason. (goal/action/outcome text frame)	• What is the goal? What is to be accomplished? • Who is trying to achieve this goal? • What actions/steps are taken to achieve this goal? • Is the sequence of actions/steps important? • What are the effects of these actions? What happens? • Were these actions successful for achieving the goal? • Are there unexpected outcomes from these actions? • Would other actions have been more effective? Could something else have been done?
A concept needs to be understood. (concept/definition text frame)	• What is the concept? • What category of things does this concept belong to? • What are its critical characteristics? • How does it work? • What does it do? • What are its functions? • What are examples of it? • What are examples of things that share some but not all of its characteristics?
A viewpoint is being argued and supported. (proposition/support text frame)	• What is the general topic or issue? • What viewpoint, conclusion, theory, hypothesis, or thesis is being proposed? • How is this proposition supported? • Are examples provided to support the proposition? • Are data provided to support the proposition? • Is expert verification provided to support the proposition? • Is a logical argument provided to support the proposition? • Does the author make a convincing case for the proposition? • What are alternative perspectives to the author's proposition?

Note. Adapted from *Classroom Strategies for Interactive Learning* (3rd ed., p. 23), by D. Buehl, 2009, Newark, DE: International Reading Association. Copyright © 2009 by the International Reading Association.

civilization, or a webpage on Beethoven? Which set of text frame questions should students be pursuing as readers of each of these different texts? Students need concerted practice with analyzing text structures and applying appropriate questioning frames as they work texts to achieve understanding. As teachers, we can employ classroom literacy strategies that tip off students to the appropriate questioning frame for the reading tasks we assign (see Table 16 in the introduction to Section 2).

> *"Students who are knowledgeable about and/or follow the author's structure in their attempts to recall a text remember more than those who do not." (Pearson & Fielding, 1991, p. 827)*

For example, if students are to read a passage about golden eagles, you should first determine which text frame will best structure their thinking. If the author emphasizes environmental hardships that the eagle encounters, devise your strategy around problem/solution questions. If the author stresses similarities and differences between the eagles and other predatory birds, structure the assignment around compare/contrast questions. If the author discusses reasons why eagles are declining in some geographical regions, work within a cause/effect frame. If the author argues for policy changes to address habitat degradation that threatens the golden eagle, stress proposition/support relationships. If the author focuses on environmental groups' initiatives to protect eagles, then structure a goal/action/outcome assignment. If the author offers general information about the characteristics of eagles, then concept/definition questions would best guide students' comprehension.

The classroom strategies presented in this book can be used effectively to signal text frames to students and to provide the support they need to read in an effective questioning frame of mind. In addition, strategies that direct student thinking toward a specific text frame can help them overcome text that is poorly written, confusing, or challenging. Struggling readers, in particular, benefit from strategies that provide them with an organized way of thinking about information that otherwise may be overwhelming.

Figure 2 provides a framework for identifying text frames in classroom materials. For example, science

Figure 2
Framework for Identifying Text Frames

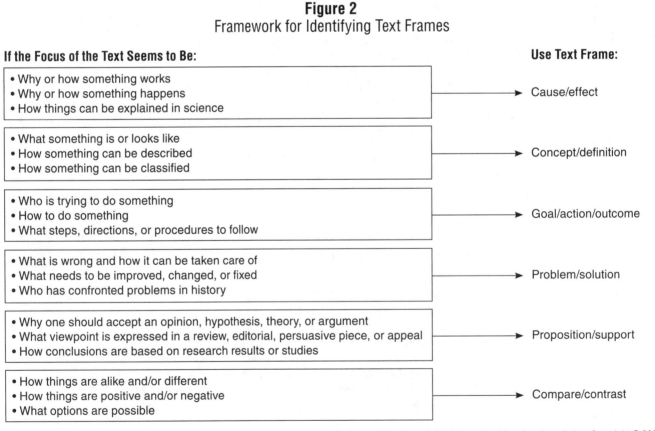

If the Focus of the Text Seems to Be:

- Why or how something works
- Why or how something happens
- How things can be explained in science

→ Use Text Frame: Cause/effect

- What something is or looks like
- How something can be described
- How something can be classified

→ Concept/definition

- Who is trying to do something
- How to do something
- What steps, directions, or procedures to follow

→ Goal/action/outcome

- What is wrong and how it can be taken care of
- What needs to be improved, changed, or fixed
- Who has confronted problems in history

→ Problem/solution

- Why one should accept an opinion, hypothesis, theory, or argument
- What viewpoint is expressed in a review, editorial, persuasive piece, or appeal
- How conclusions are based on research results or studies

→ Proposition/support

- How things are alike and/or different
- How things are positive and/or negative
- What options are possible

→ Compare/contrast

Note. Adapted from *Classroom Strategies for Interactive Learning* (2nd ed., p. 13), by D. Buehl, 2001, Newark, DE: International Reading Association. Copyright © 2001 by the International Reading Association.

texts frequently emphasize cause/effect relationships, so students focus on how certain scientific phenomena lead to specific results, whether a chemical reaction, a law of physics, or a principle in earth science. Problem/solution relationships predominate in history texts, which tend to focus on stories about people who are confronted with problems and changes. Material that outlines a chronology (e.g., a short story of a family immigrating to a new country) or a sequence of steps (e.g., directions for operating woodworking equipment, a protocol for setting up a webpage, a recipe for baking a spice cake) involves goal/action/outcome thinking. An article that presents a series of options requires a compare/contrast frame of mind. A political speech, movie review, or research article involves proposition/support thinking by providing conclusions predicated on the author's basis for justification. Finally, highly descriptive texts, such as in biology, mandate a concept/definition frame of mind for reading.

Of course, authors may employ multiple text frames to organize information in a piece of writing. For example, an author might *argue* that if we *compare* various proposals to combat global warming, certain *solutions* should be adopted as our best response. In effect, that author has combined three text frames—proposition/support, compare/contrast, and problem/solution—to structure thinking about this issue. Texts that are more complex tend to feature multiple text structures, which are often implicit rather than overtly stated. As a result, students will increasingly be called on to infer text structure as they grapple with probing relationships among factual details. Text frame questions guide readers to recognize these relationships as the foundation for what an author deems important in a text. Table 4 outlines these six text frames with materials that are commonly read in mathematics, social studies, science, and English language arts classes.

Framing Essential Questions

Consider the question, What makes a work of art great? Why do people find the painting *Guernica* by Pablo Picasso so compelling? What makes a Frank Lloyd Wright building so remarkable? Why is Edward Elgar's lyrical "Enigma Variations" such a heralded set of music? What is it about Dorothea Lange's photographs that render her images so memorable? Why do generations keep discovering magic in a novel such as Harper Lee's *To Kill a Mockingbird*? How do we explain the appeal of a Wolfgang Amadeus Mozart opera, an Emily Dickinson poem, a Michelangelo sculpture, an Akira Kurosawa film, or a Billie Holiday recording? How do we account for what makes some artistic works great?

Certainly, this is an essential question, one that cuts right to the core of understanding art and what makes some art meaningful, powerful, and enduring. It is also a question that would undoubtedly elicit a variety of possible answers, probably some disagreement, and perhaps even heated passions. In their influential guide to curricular planning, *Understanding by Design*, Wiggins and McTighe (2005) propose organizing instruction around big ideas, the central and focusing ideas within a topic that make it worthy of study, the gist of a unit that provides students with important insights into their world, the essence of learning that students retain long after their days in the classroom are over. Big ideas are those explanations, interpretations, generalizations, conclusions, and conceptual insights portrayed at the top of the diagram in Figure 1. The way to get at big ideas, Wiggins and McTighe suggest, is through essential questions.

Most of the questions that confront students in our curricula are leading questions. They direct students toward a set answer and can be helpful for clarifying key information. However, essential questions help students dig deeper into a topic. Instruction organized around essential questions considers the transcendent, overarching ideas that position students to examine critical connections or relationships within a topic area: Why exactly are we studying this? How can this be applied in the larger world? What couldn't we do if we didn't understand this? What ideas is the author exploring in this story? What is worth remembering, after time has passed, about this topic, unit, novel, or experiment?

For example, why should students read William Golding's novel *Lord of the Flies*? Why read this book and not another? What will they gain from this experience that will make a difference to them? What are the big ideas in this work? What makes this book a classic? Questions like these help teachers focus on the point of instruction. Unlike leading questions, which could help students follow key events of the plot, spotlight important vocabulary, or clarify characterization, these overarching questions tap into larger ideas that can be accessed during a unit such as a novel study of *Lord of the Flies*.

Essential questions exhibit a number of critical attributes. First, they are arguable; there may be no single obvious right answer. Such questions ask students to uncover ideas, problems, controversies, philosophical positions, or perspectives. Second, essential questions often reach across disciplinary boundaries and engender a series of ensuing and related questions that help us reach an understanding. Third, these questions often strike right at the heart of a discipline, such as what novels can tell us, whose version of history is

Table 4
Disciplinary Text Frames

Text Frame	Description
Mathematics	
Problem/solution	Procedural knowledge texts that engage students in problem solving, including story problems and scenarios that challenge students to devise solutions
Cause/effect	Logical reasoning: Analyzing math principles and their applications (deductive) and developing generalizations based on data (inductive)
Compare/contrast	Examinations of critical differentiating characteristics, such as geometric shapes or measures of center (mean, median, mode)
Proposition/support	Justifying decisions to apply specific math formulas or strategies in problem-solving situations
Goal/action/outcome	Specific algorithms that are followed to solve certain mathematical problems
Concept/definition	Development of math conceptual knowledge, such as factor, prime number, square root, quadrilateral, circumference, and relative frequency
Social Studies	
Problem/solution	Historical texts that examine problems people encountered and how they addressed them
Cause/effect	Factors that lead to certain results or conditions, such as in history or psychology
Compare/contrast	Examinations of how things are alike or different, such as cultures, policies, philosophies, and types of government
Proposition/support	Articulation of points of view, position statements, and constructed arguments or theories
Goal/action/outcome	Steps taken by people, organizations, governments, or countries that are intended to achieve a certain aim or goal
Concept/definition	Development of key social studies concepts, such as socialization, imperialism, nationalism, federalism, and democracy
Science	
Problem/solution	Investigations of problems in the natural world and scientific explanations for possible actions to redress them, such as an avian flu epidemic, loss of swampland, and disappearing habitats
Cause/effect	Examinations of what happened and why it happened or studies of what would happen if certain steps or processes were undertaken
Compare/contrast	Analyses of how certain biological or physical phenomena are alike and different
Proposition/support	Hypotheses that are tested and conclusions that are drawn from examinations of data and scientific evidence
Goal/action/outcome	Steps taken by scientists to investigate relationships and hypotheses, usually conducted as scientific experiments and research
Concept/definition	Classification of biological and physical phenomena into categories according to defining characteristics and attributes
English Language Arts	
Problem/solution	Literature that deals with characters attempting to resolve a problem, issue, dilemma, or conflict
Cause/effect	Author's use of language and communication devices that influence interpretation of meaning, such as word choice, tone, and elements of speech
Compare/contrast	Literature that presents contrasting characters to signal the author's theme; alternative styles of writing or communication
Proposition/support	Essays that present a point of view or line of argumentation with supporting evidence or logic; literature that provides a vehicle for expression of an author's ideas through plot, characterization, or theme
Goal/action/outcome	Literature that features characters who are striving to attain their dreams, desires, or personal fulfillment
Concept/definition	Development of key literary concepts, such as coming of age, social justice, metaphor, symbolism, protagonist, and haiku

Note. Adapted from "Literacy Demands in Content Classrooms" (pp. 34, 39, and 44), by D. Buehl and S. Stumpf, in *Adolescent Literacy Toolkit*, 2007, Madison: Wisconsin Department of Public Instruction. Copyright © 2007 by the Wisconsin Department of Public Instruction.

being told, what we ultimately can prove in science, and how we know what we think we know. For example, the following essential questions are germane to *Lord of the Flies*: What does it mean to be civilized? Are modern civilizations more civilized than ancient ones? What is necessary to ensure civilized behavior? Do children need to be taught to be civilized? What causes us to stop behaving in a civilized manner? As a result, essential questions are also recursive; that is, they naturally reoccur, often many times, during the study of a discipline. First graders as well as college students can offer valid aesthetic judgments about what makes a book great.

Finally, essential questions provide a focus for sifting through the information and details of a unit of study; they alert readers to organizational imprints of specific text frames: We are searching for causes, patterns, solutions, procedures, defining characteristics, or defensible arguments. Invariably, essential questions encourage student inquiry, discussion, and research, a primary expectation of the Common Core's Writing Anchor Standards 7–9. Essential questions invite students to personalize their learning and develop individual insights derived from their studies. Students frequently complain that they do not see the point of learning about a certain topic or that they won't use any of this stuff in their lives. Essential questions guide students through the curriculum and help them understand the intent behind a unit of study so they can perceive lasting value.

For example, essential questions for a history unit on manifest destiny and the westward movement of settlers in the United States could tap into cause-and-effect relationships: Why do people move? Do people migrate for the same reasons today that they did in the 19th century? Who has the right to a particular territory? Who wins and who loses during major population shifts? Questions such as these can help students focus on big ideas as they study a panorama of events in U.S. history: the Oregon Trail, the Mexican War, the California Gold Rush, the conflicts between settlers and American Indian nations in the Great Plains, and the waves of immigration to North America.

Much of our curricula is geared to telling students *what*. Essential questions engage students in asking *why*. As critical thinkers about big ideas, students begin to expect more than factual information from their learning and become accustomed to examining topics and issues in depth. Students are encouraged to adopt an inquiring approach to their reading, to explore answers that can be supported by textual evidence, and to constantly focus on understanding why in their studies. Ultimately, learning centered around essential questions is likely to be remembered over time rather than forgotten after a test has been taken.

Integrating Fact Pyramids With Essential Questions

Fact Pyramids (Buehl, 1991) provide teachers with a template for analyzing their curriculum so instruction guides comprehension toward big ideas—the understandings that we truly want students to remember over time. Teachers use Fact Pyramids as a planning tool to graphically categorize text information into three levels: (1) essential knowledge, (2) short-term information, and (3) background detail (see Figure 3 for an example).

Essential knowledge is what one would expect a literate person to know or be able to do over time; these are the "need to know" explanations, generalizations, interpretations, procedures, conclusions, and conceptual understandings. Essential knowledge remains with us years later. Such big ideas represent the point of learning, so essential knowledge resides in the point of a Fact Pyramid. Curricular standards to be met by a unit of study are reflected in these "top of the pyramid" priorities. Essential knowledge is triggered by essential questions and organized through specific text frames. Essential knowledge represents the heart of the comprehension processes of determining importance and synthesizing understanding and intersects with the Common Core's Reading Anchor Standard 2, which emphasizes central themes and ideas and their development in written texts.

Short-term information comprises the necessary facts and details we use to deepen our understandings, but these are generally forgotten over time. This information occupies much of the language of class discussion and instruction—the key vocabulary and major details—but ultimately is not important as an end in itself. The Common Core refers to short-term information as "text-based evidence," which we use to support those generalizations, interpretations, and conclusions that become memorable, but this factual baseline gradually drifts away. Often we tell students, "You need to know this," but what we are really saying is that this short-term information will be on the test. We would be hard-pressed to locate many literate adults who have retained this short-term information

> "To put it in an odd way, too many teachers focus on the teaching *and not the* learning. *They spend most of their time thinking, first, about what they will do, what materials they will use, and what they will ask students to do rather than first considering what the learner will need in order to accomplish the learning goals." (Wiggins & McTighe, 2005, p. 15)*

Figure 3
Fact Pyramid for the Crusades

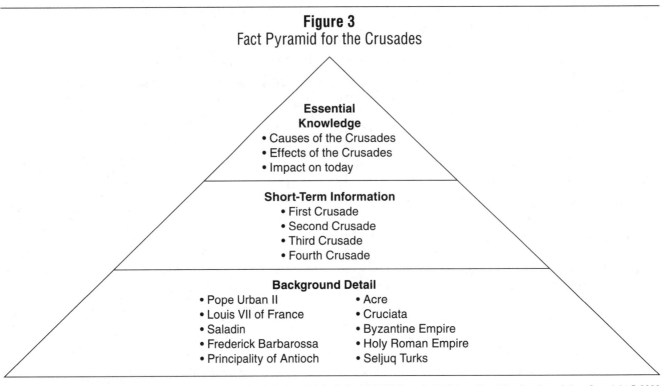

**Essential
Knowledge**
• Causes of the Crusades
• Effects of the Crusades
• Impact on today

Short-Term Information
• First Crusade
• Second Crusade
• Third Crusade
• Fourth Crusade

Background Detail

• Pope Urban II	• Acre
• Louis VII of France	• Cruciata
• Saladin	• Byzantine Empire
• Frederick Barbarossa	• Holy Roman Empire
• Principality of Antioch	• Seljuq Turks

Note. Adapted from *Classroom Strategies for Interactive Learning* (3rd ed., p. 35), by D. Buehl, 2009, Newark, DE: International Reading Association. Copyright © 2009 by the International Reading Association.

(earlier in the chapter, we identified this temporary storage as working memory). Only individuals who make repeated trips through the material, such as professionals in a particular field and teachers, tend to remember short-term information over time.

Background detail is the supporting information that provides the depth for fleshing out an understanding but certainly does not need to be learned for its own sake. A complex text supplies readers with more than headlines and boldface vocabulary. Background detail comprises the semantic glue for a text, the elaborations and examples that help illuminate understanding. Background detail can be an asset in classroom materials, but such information should not be accentuated as factlets that draw students' attention away from big ideas. Classroom questions, activities, and assessments should not ask students to be responsible for background detail. Instead, students should be expected to generalize and summarize: "Basically, what the author is telling me in these three paragraphs is...."

Using Fact Pyramids as a planning tool can help teachers make decisions about which classroom strategies best differentiate among the levels of information delivered in a text. By categorizing information in terms of the three levels, teachers can identify shortcomings in a text's organization and presentation of

ideas. Is essential knowledge readily apparent, or will students become overwhelmed by factual information and not realize the point of the material? Will students be able to synthesize understandings, or will they stumble, lost, through forests of details?

Planning With Fact Pyramids

Unfortunately, as previously discussed, classroom questioning frequently diverts attention away from essential knowledge. For example, the following item, typical in world history textbooks, asks students to process background detail to complete an assignment about the Crusades:

Identify the following:

(a) Urban II

(b) Saladin

(c) Richard I

(d) Seljuq Turks

(e) Children's Crusade

Such a question sends a faulty message to students. First, they are led to believe that all historical facts mentioned in a text are equally important. A few of us might recognize Richard I as the famous Richard the Lionheart, but most literate adults would have scant notion of the other items. Such assignments give students no direction for evaluating which information is most deserving of emphasis. In addition, students know they will forget whatever they write down about these facts within a short period of time, so they begin to cynically regard all information encountered in history as equally forgettable.

A Fact Pyramid (reproducible available in the Appendix) would help clarify important text information for students to write about and remember (see Figure 3). A history teacher might decide that the primary focus for a unit on the Crusades—what literate people should remember over time—should center on three big ideas, all structured around a cause/effect text frame:

1. *Causes of the Crusades:* European Christians regarded it a moral imperative to contest Muslim control of territory in the Middle East regarded as holy lands.

2. *Effects of the Crusades:* Years of contact between Christian and Muslim worlds led to profound changes in trade, political structures, warfare, economics, scientific knowledge, and spread of ideas.

3. *Impact on today:* Attitudes and issues created by the Crusades provide insight on understanding current tensions and conflict in the Middle East.

Short-term information for the Crusades unit might include the First, Second, Third, and Fourth Crusades. Details regarding major defining events, such as the massacre at Jerusalem, the plunder of Constantinople, the creation of Crusader states, and the Children's Crusade, will become hazy for most people over time, but an awareness of the controversies engendered by the Crusades should remain. Class discussions might also include the decline of feudalism, new technologies like gunpowder, siege warfare tactics, and the rise of nation-states.

Background information about historical figures, such as Pope Urban II, Saladin, Louis VII of France, and Frederick Barbarossa, and facts like the establishment of the Principality of Antioch, *cruciata* means marked with a cross, and details about the Byzantine and Holy Roman Empires, represent supportive information useful in broadening and enriching an understanding of this unit's big ideas. Few literate adults could successfully identify most of this information. Students should *not* be asked to identify and respond to such background detail.

Fact Pyramids provide teachers with a planning tool to spotlight what is important and worthy of being remembered over time. Fact Pyramids emphasize instruction and the selection of classroom strategies that help students determine what is important and synthesize understandings to get the point—the top of the pyramid.

> *"Along with making thoughtful decisions about what information to stress, teachers must orchestrate learning opportunities that permit students to explore these concepts more deeply and fully." (Alexander & Jetton, 2000, p. 287)*

References

Alexander, P.A., & Jetton, T.L. (2000). Learning from text: A multidimensional and developmental perspective. In M.L. Kamil, P.B. Mosenthal, P.D. Pearson, & R. Barr (Eds.), *Handbook of reading research* (Vol. 3, pp. 285–310). Mahwah, NJ: Erlbaum.

Anderson, T.H., & Armbruster, B.B. (1984). Studying. In P.D. Pearson, R. Barr, M.L. Kamil, & P.B. Mosenthal (Eds.), *Handbook of reading research* (pp. 657–679). New York: Longman.

Buehl, D. (1991). Fact pyramids. *New Perspectives: Reading Across the Curriculum, 7*(6), 1–2.

Buehl, D. (2001). *Classroom strategies for interactive learning* (2nd ed.). Newark, DE: International Reading Association.

Buehl, D. (2009). *Classroom strategies for interactive learning* (3rd ed.). Newark, DE: International Reading Association.

Buehl, D., & Stumpf, S. (2007). Literacy demands in content classrooms. In *Adolescent literacy toolkit* (pp. 33–51). Madison: Wisconsin Department of Public Instruction.

Daniels, H., & Zemelman, S. (2004). *Subjects matter: Every teacher's guide to content-area reading*. Portsmouth, NH: Heinemann.

Durkin, D. (1978). What classroom observations reveal about reading comprehension instruction. *Reading Research Quarterly, 14*(4), 481–533. doi:10.1598/RRQ.14.4.2

Jones, B.F., Palincsar, A.S., Ogle, D.S., & Carr, E.G. (1987). *Strategic teaching and learning: Cognitive instruction in the content areas*. Alexandria, VA: Association for Supervision and Curriculum Development.

National Governors Association Center for Best Practices & Council of Chief State School Officers. (2010). *Common Core State Standards for English language arts and literacy in history/social studies, science, and technical subjects*. Washington, DC: Authors.

Pearson, P.D., & Fielding, L. (1991). Comprehension instruction. In R. Barr, M.L. Kamil, P. Mosenthal, & P.D. Pearson (Eds.), *Handbook of reading research* (Vol. 2, pp. 815–860). New York: Longman.

Sousa, D.A. (2011). *How the brain learns* (4th ed.). Thousand Oaks, CA: Corwin.

Wiggins, G., & McTighe, J. (2005). *Understanding by design* (Expanded 2nd ed.). Alexandria, VA: Association for Supervision and Curriculum Development.

Suggested Reading

Buehl, D. (1991). Frames of mind. *The Exchange, 4*(2), 4–5.

CHAPTER 4

Mentoring Reading Through Disciplinary Lenses

Consider the vast range of written texts you might read during a stretch of weeks: periodicals, professional resources, news articles, technical documents, classroom materials, student work, journals, blogs, and books. Some of the texts would be considered *choice* reads; you choose to read them for purposes you identified, such as to inform or entertain yourself. Other texts could be termed *obligation* reads; you felt personally obligated to read them to satisfy certain needs or goals, or others obligated you to read them to meet demands, such as workplace requirements or college course expectations.

A highlight of my recent reading was the fourth volume of Robert Caro's (2012) monumental biography of former President Lyndon Johnson, a choice read selected to both inform and entertain. Having read the first three volumes over the years, I had been eagerly awaiting the next installment, and I was not disappointed. Caro entices readers in his introduction:

> Although the cliché says that power always corrupts, what is seldom said, but what is equally true, is that power always *reveals*. When a man is climbing, trying to persuade others to give him power, concealment is necessary: to hide traits that might make others reluctant to give him power, to hide also what he wants to do with that power; if men recognized the traits or realized the aims, they might refuse to give him what he wants. But as a man obtains more power, camouflage is less necessary. The curtain begins to rise. The revealing begins. (p. xiv)

In Chapter 1, we examined the characteristics of complex texts, and certainly Caro's prose is another prime example of text complexity. We meet sophisticated language, elaborate sentence structures, and intriguing ideas. The author tells us much in his 605 pages, requiring perseverance and frequent referrals back in the text as we incrementally assemble a sense of the people and the times. Readers have to manage the comprehension processes explained in Chapter 1, the knowledge demands emphasized in Chapter 2, and the internal textual relationships outlined in Chapter 3.

In addition, readers must mediate the way a historian thinks; how a historian constructs a history; how a historian examines the historical record; and how a historian arrives at particular explanations, interpretations, theories, and conclusions. Unsurprisingly, having majored in history as an undergraduate, I am comfortable with authors who display this kind of thinking. I expect such authors to explain why things transpired the way they did, and in this case, why Johnson and others behaved the way they did and why events happened the way they did. I track how things changed, why they changed, and how these changes impacted people. I am alert for turning points that propelled events in new and potentially redefining directions. I attempt to understand these people from a past era—their needs, their concerns, their perspectives, and their beliefs. And I am ever vigilant for distilling the lessons of history, how the past can inform who we are and how we live today. As a result, I am confident in choosing to read a history book as a choice text.

The Development of Disciplinary Literacy

This approach to thinking about texts, exhibited by me as a reader of history, can be described as reading through a disciplinary lens. This lens—my approach to comprehending the texts of history—has been honed over the years through my interests, preferences, and experiences. You likely have a comfortable lens for reading certain disciplinary texts as well. Some of you excel as readers through a scientific lens, or mathematical lens, or artistic lens, or technical lens, or literary lens, or others. You have become accomplished readers of the various texts of your discipline.

The phrase *disciplinary literacy* is increasingly being used to characterize reading and writing in the service of acquiring disciplinary knowledge, insights, and practices. It is helpful to represent the literacy development of our students as assuming three critical growth phases (T. Shanahan & Shanahan, 2008). The foundational phase, basic literacy, emphasizes gaining initial facility with how written language works and concentrates on mastery of those enabling skills that allow a reader to do what readers do: receive and comprehend written communications. And from the start, beginning readers work on comprehension; they address the same 10 Common Core reading anchor standards as high school seniors, albeit at earlier stages of sophistication. In addition, the Common Core establishes reading to inform as a priority during this phase, with a heavy expectation on informational texts for reading instruction (see Figure 4).

The second growth phase, intermediate literacy, is predominantly a streamlining and multitasking time, when readers become practiced in smoothly orchestrating their repertoire of strategies, extend their personal comprehension tool kits, sample a broader range of text genres, and build vocabularies that extend beyond the language of conversation (referred to as Tier 2 words in the Student-Friendly Vocabulary Explanations strategy). It is the need for continued work on this phase that characterizes most of our struggling readers at the middle and high school levels, and our school-wide conversations about differentiation and interventions focus on students still growing in this phase of literacy development.

Disciplinary literacy, the third growth phase, represents a significant transition from more generalized reading behaviors to highly contextualized reading demands—reading, writing, and thinking through different disciplinary lenses. Students are called on, certainly in the later elementary grades and most definitely during the middle and high school years, to delve into increasingly complex texts that reflect the knowledge, processes, and wisdom—the discourses—of a host of academic disciplines.

Disciplinary literacy, however, is not one compact set of highly skilled behaviors and routines but many. It might be helpful to portray disciplinary literacy as "towers of literacy" (Buehl, 2011a, p. 7). Students are expected to grow their capacities to access communications through texts as disparate as literary fiction, mathematics, the sciences, the social sciences, technical fields, health and fitness, and the humanities (art and music). Growth in one of these towers, such as the ability to effectively read fictional texts, does not necessarily translate into growth in the other towers, such as mathematics or the sciences. Disciplinary literacy is undertaken to facilitate acquiring disciplinary knowledge, and disciplinary literacy instruction must be embedded into disciplinary practices if students are to grow their capacities to successfully read disciplinary texts and communicate their understandings through speaking, writing, and creating in ways that conform to disciplinary expectations.

> *"Strong early reading skills do not automatically develop into more complex skills that enable students to deal with the specialized and sophisticated reading of literature, science, history, and mathematics (Perle et al. 2005)." (T. Shanahan & Shanahan, 2008, p. 43)*

Figure 4
The Contextualized Nature of Disciplinary Literacy

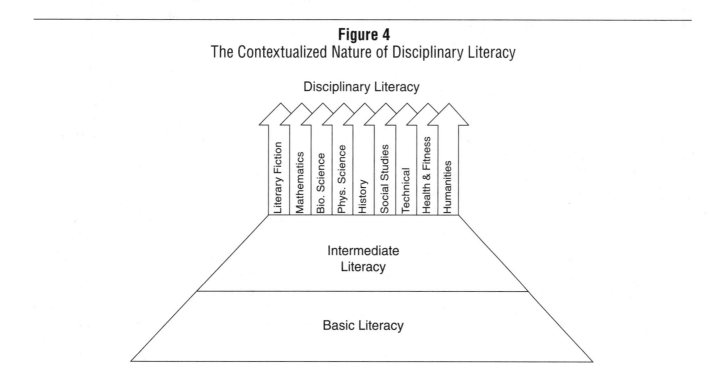

Apprenticing Disciplinary Readers and Learners

But who mentors students to build the capacity to read through different disciplinary lenses? As the research in adolescent literacy can attest, disciplinary literacy has been the neglected growth phase for our students (International Reading Association, 2012). Generally, the approach in our schools might be encapsulated as "You should be able to do this by now." As in, "Shouldn't we expect sixth graders (or ninth graders, or 12th graders) to be able to read the texts central to learning in our disciplines?" Students may receive reading assignments during the flow of disciplinary course work, but they rarely receive instructional support. Essentially, at that time when texts become increasingly diverse and complex, we tend to terminate instruction and leave students to devise effective practices on their own for making sense of disciplinary texts. Students are expected to comprehend texts dealing with sophisticated concepts—and that are more abstract, ambiguous, and subtle—by engaging in advanced literacy practices that, as Shanahan and Shanahan (2008) concluded, "are rarely taught" (p. 45).

Proficient readers might employ a number of effective stratagems to work a text as they strive to achieve an understanding: previewing a selection, rereading a difficult passage, adjusting reading rate, underlining pertinent information, tracking thoughts in the margins, using context to figure out new vocabulary, creating a graphic representation, jotting down notes, and periodically summing up understanding. But how about the majority of our students, those who have not yet developed such a degree of independence as readers? How can we interweave literacy strategies into the daily instruction of our course content? In many classrooms, this question is quite frankly not addressed; students will be left to figure out the adjustments they need to make on their own.

> "If learning to read effectively is a journey toward ever-increasing ability to comprehend texts, then teachers are the tour guides, ensuring that students stay on course, pausing to make sure they appreciate the landscape of understanding, and encouraging the occasional diversion down an inviting and interesting cul-de-sac or byway." (Duke, Pearson, Strachan, & Billman, 2011, p. 51)

The classroom strategies presented in Section 2 of this book depend on an apprentice learning model for mentoring disciplinary literacy (e.g., Schoenbach, Greenleaf, & Murphy, 2012). In their classic treatise on reading comprehension, Pearson and Gallagher (1983) coined the phrase *gradual release of responsibility* to describe this apprenticeship dynamic in the classroom. Basing their model on the ideas of the influential Russian educational theorist Lev Vygotsky (1978), Pearson and Gallagher envisioned instruction that moved from explicit modeling and instruction, to guided practice, and then to activities that incrementally position students to become independent learners.

Consider times in your life when you were treated as an apprentice learner. For me, this model reflects the natural circumstances of growing up on a Wisconsin dairy farm, which meant a childhood where work and home were interchangeable. As a youngster, much of my time was spent alongside my parents as they engaged in the varied tasks of farming: bumping along on a dusty hayrack as bales of fragrant alfalfa were piled higher and higher, trailing pails of frothy milk being carried down the barn driveway to the milk house, tagging along on the daily circuit of chores, and managing the livestock. As a farm kid, I was expected to eventually assume responsibility for many of the tasks I had been witnessing from an early age. Gradually, I was trusted at the steering wheel of the Allis Chalmers tractor, first under the supervision of my father and then more and more on my own, until I was regarded as a capable operator who could hitch up machinery and reliably accomplish fieldwork independent of my parents.

As an apprentice learner during those years, I was accorded ample opportunities to experience firsthand the work of the farm being properly executed. I was encouraged to ask questions about why things were done a certain way and what could happen if they weren't. I was granted the benefit of my parents' thinking as they solved problems while they worked. I was given guidance and supervision as I began to try my hand at a range of important jobs. I was treated like someone who was capable of handling responsibility and doing the work, and it was also clear that I was transitioning into the role of peer, someone who would be expected to take over a slice of the daily farm routine, to be on my own.

This same apprentice learning model is necessary to mentor students as they progressively develop their capacity to comprehend complex disciplinary texts. In the classroom, the gradual release of responsibility (see Figure 5) begins with teacher modeling. Students need continued opportunities to observe an expert—the teacher—at work, interacting with texts and showcasing thinking that undergirds working a text toward understanding. The first stage of the gradual release model assumes that students—novice learners of a discipline—may be confused about how to approach reading material in a particular content area or how to

Figure 5
Gradual Release of Responsibility

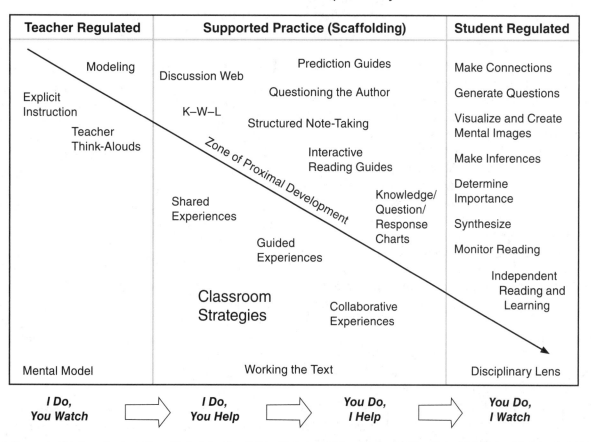

Teacher Regulated	Supported Practice (Scaffolding)	Student Regulated
Modeling	Discussion Web Prediction Guides	Make Connections
Explicit Instruction	Questioning the Author	Generate Questions
Teacher Think-Alouds	K–W–L Structured Note-Taking	Visualize and Create Mental Images
Zone of Proximal Development	Interactive Reading Guides	Make Inferences
	Shared Experiences Knowledge/ Question/ Response Charts	Determine Importance
	Guided Experiences	Synthesize
		Monitor Reading
	Classroom Strategies Collaborative Experiences	Independent Reading and Learning
Mental Model	Working the Text	Disciplinary Lens

| *I Do, You Watch* | → | *I Do, You Help* | → | *You Do, I Help* | → | *You Do, I Watch* |

Note. The bottom part of this figure is adapted from *Strategic Reading: Guiding Students to Lifelong Literacy, 6–12* (p. 45), by J.D. Wilhelm, T.N. Baker, and J. Dube, 2001, Portsmouth, NH: Boynton/Cook. Copyright © 2001 by Boynton/Cook. Adapted from *Classroom Strategies for Interactive Learning* (3rd ed., p. 9), by D. Buehl, 2009, Newark, DE: International Reading Association. Copyright © 2009 by the International Reading Association.

successfully employ a specific strategy. A think-aloud is a particularly powerful method for teachers to use to model their thinking as they work a disciplinary text. A think-aloud provides students with a window into the wisdom and strategy employed by an accomplished thinker during reading, allowing them to create a mental model of effective practices. These short sharing sessions become a means for displaying the thinking you will expect your students to try when they are confronted with similar reading demands.

Think-alouds need to underscore that the brain of an effective learner is constantly abuzz with mental activity, that thinking is not accidental but highly purposeful, and that thinking is always open to revision and reinterpretation. Even proficient readers sometimes encounter difficult texts and, like many students in your classroom, do not immediately get it. But proficient readers know appropriate reader moves—strategic responses—to make sure that they can achieve a satisfactory level of comprehension. Short texts, or excerpts from assigned classroom material such as the

textbook, make excellent sources for modeling this thinking.

Mentoring extends into the middle stage of the gradual release model, where the bulk of instructional action occurs. During this stage, as they converse with you and, most importantly, with other classmates to clarify their thinking and develop their understandings, students experiment with what you have modeled (Frey, Fisher, & Allen, 2009). This middle stage relies on scaffolding, support that is integrated within a lesson to guide student learning and prompt effective thinking. A scaffold is a temporary structure that is constructed to help

"We suspect that many students, particularly those who are especially high achieving, have benefited from close cultural models who have apprenticed them—implicitly and explicitly—into some of the necessary disciplinary knowledge and practices needed to successfully engage in sophisticated disciplinary practices." (Rainey & Moje, 2012, p. 77)

someone complete a task that would otherwise be very difficult. We use scaffolds frequently in life: to facilitate workers in erecting or repairing a building, to make it possible for painters to reach otherwise inaccessible areas, and to allow window washers dangling from high-rise offices to undertake a task unimaginable without such a device. But when the job is completed, scaffolds are dismantled; they are temporary structures.

Likewise, the classroom strategies in Section 2 of this book represent scaffolding, temporary instructional practices to help students as they embark on unfamiliar thinking but designed to fade away as students become comfortable with learning and working without this type of teacher guidance. A critical aspect of scaffolding in the classroom is teacher feedback. Students need continual dialogue with a knowledgeable mentor to help focus their efforts and problem-solve through difficulties. Students will fail at times during scaffolded lessons, but they need to realize that failure during new learning is a normal phenomenon. Helping students digest what went wrong and why, and what needs to be done the next time, is an essential component of this scaffolded zone.

The gradual release model assumes that students will need considerable work that is scaffolded before they become independent. A number of educational observers argue that this dynamic of instruction—scaffolding—is frequently not adequately achieved in disciplinary classrooms. Teachers may expect students to demonstrate independent thinking and learning before they have had sufficient practice and feedback to really get good at it. Struggling readers in particular need scaffolded lessons that remind them what effective thinkers do during learning and that guide them through challenging texts.

> "Vygotsky's ideas about actively assisting and instructing students to do complex cognitive tasks and for guiding them through the 'zone of proximal development'—the level at which they can do things with help that they cannot do alone—are apparent in highly successful programs for elementary students.... However, we rarely see these approaches used with older students." (Wilhelm et al., 2001, pp. 9–10)

The rationale of the gradual release model is to cede increasing responsibility to the students for directing their own learning. Students need regular reminders that the focal point of instruction is to empower them to accomplish important and sophisticated tasks while phasing out the support of the teacher and their classmates. The model emphasizes comprehension instruction that mentors students into becoming capable thinkers and learners when handling reading expectations with which they

have not yet developed expertise. This model is consistent with the Common Core's Reading Anchor Standard 10, which recommends scaffolding, as needed, to transition students into becoming independent, proficient readers of complex disciplinary texts.

Reading as Access

Instruction that adheres to the gradual release of responsibility model is indispensable for mentoring reading through different disciplinary lenses. But the disciplinary literacy growth phase also presumes that students are actually spending time comprehending complex texts as a regular component of their learning in different academic subjects. Students are not mentored to read complex disciplinary texts when one of these three very prevalent but flawed classroom conditions exists (Buehl, 2011a):

1. Students are expected to comprehend such texts without instruction and scaffolding.

2. Students are assigned to read such texts but do not need to depend on reaching satisfactory comprehension because they can count on being told or shown what they need to know.

3. Students are not even assigned to read such texts, and operate instead in a print-free environment, where virtually all they need to know will be delivered through telling, showing, and interactive activities.

Although the intended goal of the Common Core's reading standards is attaining the capacity for reading complex texts independently and proficiently, the first condition is a "sink or swim" scenario. Most teachers of academic disciplines recognize that a significant number of their students could find complex disciplinary texts overwhelming and would fail to learn if expected to be independent readers from these texts. Teachers may feel that their students should be able to comprehend such texts without instruction and scaffolding, and they may be frustrated that this is not so. Yet, until students have been provided necessary mentoring and support in disciplinary literacy, this first condition will remain unrealizable for many students.

The second flawed condition—assigning reading and then subsequently telling students what they need to know—might be summed up as a "hedging your bets" scenario. When teachers do not trust that many of their students will satisfactorily comprehend assigned texts, they follow up with presentations that focus more on telling rather than discussing to ensure that students get the desired content. And, of course, students—not just struggling readers but all students—pick up on this default routine very quickly. It has become a truism that students realize (and expect) that being a good listener will be the ticket to success in disciplinary classrooms. As a result, students may read assigned texts but rely on their teachers to deliver the payoff of what they will be accountable for knowing. Reading assignments may permit students to bypass comprehension and instead encourage a superficial pseudoread that concentrates on locating information to record on a worksheet or as answers to questions. In essence, this second flawed condition represents teacher awareness that "sink or swim" expectations are unrealistic. But in lieu of providing needed instruction and scaffolding, teachers rely on telling. (A variation of this second flawed condition is resorting to reading texts aloud to students, not as modeling and think-alouds but to deliver content, another exercise in listening.) Students become highly dependent on an intermediary—the teacher—to tell them what they should be developing the capacity to obtain themselves from their reading. This second condition is antithetical to meeting the Common Core's reading standards; students will not develop independence and proficiency as readers of complex texts if listening is their primary mode of learning in disciplinary settings.

The third flawed condition—not assigning reading—reflects a perception that disciplinary texts are a barrier to learning rather than significant sources for obtaining knowledge within an academic subject. This condition might be rather bluntly identified as throwing in the towel, with teachers conceding that because students struggle with comprehending complex texts, reading as a means to access disciplinary knowledge and practices will be completely sidestepped as a course expectation. Teachers may proclaim that reading is not a problematic issue in their classes because their students are not asked to do it. As detailed in Chapter 1, however, the Common Core's literacy standards represent a significant shift in expectations, in that all teachers are now accountable for the literacy development of the students in their discipline.

It is important to recognize that there are many points of access to disciplinary knowledge and insights and that reading is only one of these access points. Certainly, given the wealth of technological resources today, a 21st-century classroom should aggressively integrate viewing, creating, and interacting through technology into the flow of learning, interspersed with telling, classroom demonstrations, discussions, hands-on experiences, inquiry projects, and yes, reading. But avoidance of developing reading as an access point to learning about a discipline guarantees that many students will not build disciplinary knowledge without access to an intermediary—a well-informed and experienced expert—to tell them and show them what

they need to know. They will not have developed the capacity to inform themselves as readers.

In certain respects, this third flawed condition almost seems a reversion to preliterate times and reliance on the oral tradition, which emphasized access to a knowledgeable elder who passed on knowledge through telling and showing. One significant advantage of written texts was that learners could directly access what people know and think without proximity to these knowledgeable intermediaries. This is not to deny that intermediaries (e.g., teachers, creators of video resources) are highly valuable and critical pathways for accessing disciplinary knowledge. But critics argue that to redress the first flawed condition—the expectation of comprehension through reading without instruction and scaffolding—we have tilted too far to the second and third flawed conditions: disciplinary classrooms that do not develop independent points of access to knowledge through reading. For example, Pearson, Moje, and Greenleaf (2010) made this cogent observation about science classrooms:

> "Numerous studies over the past few decades have demonstrated that it is most helpful to teach comprehension strategies, text structures, and word-level strategies while students are engaged in reading challenging, content-rich texts. *Such skills don't stick when practiced for their own sake.*" (Heller & Greenleaf, 2007, p. 8)

> Reading about science is replaced by listening to someone talk about science….Avoiding the challenge of engaging students with texts may seem efficient, yet it ultimately undermines student learning. Instead of confronting reading problems head on, it breeds student dependence on the teacher for science knowledge and places the learner in a passive role. (p. 460)

A final comment about reading as a point of access should be acknowledged: An impressive segment of the groundbreaking research on comprehension in the 1980s examined the nature of the material students were asked to read in schools. The term *inconsiderate text* emerged from this body of research, and teachers were introduced to limitations of and issues with texts commonly assigned for disciplinary learning (Armbruster, 1984). Teachers who are disheartened by the shortcomings with many traditional texts used in disciplinary instruction, particularly textbooks, have rightfully veered away from assigning reading from texts that are arguably lacking. Complex disciplinary texts should also represent quality texts, even while recognizing that well-written textbooks can be useful sources of disciplinary information and insights. Reading Anchor Standard 9 of the Common Core envisions students reading from a broad array of complex texts as disciplinary learners.

Questioning Through Disciplinary Lenses

Mentoring reading, writing, and thinking through a disciplinary lens involves introducing students to characteristic ways of examining our world, communicating knowledge, and acting on disciplinary insights. As Fang (2012) explained,

> Recognizing disciplinary ways of using language is important because one cannot fully comprehend the texts of a specific discipline—where disciplinary knowledge is produced, stored, transmitted, and evaluated—without having a sense of how the discipline organizes knowledge though language. (p. 36)

As a result, there is distinctness to disciplinary texts; they are not mere generic informational texts. Not only do disciplinary texts exhibit specific knowledge demands and vocabulary, as examined in Chapter 2, but they are also repositories of organized thinking and distinct lines of inquiry.

> *"Disciplines have different ways of writing and speaking about the world. And because of this, discipline experts approach text with sets of expectations, reading strategies, and understandings that are firmly grounded in disciplinary knowledge."* (C. Shanahan, 2012, p. 71)

Or to put it another way, scientists ask different questions about their chosen fields of study than do historians, mathematicians, artists, musicians, fitness specialists, and other disciplinary experts. Comprehension of complex disciplinary texts, then, necessitates questioning through disciplinary lenses—questioning like a scientist, historian, mathematician, literary critic, and so forth. Questioning through a disciplinary lens pinpoints the essential questions explored by a discipline, as discussed in Chapter 3. Text frame questions, also detailed in Chapter 3, are embedded in these disciplinary-specific questions.

> *"The idea is not that content-area teachers should become reading and writing teachers, but rather that they should emphasize the reading and writing practices that are specific to their subjects, so students are encouraged to read and write like historians, scientists, mathematicians, and other subject-area experts."* (Biancarosa & Snow, 2004, p. 15)

For example, as I mentioned at the beginning of this chapter, I am comfortable with the kind of thinking displayed by authors who write through a historian's lens. I know what to expect, how to organize my thinking, and what questions I should pose to guide my comprehension. It does not mean that I am personally a historian or that we should treat our students as minihistorians. Instead, questioning like a historian provides a window into understanding facets of our life and world in a very valuable disciplinary way. Mentoring disciplinary literacy means modeling questioning the way disciplinary experts question and devising instruction that provides ongoing practice through strategies and tasks that reinforce and elicit these questions with students as they build knowledge in a discipline.

Following are several disciplinary questioning taxonomies that reflect thinking through different disciplinary lenses. Each taxonomy is a disciplinary-specific outgrowth of the baseline Self-Questioning Taxonomy (described in depth in Section 2). Questions are arrayed according to the revised Bloom's Taxonomy (Anderson & Krathwohl, 2001), meaning that students are mentored as readers of complex texts to ask disciplinary-relevant questions at all six levels of thinking: creating, evaluating, analyzing, applying, understanding, and remembering. In addition, the Common Core's literacy standards that correlate with the questions at each level of the taxonomy are identified. In many respects, these taxonomies offer teachers of a discipline seed questions from which to base modeling and classroom tasks.

Reading Through a History Lens

Examination of complex historical texts centers on five significant dynamics of historical inquiry: cause/effect, change/continuity, turning points, through their eyes, and using the past (Mandell & Malone, 2007). Questioning historical texts leads to forming arguments—conclusions, explanations, or generalizations—that can be justified by the historical record (see Table 5).

Reading Through a Literary Lens

Literary texts are indirect communications; authors use story as a vehicle for examining ideas and life experiences. Questioning of literary fiction guides readers to notice how an author is telling the story and why the author made certain choices so they can develop interpretations of what a complex literary text might mean (see Table 6).

Reading Through a Science Lens

Although thinking scientifically draws on general principles of scientific inquiry and agreement on conditions for determining scientific truths, some important distinctions exist between the biological and physical sciences that are reflected in complex texts within those disciplines. Both branches of science emphasize explaining—cause/effect dynamics—and the case that can be made for accepting such explanations (see Tables 7 and 8). In addition, biological science

Table 5
Self-Questioning Taxonomy for History Texts

Level of Thinking	Comprehension Self-Assessment	Focusing Questions	Common Core Anchor Standards for Reading
Creating	I have created new knowledge about the past.	• How has this author changed what I understand? • Why does this matter to the author? To me?	2: Main ideas 6: Author's purpose/ perspective 10: Text complexity
Evaluating	I can critically examine this author's conclusions/ interpretations/ explanations.	• Who is the author, and how has the author's perspective influenced the telling of this history? • What conclusions/interpretations/explanations does the author provide? • How did the author find out? What is the evidence? How can we evaluate this evidence? • What other conclusions/interpretations/ explanations could be justified by the evidence? • Does the author have an attitude, and if so, about what? • Whose viewpoints are not presented? What might be their perspective?	1: Explicit/implicit meanings 3: Text relationships 4: Vocabulary 6: Author's purpose/ perspective 8: Argument and support 9: Multiple texts 10: Text complexity
Analyzing	I can understand why.	• What happened? What caused it to happen? • What changed, and what remained the same? • Who benefited from the changes? Who didn't? • How does the author talk about the effect of past decisions or actions on future choices?	3: Text relationships 5: Text structure 10: Text complexity
Applying	I can use my understanding to better understand how the past influences my life and world.	• How can I connect my experiences and knowledge to what this author is telling me? • How does studying the past help me understand my life and my world?	1: Explicit/implicit meanings 4: Vocabulary 7: Visual literacy/ technology 9: Multiple texts 10: Text complexity
Understanding	I can understand what the author is telling me about the past.	• What does this author want me to understand about the past? • What questions does the author ask about the past? • How did people in this time period view their lives and world?	1: Explicit/implicit meanings 2: Main ideas 6: Author's purpose/ perspective 10: Text complexity
Remembering	I can recall specific details, information, and ideas from this text.	• What do I need to remember to make sense of the past?	1: Explicit/implicit meanings 2: Main ideas 10: Text complexity

Note. Adapted from "Reading Like an Insider," by D. Buehl, 2009, *The Exchange*, *22*(1), p. 5. Copyright © 2009 by the International Reading Association.

emphasizes conceptual organizations, such as classifying and categorizing.

Reading Through a Mathematics Lens

Mathematics texts are particularly sophisticated because readers must negotiate three methods of communicating mathematics knowledge: symbolic notation, graphic representations, and prose explanations. Within a specific text, readers must shift their questioning focus from reading to develop conceptual knowledge (the logic of the mathematics principles) to reading to develop procedural knowledge (the problem-solving processes of how to act on these understandings; see Tables 9 and 10).

Table 6
Self-Questioning Taxonomy for Literary Fiction

Level of Thinking	Comprehension Self-Assessment	Focusing Questions	Common Core Anchor Standards for Reading
Creating	I have developed an interpretation of what this story means.	• Why is the author telling me this story? • What theme or idea might the author be exploring in this story? • What does this story mean to me? • How has the author changed what I understand?	2: Main ideas 6: Author's purpose/ perspective 10: Text complexity
Evaluating	I can critically examine this story.	• Who is the author, and how has the author's perspective influenced the telling of this story? • What does the author's choice of words indicate about what the author might be thinking? • What emotions is the author eliciting? • Does the author have an attitude, and if so, about what?	1: Explicit/implicit meanings 4: Vocabulary 6: Author's purpose/ perspective 10: Text complexity
Analyzing	I can notice how the author wrote this story.	• What literary techniques does the author use? • What seems to be the purpose for using these literary techniques?	3: Text relationships 4: Vocabulary 5: Text structure 6: Author's purpose/ perspective 10: Text complexity
Applying	I can use my life experiences to understand the story.	• How can I connect this story to my life and experiences? • Why might the author have the characters say (or do) this? • What point might the author be making about the characters' actions? • Why did the author place the story in this setting?	3: Text relationships 4: Vocabulary 7: Visual literacy/ technology 9: Multiple texts 10: Text complexity
Understanding	I can understand what the author is telling me.	• How does the author have the characters interact with one another? • How do the characters feel about one another? • How do the characters' feelings and interactions change? • How does the author use conflict in this story? • How does the author resolve this conflict?	1: Explicit/implicit meanings 2: Main ideas 3: Text relationships 5: Text structure 6: Author's purpose/ perspective 10: Text complexity
Remembering	I can follow what happens in this story.	• Who are the characters? • Where does the story take place? • What are the major events of the story? • What is the sequence of these events? • What event initiates the action of the story?	1: Explicit/implicit meanings 3: Text relationships 10: Text complexity

Note. Adapted from *Classroom Strategies for Interactive Learning* (3rd ed., p. 159), by D. Buehl, 2009, Newark: DE: International Reading Association. Copyright © 2009 by the International Reading Association.

Reading Through a Technical Lens

Complex technical texts tend to be very terse and vocabulary driven and usually highly visual, as some of the information is portrayed through illustrations. Questioning a technical text derives from the very pragmatic need to use understanding to complete some desired task to achieve a certain end (see Table 11). As a result, reading tends to be hands-on: Read a segment, then apply it, then read the next segment, then apply it, and so on until the task is completed.

Table 7
Self-Questioning Taxonomy for Biological Science Texts

Level of Thinking	Comprehension Self-Assessment	Focusing Questions	Common Core Anchor Standards for Reading
Creating	I have created new knowledge about the biological world.	• How has this author changed what I understand? • How has this author corrected my previous misunderstandings?	2: Main ideas 6: Author's purpose/ perspective 10: Text complexity
Evaluating	I can critically examine this author's conclusions/theories/ explanations.	• What conclusions/theories/explanations does the author provide? • How do we know? What is the evidence? • What other conclusions/theories/explanations could be justified by the evidence?	1: Explicit/implicit meanings 2: Main ideas 6: Author's purpose/ perspective 8: Argument and support 9: Multiple texts 10: Text complexity
Analyzing	I can understand why.	• What happened? Why did it happen? How did it happen? • How does this biological concept work? • Why does this biological concept work the way it does? • What are the defining characteristics? • How is this similar to (or different from) other related biological concepts?	1: Explicit/implicit meanings 2: Main ideas 5: Text structure 7: Visual literacy/ technology 9: Multiple texts 10: Text complexity
Applying	I can use my understanding to better understand the biological world.	• How can I connect my experiences to what this author is telling me? • How can I use what this author is telling me to better understand living things? • How is what the author is telling me different from what I previously understood?	2: Main ideas 4: Vocabulary 7: Visual literacy/ technology 9: Multiple texts 10: Text complexity
Understanding	I can understand what the author is telling me about the biological world.	• What does this author want me to understand about living things? • How does the visual information help me understand what the author is telling me? • What do I currently understand about what the author is telling me?	1: Explicit/implicit meanings 2: Main ideas 6: Author's purpose/ perspective 7: Visual literacy/ technology 10: Text complexity
Remembering	I can recall specific information and ideas from this text.	• What biological concepts do I need to remember for future understandings? • What biological vocabulary do I need to become comfortable using?	1: Explicit/implicit meanings 2: Main ideas 4: Vocabulary 10: Text complexity

Note. Adapted from "Mentoring Literacy Practices in Academic Disciplines" (p. 235), by D. Buehl, in *Adolescent Literacy, Field Tested: Effective Solutions for Every Classroom*, 2009, edited by S.R. Parris, D. Fisher, and K. Headley, Newark, DE: International Reading Association. Copyright © 2009 by the International Reading Association.

Reading Through a Health and Physical Fitness Lens

Reading complex health and fitness texts is also accompanied by expectations that readers will act on the information. Questioning health and fitness texts centers on developing insights into personal health variables and how one's body works, as well as outlining possible actions a reader might take to achieve certain health and fitness goals (see Table 12).

Reading Through a Music Lens

Reading complex music texts revolves around tracking the author's references to the elements of music and

Table 8
Self-Questioning Taxonomy for Physical Science Texts

Level of Thinking	Comprehension Self-Assessment	Focusing Questions	Common Core Anchor Standards for Reading
Creating	I have created new knowledge about the physical world.	• How has this author changed what I understand? • How has this author corrected my previous misunderstandings? • How do I see the world I live in differently now?	2: Main ideas 6: Author's purpose/ perspective 10: Text complexity
Evaluating	I can critically examine this author's conclusions/theories/ explanations.	• What conclusions/theories/explanations does the author provide? • How do we know? What is the evidence? • How can we test these scientific principles? How can we collect our own evidence? • What do our observations tell us? • Are our observations consistent with the scientific principles that we are examining? • What are possible limitations of our investigations? • What other conclusions/theories/explanations could be justified by the evidence?	1: Explicit/implicit meanings 2: Main ideas 3: Text relationships 6: Author's purpose/ perspective 7: Visual literacy/ technology 8: Argument and support 9: Multiple texts 10: Text complexity
Analyzing	I can understand why.	• What happened (or happens)? Why does it happen? How does it happen? • What process do objects go through? What happens at each stage of the process? • What are the relationships that cause each effect in this process? • How can we model this process? • How can these scientific principles be demonstrated?	1: Explicit/implicit meanings 2: Main ideas 5: Text structure 7: Visual literacy/ technology 9: Multiple texts 10: Text complexity
Applying	I can use my comprehension to better understand the physical world.	• How can I connect my experiences to what this author is telling me? • How do these scientific principles explain the world I live in? • Where might I encounter these scientific principles in action? • How is what the author is telling me different from what I previously understood?	2: Main ideas 4: Vocabulary 7: Visual literacy/ technology 9: Multiple texts 10: Text complexity
Understanding	I can understand what the author is telling me about the physical world.	• What does this author want me to understand about the physical world? • What do I currently understand about what the author is telling me? • How does the visual information help me understand what the author is telling me? • Can I use my imagination to see what the author wants me to understand?	1: Explicit/implicit meanings 2: Main ideas 6: Author's purpose/ perspective 7: Visual literacy/ technology 10: Text complexity
Remembering	I can recall specific information and ideas from this text.	• What scientific principles do I need to remember for future understandings? • What science vocabulary do I need to become comfortable using?	1: Explicit/implicit meanings 2: Main ideas 4: Vocabulary 10: Text complexity

Note. Adapted from *Developing Readers in the Academic Disciplines* (p. 200), by D. Buehl, 2011, Newark, DE: International Reading Association. Copyright © 2011 by the International Reading Association.

Table 9
Self-Questioning Taxonomy for Mathematical Concepts Texts

Level of Thinking	Comprehension Self-Assessment	Focusing Questions	Common Core Anchor Standards for Reading
Creating	I have created new knowledge.	• What do I understand now that I didn't understand before about mathematics? • How does this concept help me think mathematically?	2: Main ideas 6: Author's purpose/ perspective 8: Argument and support 10: Text complexity
Evaluating	I can critically examine this mathematics concept.	• Why is this definition useful? What can we do with this concept? • How does the author use the concept in mathematics problem solving? • What kinds of problems can I solve using my understanding of this concept?	2: Main ideas 3: Text relationships 4: Vocabulary 6: Author's purpose/ perspective 8: Argument and support 9: Multiple texts 10: Text complexity
Analyzing	I can follow the logic of what the author is telling me.	• What are the defining characteristics of this concept? • How can I explain why this concept makes sense? • How does this concept relate to other mathematics concepts that I have learned?	1: Explicit/implicit meanings 2: Main ideas 5: Text structure 9: Multiple texts 10: Text complexity
Applying	I can use my mathematics understanding in some meaningful way.	• Where in my life might I encounter this mathematics concept? • What are some examples of this mathematics concept from my life? • How can I use this concept to describe, inform, or explain some part my life?	2: Main ideas 4: Vocabulary 7: Visual literacy/ technology 9: Multiple texts 10: Text complexity
Understanding	I can understand what the author is telling me.	• How can I explain the mathematics concept? In mathematics language? In everyday language? • How can I use visual information (diagrams, pictures, or graphs) about the concept to understand its definition? • What examples of this mathematical concept does the author provide?	1: Explicit/implicit meanings 2: Main ideas 4: Vocabulary 6: Author's purpose/ perspective 7: Visual literacy/ technology 10: Text complexity
Remembering	I can recall specific terms and mathematics concepts presented by the author.	• What mathematics vocabulary does the author introduce? • What definitions does the author provide for new mathematics concepts? • What are the undefined terms (e.g., *whole number, point, line, plane, group operation, set*) in the definitions? • What previous mathematics learning do I need to review to make sense of the definitions? • What do the symbols and notations mean in the definitions?	1: Explicit/implicit meanings 4: Vocabulary 9: Multiple texts 10: Text complexity

Note. Adapted from *Developing Readers in the Academic Disciplines* (p. 205), by D. Buehl, 2011, Newark, DE: International Reading Association. Copyright © 2011 by the International Reading Association.

Table 10
Self-Questioning Taxonomy for Mathematics Problem-Solving Texts

Level of Thinking	Comprehension Self-Assessment	Focusing Questions	Common Core Anchor Standards for Reading
Creating	I have created new knowledge.	• How can my understanding be used to describe, inform, or explain information, objects, or situations in a mathematical way? • How have I expanded my ability to create solutions using mathematics?	2: Main ideas 6: Author's purpose/ perspective 8: Argument and support 9: Multiple texts 10: Text complexity
Evaluating	I can monitor my effectiveness in applying this problem-solving procedure.	• Do the example problems make sense when I examine them? • What results have I obtained from applying the problem-solving procedure? • How close is the result to what I predicted or estimated? • What confusions did I encounter during problem solving? • What actions can I take to overcome any confusions?	3: Text relationships 6: Author's purpose/ perspective 8: Argument and support 10: Text complexity
Analyzing	I can follow the logic of what the author is telling me.	• What is the logical reasoning justifying the mathematics statement? • How can I use this statement to explain mathematical facts that I already know to be true? How can I use this statement as proof? • How can I link this statement to similar mathematics statements that I have learned? • Is the converse of the statement ("if B, then A") true? • What predictions or estimations do I have when I am problem solving?	2: Main ideas 4: Vocabulary 5: Text structure 8: Argument and support 9: Multiple texts 10: Text complexity
Applying	I can use my understanding for solving mathematical problems.	• What kinds of problems can I solve using this mathematics statement? • How can I apply this problem-solving procedure to a variety of problems? • What are similar mathematics statements that I have previously learned?	3: Text relationships 4: Vocabulary 7: Visual literacy/ technology 9: Multiple texts 10: Text complexity
Understanding	I can understand what the author is telling me.	• How can I explain the mathematics statement in the form "if A, then B"? • How can I rephrase the statement using other symbols or notations without changing its meaning? • How can the visual information inform my problem solving?	1: Explicit/implicit meanings 2: Main ideas 3: Text relationships 4: Vocabulary 6: Author's purpose/ perspective 7: Visual literacy/ technology 10: Text complexity
Remembering	I can recall specific terms and mathematics procedures presented by the author.	• What mathematics vocabulary does the author use? • What are the symbols, notations, and definitions of the terms used? • What mathematics statement (formula, theorem, rule, or principle) does the author introduce? • What problem-solving procedure does the author introduce? • What are the steps I need to follow in this problem-solving procedure?	1: Explicit/implicit meanings 3: Text relationships 4: Vocabulary 10: Text complexity

Note. Adapted from *Developing Readers in the Academic Disciplines* (p. 206), by D. Buehl, 2011, Newark, DE: International Reading Association. Copyright © 2011 by the International Reading Association.

Table 11
Self-Questioning Taxonomy for Technical Texts

Level of Thinking	Comprehension Self-Assessment	Focusing Questions	Common Core Anchor Standards for Reading
Creating	I have created a product or completed a task.	• What have I been able to create or accomplish? • How can I use my understanding in future applications?	2: Main ideas 6: Author's purpose/ perspective 9: Multiple texts 10: Text complexity
Evaluating	I can critically examine my completion of this task.	• To what extent have I been able to apply my understanding to complete the task? • To what extent have I been able to meet the author's expectations? • To what extent does my application of the author's instructions achieve the intended final outcome?	2: Main ideas 3: Text relationships 6: Author's purpose/ perspective 8: Argument and support 9: Multiple texts 10: Text complexity
Analyzing	I can examine the text and determine what I need to do to accomplish the task.	• What is not clear to me? What can I do to problem-solve my lack of understanding? • What visual information does the author provide? • How does the visual information help me visualize (create a mental model) of what I need to do? • How do the visuals connect to written portions of the text? To unfamiliar vocabulary? • What might happen if I do not follow the specified procedures?	3: Text relationships 5: Text structure 7: Visual literacy/ technology 8: Argument and support 10: Text complexity
Applying	I can use my previous experiences to understand the procedures and instructions.	• How can I connect my previous experiences to performing this task? • What must I read especially carefully? • What help does the author provide for understanding key terms? • What can I do to develop an understanding of unfamiliar terms?	1: Explicit/implicit meanings 4: Vocabulary 7: Visual literacy/ technology 9: Multiple texts 10: Text complexity
Understanding	I can understand how to follow the procedures and complete the task.	• What is the task that I need to accomplish? • What should the final outcome look like? • Can I imagine myself completing the procedures that the author describes?	2: Main ideas 6: Author's purpose/ perspective 7: Visual literacy/ technology 10: Text complexity
Remembering	I can follow the author's instructions.	• What steps do I need to follow? • What key terms are used? • What do I remember about these key terms?	1: Explicit/implicit meanings 3: Text relationships 4: Vocabulary 10: Text complexity

Note. Adapted from *Developing Readers in the Academic Disciplines* (p. 209), by D. Buehl, 2011, Newark, DE: International Reading Association. Copyright © 2011 by the International Reading Association.

how composers, musicians, and compositions can be understood through analysis of these elements. In addition, questioning musical texts includes application to musical performances, which act on this knowledge, as well as the reading of the symbolic musical notation—technical texts that readers must adhere to while performing (see Table 13).

Reading Through an Art Lens

Aesthetic understanding and appreciation of various art forms relate to the elements of art and principles of design. Questioning complex art texts is predicated on perceiving how an author communicates these elements when describing or explaining artworks or artists. Examination of visual artistic works is integral to

Table 12
Self-Questioning Taxonomy for Health and Physical Fitness Texts

Level of Thinking	Comprehension Self-Assessment	Focusing Questions	Common Core Anchor Standards for Reading
Creating	I have created new knowledge relevant to my personal health and physical fitness.	• How has this author changed what I previously understood about specific personal health and physical fitness issues? • How has my understanding helped me articulate new personal goals? • How has my understanding helped me identify new personal health and physical fitness routines?	2: Main ideas 3: Text relationships 6: Author's purpose/ perspective 8: Argument and support 9: Multiple texts 10: Text complexity
Evaluating	I can critically examine the author's explanations/ conclusions/ recommendations.	• What is the author's purpose for telling me this message? • What authority does the author bring to this message? • How current is the information? • How does the author support the explanations, conclusions, and recommendations?	2: Main ideas 6: Author's purpose/ perspective 8: Argument and support 10: Text complexity
Analyzing	I can explain why.	• What causes of personal health and fitness conditions does the author explain? • What effects on personal health and fitness does the author explain? • How is the author's message similar to (or different from) other texts on this topic that I have read?	2: Main ideas 5: Text structure 6: Author's purpose/ perspective 9: Multiple texts 10: Text complexity
Applying	I can connect my understanding to personal health and physical fitness concerns.	• How does what the author is telling me compare with my current behavior? • How does what the author is telling me suggest changes in my current behavior? • How can I apply what the author is telling me to personal health and fitness decisions?	3: Text relationships 6: Author's purpose/ perspective 8: Argument and support 9: Multiple texts 10: Text complexity
Understanding	I can understand what the author wants me to know about health and physical fitness.	• What does the author want me to understand about health and physical fitness issues? • How is what the author is telling me different from what I previously understood? • How does the visual information help me understand what the author is telling me?	2: Main ideas 3: Text relationships 6: Author's purpose/ perspective 7: Visual literacy/ technology 9: Multiple texts 10: Text complexity
Remembering	I can recall specific information about personal health and physical fitness from this text.	• What do I need to remember that relates to personal health and physical fitness? • What health and fitness vocabulary do I need to become comfortable using?	1: Explicit/implicit meanings 3: Text relationships 4: Vocabulary 10: Text complexity

comprehension of complex art texts, and readers frequently apply their understandings toward the creation of personal artistic works (see Table 14).

These disciplinary self-questioning taxonomies provide a foundation for the use of any of the specific classroom strategies described in Section 2. Frequent references to particular taxonomies are integrated into the strategy explanations. For more extensive discussions of reading through disciplinary lenses and in-depth considerations of the literacy demands of each of the above-mentioned disciplines, consult *Developing Readers in the Academic Disciplines* (Buehl, 2011b), which is designed to be a companion resource to this book.

Table 13
Self-Questioning Taxonomy for Music Performance

Level of Thinking	Comprehension Self-Assessment	Focusing Questions	Common Core Anchor Standards for Reading
Creating	I have created an interpretation of this music.	• What might the composer be telling listeners through this music? • How can my performance communicate this music to my listeners?	2: Main ideas 6: Author's purpose/ perspective 9: Multiple texts 10: Text complexity
Evaluating	I can critically examine my performance of this music.	• What expectations does the composer have for the musicians playing (or singing) this piece? • How have I met the composer's expectations?	1: Explicit/implicit meanings 3: Text relationships 4: Vocabulary 5: Text structure 6: Author's purpose/ perspective 8: Argument and support 10: Text complexity
Analyzing	I can understand how the composer created the musical effects of this composition.	• How does the composer use the elements of music (form, rhythm, melody, harmony, timbre, texture, and expression)? • Why did the composer make these particular musical choices?	5: Text structure 6: Author's purpose/ perspective 10: Text complexity
Applying	I can use my understanding to perform and appreciate this music.	• How can I connect my experiences to performing this music? • What emotional responses to the music does the composer seem to be indicating?	6: Author's purpose/ perspective 7: Visual literacy/ technology 9: Multiple texts 10: Text complexity
Understanding	I can understand the background of this composition.	• When did the composer write this piece, and how might the times have influenced this music? • Why did the composer write this piece, and for whom? • What do we know about the composer, and is the piece characteristic of this individual's work?	1: Explicit/implicit meanings 2: Main ideas 6: Author's purpose/ perspective 9: Multiple texts 10: Text complexity
Remembering	I can follow the composer's instructions.	• How has the composer indicated that this piece should be performed? • What attention do I need to pay to time signatures, key signatures, note values, dynamics, tempo markings, and pitches?	1: Explicit/implicit meanings 3: Text relationships 4: Vocabulary 7: Visual literacy/ technology 10: Text complexity

Note. Adapted from "Connecting Music to Literacy" (p. 3), by D. Buehl and W. Buehl, October 2008, paper presented at the Wisconsin School Music Association Conference, Madison.

References

Anderson, L.W., & Krathwohl, D.R. (Eds.). (2001). *A taxonomy for learning, teaching, and assessing: A revision of Bloom's taxonomy of educational objectives.* New York: Longman.

Armbruster, B. (1984). The problem of "inconsiderate text." In G.G. Duffy, L.R. Roehler, & J. Mason (Eds.), *Comprehension instruction: Perspectives and suggestions* (pp. 202–217). New York: Longman.

Biancarosa, G., & Snow, C.E. (2004). *Reading next—a vision for action and research in middle and high school literacy: A report to Carnegie Corporation of New York.* Washington, DC: Alliance for Excellent Education.

Buehl, D. (2009). *Classroom strategies for interactive learning* (3rd ed.). Newark, DE: International Reading Association.

Buehl, D. (2009). Mentoring literacy practices in academic disciplines. In S.R. Parris, D. Fisher, & K. Headley (Eds.), *Adolescent literacy, field tested: Effective solutions for every*

Table 14
Self-Questioning Taxonomy for Art

Level of Thinking	Comprehension Self-Assessment	Focusing Questions	Common Core Anchor Standards for Reading
Creating	I have created an understanding and/ or appreciation of this artwork.	• How have I developed an understanding and/or appreciation of specific artistic methods and ideas expressed in this artwork? • How do I personally regard this artwork? • How does this artwork speak to my interests and experiences?	2: Main ideas 6: Author's purpose/ perspective 7: Visual literacy/ technology 8: Argument and support
Evaluating	I can critically evaluate this artwork.	• What about the artwork seems to be most important to the artist? • How effective was the author in using the elements of art and principles of design? • What might the artist be communicating to people through this artwork? • How successful was the author in communicating through this artwork?	2: Main ideas 3: Text relationships 4: Vocabulary 6: Author's purpose/ perspective 7: Visual literacy/ technology 8: Argument and support 9: Multiple texts 10: Text complexity
Analyzing	I can understand how the artist created the artistic effects of this artwork.	• How does the artist use the elements of art (color, line, texture, shape, form, value, and space)? • How does the artist use the principles of design (balance, gradation, repetition, contrast, harmony, dominance, and unity)? • What is the impact of these particular artistic choices? • How did the artist's choices set the tone of the artwork? • How does the artwork compare with other works following a similar theme, method, or artistic idea?	3: Text relationships 4: Vocabulary 5: Text structure 6: Author's purpose/ perspective 7: Visual literacy/ technology 8: Argument and support 9: Multiple texts
Applying	I can use my understanding to examine this artwork.	• How can I connect my life and experiences to what I observe in this artwork? • How does the artwork strike my senses? • What emotional responses do I have to the artwork? • What is the tone of the artwork?	7: Visual literacy/ technology 9: Multiple texts 10: Text complexity
Understanding	I can understand the background of this artwork.	• What do we know about the artist, and is the piece characteristic of this individual's work? • When did the artist create this piece, and how might the times have influenced this artwork? • What do we know about why the author created this particular piece (or pieces) of this type? • How does this artwork reflect particular methods or artistic ideas?	1: Explicit/implicit meanings 2: Main ideas 5: Text structure 6: Author's purpose/ perspective 7: Visual literacy/ technology 9: Multiple texts 10: Text complexity
Remembering	I can describe the artwork.	• What elements of art (color, line, texture, shape, form, value, and space) do you observe in this artwork? • What techniques of mark making do you observe in this artwork?	3: Text relationships 4: Vocabulary 7: Visual literacy/ technology

classroom (pp. 228–238). Newark, DE: International Reading Association.

Buehl, D. (2009). Reading like an insider. *The Exchange, 22*(1), 2–5.

Buehl, D. (2011a). Constructing towers of literacy. *The Exchange, 24*(1), 6–10.

Buehl, D. (2011b). *Developing readers in the academic disciplines*. Newark, DE: International Reading Association.

Buehl, D., & Buehl, W. (2008, October). *Connecting music to literacy*. Paper presented at the Wisconsin School Music Association Conference, Madison.

Duke, N.K., Pearson, P.D., Strachan, S.L., & Billman, A.K. (2011). Essential elements of fostering and teaching reading comprehension. In S.J. Samuels & A.E. Farstrup (Eds.), *What research has to say about reading instruction* (4th ed., pp. 51–93). Newark, DE: International Reading Association.

Fang, Z. (2012). The challenges of reading disciplinary texts. In T.L. Jetton & C. Shanahan (Eds.), *Adolescent literacy in the academic disciplines: General principles and practical strategies* (pp. 34–68). New York: Guilford.

Frey, N., Fisher, D., & Allen, A. (2009). Productive group work in middle and high school classrooms. In S.R. Parris, D. Fisher, & K. Headley (Eds.), *Adolescent literacy, field tested: Effective solutions for every classroom* (pp. 70–81). Newark, DE: International Reading Association.

Heller, R., & Greenleaf, C.L. (2007). *Literacy instruction in the content areas: Getting to the core of middle and high school improvement*. Washington, DC: Alliance for Excellent Education.

International Reading Association. (2012). *Adolescent literacy: A position statement of the International Reading Association* (Rev. ed.). Newark, DE: Author.

Mandell, N., & Malone, B. (2007). *Thinking like a historian: Rethinking history instruction*. Madison: Wisconsin Historical Society Press.

Pearson, P.D., & Gallagher, M.C. (1983). The instruction of reading comprehension. *Contemporary Educational Psychology, 8*(3), 317–344. doi:10.1016/0361-476X(83)90019-X.

Pearson, P.D., Moje, E., & Greenleaf, C. (2010). Literacy and science: Each in the service of the other. *Science, 328*(5977), 459–463.

Rainey, E., & Moje, E.B. (2012). Building insider knowledge: Teaching students to read, write, and think within ELA and across the disciplines. *English Education, 45*(1), 71–90.

Schoenbach, R., Greenleaf, C., & Murphy, L. (2012). *Reading for understanding: How reading apprenticeship improves disciplinary learning in secondary and college classrooms* (2nd ed.). San Francisco: Jossey-Bass.

Shanahan, C. (2012). How disciplinary experts read. In T.L. Jetton & C. Shanahan (Eds.), *Adolescent literacy in the academic disciplines: General principles and practical strategies* (pp. 69–90). New York: Guilford.

Shanahan, T., & Shanahan, C. (2008). Teaching disciplinary literacy to adolescents: Rethinking content-area literacy. *Harvard Educational Review, 78*(1), 40–59.

Vygotsky, L.S. (1978). *Mind in society: The development of higher psychological processes* (M. Cole, V. John-Steiner, S. Scribner, & E. Souberman, Eds. & Trans.). Cambridge, MA: Harvard University Press.

Wilhelm, J.D., Baker, T.N., & Dube, J. (2001). *Strategic reading: Guiding students to lifelong literacy, 6–12*. Portsmouth, NH: Boynton/Cook.

Literature Cited

Caro, R.A. (2012). *The years of Lyndon Johnson: The passage of power*. New York: Alfred A. Knopf.

Classroom Strategies for Scaffolding Learning

Integrating Strategies and Instruction

What are promising literacy practices that address the Common Core's literacy standards and embed comprehension instruction into the daily routines of teaching and learning? Section 2 features a range of strategies that integrate proficient reader development into the rhythm of disciplinary learning. Each of these strategies can be considered a prototype—a blueprint for scaffolding learning that can be adapted for application in different academic disciplines, from elementary school through high school. These classroom strategies represent innovative ideas for supporting learning in diverse classrooms with students who exhibit a variety of learning needs.

Embedding Strategies in Classroom Lessons

The classroom teaching strategies featured in this section are categorized according to how they might be incorporated with the flow of a lesson. Each classroom strategy is introduced with a Strategy Index correlated with the three phases of instruction:

1. *Frontloading learning:* Before-reading scaffolding
2. *Guiding comprehension:* During-reading scaffolding
3. *Consolidating understanding:* After-reading scaffolding

The strategies for frontloading learning prepare students for successful reading. In particular, they address teaching to the match—matching knowledge demands of a text with the background knowledge students bring to a text. The comprehension processes that receive primary emphasis are making connections and generating questions, and frontloading strategies also cue purpose for reading, which sets up determining importance.

The strategies for guiding comprehension prompt student thinking during reading and learning. All seven comprehension processes are integrated into this phase of a lesson: making connections, generating questions, creating visual and sensory images, making inferences, determining importance, synthesizing, and monitoring reading.

The strategies for consolidating understanding engage students in refining their comprehension and applying new learning to meaningful situations. Although all seven comprehension processes continue to be integral to the strategies in this phase of a lesson, synthesizing (summarizing understanding and personalizing new learning) is especially critical during this phase.

As you use the classroom strategies described in this book, notice how they might be embedded in various phases of lesson planning. For example, a frontloading strategy such as K–W–L Plus is an excellent way to prepare students for new learning because it encourages them to activate what they know and focus their attention on questions for new learning. A guiding comprehension strategy such as Interactive Reading Guides prompts students to selectively read and meaningfully organize important information. The Discussion Web provides students with a means to analyze argumentation in a text as they sort evidence that supports either side of a question. The web then becomes a graphic resource for supporting a position on the question through the use of text-based evidence, both in discussion and in written follow-up activities.

Three guidelines can help teachers make effective decisions for implementing these strategies with their students. First, remember that student learning drives strategy selection. A classroom strategy may work well with some complex texts but be a poor fit with others. Once you decide what students need to know and be able to do, consider which strategies would be appropriate to frontload learning, guide comprehension, and consolidate understanding. Make sure the classroom strategy is aligned with students' goals for learning and the demands of the texts they will be reading.

Second, it is the students' thinking that counts, not the specific classroom strategy. The strategies are designed to prompt the comprehension processes of proficient readers and learners, but merely following the steps of a strategy does not guarantee that students will automatically engage in this thinking. The classroom strategies in this book do not lead magically or inevitably to success. It is easy for students to fall into a routine of going through the motions. Be alert for students just "doing" rather than thinking and schedule frequent metacognitive debriefing sessions that focus students on evaluating their own understandings.

Third, tailor the classroom strategy to match your students and your academic discipline. Although these classroom strategies are conveniently outlined as a series of steps, be aggressive in adapting these ideas so the specific needs of your students and the demands of your curriculum are factored in. Again, these strategies are prototypes that will look somewhat different in their application depending on the nature of the content and the demands of disciplinary thinking. How can a strategy be customized to support learning in a world language classroom? How might the same strategy be tweaked to support learning in science? Although the comprehension processes are universal, specific instructional applications will vary.

Metacognitive Conversations

Although classroom strategies like the ones presented in this section are becoming more commonplace in classrooms, researchers are concerned that students do not necessarily own them. Indeed, the Common Core's literacy standards are predicated on students reading complex texts proficiently and independently—in other words, internalizing strategies so they no longer need scaffolded instruction for support. If students are not privy to the insider thinking that made a particular strategy effective, they may not become more independent learners; instead, they will continue to depend on constant guidance from teachers to effectively learn course content.

What were you thinking? is the preeminent question that governs the learning in our classrooms. But if students are not accorded frequent opportunities to listen in on the thinking of successful learners, then how learning unfolds may remain a mystery for them. Their struggles and failures may lead many students to conclude that they lack the ability to learn the material. If students are regularly supplied with strong mental models for thinking as they read and learn across the curriculum, they can gradually emulate such effective thinking themselves. Therefore, making thinking public must assume a central role in classroom learning.

Researchers refer to these public discussions of thinking as *metacognitive conversations* (Schoenbach, Greenleaf, & Murphy, 2012). Metacognition is a state of awareness about one's thinking; people who are metacognitive not only track *what* they are thinking but also monitor *how* they constructed their thoughts and *why* they decided on specific strategies to best achieve comprehension. Metacognitive learners are in personal control of their learning.

Metacognitive conversations invite students into the dialogue about thinking. The teacher's objective is ongoing classroom talk not only about what students are thinking but also about how they arrived at their thoughts. When students provide a response in your classroom, they should immediately expect a follow-up: "Talk about how you figured that out." "Tell us more about your thinking." These text-based discussions ask students to notice and then reconstruct their thinking as they read. Students who achieved comprehension fairly rapidly are not always cognizant of what it was they did that served them well. Asking them to articulate their thinking reimmerses them into their thought processes, which may lead them to discover further ideas about a text.

Metacognitive conversations are especially critical for students who struggle with learning. Many of our students observe the people around them "getting it" on a daily basis, without truly knowing what they could do differently that would help them achieve a better understanding. As a result, many students question their intelligence and adopt a fatalistic approach to reading: "I probably won't be able to understand it no matter what I try."

Metacognitive conversations involve all students in the inside game of learning—the how and why as well as the what. The more students are able to eavesdrop on the mental deliberations of others, and contribute their own versions of possible ways to think about a text, the more comfortable all students will become with tracking and adjusting their thinking during learning. Teachers should schedule regular debriefing sessions during classroom lessons that prompt metacognitive conversations. Students need to recognize how the structure of a lesson enhanced their learning and cued proficient reader behaviors such as making connections to background knowledge, posing questions to oneself and of the author, and determining what is most important in an author's message. Debriefing sessions focus discussions on how the classroom activities led to comprehension. Without a debriefing session, the students will leave the classroom still unduly dependent on a well-organized lesson to guide their learning. If students are to transition into increasingly independent learning, they need to regularly talk about their own thinking during the course of an effective lesson.

Metacognitive conversations can be categorized as external conversations: They take place in public, they are social in that multiple learners are included in the discussions, and students are not compelled to infer the direction of thought that led other students to their interpretations and conclusions. Ultimately, these metacognitive conversations need to become self-programmed as internal conversations—the mental dialogues we have with ourselves that shape our thinking as we read and learn. A variety of methods can be used with students to prompt internal metacognitive conversations.

Asking students to talk about their thinking in journal entries or learning logs is a popular strategy.

Metacognitive conversations are a natural fit for classroom discussions about learning. These critical discussions need to assume a permanent and organic role in classroom routines. Students become privileged to the inner workings of effective minds at work, allowing them to experiment with their own thinking as learners. In addition, students become increasingly comfortable with using one another as learning resources, as discussions center less on "tell me the right answer" and more on "tell me how you decided that was the right answer."

Indexing the Strategies

To assist teachers in their instructional planning, each classroom strategy is identified by a Strategy Index, found in the lower outside corner of the page on which the strategy is introduced. The Strategy Index highlights the strengths of the particular strategy in terms of instructional focus, text frames, and comprehension processes.

Instructional focus refers to how the strategy can be integrated into a lesson: frontloading learning (before-reading scaffolding), guiding comprehension (during-reading scaffolding), and consolidating understanding (after-reading scaffolding). As an additional planning resource, Table 15 presents the instructional focus for all of the strategies in a single chart.

Text frames refers to the way thinking is organized during reading and learning activities. Chapter 3 outlined six basic text frames that condition a student's frame of mind during the lesson: cause/effect, concept/definition, problem/solution, compare/contrast, proposition/support, and goal/action/outcome. Text frames help students ask themselves the right questions about

Table 15
Classroom Strategies Indexed by Instructional Focus

Instructional Focus	Classroom Strategies		
Frontloading learning	• Analogy Charting • Anticipation Guides • B/D/A Questioning Charts • Brainstorming Prior Knowledge • Chapter Tours • Character Quotes • Concept/Definition Mapping	• Connect Two • Follow the Characters • Guided Imagery • Hands-On Reading • History Change Frame • Inquiry Charts • K–W–L Plus • Math Reading Keys	• Mind Mapping • Quick-Writes • Science Connection Overview • Self-Questioning Taxonomy • Story Impressions • Student-Friendly Vocabulary Explanations
Guiding comprehension	• Analogy Charting • Anticipation Guides • Author Says/I Say • B/D/A Questioning Charts • Chapter Tours • Character Quotes • Concept/Definition Mapping • Connect Two • Double-Entry Diaries • First-Person Reading	• Hands-On Reading • History Change Frame • Inquiry Charts • Interactive Reading Guides • Knowledge/Question/ Response Charts • K–W–L Plus • Math Reading Keys • Mind Mapping • Power Notes	• Pyramid Diagram • Questioning the Author • Role-Playing as Readers • Science Connection Overview • Self-Questioning Taxonomy • Story Mapping • Structured Note-Taking • Text Coding • Three-Level Reading Guides
Consolidating understanding	• Analogy Charting • Anticipation Guides • Author Says/I Say • B/D/A Questioning Charts • Concept/Definition Mapping • Connect Two • Different Perspectives for Reading • Discussion Web • Double-Entry Diaries • First-Person Reading • Follow the Characters • Guided Imagery	• Inquiry Charts • Interactive Reading Guides • Knowledge/Question/ Response Charts • K–W–L Plus • Magnet Summaries • Mind Mapping • Paired Reviews • Power Notes • Pyramid Diagram • Questioning the Author • Quick-Writes	• RAFT • Role-Playing as Readers • Save the Last Word for Me • Story Impressions • Story Mapping • Structured Note-Taking • Student-Friendly Vocabulary Explanations • Three-Level Reading Guides • Vocabulary Overview Guide • Word Family Trees • Written Conversations

the material as they learn. As an additional planning resource, Table 16 presents text frames for all the strategies in a single chart.

Comprehension processes refers to characteristics of proficient reading that were outlined in Chapter 1: making connections, generating questions, creating mental images, making inferences, determining importance, and synthesizing. As an additional planning resource, Table 17 presents the comprehension processes for all the strategies in one handy chart.

Table 16
Text Frames and Corresponding Classroom Strategies

Text Frame	Classroom Strategies		
Cause/effect	• Anticipation Guides • Author Says/I Say • B/D/A Questioning Charts • Double-Entry Diaries • First-Person Reading • Follow the Characters • Hands-On Reading	• History Change Frame • Interactive Reading Guides • Knowledge/Question/ Response Charts • Questioning the Author • Quick-Writes • RAFT	• Science Connection Overview • Self-Questioning Taxonomy • Story Impressions • Structured Note-Taking • Text Coding • Three-Level Reading Guides • Written Conversations

Concept/definition	• Analogy Charting
	• Brainstorming Prior
	  Knowledge
	• Chapter Tours
	• Concept/Definition Mapping
	• Connect Two
	• Double-Entry Diaries
	• Guided Imagery
	• Interactive Reading Guides
	• Knowledge/Question/
	  Response Charts
		• Magnet Summaries
		• Math Reading Keys
		• Mind Mapping
		• Paired Reviews
		• Power Notes
		• Pyramid Diagram
		• Quick-Writes
		• RAFT
		• Science Connection Overview
			• Self-Questioning Taxonomy
			• Story Impressions
			• Structured Note-Taking
			• Student-Friendly Vocabulary
			  Explanations
			• Text Coding
			• Three-Level Reading Guides
			• Vocabulary Overview Guide
			• Word Family Trees

Problem/solution	• Anticipation Guides • Double-Entry Diaries • Hands-On Reading • History Change Frame • Interactive Reading Guides • Knowledge/Question/ Response Charts	• Math Reading Keys • Paired Reviews • Quick-Writes • RAFT • Self-Questioning Taxonomy	• Structured Note-Taking • Text Coding • Three-Level Reading Guides • Written Conversations

Compare/contrast	• Analogy Charting
	• Author Says/I Say
	• B/D/A Questioning Charts
	• Different Perspectives for
	  Reading
	• Discussion Web
	• Double-Entry Diaries
	• History Change Frame
		• Inquiry Charts
		• Interactive Reading Guides
		• Knowledge/Question/
		  Response Charts
		• Mind Mapping
		• Paired Reviews
		• Pyramid Diagram
		• Quick-Writes
			• RAFT
			• Self-Questioning Taxonomy
			• Structured Note-Taking
			• Student-Friendly Vocabulary
			  Explanations
			• Text Coding
			• Three-Level Reading Guides
			• Written Conversations

Proposition/support	• Anticipation Guides • Author Says/I Say • Character Quotes • Discussion Web • Double-Entry Diaries • First-Person Reading • Follow the Characters	• Inquiry Charts • Interactive Reading Guides • Knowledge/Question/ Response Charts • Paired Reviews • Quick-Writes • RAFT	• Role-Playing as Readers • Save the Last Word for Me • Self-Questioning Taxonomy • Structured Note-Taking • Text Coding • Three-Level Reading Guides • Written Conversations
Goal/action/outcome	• Chapter Tours • Hands-On Reading • History Change Frame • Inquiry Charts • Interactive Reading Guides • Knowledge/Question/ Response Charts	• K–W–L Plus • Math Reading Keys • Questioning the Author • Quick-Writes • RAFT	• Story Mapping • Structured Note-Taking • Text Coding • Three-Level Reading Guides

Table 17
Classroom Strategies Indexed by Comprehension Process

Comprehension Process	Classroom Strategies		
Making connections to prior knowledge	• Analogy Charting • Anticipation Guides • Author Says/I Say • Brainstorming Prior Knowledge • Chapter Tours • Concept/Definition Mapping • Connect Two • Different Perspectives for Reading • Double-Entry Diaries • Hands-On Reading	• History Change Frame • Inquiry Charts • Interactive Reading Guides • Knowledge/Question/ Response Charts • K–W–L Plus • Math Reading Keys • Mind Mapping • Paired Reviews • Questioning the Author • Quick-Writes • RAFT	• Role-Playing as Readers • Save the Last Word For Me • Science Connection Overview • Self-Questioning Taxonomy • Story Impressions • Student-Friendly Vocabulary Explanations • Text Coding • Three-Level Reading Guides • Vocabulary Overview Guide • Word Family Trees • Written Conversations
Generating questions	• Analogy Charting • Anticipation Guides • Author Says/I Say • B/D/A Questioning Charts • Brainstorming Prior Knowledge • Chapter Tours • Different Perspectives for Reading • Double-Entry Diaries • Follow the Characters	• Hands-On Reading • History Change Frame • Inquiry Charts • Interactive Reading Guides • Knowledge/Question/ Response Charts • K–W–L Plus • Math Reading Keys • Mind Mapping • Paired Reviews	• Questioning the Author • Role-Playing as Readers • Save the Last Word for Me • Science Connection Overview • Self-Questioning Taxonomy • Story Impressions • Story Mapping • Text Coding • Three-Level Reading Guides • Written Conversations
Creating mental images	• Analogy Charting • Chapter Tours • Character Quotes • Different Perspectives for Reading • Double-Entry Diaries • First-Person Reading	• Follow the Characters • Guided Imagery • Hands-On Reading • Interactive Reading Guides • Mind Mapping • Paired Reviews	• RAFT • Role-Playing as Readers • Self-Questioning Taxonomy • Student-Friendly Vocabulary Explanations • Text Coding
Making inferences	• Analogy Charting • Anticipation Guides • Author Says/I Say • Chapter Tours • Character Quotes • Connect Two • Different Perspectives for Reading • Discussion Web • Double-Entry Diaries • First-Person Reading • Follow the Characters	• Guided Imagery • Hands-On Reading • Inquiry Charts • Interactive Reading Guides • Knowledge/Question/ Response Charts • K–W–L Plus • Math Reading Keys • Mind Mapping • Paired Reviews • Questioning the Author • RAFT	• Role-Playing as Readers • Save the Last Word for Me • Self-Questioning Taxonomy • Story Mapping • Student-Friendly Vocabulary Explanations • Text Coding • Three-Level Reading Guides • Vocabulary Overview Guide • Word Family Trees • Written Conversations
Determining importance	• Analogy Charting • Anticipation Guides • Author Says/I Say • Chapter Tours • Connect Two • Discussion Web • Double-Entry Diaries • Follow the Characters • Hands-On Reading • History Change Frame	• Inquiry Charts • Interactive Reading Guides • Knowledge/Question/ Response Charts • K–W–L Plus • Magnet Summaries • Mind Mapping • Paired Reviews • Power Notes • Pyramid Diagram	• Questioning the Author • Quick-Writes • Science Connection Overview • Self-Questioning Taxonomy • Story Mapping • Structured Note-Taking • Text Coding • Three-Level Reading Guides • Vocabulary Overview Guide • Written Conversations
Synthesizing	• Analogy Charting • Anticipation Guides • Author Says/I Say • B/D/A Questioning Charts • Chapter Tours • Character Quotes • Concept/Definition Mapping • Connect Two • Different Perspectives for Reading • Discussion Web • Double-Entry Diaries	• First-Person Reading • Follow the Characters • Inquiry Charts • Interactive Reading Guides • Knowledge/Question/ Response Charts • K–W–L Plus • Magnet Summaries • Mind Mapping • Paired Reviews • Power Notes • Pyramid Diagram	• Quick-Writes • RAFT • Role-Playing as Readers • Save the Last Word for Me • Self-Questioning Taxonomy • Story Mapping • Structured Note-Taking • Student-Friendly Vocabulary Explanations • Text Coding • Three-Level Reading Guides • Written Conversations

Notice that most classroom strategies emphasize more than one comprehension process, text frame, or instructional focus. For example, the second classroom strategy in this section is Anticipation Guides. As shown on the lower outside corner of this strategy's opening page, in the Strategy Index under "Instructional Focus," all three are highlighted because this strategy can be used to frontload instruction, to guide student comprehension as they read, and to synthesize their understandings after reading. The three highlighted boxes under "Text Frames"—"Cause/Effect," "Problem/ Solution," and "Proposition/Support"—indicate that Anticipation Guides are especially effective for exploring these relationships during a lesson. Five comprehension processes are highlighted because phases of the Anticipation Guides engage students in making connections, generating questions, inferring, determining importance, and synthesizing.

Finally, each strategy is cross-referenced with the Common Core's literacy standards: reading, writing, speaking and listening, and language. The specific Common Core standards that are addressed through the application of a strategy are detailed in a final section for each strategy entitled "Meets the Standards." All the strategies and their variations meet the challenges of Reading Anchor Standard 10—developing independent and increasingly proficient readers of complex literary and informational texts. It becomes clear that a single strategy has the potential to provide students with experiences that can meet numerous Common Core standards. Table 18 presents this Common Core literacy standards information for all the strategies in a single chart.

Reference

Schoenbach, R., Greenleaf, C., & Murphy, L. (2012). *Reading for understanding: How reading apprenticeship improves disciplinary learning in secondary and college classrooms* (2nd ed.). San Francisco: Jossey-Bass.

Table 18
Classroom Strategies Indexed by the Common Core's Anchor Standards for Literacy

Classroom Strategy	Reading	Writing	Speaking and Listening	Language
Analogy Charting	1, 2, 4, 7, 9, 10	2, 9	1, 2, 4	5, 6
Anticipation Guides	1, 2, 5, 6, 8, 10	1, 2, 9	1, 3, 4	5
Prediction Guides	1, 2, 5, 6, 8, 10	1, 2, 9	1, 3, 4	5
Author Says/I Say	1, 2, 6, 7, 8, 9, 10	1, 9	1, 2, 3, 4	5
Say Something Read-Aloud	1, 2, 10		1, 4	5
B/D/A Questioning Charts	1, 2, 4, 6, 8, 9, 10	2, 7, 8, 9	1	4, 5
Brainstorming Prior Knowledge	7, 9, 10	2	1	5, 6
Alphabet Brainstorming	7, 9, 10		1	5, 6
Knowledge Ladders	7, 9, 10		1	5, 6
Knowledge Mapping	7, 9, 10		1	5, 6
LINK	9, 10	2	1	5, 6
Chapter Tours	2, 3, 5, 6, 7, 10	1, 2, 9	1, 2, 4	4, 5, 6
Character Quotes	1, 2, 4, 6, 8, 10	2	1	5, 6
Reading With Attitude	1, 2, 4, 6, 8, 10		1, 3, 4	5
Concept/Definition Mapping	1, 2, 4, 7, 9, 10	2, 9	1, 2, 4	4, 5, 6
Frayer Model	1, 2, 4, 7, 9, 10	2, 9	1, 2, 4	4, 5, 6
Connect Two	1, 2, 4, 9, 10	2, 9	1, 3, 4	4, 5, 6
Possible Sentences	1, 2, 4, 9, 10	2, 9	1, 3, 4	4, 5, 6
Different Perspectives for Reading	1, 2, 6, 7, 8, 9, 10	2, 9	1, 3, 4	5
Discussion Web	1, 2, 3, 6, 7, 8, 9, 10	1, 9	1, 2, 4	5
Point–Counterpoint Charts	1, 2, 3, 6, 7, 8, 9, 10	1, 9	1, 2, 4	5
Double-Entry Diaries	1, 2, 3, 5, 6, 7, 8, 9, 10	1, 2, 9	1, 3	5
First-Person Reading	1, 2, 3, 4, 6, 7, 8, 9, 10	1, 2, 9	1, 2, 3, 4	5
Eyewitness Testimony Charts	1, 2, 3, 4, 6, 7, 8, 9, 10	1, 2, 9	1, 2, 3, 4	5
First Impressions	1, 2, 3, 4, 6, 7, 8, 9, 10	1, 2, 9	1, 2, 3, 4	5
You Ought to Be in Pictures	1, 2, 3, 6, 7, 8, 9, 10	1, 2, 9	1, 2, 3, 4	5
Follow the Characters	1, 2, 3, 5, 6, 7, 8, 10	1, 2, 9	1, 2, 4	5

(continued)

Classroom Strategy	Reading	Writing	Speaking and Listening	Language
Guided Imagery	1, 2, 3, 4, 5, 7, 9, 10	2, 9	1, 2, 4	5, 6
Hands-On Reading	1, 2, 3, 4, 5, 6, 7, 8, 10	2, 9	1, 2, 4	4, 5, 6
History Change Frame	1, 2, 3, 4, 5, 7, 10	1, 2, 9	1, 2, 4	5, 6
History Memory Bubbles	1, 2, 3, 4, 5, 7, 10	1, 2, 9	1, 2, 4	5, 6
Inquiry Charts	1, 2, 6, 7, 8, 9, 10	1, 2, 7, 8, 9	1, 2, 4	5, 6
Interactive Reading Guides	1, 2, 3, 4, 5, 6, 7, 8, 9, 10	1, 2, 9	1, 2, 4	4, 5, 6
Knowledge/Question/Response Charts	1, 2, 6, 7, 8, 9, 10	2, 9	1, 3, 4	5
K–W–L Plus	1, 2, 3, 6, 7, 8, 9, 10	1, 2, 9	1, 2, 4	5, 6
Confirming to Extending Grid	1, 2, 3, 6, 7, 8, 9, 10	1, 2, 9	1, 2, 4	5, 6
Magnet Summaries	1, 2, 3, 4, 5, 10	2, 9	1, 3, 4	4, 5, 6
Math Reading Keys	1, 2, 3, 4, 5, 6, 7, 8, 9, 10	1, 2, 9	1, 2, 4	4, 5, 6
Review/New Charts	1, 2, 3, 4, 6, 8, 9, 10	2, 9	1, 2, 4	4, 5, 6
Mind Mapping	1, 2, 3, 4, 5, 7, 10	2, 9	1, 2, 4	4, 5, 6
Paired Reviews	1, 2, 3, 4, 5, 6, 8, 9, 10	1, 9	1, 3, 4	4, 5, 6
Line-Up Reviews	1, 2, 3, 4, 5, 6, 8, 9, 10	1, 9	1, 3, 4	4, 5, 6
Paired Verbal Fluency	1, 2, 3, 4, 5, 6, 8, 9, 10		1, 3, 4	4, 5, 6
Reflect/Reflect/Reflect	1, 2, 3, 4, 5, 6, 8, 9, 10		1, 3, 4	4, 5, 6
Think/Pair/Share	1, 2, 3, 4, 5, 6, 8, 9, 10		1, 3, 4	4, 5, 6
3-Minute Pause	1, 2, 3, 4, 5, 6, 8, 9, 10	1, 9	1, 3, 4	4, 5, 6
Power Notes	1, 2, 3, 5, 7, 8, 10	1, 2, 9	1, 2, 4	5, 6
Power Notes and Concept Maps	1, 2, 3, 5, 7, 8, 10	1, 2, 9	1, 2, 4	5, 6
Pyramid Diagram	1, 2, 3, 5, 6, 7, 8, 10	2, 9	1, 2, 3, 4	5, 6
Questioning the Author	1, 2, 3, 4, 5, 6, 7, 8, 9, 10	1, 2, 9	1, 3, 4	4, 5, 6
Elaborative Interrogation	1, 2, 3, 4, 5, 6, 7, 8, 9, 10	1, 2, 9	1, 3, 4	4, 5, 6
Question–Answer Relationships	1, 2, 3, 4, 5, 6, 7, 8, 9, 10	1, 2, 9	1, 3, 4	4, 5, 6
Quick-Writes	1, 2, 3, 4, 5, 6, 8, 9, 10	1, 2, 9, 10	1, 3, 4	5, 6
Admit and Exit Slips	1, 2, 3, 4, 5, 6, 8, 9, 10	1, 2, 9, 10	1, 3, 4	5, 6
Learning Logs	1, 2, 3, 4, 5, 6, 8, 9, 10	1, 2, 9, 10	1, 3, 4	5, 6
Template Frames	1, 2, 3, 4, 5, 6, 8, 9, 10	1, 2, 9, 10	1, 3, 4	5, 6
RAFT	1, 2, 3, 6, 8, 9, 10	1, 2, 9, 10	1, 2, 4	5, 6
Role-Playing as Readers	1, 2, 3, 4, 5, 6, 8, 9, 10	1, 2, 9	1, 3, 4	4, 5, 6
Point-of-View Study Guides	1, 2, 3, 4, 5, 6, 8, 9, 10	1, 2, 9	1, 3, 4	4, 5, 6
Readers Theatre	1, 4, 6, 8, 9, 10	1, 2, 9	1, 4	5, 6
Vocabulary Interviews	1, 2, 3, 4, 5, 6, 8, 9, 10	1, 2, 9	1, 3, 4	4, 5, 6
Save the Last Word for Me	1, 2, 3, 6, 8, 10	1, 2, 9, 10	1, 3, 4	5
Science Connection Overview	1, 2, 3, 4, 5, 6, 7, 10	2, 9	1, 2, 4	4, 5, 6
Self-Questioning Taxonomy	1, 2, 3, 4, 5, 6, 7, 8, 9, 10	1, 2, 9	1, 2, 4	5, 6
Story Impressions	1, 2, 3, 4, 5, 6, 9, 10	2, 9	1, 3, 4	4, 5, 6
Story Mapping	1, 2, 3, 4, 5, 6, 7, 8, 10	1, 2, 9	1, 2, 4	5
Structured Note-Taking	1, 2, 3, 5, 6, 7, 8, 10	1, 2, 9	1, 2, 4	5, 6
Proposition/Support Outlines	1, 2, 3, 5, 6, 7, 8, 10	1, 2, 9	1, 2, 4	5, 6
Pyramid Notes	1, 2, 3, 5, 6, 7, 8, 10	1, 2, 9	1, 2, 4	5, 6
Student-Friendly Vocabulary Explanations	4, 7, 10	2, 9	1, 2, 4	4, 5, 6
Text Coding	1, 2, 3, 4, 5, 6, 7, 8, 10	2, 9	1, 3, 4	4, 5, 6
Three-Level Reading Guides	1, 2, 3, 4, 5, 6, 8, 9, 10	1, 2, 9	1, 3, 4	4, 5
Vocabulary Overview Guide	1, 2, 3, 4, 7, 9, 10	2, 9	1, 2, 4	4, 5, 6
Word Family Trees	4, 7, 9, 10	2, 9	1, 2, 4	4, 5, 6
Written Conversations	1, 2, 3, 4, 6, 8, 9, 10	1, 2, 9, 10	1, 3, 4	5, 6

Note. The italicized strategies are discussed in the strategy pages with the preceding roman title.

Analogy Charting

"You mean it's like...?" Students' eyes light up. The concept that you are teaching comes alive. An analogy that relates to your students' lives has helped them make a connection. Teachers know that analogies are a powerful way to help students understand new information or concepts:

- "Cells are the building blocks of your body like bricks are the building blocks of this school."
- "The judicial branch of government functions like umpires in baseball."
- "Punctuation marks in a sentence are like traffic signs."

Analogies help students link new learning to familiar concepts. Chapter 2 outlined three types of knowledge that students bring to their comprehension of written texts: text-to-self, text-to-text, and text-to-world. Text-to-self knowledge is especially powerful because students can see how their personal lives intersect with what an author is telling them. Analogies take advantage of text-to-self knowledge by suggesting ways students may draw on their personal experiences as a bridge to understanding new and unfamiliar territory.

Analogy Charting (Buehl, 1995; Buehl & Hein, 1990) is a classroom strategy that provides a visual framework for students to analyze key relationships in an analogy in depth. Analogies are based on the compare/contrast text frame, and as students explore relationships by making connections to already known ideas, they broaden their understanding of important concepts and vocabulary. Analogy Charting can be used with students to introduce a topic, guide comprehension while reading, or synthesize understanding as they return to the text for rereading.

Using the Strategy

Authors frequently use metaphorical comparisons to help the reader gain insight into what they are describing or explaining. Analogy Charting extends that practice by using analogy to help students perceive similarities and differences between a new concept and something familiar in their lives.

1 Determine what students already know to establish an analogous relationship to the new concept to be introduced. Selecting a familiar concept can provide a foundation for understanding the new concept. For example, students studying the concept of colony in history class can readily relate it to a highly familiar situation: being a dependent child in a family.

In literature, students may be asked to examine a fictional character through comparison with a well-known person, a movie figure, or a previously encountered fictional character. Another option is to compare settings or events; for example, how is the society of George Orwell's novel *1984* analogous to the society of the present-day United States? In history, how is the relocation of Japanese Americans into internment camps during World War II analogous to the displacement of American Indians onto reservations? In science, students can explore analogous relationships between oceans and the earth's atmosphere.

2 Introduce the Analogy Chart (reproducible available in the Appendix) and provide copies for students to complete as you examine the analogy. Brainstorm with students to generate ideas about specific characteristics or properties common to both concepts. Enter these in the "Similarities" column. Students might offer that a colony and a dependent child share the following characteristics: They rely on a parent figure for their needs, they must follow rules or laws set by others, they are related or somehow connected to the parent figure, they sometimes have feelings of resentment and a desire to be independent and on their own, and they even share language, such as *mother* and *mother country* (see the Analogy Chart for History).

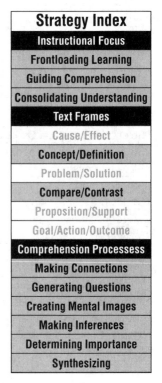

Strategy Index

Instructional Focus
Frontloading Learning
Guiding Comprehension
Consolidating Understanding
Text Frames
Cause/Effect
Concept/Definition
Problem/Solution
Compare/Contrast
Proposition/Support
Goal/Action/Outcome
Comprehension Processess
Making Connections
Generating Questions
Creating Mental Images
Making Inferences
Determining Importance
Synthesizing

Analogy Chart for History

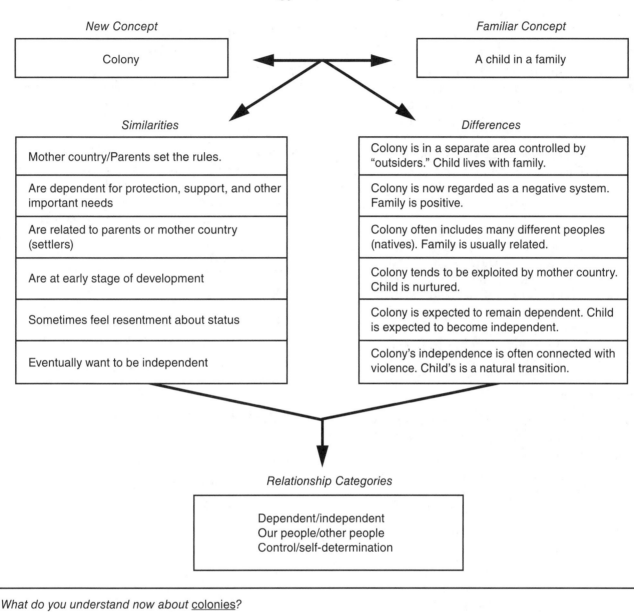

New Concept

Colony

Familiar Concept

A child in a family

Similarities

Mother country/Parents set the rules.
Are dependent for protection, support, and other important needs
Are related to parents or mother country (settlers)
Are at early stage of development
Sometimes feel resentment about status
Eventually want to be independent

Differences

Colony is in a separate area controlled by "outsiders." Child lives with family.
Colony is now regarded as a negative system. Family is positive.
Colony often includes many different peoples (natives). Family is usually related.
Colony tends to be exploited by mother country. Child is nurtured.
Colony is expected to remain dependent. Child is expected to become independent.
Colony's independence is often connected with violence. Child's is a natural transition.

Relationship Categories

Dependent/independent
Our people/other people
Control/self-determination

What do you understand now about <u>colonies</u>?
I can see why people in a colony would feel resentful, because in a way they were treated like children. They didn't get to set their own rules and laws, and they had to rely on "the mother country" for practically everything, like money and protection. Children get to grow up and live their own lives, but colonies were expected to be "children" forever, so no wonder they often had to fight to get their freedom.

Note. Adapted from *Classroom Strategies for Interactive Learning* (p. 26), by D. Buehl, 1995, Schofield: Wisconsin State Reading Association. Copyright © 2001 by the International Reading Association.

3 Next, ask students to brainstorm how the two concepts are different and enter these in the "Differences" column. This is a vital step because it will ensure that students do not overgeneralize how the two concepts are alike, and it will reinforce that analogous relationships are not identical relationships. Initially, steps 2 and 3 need to be modeled extensively by the teacher, but after students become practiced with the strategy, have them complete individual copies of a blank Analogy Chart with partners or in collaborative groups.

Students may note the following in our history example: (a) a colony is usually separated geographically from the parent figure, whereas a child usually lives with the parent figure in a family group; (b) a colony is regarded as a negative system, whereas families are not; and (c) a colony's independence has historically been associated with violence, which is not characteristic of children coming of age in most families.

4 Discuss with students categories that make up the basis for the comparison. For example, some relationships (e.g., both rely on the "parent" for protection and other basic needs; both represent an early stage of development; a colony is expected to remain dependent, but a child is expected to become independent) might be labeled as "dependent/independent," while other similarities might be labeled as "our people/other people" or "control/self-determination."

5 Have students write a summary statement about the similarities of the new concept and the familiar concept using their Analogy Charts. Students may write about how children and colonies often depend a great deal on the parent, how they eventually grow up or mature and want to assume control over themselves, how they may feel exploited, or how resentments lead to arguments or violence in the process of gaining independence.

Advantages

- Students enhance their understanding of new concepts or vocabulary through the analysis of familiar analogous concepts.
- Students bridge knowledge demands of new material by activating related experiences and background, which can compensate for academic knowledge gaps.

- Students gain practice in writing well-organized summaries that follow a compare/contrast text frame.

Meets the Standards

Analogy Charting promotes careful reading and rereading of an author's message (R.1); discerning main ideas and summarizing (R.2); interpreting word meaning, especially the use of figurative language (R.4); integrating ideas into visual representations (R.7); comparing and contrasting to other sources of knowledge (R.9); and mentoring the reading of complex literary and informational texts (R.10). In addition, the collaborative conversations develop expressing and defending thinking using visual displays (SL.1, SL.2, SL.4). Summarization writing provides practice using text-based evidence in explaining (W.2) and drawing evidence from texts for analysis and reflection (W.9). Attention to word relationships addresses vocabulary development (L.5) and acquiring domain-specific vocabulary (L.6).

References

Buehl, D. (1995). *Classroom strategies for interactive learning.* Schofield: Wisconsin State Reading Association.

Buehl, D., & Hein, D. (1990). Analogy graphic organizer. *The Exchange, 3*(2), 6.

Suggested Readings

Bean, T.W., Singer, H., & Cowan, S. (1985). Analogical study guides: Improving comprehension in science. *Journal of Reading, 29*(3), 246–250.

Cook, D.M. (Ed.). (1989). *Strategic learning in the content areas.* Madison: Wisconsin Department of Public Instruction.

Anticipation Guides

Suppose you have planned a special evening at a gourmet restaurant. As you look forward to your dining, which of the following statements reflect your expectations?

- Gourmet meals are very expensive.
- Gourmet meals feature elaborate recipes that are difficult to prepare at home.
- Gourmet dining is a relaxing experience with outstanding service.
- Gourmet meals feature small portions.
- Gourmet foods are delicious but fattening.

After dinner, as you drive home from the restaurant, you will likely appraise whether your actual experience was consistent with your expectations.

The Anticipation Guide (Herber, 1978) is a frontloading strategy that forecasts major ideas in a passage through statements that activate students' thoughts and prior knowledge. Before reading a selection, students respond to statements that challenge or support their preconceived thoughts about key concepts in the passage. Students then explain or elaborate on their responses in collaborative group and whole-class discussions. This process arouses interest, sets purposes for reading, and encourages raising questions—all important facets of comprehension. When students have completed their reading, they return to the Anticipation Guide to evaluate their understandings of the material and to correct misconceptions that surfaced during their initial deliberations.

Using the Strategies

An Anticipation Guide engages students in examining their knowledge and beliefs about a topic and then prompts them to reassess their thinking after reading a text. Anticipation Guides can effectively scaffold complex texts in all disciplines and are equally successful with print and nonprint media. Prediction Guides, a closely related strategy, are also described.

1 Identify the major ideas and concepts in a text that the students will be reading. For example, a science teacher may decide that students studying wetlands should focus attention on the following essential knowledge as they read:

- Wetlands feature a highly diverse range of plant and animal life.
- Wetlands are an indispensable ecosystem that is crucial for water purification.
- Wetlands provide flood control and protect coastlines against major storms, including hurricanes.
- Draining wetlands can harm a region's ecology.
- Wetlands are threatened, and degradation of wetlands is a significant environmental problem.

2 Predict what students might already know about the topic to ensure that they can thoughtfully respond to items on an Anticipation Guide. If students lack sufficient background knowledge, they may resort to an "I don't know" posture as they go through the statements in the guide. In addition, factor in students' experiences and beliefs that will be either supported or challenged by the reading. Most students will have some experiences with and knowledge about wetlands. Some may have opinions about the usefulness of such regions to people, and others may be apprised of environmental concerns regarding losing wetlands.

3 Create an Anticipation Guide with four to six statements that challenge or modify students' preexisting understandings. Statements should be idea-level relationships, not merely statements of fact (see the Anticipation Guide for Science). Otherwise, reading becomes reduced to "look for answers" skimming instead of careful reading to marshal support for explanations, generalizations, conclusions, or debatable positions. For example, "Swamps and marshes are examples of wetlands" is a factual statement that elicits a mere yes-or-no response but little discussion. Develop statements that reflect

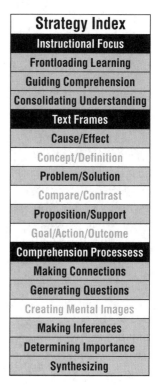

Strategy Index

Instructional Focus
Frontloading Learning
Guiding Comprehension
Consolidating Understanding

Text Frames
Cause/Effect
Concept/Definition
Problem/Solution
Compare/Contrast
Proposition/Support
Goal/Action/Outcome

Comprehension Processess
Making Connections
Generating Questions
Creating Mental Images
Making Inferences
Determining Importance
Synthesizing

Anticipation Guide for Science

Wetlands

- Read the following statements about wetlands regions like swamps and marshes.
- Consider what you know or have heard about each statement. Check the statements you think might be supported by the scientific evidence.
- Talk with your group members about why you made your choices. Be prepared to share any information you know or have heard about wetlands as your group discusses the following six statements:

___ 1. Wetlands flood easily, making them a hazard to neighboring properties.

___ 2. Wetlands improve water quality in a region.

___ 3. Swamps and marshes are essentially wastelands where limited plants and animals can survive.

___ 4. Draining wetlands is a promising way to increase productive farmland.

___ 5. We have fewer wetlands areas in the United States today.

___ 6. Wetlands can provide protection from natural disasters.

Anticipation Guide for Literature

The Call of the Wild

What do you think about human nature? What does the author (Jack London) think?

- Check the column labeled "You" for those statements you could agree with. Think about why and be prepared to support your positions with examples.
- After reading, check the column labeled "Jack London" for those statements with which you feel he would agree. Be prepared to cite specific evidence from the text to support your interpretation.

You	Jack London	
___	___	1. Only the strong survive in this world.
___	___	2. People must live in harmony with their environment.
___	___	3. Greed makes people cruel.
___	___	4. The primitive instinct exists in all people.
___	___	5. Much of what happens to people is the result of fate.
___	___	6. People will adapt to their surroundings and survive.

Note. Developed by Sarah Conroy, 1993, Madison East High School, Madison, WI, and adapted from *Classroom Strategies for Interactive Learning* (p. 30), by D. Buehl, 1995, Madison: Wisconsin State Reading Association. Copyright © 2001 by the International Reading Association.

text frames emphasized by the author. Cause/effect, problem/solution, and proposition/support text frames especially lend themselves to relationship statements. Notice how the six statements in the science example follow a problem/solution text frame because they concern environmental problems solved by wetlands or problems resulting from the loss of wetlands. The most effective statements are those about which students have some knowledge but not necessarily a complete understanding. If possible, include a statement that taps into possible misconceptions or common misunderstandings about the topic.

As a second example, to prepare students in a literature class for the major themes of Jack London's novel *The Call of the Wild*, an English language arts teacher can create an Anticipation Guide that draws out student perspectives on ideas and themes explored by the author (see the Anticipation Guide for Literature).

4 Project the Anticipation Guide or provide copies as individual student handouts. Leave space for individual or group responses. Students first complete the guide individually and then share their thinking with partners or in collaborative groups. As each statement is discussed, have students provide justification for their decision; ask them to talk about their thinking and share their insights and knowledge. After these decentralized conversations, call on students to contribute thoughts and information in a whole-class discussion.

5 As students read the selection, ask them to identify places in the text that confirm, elaborate, or reject each of the statements in the Anticipation Guide. If students are reading material that can be marked, instruct them to underline or highlight sections that are germane to each statement and annotate with the number of the item that this section concerns. Or they can affix sticky notes to textbook pages alongside information that supports or rebuts each statement. This stage is critical for locating text-based evidence that allows further evaluation of the statements.

In our literature example, students track the author's treatment of the themes identified in the Anticipation Guide. Chapter by chapter, they are alert for instances, actions, character behaviors, or narrator comments that possibly signal how London may be developing the ideas through literary means. Students meet with partners after reading a chapter to confer, compare notes, and begin to articulate interpretations that can be supported by details in the story. These evolve into whole-class discussions of theme.

6 After students complete the reading, have them return to the statements in the Anticipation Guide to determine how they have changed their thinking. With partners or in collaborative groups, have them locate the information from the text that supports or rejects each statement. Students then edit the Anticipation Guide by rewriting any statement to make it consistent with what the author has told them in the selection. To solidify learning, follow up with a writing assignment by asking students to either explain the support for one of the guide's statements or create an argument for or against a statement, citing specific evidence from the text as support.

Another option is to include two columns in the Anticipation Guide for responses: one for students and one for the author. After reading the passage, students then compare their thoughts on each statement with those of the author. This is especially effective when responding to ideas presented in literature (see the Anticipation Guide for Literature). In this case, students determine the extent to which they accept London's basic premises on human nature as he illustrates them in his novel. Then, as an assignment, have students explain or argue their positions with text-based support.

Prediction Guides

Prediction Guides are a variation of this strategy. Predictions are a natural human response to the avalanche of phenomena that we encounter in our lives. Our hours hum with predictions: How long will it take to prepare this meal? How will students respond to this particular lesson? How will my spouse like the gift I

selected? How much longer will it be before we have to trade in this increasingly unreliable car?

Making predictions is also a core strategy for reading comprehension. Proficient readers constantly attempt to read ahead of an author—picking up clues and predicting what might unfold. Predictions are a category of inference: When we predict, we are going beyond what is explicitly stated to anticipate what, where, why, how, who, and if.

1 Establish with students the characteristics of solid predictions. Predictions are not haphazard shots in the dark, nor are they merely opinions. Instead, a good prediction is grounded in two ways. First, the prediction must be consistent with the available evidence. Students making a prediction must be able to cite relevant information from a text that lends support to the reasonableness of their hunch. Second, the prediction must be consistent with previous knowledge and experiences. What we already know about a situation, or what has happened previously in similar circumstances, allows us to conjecture about this particular instance.

As students explore various predictions, introduce a critical proviso: Although a prediction may be thoughtful and well founded, it still may turn out to be incorrect. Many excellent predictions fail to be realized. Emphasize that predicting is sophisticated thinking that draws on incomplete information. The process of confirming and rejecting predictions is an essential dynamic of comprehension and the essence of active reading.

2 Model predicting as a think-aloud. Select a short text that can be projected, or provide students with a copy. As you think aloud, speculate what you think the author might say next, where you think a story might be heading, or other aspects that you might be wondering about. Show how various statements or hints in the text prompt your predictions and also how your personal knowledge and experiences guide and shape your predictions.

3 Create a Prediction Guide that features a series of statements about the topic that may or may not be validated in the text. For example, the newspaper article "Calories Are Everywhere, yet Hard to Track" (Brody, 2012) could elicit predictions regarding the consumption of calories in our diet (see the Prediction Guide for Health). Students complete the guide individually and then talk about their predictions with partners or in collaborative groups before sharing with the entire class. The first stage involves making predictions about whether the author will confirm each statement. This stage engages students in searching their

Prediction Guide for Health

Calories

You will be reading an article from *The New York Times* entitled "Calories Are Everywhere, yet Hard to Track." Under "Your Prediction," add a check mark for each of the statements below that you predict the author will say. Share your predictions with a partner. Then, read the article to confirm or reject your predictions, and add a check mark for each confirmed one under "Confirmed by the Author."

Your Prediction	Confirmed by the Author	
____	____	1. The daily diet for most Americans includes eating too many calories.
____	____	2. Our bodies can tell us when we've eaten enough calories.
____	____	3. The size of food portions has gone up, increasing the calories we take in.
____	____	4. People are pretty reliable in their estimates of how many calories are contained in a food item.
____	____	5. Eating organic foods is a way to cut back on the calories we consume.
____	____	6. People misunderstand nutrition labels on food products regarding the number of calories.

Prediction Guide for Music

Classic Violins

Stradivarius and Guarneri are two names that stand out as classic violins made centuries ago. Rank order the following statements according to your understandings of the quality of classic violins compared with violins made in recent years. Rank the statements from 1 to 6, with 1 being the statement you would argue is *most* likely to be true, and 6 being the *least* likely to be true. Be prepared to share <u>why</u> you ranked the statements as you did.

Rank

_____ a. Classic violins have better workmanship than modern violins.

_____ b. There is really no difference in the quality of sound between a classic violin and a well-made modern violin.

_____ c. People believe classic violins are superior because they expect that to be true.

_____ d. There is something special about the materials and techniques used to construct classic violins.

_____ e. Classic violins sound better because world-class musicians are the individuals who play them.

_____ f. It depends on the individual instrument as to whether a classic violin is superior in sound to a modern violin (excluding, of course, damaged instruments).

personal knowledge and experience base to justify their predictions.

Another variation is to have students rank order the statements, starting with 1 for the statement that they feel is most supportable, and so forth, until the highest number is given to the statement that they think is least supportable (see the Prediction Guide for Music).

4 Students read the assigned material to discover which of their predictions will be supported by the author. Students need to search for textual evidence that can back up a prediction or contradict it. The Prediction Guide gives students a clear purpose for reading, which parallels what proficient readers do as a matter of habit: reading to substantiate predictions.

5 Students rejoin their groups or partners to complete the second stage of the Prediction Guide: checking those statements confirmed by the author.

Because the guide's statements should not be merely lifted from the text verbatim, students will need to summarize and make inferences to ascertain whether the author did indeed confirm or reject each statement. With rank-ordered Prediction Guides, students negotiate to rerank the statements, making their new ranking consistent with their understanding of how the author would rate them, based on evidence from the text. As with Anticipation Guides, follow up with a writing assignment that engages students in explaining or arguing their thinking by citing specific evidence from the text.

6 Ask students to generate their own predictions from a text by examining the title, headings and subheadings, pictures, and other salient information. They can also be asked to pause at the end of prescribed paragraphs or sections, or at the end of chapters, to consider possible predictions that they feel are justified by their reading so far. Model appropriate predicting language, as in the following examples:

- "From the title/paragraph, I predict this chapter will be about...."
- "The reason I believe this is...."
- "Based on..., I predict this story will...."
- "I think this because...."
- "My prediction was confirmed because...."
- "My prediction was not confirmed because...."

Advantages

- Students are cued into the major ideas of a selection before they start reading.
- Students activate their background knowledge about a topic before they read, which they can share with classmates.
- Students are motivated to read to determine whether the text will confirm or contradict their conjectures.
- Students' misconceptions about a topic are openly addressed and more likely to change after reading and discussing the new material.
- Students learn to risk airing their ideas as they come to understand that many reasonable predictions will not be confirmed by a text.
- Students receive valuable practice in citing text-based evidence to support their interpretations of the statements in the guide.

Meets the Standards

Anticipation and Prediction Guides promote careful reading of an author's message (R.1), discerning main ideas (R.2), analyzing text structure (R.5), tracking the author's perspective and purpose (R.6), supporting argumentation (R.8), and mentoring the reading of complex literary and informational texts (R.10). In addition, the collaborative conversations develop expressing and defending thinking with supporting evidence (SL.1, SL.3, SL.4). Follow-up writing tasks provide practice in using text-based evidence in arguing (W.1) or explaining (W.2), and drawing evidence from texts for analysis and reflection (W.9). Attention to word relationships (i.e., cause/effect language) addresses vocabulary development (L.5).

References

Buehl, D. (1995). *Classroom strategies for interactive learning.* Madison: Wisconsin State Reading Association.

Herber, H.L. (1978). *Teaching reading in content areas* (2nd ed.). Englewood Cliffs, NJ: Prentice Hall.

Literature Cited

Brody, J.E. (2012, March 19). Calories are everywhere, yet hard to track. *The New York Times*, p. D7.

Suggested Readings

Bean, T.W., Readence, J.E., & Baldwin, R.S. (2007). *Content area literacy: An integrated approach* (9th ed.). Dubuque, IA: Kendall/Hunt.

Nichols, J.N. (1983). Using prediction to increase content area interest and understanding. *Journal of Reading, 27*(3), 225–228.

Author Says/I Say

Hmmm, jet lag.... The author of this article says that sleep cycles are not the only body system disrupted by jet lag. Traveling across several time zones also impacts the body's digestive system, temperature, and hormone secretions. I certainly noticed this phenomenon personally. Not only did I feel sleep deprived, but I also had an unsettled stomach for several days after that first flight to England. I was fatigued and generally under the weather until I was able to adjust to London time. This information underscores that jet lag is more than merely not getting enough sleep one night. Jet lag disrupts the way your body is used to functioning. The author goes on to criticize a jet lag diet for being nutritionally problematic as well as highly inconvenient. But I tried such a diet the second time I flew to England, and it seemed to work remarkably well.

Imagine eavesdropping into the thinking of a reader immersed in the flow of comprehension of a newspaper article offering advice on jet lag. On one level, the reader attends to the words of the author, who dedicated time to compose this message. But invariably, as readers, we cannot help but personalize what an author tells us. We find ourselves talking through an author's message, interjecting our own thoughts and experiences, as we customize our understanding of what a text means.

We recognize these internal dialogues with ourselves as a familiar daily mental routine. Reading is, in many respects, a conversation with another person. Although the author is not physically present, this individual is definitely talking to us, the readers, to tell a story, to inform and enlighten, or even to influence. As we track what an author has to say to us, we cannot help but talk back. We remind ourselves of how our lives connect to the author's words. We factor in something from our personal knowledge banks. In some cases, we may even want to argue or disagree. And as this exchange between the author and the reader unfolds, we periodically take stock of our thinking. We register what we understand, we sum up key thoughts and ideas, and we periodically draw conclusions and make judgments.

Using the Strategies

The Author Says/I Say strategy is a variation of a strategy developed by Beers (2003), which uses a chart to guide students in constructing meaning from a written text. The Say Something Read-Aloud, a related strategy, is also presented.

1 Introduce the Author Says/I Say Chart (reproducible available in the Appendix). The chart is devised so readers connect what they are wondering with what an author says. In addition, readers are prompted to weigh in with what they are thinking. The final column returns students to what they were wondering, as they sum up what they now understand. In effect, five key comprehension processes are elicited: questioning ("I wonder…"), determining importance ("The author says…"), making connections to prior knowledge and inferring ("I say…"), and synthesizing new understandings ("And so…").

2 Model this strategy with a think-aloud. For example, an article on food safety (Shute, 2007) provides an excellent opportunity to demonstrate all of these phases of thinking using the Author Says/I Say strategy (see the Author Says/I Say Chart for a Culinary Arts Article).

This article focuses on what people can do to avoid becoming ill from the food they eat. I wonder how serious a problem this is. The author says that 76 million Americans become sick from food-related illnesses each year, and 5,000 die. I had no idea that "bad" food was this extensive, although I remember reading about deaths from spinach and pet food that were contaminated. It seems that we take our food supply for granted and need to be much more careful about checking what we eat.

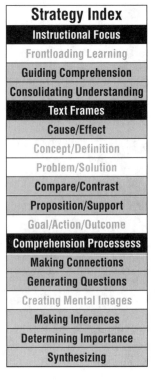

Strategy Index

Instructional Focus
Frontloading Learning
Guiding Comprehension
Consolidating Understanding
Text Frames
Cause/Effect
Concept/Definition
Problem/Solution
Compare/Contrast
Proposition/Support
Goal/Action/Outcome
Comprehension Processes
Making Connections
Generating Questions
Creating Mental Images
Making Inferences
Determining Importance
Synthesizing

Author Says/I Say Chart for a Culinary Arts Article[a]

I Wonder...	The Author Says...	I Say...	And So...
How widespread is unsafe food?	Each year, 76 million Americans get sick from food causes, 300,000 are hospitalized, and 5,000 die.	I remember tainted spinach killing some people, and I also recall pet food that was contaminated.	It seems like we are taking food safety for granted when we really shouldn't be!
How can we prevent getting sick from food?	The only way to be sure you don't get sick from food is to not eat.	I don't think the author is really serious about this.	I think the author is really saying that we will always face a danger of getting sick from food.
	The best defense is in the kitchen. We should wash all foods, even organic.	I don't always wash fruits and vegetables, and I've heard that kitchen counters and cutting boards harbor lots of germs.	I need to change my habits when preparing foods, wash everything more thoroughly, and wash my hands more around food.
	Cooked foods are safer than eating foods that are uncooked.	I know you have to thoroughly cook meats like hamburger, but I thought uncooked vegetables have more vitamins than cooked vegetables.	I need to be extra careful with raw foods, especially fruits and vegetables that are eaten uncooked.
Is organic food safer?	Organic food is freer of pesticides, herbicides, and antibiotics but still can be contaminated by bacteria, metals, and other dangerous substances.	People assume that organic food is safe, and organic farmers try to use natural and nontoxic growing methods.	We can't assume any food is free of problems, although organic foods might present fewer problems.
Is buying locally grown food safer?	Many foods produced in other countries are grown in poor sanitation conditions and could contain pesticides banned in the United States.	I know DDT has long been banned in the United States but is still sold to countries that sell us food.	It is a good idea to know where the food you eat is produced.

Note. Adapted from "Author Says/I Say," by D. Buehl, June 2007, *OnWEAC*, retrieved from www.weac.org/News/2006–07/june07/readingroom.htm. Copyright © 2007 by Doug Buehl.
[a]Shute, N. (with Baldauf, S., & Voiland, A.). (2007). Better safe than sorry. *U.S. News & World Report, 142*(19), 67–70, 72.

As you talk your way through the text, emphasize how statements by the author spark your thinking about food safety. Reading becomes an interchange between the author and the reader because both have something to say about the topic. The key is the "And So..." column, which registers how you have pulled your thinking together into ideas that you learned from this text. This column for summarizing prompts students to verbalize what they will take away from the text.

3 Provide ample opportunities for students to practice using this strategy to enhance their comprehension of potentially problematic texts. One method involves asking students to use sticky notes to record those questions they notice themselves wondering about—before, during, and after reading. Then, instruct them to focus on five questions that seem to be the most significant. These questions are then charted on the Author Says/I Say Chart.

A variation of this chart focuses directly on argumentation. This three-column chart starts with identifying key arguments made by the author, which are recorded in the "The Author Argues..." column. Readers then respond and sum up their thinking about the argument in the other two columns (see the Author Argues/I Say Chart for the Seneca Falls Declaration).

Say Something Read-Aloud

The Say Something strategy (Gaither, 1997) is another variation that allows students to "talk back" to an author.

1 Partners switch off with oral reading of paragraphs from classroom materials. For example, history students read a history textbook passage about life during the Great Depression. One student reads the first paragraph aloud while the partner follows along and listens. When the reader finishes, the listener must

Author Argues/I Say Chart for the Seneca Falls Declaration

The Author Argues...	I Say...	And So...
"The history of mankind is a history of repeated injuries and usurpations on the part of man toward woman, having in direct object the establishment of an absolute tyranny over her."[a]	I hear about women being treated unfairly or being victimized nearly every day. Women still have very few rights in many parts of the world.	I know we've made progress in this country, but I would argue that we still don't have full equality. And *tyranny* is a good word to describe what a lot of women have to put up with in many countries.

[a]From *An American Primer*, edited by Daniel J. Boorstin, 1966, Chicago: University of Chicago Press. Copyright © 1966 by the University of Chicago Press.

say something about what was read: comment on interesting material, make a prediction, wonder about something stated, identify confusing information, or relate information from the paragraph to personal background experiences or knowledge.

2 Ask partners to switch roles and continue with the next paragraph. Unlike round-robin reading—one student reading while the rest of the class listens— paired reading involves half the class reading while partners listen. Because all students are either reading aloud or listening and commenting, the sound level in the classroom accords a measure of privacy to individual readers, which is especially helpful to struggling readers who may need assistance from their partners as they read. The Say Something Read-Aloud strategy provides a more interactive format for classroom read-alouds and allocates students more opportunities to practice oral reading fluency. The strategy stimulates conversation about a passage and encourages students to make connections as they read and work on clarifying information that is difficult or confusing.

Advantages

- Students are continually reminded that reading involves a mental conversation between an author and a reader; both need to contribute to the conversation if the reader's comprehension is to occur.
- Students are provided with cues that guide them into accessing implicit layers of meaning that necessitate inferential thinking.
- Students verbalize their understandings as they sum up what they have gained from their reading.

Meets the Standards

The Author Says/I Say and Say Something Read-Aloud strategies promote careful reading of an author's message (R.1), discerning main ideas and summarizing (R.2), tracking the author's perspective and purpose (R.6), integrating ideas into visual representations (R.7), supporting argumentation (R.8), comparing and contrasting to other sources of knowledge (R.9), and mentoring the reading of complex literary and informational texts (R.10). In addition, the collaborative conversations develop expressing and defending thinking with supporting evidence using visual displays (SL.1–4). Follow-up writing tasks provide practice in using text-based evidence in arguing (W.1) and drawing evidence from texts for analysis and reflection (W.9). Attention to word relationships and nuances in word meanings addresses vocabulary development (L.5).

References

Beers, K. (2003). *When kids can't read, what teachers can do: A guide for teachers, 6–12.* Portsmouth, NH: Heinemann.

Buehl, D. (2007, June). Author says/I say. *OnWEAC.* Retrieved from www.weac.org/News/2006-07/june07/readingroom.htm

Gaither, P. (1997, May). *Caught in the act: Strategies to engage readers with informational text.* Paper presented at the 42nd annual convention of the International Reading Association, Atlanta, GA.

Literature Cited

Boorstin, D.J. (Ed.). (1966). *An American primer.* Chicago: University of Chicago Press.

Shute, N. (with Baldauf, S., & Voiland, A.). (2007). Better safe than sorry. *U.S. News & World Report, 142*(19), 67–70, 72.

B/D/A Questioning Charts

"Any questions?" Questioning is an integral part of our daily routines, and sometimes it seems like we are constantly invited to pose questions. We outline instructions for the babysitter: Any questions? Our doctor describes procedures for taking a new medication: Any questions? We purchase a new product and scan through the explanations for use: Any questions? Our supervisor at work assigns us a project to complete: Any questions? We leave our spouse directions for assembling the evening meal: Any questions? The questioning goes on and on.

Consider how your mind literally buzzes with questions as you contemplate the reading of a long-awaited new novel. Even before you open the volume and dig in, you are wondering about a host of things. Some of your inquisitiveness concerns the content of the book: What is the plot, how will the story line unfold, and what might I expect will happen as I read along? But you will also be wondering about the actual experience of reading this book: Will I enjoy it as much as I anticipate, will I find the events and characters predictable or refreshing, will I admire how this author uses language or crafts the suspense, and will I find that I cannot put the book down or that I'm disappointed? If you have sampled this author's work before, you are also probably wondering how this book will stack up against the others you have read.

Of course, the questions keep coming once you slip into the pages. And our questions don't end when we reach that last page and set the book aside. Likely, we are still wondering: Could this story really be plausible? Did the author base this book on actual people or historical events? And on a more personal level, we might savor where our imaginations transported us: Would I have made the same decisions as the protagonists in the novel? What would it have been like if I had been a character in this story myself? What has this author got me thinking?

Asking questions is our particularly human way of navigating our understanding, of making sense. Asking questions is how we zigzag our way between knowing and not knowing. But our students would probably offer a dramatically different take on questions. For the most part, students perceive questioning as an interrogation by others; they are regularly confronted in school with the task of answering the queries of somebody else: a teacher, a textbook editor, or an exam developer. In many classrooms, the balance between question posing and question responding is badly askew. As a result, students receive inadequate practice in generating their own questions about new learning, and instead they relegate their reading to a superficial "looking for answers."

Using the Strategy

The B/D/A Questioning Chart (adapted from Laverick, 2002) transitions students to assume the intellectual work of questioning *before*, *during*, and *after* reading. Using this strategy is most effective after students have been introduced to and had ample practice using Questioning the Author (see the Questioning the Author strategy pages), which provides an excellent basis for the kind of questions that facilitate working a text.

1 Introduce the concepts of thick and thin questions (Buehl, 2005). We ask ourselves thin questions to clarify things the author says. We ask ourselves thick questions to ponder deeper ideas, which may take us far beyond the text that started our thinking. Model thick and thin questions that guide your understanding of a short text. For example, while reading a newspaper article aloud on a topic such as the avian flu, note thin questions that occur to you: What does the author say causes avian flu? How can it infect humans? What worries public health officials about it? Questions such as these are specific to the text and help guide you in clarifying the author's message. Thin questions revolve around "What is the author telling us?" and especially address the Common Core's Reading Anchor Standard 1.

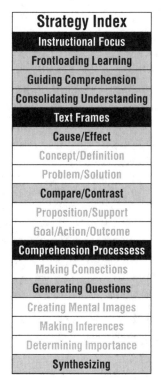

Strategy Index

Strategy Index
Instructional Focus
Frontloading Learning
Guiding Comprehension
Consolidating Understanding
Text Frames
Cause/Effect
Concept/Definition
Problem/Solution
Compare/Contrast
Proposition/Support
Goal/Action/Outcome
Comprehension Processess
Making Connections
Generating Questions
Creating Mental Images
Making Inferences
Determining Importance
Synthesizing

Thin questions may target clarification of key vocabulary (e.g., What exactly is a pandemic?) or clarification of an important fact (e.g., What was the Spanish flu outbreak in 1918?). The author may provide a direct answer to some of your thin questions, you may have to infer the answers to others, and still others may be unanswered because the author is depending on the reader to access background knowledge to fill in the missing information. Underscore these different varieties of thin questions as you talk with students; some excellent thin questions will be unanswerable using the text alone, necessitating that other sources be consulted (time to google).

Thick questions investigate the question, What is the meaning of what the author tells us? They are often triggered by asking *why* or speculating *whether* or *if.* Demonstrate thick questions that extend thinking beyond the text: Why are governments apparently not very well prepared to meet epidemic threats such as the avian flu? Are there really effective ways to protect ourselves? Will we someday experience a pandemic like the Spanish flu of 1918 when millions died? When are these public health warnings real, and when are they exaggerated? Am I, or someone close to me, at risk of being struck with a disease like the avian flu?

Thick questions are often the ones we care most about as we personalize our understandings and learning. Thick questions represent the upper layers of Bloom's Taxonomy (revised in Anderson & Krathwohl, 2001), such as application, analysis, evaluation, and synthesis (see the Self-Questioning Taxonomy strategy pages), when we truly engage with new ideas. Thick questions lead to rich conversation, divergent viewpoints, and further exploration of ideas. Are people today becoming more susceptible to dangerous diseases like the avian flu? Why might this be so? What can be done to diminish such risks? Are we likely to undertake these necessary steps? Why, or why not? What can I personally do?

2 Select a short text related to the curriculum and model how generating questions is a natural component of our thinking when we read. Explain that before we begin a text, we pose a range of generic questions, such as, What will this text be about? How much do I already know about this topic? How challenging will this be to read? and so forth. Ask students to peruse salient textual features that can elicit specific questions. The title of a newspaper article, such as "In Adolescents, Addiction to Tobacco Comes Easy" (Brody, 2008), might lead a reader to wonder, Why would adolescents be more vulnerable to tobacco addiction, and how easy is it for adolescents to become addicted? (See the B/D/A Questioning Chart for a Teen Smoking article.) The opening introduction, headings, photos, visual displays, and features such as pull quotes also provide grist for questions before reading. For example, a heading that states "New Strategies Needed" leads easily to the question, What are the new strategies advocated by this author?

Have students record their questions in the "Before Reading" column on a B/D/A Questioning Chart (reproducible available in the Appendix). Then, allot a few minutes for partner or collaborative group conversations; have students talk about their questions, which will stimulate sharing about things they already might know or have heard about the topic. As a result, students provide their own frontloading prompts for activating and pooling their prior knowledge.

B/D/A Questioning Chart for a Teen Smoking Article[a]

What questions helped you work your understanding?

Before Reading	During Reading	After Reading
• Why would adolescents be more vulnerable to tobacco addiction? • How easy is it for adolescents to become addicted?	• Can teens really get hooked from the first cigarette? • How many teens smoke? • Is teen smoking on the rise? • What can schools do? • Why is there more smoking in movies?	• Will we discover how to predict tobacco addiction? • How can we tell if someone has an addictive personality? • Are cigarettes too available for purchase? • Will we ever eliminate dangerous habits such as smoking?

What do you understand now that you didn't understand before?

Teens can become addicted to tobacco almost immediately, even infrequent smokers, and as a result are highly likely to continue smoking into adulthood.

[a]Brody, J.E. (2008, February 12). In adolescents, addiction to tobacco comes easy. *The New York Times*, p. D7.

3 Next, read an introductory paragraph(s) aloud and, again, think aloud about questions that have you wondering. Enter these in the "During Reading" column of the chart. For example, you might wonder, Can teens really get hooked from the first cigarette? How many teens currently smoke? Is this number going up?

Assign students to then work independently on reading the rest of the text, recording their questions about the material. Set a target number of questions (e.g., six to eight for the passage) or designate a question for every couple of paragraphs. Mandate a number of thick questions to encourage students to go beyond merely clarification.

4 When students have completed this phase, have them categorize their questions, using the following three codes:

✓ = Questions that you feel the author has resolved for you and that you can provide satisfactory answers for

~ = Questions that you feel the author has partially resolved for you but that you have not yet arrived at satisfactory answers for

? = Questions not resolved by the author that remain as hanging questions

Students then meet with partners or in collaborative groups to talk about their understandings of the text by sharing their questions and elaborating on possible responses. Have them start with the questions that they could check off as resolved, indicating where in the text the author provided a satisfactory answer. Next, they move to the so-so questions that were partially dealt with, again indicating pertinent sections of the text while explaining what was missing that they are still seeking to know. Finally, based on their understanding of the text and their background knowledge, students tackle the unanswered questions, with the group first confirming that the author did not address the question and then speculating on possible responses.

Come together as a whole class and continue the conversation. First, ask students to verbalize and document their answered questions (what they learned from the author). Next, transition to the partially answered questions (what they learned but still seek to know). Finally, raise the hanging questions (what they still don't know), which now take the discussion beyond the text. Be alert to significant parts of the text that do not surface in these conversations, as these may be problematic sections that students have avoided. If so, ask if anyone had questions related to those segments to guide examination of that material. If no questions are offered, direct students to reread the overlooked

segment and generate questions that work that portion to an understanding.

5 The third questioning phase involves those lingering questions after a text has been read. Emphasize that as inquisitive people, we will likely finish a text and realize that some of our questions remain unresolved. Additional exploration and reading in the future will be necessary to flesh out satisfactory answers. Ask students to decide on one or two questions that are significant hanging questions for them. Each student records their personal "to be continued" questions in the "After Reading" column. After a quick partner share, solicit questions during a whole-class wrap-up. For instance, students might be wondering whether dangerous personal habits like smoking will ever really diminish in our culture.

These after-reading questions could be left hanging because the students have registered possible further directions for future knowledge building. Or these questions could form the basis for an inquiry search, as students then consult additional sources to try to address their unanswered questions.

6 As a final stage, prompt students to verbalize their learning by summarizing key insights in the "What do you understand now that you didn't understand before?" section at the bottom of the chart. Again, ask students to share with a partner, and then generate a list of important understandings from the class.

7 Provide students with multiple opportunities to identify the questions they generated in the service of working their comprehension of a complex text. Students can track their questions on sticky notes or as marginal notations (see the Questioning the Author strategy pages).

Advantages

- Students experience a significant and valuable role reversal by becoming the questioners themselves.
- Students gain essential practice with and feedback on becoming question posers rather than merely question responders.
- Students are encouraged to be curious and critical readers who ponder what an author is telling them.
- B/D/A Questioning Charts provide students with a visual reminder of the progress of their thinking as they explore a new text.

Meets the Standards

The B/D/A Questioning Charts strategy promotes careful reading and rereading of an author's message

(R.1), discerning main ideas (R.2), clarifying vocabulary (R.4), tracking the author's perspective and purpose (R.6), integrating ideas into visual representations (R.7), supporting argumentation (R.8), connecting with other sources of knowledge (R.9), and mentoring the reading of complex literary and informational texts (R.10). In addition, the collaborative conversations develop expressing and defending thinking with supporting evidence (SL.1). Follow-up writing tasks provide practice in using text-based evidence in summarizing (W.2) and drawing evidence from texts for analysis and reflection (W.9), with the option of further inquiry and research (W.7, W.8). Attention to word relationships and nuances in word meanings addresses vocabulary development (L.4, L.5).

References

Anderson, L.W., & Krathwohl, D.R. (Eds.). (2001). *A taxonomy for learning, teaching, and assessing: A revision of Bloom's Taxonomy of educational objectives.* New York: Longman.

Buehl, D. (2005, November). Thick and thin questions. *OnWEAC.* Retrieved from www.weac.org/News/2005-06/nov05/readingroomnov05.htm

Laverick, C. (2002). B-D-A strategy: Reinventing the wheel can be a good thing. *Journal of Adolescent & Adult Literacy, 46*(2), 144–147.

Literature Cited

Brody, J.E. (2008, February 12). In adolescents, addiction to tobacco comes easy. *The New York Times*, p. D7.

Brainstorming Prior Knowledge

What do you know about Antarctica, earthworms, ultraviolet light, and Elizabeth I of England? Chances are, if you were going to read a passage about any of these topics, you would spend a few moments reconnoitering in your mind what you already know. You would take stock of your prior knowledge.

Suppose you are paging through a magazine and chance upon an article entitled "Lasers: The Promise of a 21st-Century Technology." What do you anticipate this author will talk about? Laser tools? Laser surgery? Laser scanners and printers? Laser treatments? Laser light displays? Laser weapons? The principles behind a laser as a beam of light?

Like any proficient reader, you predict the article's content by recalling your pertinent prior knowledge that might relate to new material in the article. In Chapter 2, we emphasized the critical role of knowledge in meeting the demands of complex texts. In the classroom, teachers need to assess what students already know about a topic and help them access this useful knowledge as a necessary precursor to comprehension. Frontloading activities that help students connect to prior knowledge jump-start learning about a topic.

Using the Strategies

Brainstorming strategies provide a promising framework for eliciting students' prior knowledge before learning. Several classroom variations may be used: LINK (list, inquire, note, and know), Knowledge Mapping, Knowledge Ladders, and Alphabet Brainstorming. With the ubiquity of handheld technology, a brief proviso about the use of these strategies needs to be mentioned: They are intended to engage students in brainstorming what they know and have learned, and should not devolve into "look it up" googling activities.

LINK

LINK (Vaughan & Estes, 1986) is a brainstorming strategy that encourages student-directed discussion about their knowledge of a topic.

1 Decide on a keyword or concept related to the material that will trigger responses from your students. Write this cue on the whiteboard. Allow two to three minutes for students to list on paper as many meaningful associations as occur to them. For example, the prompt "What words or phrases come to mind when you think of cloning?" might trigger prior knowledge for students preparing to read a science selection on this topic. Next, partner students and have them briefly talk about their associations, and then have them expand their lists by working in teams of four to add items that did not appear on either list. In addition, the partner interludes provide an opportunity for students to vet each other's items for possible accuracy before sharing with the whole class.

Solicit an association from each set of partners and write these around the cue term on the whiteboard. When all partners have offered an association, allow students to respond with further associations. During this stage, student contributions are listed without any comments from either you or the students, including those offering the associations. Our cloning example would likely generate a rich assortment of associations: pets, sheep, stem cells, South Korea, human organs, genetics, science fiction, Dolly, ethics, twins, Star Wars, and so forth.

2 Encourage students to inquire about the associations arrayed about the topic: "Which items would you not be comfortable talking about?" A useful conversation starter is calling on students, who can respond, "I would like someone to talk more about...." Students may ask their peers for clarification or elaboration of some items or ask for examples or definitions. They may also challenge some items. However, all inquiries are directed between the students, not to the teacher. Langer (1981) advocates that the teacher initiate the discussion by selecting a

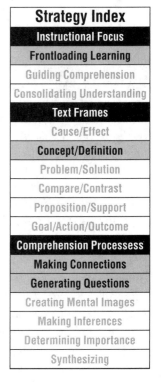

Strategy Index
Instructional Focus
Frontloading Learning
Guiding Comprehension
Consolidating Understanding
Text Frames
Cause/Effect
Concept/Definition
Problem/Solution
Compare/Contrast
Proposition/Support
Goal/Action/Outcome
Comprehension Processess
Making Connections
Generating Questions
Creating Mental Images
Making Inferences
Determining Importance
Synthesizing

response and asking, "What made you think of...?" This prompts students to converse with one another as they explore their understandings.

3 During the inquiry process, students interact both to share and to extend their understandings of the topic. To help students assume this responsibility, establish some ground rules. Remind students to be respectful of one another during their inquiries, taking care not to embarrass or belittle classmates as they examine or challenge items. Emphasize that we all "hear things that are not necessarily accurate." A benefit of brainstorming is surfacing misconceptions, which can then be tested and revised through reading.

4 When students have completed their inquiries and comments about the items, cover the items and ask students to turn over their papers and note what they have learned about the topic. One variation is to have them explain the concept. What they write is based on both their prior experience and the class discussion during the inquiry. Students are now ready to read the passage. After reading, ask them to note what they have learned from the new material. A variation is List/Group/Label (Taba, 1967), whereby students work in teams to group items by common characteristics. Provide teams with small slips of paper so they can record items, physically shift them into groups, and decide on an appropriate label for each grouping.

Knowledge Mapping

With Knowledge Mapping (Buehl, 2011), one creates a visual concept map of meaningful words and phrases associated with a key topic. This strategy is an especially effective means of orchestrating a student-led review of prior learning of disciplinary topics.

1 Again, decide on an appropriate cue word and have students work with partners or in teams to generate four to six highly meaningful words and phrases that provide useful knowledge about the term. For example, ask students to map their knowledge of *aerobic exercise* before reading about this topic (see the Knowledge Map for *Aerobic Exercise*). Team members need to clearly explain to each other how each association is meaningfully connected to the key concept, in preparation for sharing with the whole class.

2 Students explain their maps to the class and elaborate on the relationships of all the terms and phrases they included. Each member of the group should be prepared to contribute to the explanations. As an alternative, more expansive Knowledge Maps can be constructed on chart paper and posted in the room for a class gallery walk through meaningful connections, with follow-up conversations (as in the LINK

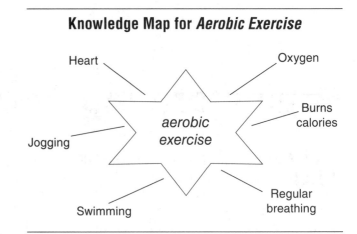

Knowledge Map for *Aerobic Exercise*

strategy discussed previously) in which students inquire about items on specific maps. A third variation is a teacher-constructed class Knowledge Map, with solicitation of individual items from each team.

3 This strategy can also be jigsawed, with teams given different cue words so multiple concepts are mapped. For example, while some teams work on mapping *aerobic exercise*, other teams could be mapping *anaerobic exercise*, leading to a compare-and-contrast follow-up discussion.

Knowledge Ladders

Knowledge Ladders (Buehl, 2011) are a more extensive brainstorming option, with the added challenge (and playfulness) of using the letters of the cue word to construct meaningful associations. Like Knowledge Mapping, this strategy is largely predicated on student review of prior learning.

1 Decide on an appropriate cue word or phrase, which ideally should consist of about eight to 12 letters to extend the number of possible meaningful links. Display the term or phrase in a vertical column. For example, science students work with partners or in teams to construct a Knowledge Ladder for *amphibian*. Because this word has nine letters, students are expected to come up with nine "rungs" for their ladder (see the Knowledge Ladder for *Amphibian*). A letter can appear in any part of a meaningful word or phrase. When completed, the array of items should clearly communicate key facets of the target concept. Students practice clearly explaining the item on each rung and its relationship to the key concept.

2 Similar to the process for Knowledge Mapping discussed previously, partners or teams explain to their classmates the relationships of items in their Knowledge Ladders. Again, these can be posted

l**A**ys eggs
sala**M**ander
Ponds
losing **H**abitats
sw**I**ms
cold **B**looded
l**I**ves near water
vertebr**A**te
Newts

around the room for a student gallery walk, followed by inquiry elaborations. Students will likely be immersed in a rich language experience because sometimes as many as 20 to 30 various terms may surface that have relevance to the topic.

Alphabet Brainstorming

Alphabet Brainstorming (Ricci & Wahlgren, 1998) is effective when students have extensive background knowledge, especially when they are engaged in looking back over previous instruction and learning. The resulting chart serves as a prompt for reviewing terms, facts, or events.

1 Provide each student with a blank Alphabet Brainstorming Chart (reproducible available in the Appendix). Because this activity involves rigorous review, have students work in collaborative teams, although each individual student should fill in a personal copy of the chart. Select only broad topic areas for a prompt, such as the Civil Rights movement to prompt students to activate prior learning about this era in U.S. history (see the Alphabet Brainstorming on the Civil Rights Movement example).

2 Students work with partners or in groups to generate a related term or meaningful association that begins with each letter of the alphabet. Ask students to fill in as many boxes as possible within a designated time period (usually about seven to eight minutes). One variation is to have students generate as many items as they can from memory in five minutes, written in one color of ink. Then, in the remaining time, have them add items in a different color using any available resources.

3 Ask teams to explain their terms with the entire class and briefly justify how each term fits with the topic. In particular, students will want to hear if other groups came up with associations for difficult letters. In the Civil Rights Movement example, some groups might have thought of "Malcolm X" for the usually problematic *X* slot on the chart.

4 After reading and expanding their understandings, teams can return to their alphabet charts and add new meaningful items related to the topic of study in a different color ink (to signal new learning).

Advantages

- Students prepare for the study of new material and the knowledge demands of complex texts. Students

Alphabet Brainstorming on the Civil Rights Movement

A Affirmative action	B Bus boycott	C Civil Rights Act of 1964	D Discrimination	E Equal rights	F Freedom riders	G George Wallace
H Fair housing	I "I Had a Dream"	J Jail	K Ku Klux Klan	L Lunch counter	M Martin Luther King, Jr.	N Nonviolent protests
O	P Poll tax	Q Quotas	R Rosa Parks	S Segregation	T	U Universities
V Voting rights	W "We Shall Overcome"	X Malcolm X	Y Andrew Young	Z		

are more motivated to read material that can be related to something they already know.

- Students share background knowledge with their peers so all students can begin reading with some familiarity of the topic.
- Student misconceptions about the material that appear during brainstorming are in the open to be corrected during instruction.
- Students assume the responsibility for raising questions, seeking clarifications, and engaging in discussion about the topic.
- Students can revisit their lists after learning to add new information or to eliminate erroneous information.

Meets the Standards

Brainstorming Prior Knowledge promotes connecting with other sources of knowledge (R.9) and mentoring the reading of complex literary and informational texts (R.10), and some strategies involve integrating ideas into visual representations (R.7). In addition, the collaborative conversations develop expressing and defending thinking with supporting evidence (SL.1). Follow-up writing tasks provide practice in explaining and summarizing (W.2). Domain-specific vocabulary development is particularly emphasized, as well as word relationships (L.5, L.6).

References

Buehl, D. (2011). *Developing readers in the academic disciplines*. Newark, DE: International Reading Association.

Langer, J.A. (1981). From theory to practice: A prereading plan. *Journal of Reading, 25*(2), 152–156.

Ricci, G., & Wahlgren, C. (1998, May). *The key to know "PAINE" know gain*. Paper presented at the 43rd annual convention of the International Reading Association, Orlando, FL.

Taba, H. (1967). *Teacher's handbook for elementary social studies*. Reading, MA: Addison-Wesley.

Vaughan, J.L., & Estes, T.H. (1986). *Reading and reasoning beyond the primary grades*. Boston: Allyn & Bacon.

Chapter Tours

Notice how this next painting exhibits several characteristics of Monet's later masterpieces. The subject (water lilies), the brush technique, and the use of color—all are associated with canvases completed by Monet in the 1920s....

Think about your experiences with being escorted on a guided tour of an art gallery, a museum, a national park, or a historical site. A guided tour provides a knowledgeable introduction to what is being viewed, helps you focus on what is interesting or important, offers insights or experiences that enhance appreciation, and provides a framework for understanding. In contrast, unless you are already quite knowledgeable, you will probably miss significant elements of the experience if you wander about by yourself. This is also true of students struggling to make sense of complex texts, especially textbooks. Chapter Tours can provide them with enough direction and background that they can successfully work a text to achieve understanding and learn what is important.

Using the Strategy

A Chapter Tour, a frontloading technique, guides or talks readers through a chapter or selection and points out features of the text that warrant special attention. An effective tour should set up readers for comprehension by stimulating connections to prior knowledge, self-questioning, imagining, inferring, determining importance, and ultimately, synthesizing understanding. In particular, a tour should mentor reading through a disciplinary lens and focus on disciplinary-specific questioning (see Tables 5–14 in Chapter 4 for taxonomies for different disciplines).

1 To underscore the importance of frontloading before reading, provide students with a short text that might appear obscure if they had not been alerted to the general topic. For example, display a passage such as the following and provide students with just enough time for a single reading:

> Your first decision is to choose the size you desire. Once you have made your selection, examine the general shape to determine where to start. The initial incision is always at the top, and you should continue until you can lift it cleanly. The removal of the interior portion can be fun, although some people regard this as the least enjoyable aspect. Once the shell is empty, you can begin to craft a personality. Some prefer a forbidding likeness, whereas others follow a more humorous direction. Finally, arrange for a source of illumination. Enjoy your results while you can, for your work will soon begin to sag.

Ask volunteers for hunches about the passage. As students offer their ideas, have them cite clues from the passage that triggered their theories. A variety of explanations about the selection may be offered and justified. Then, allow students to reread the passage with the prompt *Halloween*. Students will quickly recognize that the passage describes a cultural event: carving a pumpkin into a jack-o'-lantern.

Discuss with students the frustrations they encountered when trying to read the passage without frontloading. Because students were not sure what part of their memory to access, they may not have been able to make sense of the text without the Halloween clue. Follow up with similar passages, each time encouraging students to search their memory banks for connections to apply to the material. Students will realize that reading is much more efficient and successful if they frontload before tackling a text.

2 Preview a typical textbook chapter to examine how the text is structured to facilitate thinking in a disciplinary manner. Some texts are very overt in guiding students in reading through a disciplinary lens, and others are less obvious, appearing instead to be dense jumbles of information rather than coherent communications. As part of the preview process, take special notice of ways the chapter forecasts text

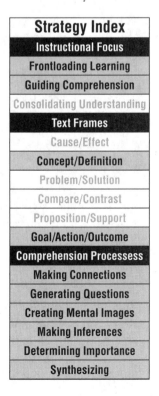

Strategy Index

Strategy Index
Instructional Focus
Frontloading Learning
Guiding Comprehension
Consolidating Understanding
Text Frames
Cause/Effect
Concept/Definition
Problem/Solution
Compare/Contrast
Proposition/Support
Goal/Action/Outcome
Comprehension Processess
Making Connections
Generating Questions
Creating Mental Images
Making Inferences
Determining Importance
Synthesizing

structure, such as cause/effect, and how it signals key concepts and ideas. (See Chapter 3, especially the section on text frames.)

Also, identify salient features that students might overlook during their reading. Many textbooks present information in a variety of visual formats other than written language and may offer study aids that guide learning in a chapter. Yet, unless attention is specifically called to these textual features, students often skip them while reading to complete an assignment.

3 Create a Chapter Tour that prompts students to think through a disciplinary lens as they examine these features while reading. For example, students reading a U.S. history textbook can easily become immersed in the voluminous details and miss major themes or ideas. A Chapter Tour can help them focus on changes and cause/effect dynamics, two concepts that predominate in thinking through a historian's lens (see the Chapter Tour for History).

4 Have students complete a Chapter Tour as an introduction to the textbook. An effective way of using a Chapter Tour is to allow the students to work with partners so they can verbalize what they are discovering about the way a specific textbook works (see the Interactive Reading Guides strategy pages). Develop variations of the Chapter Tour for subsequent chapters to remind students of critical elements in the text and to include additional aspects that you want brought to their attention.

5 Reinforce the necessity of getting a first read before undertaking any reading task. A sports analogy can provide a powerful illustration:

> Before a football quarterback runs a play, he takes time at the line of scrimmage to read the defense. He wants to know what to expect, and he wants to make predictions of what might happen. He also wants to anticipate strategies he can use during the play to be successful.

A first read, or preview, is a self-guided Chapter Tour. This initial sweep through the material requires an active and aggressive mind-set that targets the following:

- *Topic:* What is the selection about? What do I already know about this topic? What do I predict I should know after reading this?
- *Main idea:* What is the point of this material? Why did the author write this? How might this material be useful to me? What should be my focus? What does the author want me to understand?

- *Major themes:* What are the author's key arguments or conclusions? If this material were summarized, what are the central thoughts that connect most of the details? What does this author apparently believe?
- *Structure:* How is this material put together? How is it sectioned or subdivided? Where do I need to allocate my most careful attention?
- *Salient details:* Are there any facts that call for special attention? What stands out in the material? Is there text in boldface or italic type, quotations, or capital letters? Are there any key phrases that seem important? How familiar is this material? What details do I already know?
- *Style:* What do I notice about the author's writing style? How complicated are the sentences? How dense is the vocabulary? How smoothly does the prose flow? How carefully will I need to read and perhaps reread?
- *Tone/attitude/mood:* Does the author have an attitude toward this material? Can I detect any emotion in the material? What tone can I sense: anger, humor, enthusiasm, criticism, sarcasm, irony, reasoning, persuasion, inspiration, or explanation? If the author were doing a live presentation of this material, what would it be like?

Advantages

- Students are mentored to read through a disciplinary lens.
- Students learn to personally engage in frontloading before they read.
- Students are conditioned to make predictions about a passage and then read to confirm or reject them.
- Students are provided with an "expert guide" to alert them to how to uncover what is most important in a chapter and to make more systematic use of textual features.
- This strategy can be applied to text materials in all disciplines and is appropriate for students from elementary through high school levels.

Meets the Standards

The Chapter Tours strategy promotes discerning main ideas (R.2), examining interrelationships of details or ideas (R.3), analyzing text structure (R.5), tracking the author's perspective and purpose (R.6), examining visual representations (R.7), and mentoring the reading of complex literary and informational texts (R.10). In addition, the collaborative conversations develop discussion skills (SL.1). Follow-up writing provides practice in using text-based evidence in supporting summarizing and explaining (W.2). Vocabulary development

Chapter Tour for History

Facts! Facts! Facts!

History textbooks seem to be crammed with never-ending facts: names, dates, places, and events. This Chapter Tour will help you see beyond the facts—to identify the important "thinking like a historian" themes (cause/effect, change, turning points, through their eyes, using the past). A Chapter Tour helps you uncover major historical ideas and avoids close attention to details. Ask yourself, What's the point of all of this? What would historians want you to understand? To get the big picture of what a chapter is about, take a tour of the text first.

Surveying a Chapter Before Reading

1. What is the title of the chapter?

    • Based on the words in the title, predict which of the five "thinking like a historian" themes (listed above) will be emphasized and explain your thinking.

2. Each chapter begins with an Introduction section, which usually focuses on a brief story about a person or people related to the themes of the chapter. Who are the people featured in this Introduction?

    • Examine the photographs on these first two pages. Now, skim the Introduction. What do these people have to do with *industry*, a word from the chapter title?

3. Each chapter begins with an essential question that will be examined. Find the essential question displayed below the chapter title. Explain how this question seems to focus on the historian themes of change and cause/effect.

4. Chapter 25 is organized into the Introduction plus six other sections. Page through the chapter and list the headings of those six sections. (*Note:* They are numbered and printed in red.)

    • Look at keywords in these headings and predict how each section might deal with the historian theme of change.

5. Now, go back and find the first section of Chapter 25. Quickly scan the two pages of the first section. Notice that the material is divided into smaller topics, each identified by a subheading. Write the two subheadings for this section.

    • Historians use the vocabulary words that are highlighted in blue and briefly explained in the margins. Locate the two historian words in this section, write them down, and read the explanations.

    • The vocabulary explanations signal important changes in what area: population, environmental, economic, technological, political, or cultural? Tell why.

6. Look over the photographs in this chapter and think about changes and possible problems connected to these changes.

    • Select one of the photographs for closer examination. Read the caption below the photo.

    • Write down one thing you already know that is connected to this photo.

    • What change or problem seems to be shown in this photo?

    • Thinking like a historian, what is something about this chapter that you are wondering as you examine the photographs?

7. This book features a number of visual information displays, such as maps, charts, and tables. Find one visual display in this chapter. What is the general topic of this visual? Examine it and decide, What change or changes is this visual detailing?

8. The chapter features a case study, an extended example of industrialization. The case study is an additional part of the chapter and is broken into several segments. Locate the case study and identify the topic.

    • Examine the title in each segment and the photographs. Then, look carefully at the primary document excerpt in the last segment (the newspaper). Predict what the story will be about in this case study.

9. Locate the Chapter Summary page (in yellow), where a brief summary of each section is provided. Reread the essential question that you wrote for #3 above. Now, skim the summary. What issues seem to be covered in this chapter that are connected to the essential question?

10. Each chapter ends with a Reading Further section that explores some topic related to the chapter in more depth. Read the introductory paragraph (in bold type), examine the pictures, and read the captions. What topic is discussed in this section?

    • What does this topic seem to have to do with the historian themes of change and cause/effect?

    • There are many primary-source quotes throughout the textbook. These quotes are each taken from a primary source—material that was written during the time period covered by the chapter. Locate one of the primary-source quotes in this section and read it.

    • Who is quoted here, and what change does this person talk about?

Note. Designed for *History Alive! The United States Through Industrialism* (pp. 353–370), by the Teachers' Curriculum Institute, 2011, Palo Alto, CA: Author. Copyright © 2011 by the Teachers' Curriculum Institute.

includes attention to word relationships (L.5) and acquiring domain-specific vocabulary (L.6).

Literature Cited

Teachers' Curriculum Institute. (2011). *History alive! The United States through industrialism*. Palo Alto, CA: Author.

Suggested Readings

Cunningham, D., & Shablak, S.L. (1975). Selective reading guide-o-rama: The content teacher's best friend. *Journal of Reading, 18*(5), 380–382.

Wood, K.D., Lapp, D., Flood, J., & Taylor, D.B. (2008). *Guiding readers through text: Strategy guides for new times* (2nd ed.). Newark, DE: International Reading Association.

Character Quotes

Give me liberty or give me death!

Ask not what your country can do for you—ask what you can do for your country.

We have nothing to fear but fear itself.

I have a dream that one day this nation will rise up and live out the true meaning of its creed. (These first four quotes can be found on the Great American Documents website: www.greatamericandocuments.com/speeches.)

I'm the most terrific liar you ever saw in your life. It's awful. (Salinger, 1951, p. 16)

One of my troubles is, I never care too much when I lose something—it used to drive my mother crazy when I was a kid. (Salinger, 1951, p. 91)

It was one of the worst schools I ever went to. It was full of phonies. And mean guys. You never saw so many mean guys in your life. (Salinger, 1951, p. 170)

Just because somebody's dead, you don't just stop liking them, for God's sake—especially if they were about a thousand times nicer than the people you know that're alive and all. (Salinger, 1951, p. 174)

Note the power of expressive language! From the stirring rhetoric of Patrick Henry, John F. Kennedy, Franklin Delano Roosevelt, and Martin Luther King, Jr., to the introspective musings of Holden Caulfield in J.D. Salinger's (1951) *The Catcher in the Rye*, our words are a significant way that we reveal ourselves to others.

Using the Strategies

Character Quotes (Buehl, 1994; adapted from Blachowicz, 1993) is a strategy that helps students develop insights about a character by examining what he or she says. Character Quotes can be used to examine fictional characters in literature, real-life individuals in biographies, and authors—all of whom present themselves through their words. In addition, Reading With Attitude, an extension of Character Quotes, develops readers' sensitivity to the author behind the words.

1 Preview the text to identify several quotes by a character, historical figure, or author that illustrate different facets of the individual's personality. Select quotes that encourage students to develop varying descriptions of the kind of person this individual might be. Write each quote on a separate slip of paper or index card. For example, students preparing to read the classic *The Diary of a Young Girl* by Anne Frank (1995) will encounter an introspective adolescent who struggles with fears of being discovered while coping with the intense pressures of living in close proximity to her family and others (see the Character Quotes From *The Diary of a Young Girl: The Definitive Edition*). Students in a history class studying the development of the American West can be introduced to an American Indian point of view through quotes taken from Nez Perce leader Chief Joseph's speech of surrender to the U.S. government troops in 1877 (see the Character Quotes From Chief Joseph).

2 Students work with partners or in collaborative groups, each partnership or group having a different quote to consider from the same text. Ask them to generate as many words as possible that describe their impression of this person based on the quote. For example, groups working on quotes from *The Diary of a Young Girl* might come up with *studious, sensitive, worried, resentful, witty, well educated, misunderstood, outsider, gets picked on, dissatisfied, wants to be better, strong-willed, stressed out, depressed,* or *lonely*.

3 After each pair or group has generated a list of descriptors, they read their quote to the entire class and share the list of character qualities and traits that they associate with that character. They also talk about why they arrived at these traits, supporting their interpretations with specific language from the quote. As they share, record the qualities and traits for the class and inform them that all of the quotes were uttered by the same individual. A variation is to distribute quotes from two or more characters or figures, with teams examining different individuals.

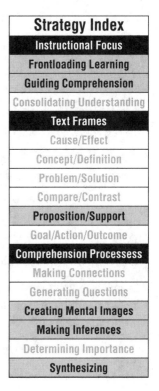

Strategy Index

Instructional Focus

Frontloading Learning

Guiding Comprehension

Consolidating Understanding

Text Frames

Cause/Effect

Concept/Definition

Problem/Solution

Compare/Contrast

Proposition/Support

Goal/Action/Outcome

Comprehension Processess

Making Connections

Generating Questions

Creating Mental Images

Making Inferences

Determining Importance

Synthesizing

Character Quotes From *The Diary of a Young Girl: The Definitive Edition*[a]

- My report card wasn't too bad. I got one D, a C– in algebra and all the rest B's, except for two B+'s and two B–'s. My parents are pleased, but they're not like other parents when it comes to grades. They never worry about report cards, good or bad…. I'm just the opposite. I don't want to be a poor student. (p. 17)

- Not being able to go outside upsets me more than I can say, and I'm terrified our hiding place will be discovered and that we'll be shot. That, of course, is a fairly dismal prospect. (p. 28)

- I don't fit in with them, and I've felt that clearly in the last few weeks. They're so sentimental together, but I'd rather be sentimental on my own. (p. 29)

- A few nights ago I was the topic of discussion, and we all decided I was an ignoramus. As a result, I threw myself into my schoolwork the next day, since I have little desire to still be a freshman when I'm fourteen or fifteen. The fact that I'm hardly allowed to read anything was also discussed. (p. 38)

- Mother and I had a so-called "discussion" today, but the annoying part is that I burst into tears. I can't help it….At moments like these I can't stand Mother. It's obvious that I'm a stranger to her; she doesn't even know what I think about the most ordinary things. (p. 41)

- They criticize everything, and I mean everything, about me: my behavior, my personality, my manners; every inch of me, from head to toe and back again, is the subject of gossip and debate. Harsh words and shouts are constantly being flung at my head, though I'm absolutely not used to it. (p. 44)

- Night after night, green and gray military vehicles cruise the streets. They knock on every door, asking whether any Jews live there. If so, the whole family is immediately taken away….It's impossible to escape their clutches unless you go into hiding. (p. 69)

- In bed at night, as I ponder my many sins and exaggerated shortcomings, I get so confused by the sheer amount of things I have to consider that I either laugh or cry, depending on my mood. Then I fall asleep with the strange feeling of wanting to be different than I am or being different than I want to be, or perhaps of behaving differently than I am or want to be. (p. 72)

[a]Frank, A. (1995). *The diary of a young girl: The definitive edition* (O.H. Frank & M. Pressler, Eds.; S. Massotty, Trans.). New York: Doubleday.

Character Quotes From Chief Joseph

- I want to have time to look for my children and see how many I can find. Maybe I shall find them among the dead. (p. 554)

- I am tired; my heart is sick and sad. From where the sun now stands, I will fight no more forever. (p. 554)

- You might as well expect the rivers to run backward as that any man who was born free should be contented penned up and denied liberty to go where he pleases. (p. 555)

- Good words will not give my people good health and stop them from dying. Good words will not get my people a home where they can live in peace and take care of themselves. I am tired of talk that comes to nothing. (p. 554)

- We only ask an even *chance* to live as other men live. We ask to be recognized as men. We ask that the same law shall work alike on all men. (p. 555)

- All men were made by the same Great Spirit Chief. They are all brothers. The earth is the mother of all people, and all people shall have equal rights upon it. (p. 555)

- Let me be a free man—free to travel, free to stop, free to work, free to trade where I choose, free to choose my own teachers, free to follow the religion of my fathers, free to think and talk and act for myself—and I will obey every law, or submit to the penalty. (p. 555)

Note. The quotes are from *The American Spirit: United States History as Seen by Contemporaries* (2nd ed.), edited by T. Bailey, 1967, Boston: Heath. Copyright © 1967 by Heath.

4 Involve students in making generalizations about the character or individual. Students work in their groups to write a preliminary personality profile of this character by drawing on the qualities and traits listed by the entire class. The profile should contain four or five statements that integrate important qualities from the list.

Provide an opening stem as a template to assist students in organizing their personality profile. The following is the opening stem for a profile on Chief Joseph's quotes:

> Chief Joseph was the type of person who ___. He also seemed to be ___. Other traits of his personality included ___. His words show that he experienced ___.

5 Students read the story, biography, or other selection. Afterward, they return to their personality profiles to discuss what new qualities or traits they might add and how they would change the profile to make it match their understanding of the character or individual better. Ask students to select further quotes from the text that provide new information about their character, or have them identify representative quotes that lead to understanding a second character or individual.

Reading With Attitude

Reading With Attitude (Buehl, 2004), an extension of Character Quotes, tunes in readers to the emotional content of a text and helps them detect the author's attitude and perspective.

1 Introduce students to three ways of tracking emotions in a written text:

1. *Character emotions:* Readers notice emotions displayed by the people or characters featured in a text. (People/Characters feel....)

2. *Reader emotions:* Readers monitor their own personal emotional responses to what they are reading. (I feel....)

3. *Author emotions:* Readers recognize emotions expressed or implied by the author of a text. (The author feels....)

Inform students that some emotions in a text are readily apparent, but the emotional content of a text is frequently not directly stated and, as a result, must be inferred by a reader. In particular, readers of prose fiction need to be sensitive to an author's word choice as they search for character emotions. The specific language chosen by an author can signal an implied emotional dynamic.

Provide practice in detecting all three kinds of emotions as students read. Ask them to mark or record on sticky notes any language and situations that indicate underlying feelings. For example, marking for character emotions in the short story "House of Snow" by Kate Wesselman (1993) reveals a number of significant hints about the relationship between the narrator in the story—a young girl—and her father, which is never directly stated. Students then write down what they are wondering about the unstated emotions:

- "Would I like to see him?" (p. 1). (Why would there be a question of whether the girl would want to see her father?)
- "Dad was fidgety" (p. 1). (Why? What was he feeling?)
- "I'd prepared for weeks" (p. 1). (Was she excited to be meeting her father, or was she anxious or unsure?)
- "I realized his fingertips were squared off on top, like mine" (p. 1). (Was she wondering how much she was like her father?)
- "His eyes danced" (p. 1). (How did he feel about his many travels about the world?)
- "He sighed" (p. 2). (How was he feeling about not knowing his own daughter?)

3 Character and reader emotions are often the easiest for students to discern when reading a text. However, author emotions are often less obvious and must be inferred. Authors may lead a reader toward certain ideas or conclusions that greatly influence how a text is understood and how a reader thinks about a topic. Some authors are up-front in communicating the perspective they bring to their writing so readers know who is talking to them and can factor this insight into their understanding. But many authors leave their personal imprint on a text unstated so readers must figure out on their own the extent of an author's beliefs, prejudices, and experiences as reflected in the author's message. Therefore, have students identify author emotions by asking, "Does the author have an attitude?" Students consider whether an author is displaying an attitude, such as a viewpoint, an opinion, a perspective, or a bias. Most students can understand or readily identify with "having an attitude" about something, and locating the author's attitude is an essential component to critical reading.

Prompt students to ask, when considering any written text (fiction or nonfiction), whether the author has an attitude. For example, while examining the following excerpt from a history textbook, they can ask themselves, Does the author have an attitude about César Chávez?

> One of the most notable campaigns for Latino rights in the 1960s was the farmworker struggle in California. César Chávez, a farmworker born in Arizona, was one

Reading With Attitude Chart for *Night*[a]

Quote	Character's Emotion	Author's Emotion	Reader's Emotion
"The gates of the camp opened. It seemed that an even darker night was waiting for us on the other side." (p. 80)	Elie was scared of his future. The unknown of his and his father's fate weighed heavily on him.	The author is foreshadowing the dark and difficult destiny that awaits them at Auschwitz. He is telling us that he felt fear.	I was worried about Elie and his father. I know what would likely happen to them when they were moved to Auschwitz.

Note. Adapted, with permission, from a Reading With Attitude Chart by K. DeVries and R. Knoll, Madison, WI.
[a]Wiesel, E. (1982). *Night* (S. Rodway, Trans.). New York: Bantam.

of the principal leaders of this effort to improve the lives of migrant workers....

Like Martin Luther King Jr., Chávez relied on nonviolence in the struggle for equal rights. Among other tactics, he used hunger strikes as a political tool. He fasted several times over the years to draw attention to the plight of farmworkers and to pressure employers to improve working conditions. (Teachers' Curriculum Institute, 2008, pp. 609–610)

Students may note favorable language, such as "notable," "improve…lives," and "nonviolence," as well as a respectful comparison to King, as indicators that the author has an approving attitude toward Chávez and perhaps workers in general.

4 Provide each student with a Reading With Attitude Chart (reproducible available in the Appendix), which combines the Character Quotes strategy with tracking the emotional content of a text (see the Reading With Attitude Chart for *Night*). Designate particularly evocative quotes from the text for examination or ask students to select quotes that they perceive as having significant emotional content. The quotes provide the basis for group and class discussions, as well as writing tasks that analyze author perspectives.

Advantages

- Students are introduced to several important facets of a character's or individual's personality before they begin reading.

- Students are involved in actively predicting major themes and issues of a story or selection.

- Students become conditioned to search for implicit meanings of a text and strengthen their ability to make inferences.

- Students tune in to the voice talking to them through print so they can become critical readers and deepen their understanding. All students need extensive practice with a variety of texts to determine author perspective and bias, to determine the extent

to which they can trust an author's judgment and version of the truth.

Meets the Standards

The Character Quotes and Reading With Attitude strategies promote careful reading of an author's message (R.1), discerning main ideas (R.2), interpreting word meaning (R.4), tracking the author's perspective and purpose (R.6), supporting argumentation (R.8), and mentoring the reading of complex literary and informational texts (R.10). In addition, the collaborative conversations develop expressing and defending thinking with supporting evidence (SL.1, SL.3, SL.4). Follow-up writing tasks provide practice in using text-based evidence in arguing and drawing evidence from texts to support analysis (W.1, W.9). Nuances in word meanings and word relationships emphasize vocabulary development (L.5).

References

Blachowicz, C. (1993, November). *Developing active comprehenders*. Paper presented to the Madison Area Reading Council, Madison, WI.

Buehl, D. (1994). You said it: Colorful quotes can be the voice of a character's soul. *WEAC News & Views, 29*(11), 21.

Buehl, D. (2004). Does the author have an attitude? *OnWEAC, 4*(5), 13.

Literature Cited

Bailey, T. (Ed.). (1967). *The American spirit: United States history as seen by contemporaries* (2nd ed., pp. 554–555). Boston: Heath.

Frank, A. (1995). *The diary of a young girl: The definitive edition* (O.H. Frank & M. Pressler, Eds.; S. Massotty, Trans.). New York: Doubleday.

Salinger, J.D. (1951). *The catcher in the rye*. New York: Little, Brown.

Teachers' Curriculum Institute. (2008). *History alive! Pursuing American ideals*. Palo Alto, CA: Author.

Wiesel, E. (1982). *Night* (S. Rodway, Trans.). New York: Bantam.

Wesselman, K. (1993). House of snow. *Nimrod: International Journal of Prose & Poetry, 37*(1), 1–14.

Concept/Definition Mapping

"Let's see...*harbinger*...um...presage...forerunner, herald...a person sent in advance to secure accommodations. I'm still not sure that I have a feel for this word *harbinger*." "Look it up in the dictionary!"

Students are conditioned throughout their schooling to follow this advice, but for many students, using the dictionary means fixating on very narrow and sometimes vague statements to define a word. These dictionary definitions contain little elaboration and may not connect at all to what students already know about a word. In contrast, Beck, McKeown, and Kucan (2008) recommend vocabulary instruction that is frequent, rich, and extended and engages students to reach beyond mere identification of a definition (see the Student-Friendly Vocabulary Explanations strategy pages). Students need a classroom environment that prompts them to assume true ownership of words for more precise written and spoken expression.

Concept/Definition Mapping (Schwartz & Raphael, 1985) helps enrich understanding of a word or concept. Concept/Definition Maps are graphic displays that focus attention on explaining the key components of a student-friendly explanation: the class or category, the properties or characteristics, and illustrations or examples. The strategy also encourages students to call on their personal knowledge when understanding new words. The Frayer Model, a related strategy, identifies nonexamples of a concept as well as examples.

Using the Strategies

Concept/Definition Mapping is an excellent strategy for teaching key vocabulary and concepts in all content disciplines. These graphic representations are especially useful for teaching academic vocabulary, sometimes referred to as Tier 3 words (see the discussion of Tier 2 and Tier 3 words in the Student-Friendly Vocabulary Explanations strategy pages).

1 Display a blank Concept/Definition Map (reproducible available in the Appendix). Point out questions that a complete definition would answer:

- *Category:* What is it?
- *Characteristics or properties:* What is it like?
- *Illustrations:* What are some examples of it?

Model how to use the Concept/Definition Map by selecting a familiar concept and soliciting the relevant information for the map from the class. For example, students responding to a map for *cheese* might identify the category as food or dairy product. Properties such as "usually soft," "usually yellow or white," "made from milk," and "kept cold" could be entered into the boxes under "What is it like?" As illustrations, students might offer cheddar, Swiss, mozzarella, and Gruyère as examples.

2 Present a key term or concept from material students are learning. Have them work in pairs to create a Concept/Definition Map for the new concept. Instruct them to use information from the reading passage, a glossary or dictionary, or their own background knowledge to complete the map. For example, science students studying types of living organisms might be given the concept of heterotroph to map (see the Concept/Definition Map for Science). The textbook identifies *heterotroph* as one of two types of living organisms, contrasted with *autotroph*. Have students note the properties of a heterotroph from the reading: needs energy from food to survive, cannot make its own food in its cells, may eat plants (autotrophs) to satisfy its need for food, and may eat other heterotrophs to satisfy its need for food. Have students locate examples of heterotrophs to be listed on the bottom of the graphic: humans, animals, fungi, and some bacteria.

Using the map, pose questions for student analysis of the concept. For example, are people who are vegetarians heterotrophs? How about people who are vegans or carnivores? Some students may draw from their background knowledge that some plants, such

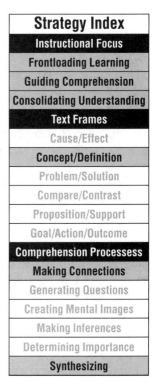

Strategy Index
Instructional Focus
Frontloading Learning
Guiding Comprehension
Consolidating Understanding
Text Frames
Cause/Effect
Concept/Definition
Problem/Solution
Compare/Contrast
Proposition/Support
Goal/Action/Outcome
Comprehension Processes
Making Connections
Generating Questions
Creating Mental Images
Making Inferences
Determining Importance
Synthesizing

Concept/Definition Map for Science

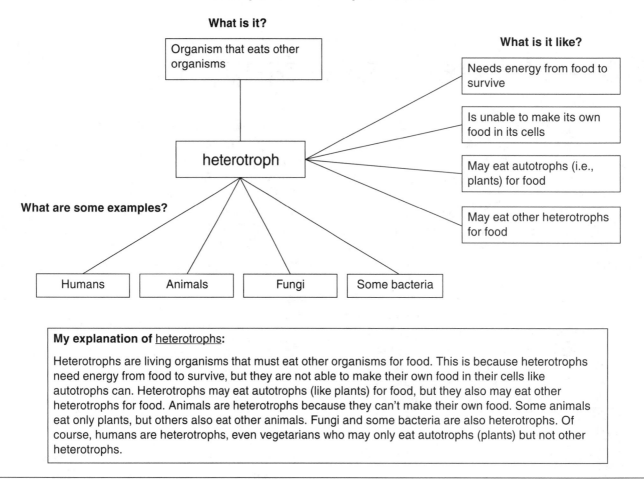

What is it?

Organism that eats other organisms

heterotroph

What is it like?

Needs energy from food to survive

Is unable to make its own food in its cells

May eat autotrophs (i.e., plants) for food

May eat other heterotrophs for food

What are some examples?

Humans | Animals | Fungi | Some bacteria

My explanation of heterotrophs:

Heterotrophs are living organisms that must eat other organisms for food. This is because heterotrophs need energy from food to survive, but they are not able to make their own food in their cells like autotrophs can. Heterotrophs may eat autotrophs (like plants) for food, but they also may eat other heterotrophs for food. Animals are heterotrophs because they can't make their own food. Some animals eat only plants, but others also eat other animals. Fungi and some bacteria are also heterotrophs. Of course, humans are heterotrophs, even vegetarians who may only eat autotrophs (plants) but not other heterotrophs.

---

as the Venus flytrap, eat insects. Does that make the Venus flytrap a heterotroph? These questions lead to further elaboration of the Concept/Definition Map and provide grist for additional inquiry and research.

3 When students have finished constructing their Concept/Definition Maps, have them use the maps to write a complete definition of the concept in the "my explanation" box. Emphasize that the definition should explain the category of the word, its properties or characteristics, and specific examples and will comprise several sentences instead of simple dictionary statements (see Concept/Definition Map for Science).

4 Assign students to create Concept/Definition Maps for additional key terms and concepts from their reading that can be used to solidify their understanding of Tier 3 vocabulary and create a resource for review.

Frayer Model

Experiences with not only examples but also non-examples, which share some but not all necessary

characteristics, enable students to construct rich and sophisticated meanings of disciplinary concepts. The Frayer Model (Frayer, Fredrick, & Klausmeier, 1969) helps students differentiate between characteristics that define the concept and those that are merely associated with it, and distinguish between items that represent the concept and items that are lacking some key characteristic of the concept.

1 Generate pairs of examples and nonexamples that exhibit major defining characteristics or attributes of a new concept. For example, a math teacher elaborating on the concept of equation might present the following pairs:

Example	Nonexample
$5 + 3 = 8$	$3 + 7$
$3x - 2y = 7z$	$5x + 2y - 3z$
$144 \div 6x = 12$	$27 \div 3 > 5$

Present a pair to students and ask them to determine the characteristics that differentiate the two lists.

For example, students might note that all of the equations (the examples) have equal signs. Note that initial determinations should be considered hypotheses that will be subject to revision as the process goes on and students analyze more pairs.

Provide additional examples and nonexamples, including some that might add more specific defining characteristics. This allows students to test their hypotheses and refine their understanding of the new concept. For example, if they encounter a nonexample such as $20 + 53 = 72$, they will realize that there is more to the definition than merely the presence of equal signs. Nonexamples such as $x + 3y \neq 105$ and $22 - y < 30$ underscore that not all mathematical expressions are necessarily equations. Furthermore, a nonexample such as $12 \div 4 \leq 3$ shows students that an expression could be true but may not be an equation. Ask students to revise the list of characteristics or attributes of the equation concept. They now might observe that equations must have two sides, that the two sides must result in the same value, and that an equal sign must be between the two sides. Record and, as necessary, rearrange these essential and nonessential characteristics on a blank Frayer Model (reproducible available in the Appendix).

2 To further establish the concept, assign students to work in pairs to generate their own examples and nonexamples of the concept. To initiate this phase of the strategy, provide students with a list of several possible examples and additional nonexamples. After they are labeled, have each pair of students continue locating or creating their own examples and nonexamples. These are then shared with the entire class, and students receive feedback on their choices. These are entered in the bottom two boxes of the Frayer Model.

Ask students to write an explanation of the concept of equation that includes all key or defining characteristics, such as the following:

> An equation has two sides separated by an equal sign. The numbers on each side must end up equaling the same value. It doesn't matter whether you add, subtract, multiply, or divide on either side, as long as both sides result in the same value.

3 Carefully analyze the defining attributes of a concept that you will be teaching to your students. For example, for a science concept like reptile, the essential characteristics would include animal, cold-blooded, and vertebrate. If students bring some knowledge about a concept before reading, brainstorm with the class to create a list of known characteristics or attributes of the concept. Ask students to posit possible examples and nonexamples.

Students then read a selection about the concept, using blank Frayer Models to track key information related to the concept. Note that students will be reading to confirm, reject, and extend the information generated by the class. You may wish to have students work in pairs as they read and complete the graphic organizer.

When everyone has completed their reading, have the students return to the original items they generated. Check off the examples and characteristics that students were able to confirm by the reading, with students citing evidence from the text to support their decisions. Some items from their list may need to be moved to the nonessential and nonexamples sections. Students record the new information they learned from the reading in the appropriate section on the model. Further research may be needed to clarify some possible examples.

For a concept that is likely unfamiliar to most students, the Frayer Model analysis can occur when students are asked to reread a text and collaborate with partners to determine the key conceptual information. For example, geometry students used the Frayer Model to clearly define the concept of parallelogram (see the Frayer Model for Math). As students explore the concept during subsequent lessons, additional defining characteristics and examples surface that are then added to the model, which becomes a valuable vocabulary resource for reinforcement of key disciplinary concepts over time.

Advantages

- Students expand their understandings of key academic vocabulary and concepts beyond simple definitions.
- Students construct a visual representation of a concept's definition that helps them remember it.
- Students develop precise and extended definitions of essential disciplinary concepts.
- Students are encouraged to integrate their background knowledge when developing vocabulary explanations.

Meets the Standards

Concept/Definition Mapping and the Frayer Model promote careful reading and rereading of an author's message (R.1); discerning main ideas and summarizing key concepts (R.2); interpreting word meaning, and use of figurative language (R.4); integrating ideas into visual representations (R.7); comparing and contrasting with other sources of knowledge (R.9); and mentoring the reading of complex literary and informational texts (R.10). In addition, the collaborative conversations develop expressing and defending thinking using visual displays (SL.1, SL.2, SL.4). Summarizing writing

Frayer Model for Math

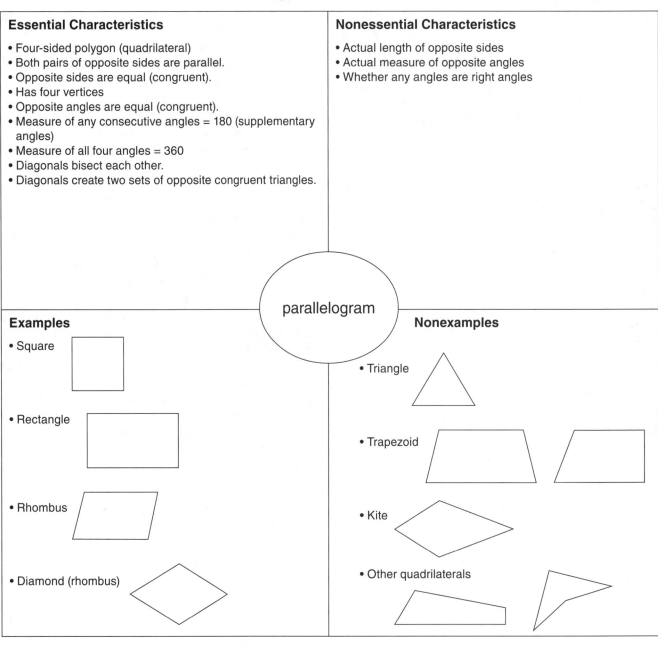

Essential Characteristics

- Four-sided polygon (quadrilateral)
- Both pairs of opposite sides are parallel.
- Opposite sides are equal (congruent).
- Has four vertices
- Opposite angles are equal (congruent).
- Measure of any consecutive angles = 180 (supplementary angles)
- Measure of all four angles = 360
- Diagonals bisect each other.
- Diagonals create two sets of opposite congruent triangles.

Nonessential Characteristics

- Actual length of opposite sides
- Actual measure of opposite angles
- Whether any angles are right angles

parallelogram

Examples

- Square
- Rectangle
- Rhombus
- Diamond (rhombus)

Nonexamples

- Triangle
- Trapezoid
- Kite
- Other quadriaterals

---

provides practice in using text-based evidence in explaining (W.2), and drawing evidence from texts for analysis and reflection (W.9). Vocabulary development includes determining and clarifying key vocabulary (L.4), attention to word relationships (L.5), and acquiring domain-specific vocabulary (L.6).

References

Beck, I.L., McKeown, M.G., & Kucan, L. (2008). *Creating robust vocabulary: Frequently asked questions and extended examples.* New York: Guilford.

Frayer, D.A., Fredrick, W.C., & Klausmeier, H.J. (1969). *A schema for testing the level of cognitive mastery* (Working Paper No. 16). Madison: Wisconsin Research and Development Center for Cognitive Learning, University of Wisconsin.

Schwartz, R.M., & Raphael, T.E. (1985). Concept of definition: A key to improving students' vocabulary. *The Reading Teacher, 39*(2), 198–205.

Suggested Reading

Santa, C., Havens, L., Franciosi, D., & Valdes, B. (2012). *Project CRISS: Helping teachers teach and learners learn* (4th ed.). Kalispell, MT: Lifelong Learning.

Connect Two

The checkerspot butterfly—a colorful photograph splashed across the newsprint immediately snags your attention. A quick scan of the accompanying newspaper article reveals the following prominent vocabulary terms: *invasive, habitat, greenhouse gases, extinction, assisted migration, biodiversity, ecological, ice age, species, transported,* and *conservation biologist.* Consider for a moment how an author might put these terms into play in a news story about butterflies. Given what you know about each of these words, how might they contribute to the development of the author's message? Which terms might you expect to find linked in some way in this article? Perhaps *extinction* and *species*, or *biodiversity* and *habitat*? What other potential combinations occur to you?

As readers, we realize that a flow of significant vocabulary guides our thinking through written texts. Of course, our comprehension of complex texts hinges on the knowledge of key vocabulary that we bring to our reading. But we are also called on to inventory our partial knowledge of words, our hunches about words that are still unfamiliar to a degree, and our predictions about words based on our attempts to glean an overall sense of meaning from a passage. Finally, we realize that vocabulary words operate as semantic networks, not as isolated packets of definitional information. Words are better understood in conjunction with their companion words—"fellow traveler" terms with which they share some relationship. In their natural environment, words do not exist alone; instead, they are interwoven into extended language to craft meaningful communications.

Using the Strategies

Connect Two (Blachowicz, 1986) is a strategy that helps students explore the key vocabulary of a passage before they begin reading. It encourages them to make predictions about the probable meaning of a passage based on what they know or can anticipate about a number of keywords or terms. Then, when students begin reading, they have already previewed major ideas of a text. A related strategy is Possible Sentences (Moore & Moore, 1986).

1 Identify 10 to 15 key concepts or terms in material that students will be reading. Include terms that will be familiar, as well as those that may be obstacles in their reading. Focus on words that are related to important ideas in the story or selection. The words you choose to draw attention to should help guide readers through central ideas or events in the text. Pay special attention to words that readers tend to encounter in written texts rather than through spoken language (Tier 2 words; see the Student-Friendly Vocabulary Explanations strategy pages for a discussion of academic vocabulary). In addition, highlight words that represent disciplinary concepts (Tier 3 words). In our opening scenario, *invasive* and *migration* are examples of significant Tier 2 words, and *biodiversity* and *habitat* are examples of important Tier 3 words.

2 Present these words to students as a group rather than a series of stand-alone new vocabulary terms. Exclusion Brainstorming is one method for initial exploration of a core group of words. For this activity, intersperse words that are *not* found in the text—and do not necessarily seem consistent with topics in the reading—with the set of words you selected from the passage. In our butterflies example, we might provide the following array of words for students to examine: *invasive, habitat, cholesterol, greenhouse gases, extinction, assisted migration, teleprompter, biodiversity, ecological, asphalt, species,* and *conservation biologist.*

Introduce this set of words by noting that several were taken from a selection that the class will be reading (in this case, on the topic of the checkerspot butterfly). In groups, have students speculate which words are the odd ones that do not appear in the article and should be struck from the list. As students deliberate, they begin to anticipate possible themes of the

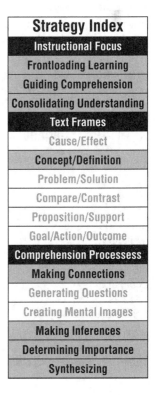

Strategy Index

Instructional Focus

Frontloading Learning

Guiding Comprehension

Consolidating Understanding

Text Frames

Cause/Effect

Concept/Definition

Problem/Solution

Compare/Contrast

Proposition/Support

Goal/Action/Outcome

Comprehension Processess

Making Connections

Generating Questions

Creating Mental Images

Making Inferences

Determining Importance

Synthesizing

butterfly article and to identify likely vocabulary that could communicate those themes. As students share knowledge about the words in this set, they are likely to decide that words like *cholesterol*, *teleprompter*, and *asphalt* do not seem as likely to be used as the others. The key dynamic here is the collaborative discussion about word knowledge, not that students discover all the superfluous terms. Some words that are actually in the article might be struck because these words might appear in unexpected ways in the text or because students lack sufficient knowledge of them. Or students might suppose that *asphalt* belongs because a butterfly's habitat could be covered with asphalt.

3 Present the key vocabulary arranged into two columns. Place words that might be more challenging or unfamiliar in Column A (see the Connect Two for Science). Related but more common words are listed in Column B. Students work with partners to create five sets of pairs, each pair consisting of a link between a word from each column. For each pair, they must explain how the two words might be meaningfully connected. Then, students create a sentence that puts the two words in play with each other. These sentences should represent ideas that students predict might occur in an article on butterflies that contains such a core group of words.

For example, *extinction* from column A might be paired with *global warming* from column B. The explanation of this pair's connection might be "Global warming is making it harder for some plants and animals to survive, which could cause their extinction." A predictive sentence illustrating this pair could be "Global warming is threatening to cause the extinction of the checkerspot butterfly." Of course, other partners could pair these terms differently. *Greenhouse gases* might be paired with *global warming*, or *polar bears*

Connect Two for Science

Checkerspot Butterfly

Column A	Column B
invasive	ice age
habitat	transported
greenhouse gases	range
extinction	climate
assisted migration	preserves
biodiversity	global warming
ecological	grassland
species	carbon dioxide
conservation biologist	polar bears

Note. From *Classroom Strategies for Interactive Learning* (3rd ed., p. 71), by D. Buehl, 2009, Newark, DE: International Reading Association. Copyright © 2009 by the International Reading Association.

---

with *extinction*. The intent behind Connect Two is to engage students in conversations about their vocabulary knowledge that focus on relationships between words as they might occur within a topic of study.

4 Students read the text. Ask them to track how the author employed the words in columns A and B.

5 When they have completed their reading, students continue their vocabulary exploration. Select six to eight of the terms to receive more in-depth emphasis. For example, you might select *invasive*, *habitat*, *assisted migration*, *extinction*, *biodiversity*, and *conservation biologist*. Partners then write statements using each word to summarize one important understanding about the topic. Each statement is built around a different key term, and each statement must say something different about the topic. When these statements are completed, students will have practiced their new vocabulary by embedding these terms into a written summary of the article about the checkerspot butterfly. A sample summary might begin as follows:

> Invasive plants have taken over places in the San Francisco Bay area, replacing the plants that the checkerspot butterfly depends on to live. The habitat for the checkerspot butterfly has changed, and fewer of them can be seen in the San Francisco Bay area. One proposal to help the butterfly is assisted migration, which involves moving the butterflies to a new area that has the habitat they need.

This phase of vocabulary development asks students to experiment with integrating these words with their own language, in a highly contextualized manner, by talking about their understanding of a now-familiar passage. Because they have the author's use of the word as a model, they are more apt to be comfortable with using the words themselves.

Possible Sentences

Possible Sentences (Moore & Moore, 1986) is a variation that involves students in discovering the accuracy of their predictions about key vocabulary.

1 Select 12 to 15 target vocabulary terms, using criteria similar to Connect Two. Have students work with partners to write a series of sentences that they predict could reasonably appear in the text to be read (see the Possible Sentences for Social Studies). Like Connect Two, each sentence should link at least two of the terms from the list.

Some terms would connect to knowledge students bring to the reading. For example, students preparing to read a passage on the Mayan civilization might know some geography related to where the Mayans lived (Mesoamerica or the Yucatán Peninsula) or that

Possible Sentences for Social Studies

Mayan Culture

Key Terms

Yucatán	Long Count Calendar	jaguar god
temples	Chichén Itzá	city-state
adobe	priests	slaves
agriculture	cacao	hieroglyphs
sacrifice	Mesoamerica	astronomy
pyramids		

Possible Sentences

DK 1. The pyramids of the Mayans were built by slaves.

T 2. The Mayans lived in an area of Mesoamerica called Yucatán.

T 3. Cacao was a main product of Mayan agriculture.

F 4. Chichén Itzá was a famous Mayan king who ruled in a city-state.

F 5. The Long Count Calendar was written in hieroglyphs and said the world would end in the year 2012.

DK 6. The Mayans offered sacrifices to the jaguar god.

Key:

T = true based on the reading.

F = false based on the reading; needs to be rewritten.

DK = don't know, not mentioned in the reading.

---

the Mayans constructed pyramids. For terms that are unfamiliar, encourage students to predict a probable meaning and to construct possible sentences. Students may go with a hunch that cacao (from which chocolate is derived) was a product of Mayan agriculture. They may not know about Chichén Itzá or hieroglyphs, so they would offer credible guesses based on these key terms.

2 Have students read the passage and check the accuracy of the possible sentences. They should evaluate each possible sentence in terms of whether it is true (the text confirms their prediction) or false (the text presents a contrary use of the terms), or they don't know (the statement can be neither proved nor disproved based on the text). For example, some possible sentences in the Mayan example are directly contradicted by the text: The reading reveals that Chichén Itzá was a location famous for Mayan pyramids and was not a person and that scholars disagree that the Mayan calendar forecasted the end of the world in 2012. Other possible sentences were not clearly dealt with in the text. For example, the text does not reveal whether Mayan workers or slaves erected the pyramids.

3 After students have read the passage and evaluated their possible sentences, they again work with partners to rewrite their sentences to be consistent with the reading. Have students locate relevant portions of the text to defend their corrections. In effect, students are constructing summary statements that reflect their understandings.

Students may find that some statements need to be expanded to two or three sentences to accurately reflect the text. Students may also generate new sentences to add to their original statements. For example, sentence 5 in the example might be repaired by students to read, "The Long Count Calendar was written in hieroglyphs and was carved on monuments in buildings like temples. Mayans viewed time in cycles, and their calendar was based on extremely accurate astronomical observations." Emphasize that exact statements copied from the text are unacceptable; students need to paraphrase their understandings of these terms in their own words. Again, each sentence should contain at least two of the target terms.

Advantages

- Students become acquainted with key terms and vocabulary from a passage before they begin to read.

- Students are encouraged to draw on their partial knowledge of words to speculate about possible meanings in the context of a core group of words about a theme or topic.

- Students encounter new vocabulary as extended families of words that are related to one another rather than as definitions that need to be memorized.

- Students are involved in a process that helps them establish their purposes for reading.

- Students activate what they know about information before they read and are able to share background knowledge with their classmates.

Meets the Standards

Connect Two and Possible Sentences promote careful reading and rereading of an author's message (R.1), discerning main ideas and summarizing (R.2), interpreting word meaning (R.4), comparing and contrasting with other sources of knowledge (R.9), and mentoring the reading of complex literary and informational texts (R.10). In addition, the collaborative conversations develop expressing and defending thinking (SL.1, SL.3, SL.4). Follow-up writing provides practice in using text-based evidence in summarizing and explaining (W.2) and drawing evidence from texts for analysis and reflection (W.9). Vocabulary development includes determining and clarifying key vocabulary (L.4), attention to word relationships (L.5), and acquiring domain-specific vocabulary (L.6).

References

Blachowicz, C.L.Z. (1986). Making connections: Alternatives to the vocabulary notebook. *Journal of Reading, 29*(7), 643–649.

Buehl, D. (2009). *Classroom strategies for interactive learning* (3rd ed.). Newark, DE: International Reading Association.

Moore, D.W., & Moore, S.A. (1986). Possible sentences. In E.K. Dishner, T.W. Bean, J.E. Readence, & D.W. Moore (Eds.), *Reading in the content areas: Improving classroom instruction* (2nd ed., pp. 174–179). Dubuque, IA: Kendall/Hunt.

Suggested Reading

Readence, J.E., Moore, D.W., & Rickelman, R.J. (2000). *Prereading activities for content area reading and learning* (3rd ed.). Newark, DE: International Reading Association.

Different Perspectives for Reading

"That's not my take on that article!" Two individuals sparring over their understandings of a particular text is a frequent and unsurprising occurrence. Look at the potential for spirited discussion that arrives each day in the morning news feed: an editorial about the glass ceiling for women executives, an exposé on the flaws of capital punishment, a movie review of the most recent action blockbuster, an article about substituting holistic health practices for drug treatments, a discussion of the mayor's comments about raising bus fares, a travel column recommending must-see spots in Europe, a feature article on the role of technology in today's classrooms, a report about teenagers who are lobbying the city for a skateboard park, an analysis of unlimited money in elections—the list goes on.

What would influence your comprehension in each of these reading situations? Chances are, you would read through a variety of personal lenses, which would create a perspective derived from your experiences, values, and attitudes that guide your comprehension of the text. Socioeconomic status, gender, political persuasion, age, ethnic identity, marital status, career history, educational background, and specific life experiences all factor into your perspective as you read. Thus, two people can read the same article and come away with different but equally valid interpretations of what the text means.

Because students, too, are individuals with different background experiences, beliefs, and understandings about the world, no two students will read and comprehend a passage in exactly the same way. A student whose grandparents are dairy farmers will understand a passage about organic milk in a decidedly different way than a student whose only connection to cows may be through cartoon portrayals. Likewise, a student who has visited Arizona will comprehend a story about the desert with a different appreciation than a student who has never left New York City. Strategies that broaden one's perspective about a topic will help students read with a greater depth of comprehension and appreciation.

Using the Strategy

Different Perspectives for Reading (McNeil, 1984) uses a graphic organizer to guide students through multiple readings of a text so they factor in different thinking perspectives in addition to their own.

1 After appropriate frontloading instruction, students read a story, article, or selection for the first time.

2 Identify different perspectives for a second, more in-depth reading of the text. Choose perspectives that are connected to the important ideas or concepts of the passage. For example, different perspectives in a world history textbook passage about the French Revolution might include those of a merchant, a peasant woman, a revolutionary, a parish priest, and a nobleman. For fictional material, assign students the perspective of a character other than the narrator in a story. For example, in the novel *To Kill a Mockingbird* by Harper Lee, the perspective is that of the young girl, Scout; however, other perspectives to consider are those of her brother, Jem; the family cook, Calpurnia; the elderly neighbor, Mrs. Dubose; the lawyer, Atticus Finch; the wronged man, Tom Robinson; or the phantom neighbor, Boo Radley.

3 Introduce the Different Perspectives Graphic Outline (reproducible available in the Appendix) and provide students with individual copies. Divide the class into collaborative groups of three or four and assign each team a different perspective. Ask students to identify the issues, feelings, effects, or concerns surrounding that particular perspective. For students studying the French Revolution, ask them to wonder, Why would the revolution be a concern for a priest or merchant? How would the revolution affect the needs of a peasant woman or nobleman? Students might decide that a priest would need respect for the religion, income for

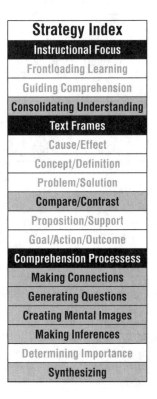

Strategy Index

Instructional Focus
Frontloading Learning
Guiding Comprehension
Consolidating Understanding
Text Frames
Cause/Effect
Concept/Definition
Problem/Solution
Compare/Contrast
Proposition/Support
Goal/Action/Outcome
Comprehension Processess
Making Connections
Generating Questions
Creating Mental Images
Making Inferences
Determining Importance
Synthesizing

Different Perspectives Graphic Outline for the French Revolution

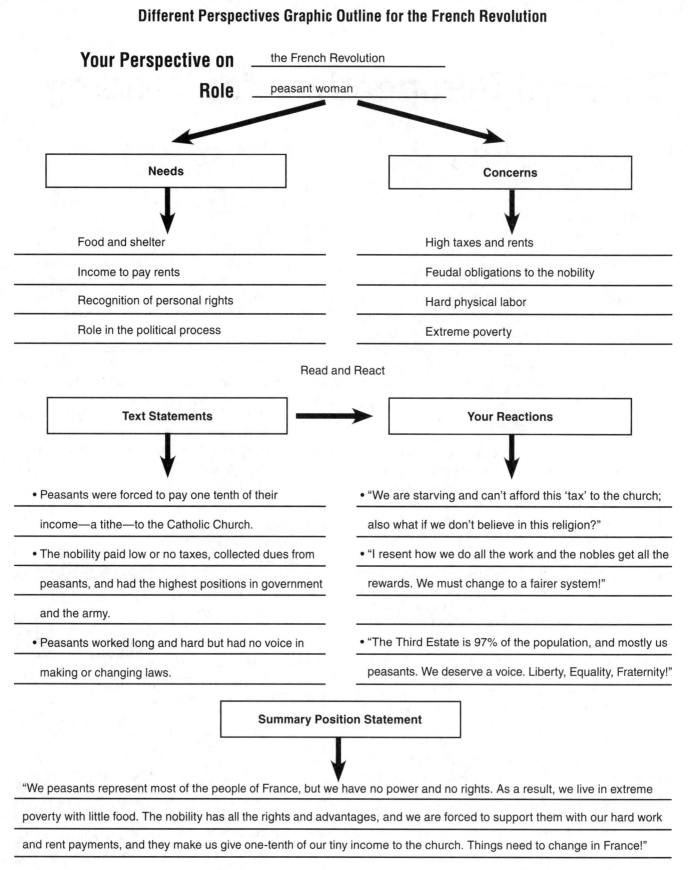

Your Perspective on _the French Revolution_

Role _peasant woman_

Needs	Concerns
Food and shelter	High taxes and rents
Income to pay rents	Feudal obligations to the nobility
Recognition of personal rights	Hard physical labor
Role in the political process	Extreme poverty

Read and React

Text Statements	→	Your Reactions

Text Statements

• Peasants were forced to pay one tenth of their income—a tithe—to the Catholic Church.

• The nobility paid low or no taxes, collected dues from peasants, and had the highest positions in government and the army.

• Peasants worked long and hard but had no voice in making or changing laws.

Your Reactions

• "We are starving and can't afford this 'tax' to the church; also what if we don't believe in this religion?"

• "I resent how we do all the work and the nobles get all the rewards. We must change to a fairer system!"

• "The Third Estate is 97% of the population, and mostly us peasants. We deserve a voice. Liberty, Equality, Fraternity!"

Summary Position Statement

"We peasants represent most of the people of France, but we have no power and no rights. As a result, we live in extreme poverty with little food. The nobility has all the rights and advantages, and we are forced to support them with our hard work and rent payments, and they make us give one-tenth of our tiny income to the church. Things need to change in France!"

Note. Adapted from *Classroom Strategies for Interactive Learning* (3rd ed., p. 74), by D. Buehl, 2009, Newark, DE: International Reading Association. Copyright © 2009 by the International Reading Association.

the church, and sufficient parishioners. Merchants would need economic and political stability, markets for their products, and lower taxation. They would be concerned with constant change in the government and periods of lawlessness. The nobility would be concerned about loss of estates, decreased political power, and possible execution.

4 Have the groups reread the material to identify specific statements or information that would be of special interest to their assigned perspective. Have them write this information on the graphic outline, along with comments based on their assigned perspective. For example, students rereading the history passage from a peasant woman's perspective might react as follows: "How can we peasants be expected to provide the church with one-tenth of our income when we are already in poverty and starving?" (See the Different Perspectives Graphic Outline for the French Revolution.)

5 Discuss with the whole class new insights gained through looking at the text through a variety of viewpoints. To bring their thoughts together, ask students to write a position statement summarizing the feelings of an individual with a particular perspective and explaining their assigned point of view. The position statements offer an excellent preparation for a "town hall" discussion of key ideas or concepts as groups argue their thinking through role-playing their assigned perspective.

Advantages

- Students receive reinforcement that a number of legitimate interpretations, conclusions, and generalizations may be drawn from a specific text.

- Students read with more emotional attachment while using this strategy and develop empathy for points of view other than their own.

- Students are given a structure to reread materials and to spotlight ideas and information that may have been overlooked in the first reading.

- Students are provided practice with identifying text-based evidence that supports alternative ways of thinking about a text.

Meets the Standards

Different Perspectives for Reading promotes careful reading and rereading of an author's message (R.1), discerning main ideas and summarizing (R.2), tracking the author's perspective and purpose (R.6), integrating ideas into visual representations (R.7), supporting argumentation (R.8), comparing and contrasting with other sources of knowledge (R.9), and mentoring the reading of complex literary and informational texts (R.10). In addition, the collaborative conversations develop expressing and defending thinking (SL.1, SL.3, SL.4). Summarizing writing provides practice in using text-based evidence in explaining (W.2) and drawing evidence from texts for analysis and reflection (W.9). Attention to word relationships addresses vocabulary development (L.5).

References

Buehl, D. (2009). *Classroom strategies for interactive learning* (3rd ed.). Newark, DE: International Reading Association.

McNeil, J.D. (1984). *Reading comprehension: New directions for classroom practice*. Glenview, IL: Scott Foresman.

Suggested Reading

Cook, D.M. (Ed.). (1989). *Strategic learning in the content areas*. Madison: Wisconsin Department of Public Instruction.

Discussion Web

Consider the array of political discussions in which you have participated. At times, you undoubtedly have been involved in passionate and highly emotional exchanges; at other times, quietly reasoned, earnestly argued conversations have taken place. All such discussions reflect a basic underlying principle, that oft-repeated truism: There are two sides to every question. Through exchanges with others, we have the opportunity to refine our thinking, respond to challenges to our viewpoints, and acknowledge alternative ideas.

Teachers know that classroom discussions are an important way to encourage students to think, but involving the entire class in a discussion can be difficult. Too often, only a few students are willing to contribute, and as a result, they monopolize the conversation. What starts as a discussion ends as a dialogue between the teacher and a handful of students. Meanwhile, the rest of the class sits passively, perhaps not listening or not paying much attention to what is being said.

Argumentation occupies a primary role in the Common Core's literacy standards—in reading, in writing, and in speaking and listening. Tracking and evaluating an argument, weighing the support marshaled for a position or point of view, and drawing one's own evidence-based conclusions are all hallmarks of critical reading.

Using the Strategy

The Discussion Web (Alvermann, 1991) is a collaborative strategy designed to include all students in active participation in class discussions. The Discussion Web incorporates all four facets of communication (reading, writing, speaking, and listening) and provides students with multiple opportunities to interact as they examine and construct arguments based on their reading. Point–Counterpoint Charts (Buehl, 2011) are a variation that incorporates prior knowledge brainstorming.

1 Choose a selection that develops opposing viewpoints, such as an article that deals with a controversial issue or a story that elicits conflicting interpretations of a character's action. Frontload instruction by activating students' relevant background knowledge for the selection and setting their purposes for reading (see the Brainstorming Prior Knowledge strategy pages).

2 After students read the selection, introduce the Discussion Web (reproducible available in the Appendix) and a focusing question for consideration. For example, students reading a history textbook passage on the Industrial Revolution might be asked, "Did the Industrial Revolution help working people?" (See the Discussion Web for the Industrial Revolution.) Students in a literature class reading *The Red Badge of Courage* by Stephen Crane might be asked, "Was Henry Fleming a coward for running?" Middle school students reading the novel *Hatchet* by Gary Paulsen might be asked, "Could Brian have survived in the wilderness without the hatchet?"

3 Assign students to work with partners to develop the opposing sides of the question. As they work, the pairs flesh out the arguments for both sides on a blank Discussion Web, going back and rereading the text to identify supportive evidence. During this phase, the emphasis is on fact finding—detailing the strongest possible arguments on both sides of the web. These yes/no statements provide the reasons for supporting or rejecting the central question. Remind students to set aside their personal beliefs to ensure that both positions are represented fully and fairly.

After analyzing the actions of the main character in *The Red Badge of Courage*, for example, students may outline the following arguments about his cowardice:

> Henry ran at the beginning of the battle, he misled others about his running, and he felt shame for running. However, Henry was experiencing his first battle, he had never before been under fire, many others ran as well, and there was much confusion during the battle.

Strategy Index
Instructional Focus
Frontloading Learning
Guiding Comprehension
Consolidating Understanding
Text Frames
Cause/Effect
Concept/Definition
Problem/Solution
Compare/Contrast
Proposition/Support
Goal/Action/Outcome
Comprehension Processes
Making Connections
Generating Questions
Creating Mental Images
Making Inferences
Determining Importance
Synthesizing

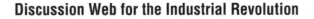

Discussion Web for the Industrial Revolution

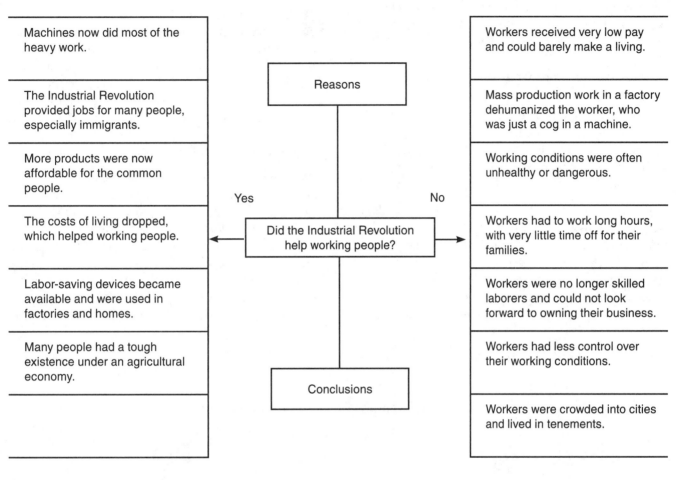

Machines now did most of the heavy work.		Workers received very low pay and could barely make a living.
The Industrial Revolution provided jobs for many people, especially immigrants.	**Reasons**	Mass production work in a factory dehumanized the worker, who was just a cog in a machine.
More products were now affordable for the common people.		Working conditions were often unhealthy or dangerous.
The costs of living dropped, which helped working people.	Yes Did the Industrial Revolution help working people? No	Workers had to work long hours, with very little time off for their families.
Labor-saving devices became available and were used in factories and homes.		Workers were no longer skilled laborers and could not look forward to owning their business.
Many people had a tough existence under an agricultural economy.	**Conclusions**	Workers had less control over their working conditions.
		Workers were crowded into cities and lived in tenements.

Note. From *Classroom Strategies for Interactive Learning* (p. 44), by D. Buehl, 1995, Madison: Wisconsin State Reading Association. Copyright © 2001 by the International Reading Association.

4 After partners complete the preliminary work on their Discussion Webs, assign each set of partners to collaborate with another pair, forming a new group of four. Ask them to deliberate toward a consensus on the question. Additional arguments on both sides of the question are added to the Discussion Web at this time, and when the group reaches a conclusion, it is written at the bottom of the web. For example, one group might conclude that in *Hatchet*, although Brian could have gotten fire from other means and may have adapted to his plight by using different strategies, he probably would not have survived without the hatchet. A second group might argue that Brian's ingenuity and common sense involving the hatchet could have been applied in other ways, which would have helped him survive without it. Again, groups need to be prepared to cite evidence from the text to support their arguments.

5 Each group of four is now ready to present its conclusions to the entire class. Allow three minutes for a spokesperson from each group to discuss one reason for their conclusion, which reduces the likelihood that the last groups to report will have no new ideas to offer. Encourage spokespersons to mention any dissenting viewpoints from their group discussions. In a discussion about the Industrial Revolution, some groups will decide that industrialization was progress and that working people ultimately benefited from innovations in industry. Other groups will likely deplore the unsafe and unhealthy conditions in which people worked and their exploitation by factory owners.

6 Students are now prepared to write their own personal position statements regarding the focusing question. The Discussion Web provides an organized guide to information and arguments that may be included in the writing. Students are thus able to develop their own ideas as well as reflect on the contributions of their classmates as they write their interpretations. A key expectation is for students to cite text-based evidence from their reading to support their stated position. In addition, students are prepared from the Discussion Web and their conversations to acknowledge counterarguments to their position and to effectively rebut these opposing viewpoints.

Point–Counterpoint Charts

Point–Counterpoint Charts (Buehl, 2011) are a variation of the Discussion Web. The Thumbs Up! Thumbs Down! Chart (reproducible available in the Appendix) combines student brainstorming of prior knowledge of a topic, which is then compared with what an author argues as positives and negatives about the topic.

1 During the initial brainstorming phase, students engage in a variation of the LINK strategy (see the Brainstorming Prior Knowledge strategy pages). They are asked to create two lists—one for positive statements and the other for negatives—related to a given prompt. For example, students might be asked to brainstorm possible positive effects of bacteria for

humans as well as negatives. Provide students with up to three minutes for this initial phase.

2 Have students team with a partner to talk about their items. In addition, ask them to work together to come up with at least one new item for each list. Then, during a whole-class discussion, solicit an item from each set of partners, first focusing on positives and then moving to negatives. As you record the items on the whiteboard, each student also records each item on a blank Thumbs Up! Thumbs Down! Chart (see the Thumbs Up! Thumbs Down! Chart for Bacteria).

3 Students read a text that provides additional information about the topic. This is an excellent opportunity for use of multiple texts, where perhaps three or four different texts can be available for students to deepen their knowledge about a topic. If texts can be annotated, have students text code either + or − in the margins next to where the author mentions relevant details or offers pertinent arguments. After reading, again team students with a partner and have them decide

---

Thumbs Up! Thumbs Down! Chart for Bacteria

Topic: Effects of Bacteria on Humans

Your Ideas/Arguments/Evidence For	Your Ideas/Arguments/Evidence Against
• There are good bacteria. • They are used in foods such as yogurt. • We already have some in our bodies. • I think it is how they make cheese. • Bacteria make dead plants rot and turn into soil. • You can build up your resistance to bacteria.	• They are harmful germs. • You could get sick or even die. • They cause infections. • You need antibiotics to kill them. • We now have super bacteria that resist drugs. • You can get food poisoning from them. • E. coli on vegetables causes illness and can kill you. • They can get in cuts or wounds. • Wash your hands or use hand sanitizer to get rid of them. • They cause food to spoil.
The Author's Ideas/Arguments/Evidence For	**The Author's Ideas/Arguments/Evidence Against**
• Humans consist of microbiomes that include bacteria. • Bacteria in humans outnumber human cells 10 to 1. • Humans could not live without bacteria. • Healthy humans are hosts for thousands of bacteria types. • Many essential life functions, such as digestion, need bacteria. • Gut bacteria break down carbohydrates. • Skin bacteria are vital for moisturizing the skin. • E. coli naturally lives in human intestines. • Antibiotics wipe out both good and dangerous bacteria. • Antibacterial soap kills both good and harmful bacteria.	• Mouth bacteria cause plaque, leading to tooth decay. • Good bacteria can become harmful with bad hygiene. • Good bacteria can cause harm in weak immune systems. • Bacteria cause strep throat and pneumonia. • Some bacteria cause botulism (lethal food poisoning). • Millions of people have died from bacterial diseases. • Poor sanitation often leads to bacterial outbreaks. • Antibiotic overuse can lead to mutated resistant forms. • We may run out of antibiotic options for new strains. • Deadly new bacterial diseases may lead to a pandemic.

---

what should be written in the bottom two boxes of the Thumbs Up! Thumbs Down! Chart.

4 During a whole-class discussion, ask students to cite from the text to support their thumbs-up and thumbs-down understandings. As part of the discussion, ask students to determine where their author falls in the debate: more on the positive side, the negative side, or fairly evenhanded in the treatment of the topic. Refer back to the brainstormed items during this phase and ask students to decide which of their items were consistent with their text, which were contradicted, and which were not considered.

5 Students are now prepared to write a position statement reflecting the weight of the evidence taken from their reading. Stress that their arguments are not intended to be merely opinion pieces but justifiable positions that can be solidly supported by evidence from their study. For our science example, students would explore our complicated corelationships as humans with ever-present bacteria.

Advantages

• Students are active participants in discussion and develop collaboration skills.

• Students have a framework for evaluating both sides of an issue or question and are encouraged to process opposing evidence and information before asserting their viewpoints.

• Students write arguments using well-organized support for their positions.

Meets the Standards

The Discussion Web and Point–Counterpoint Charts promote careful reading and rereading of an author's message (R.1), discerning main ideas (R.2), examining interrelationships of details or ideas (R.3), tracking the author's perspective and purpose (R.6), integrating ideas into visual representations (R.7), supporting argumentation (R.8), comparing and contrasting with multiple texts (R.9), and mentoring the reading of complex literary and informational texts (R.10). In addition, the collaborative conversations develop expressing and defending thinking using visual displays (SL.1, SL.2, SL.4). Follow-up writing provides practice in using text-based evidence in supporting arguments (W.1) and drawing evidence from texts for analysis and reflection (W.9). Vocabulary development includes attention to word relationships (L.5).

References

Alvermann, D.E. (1991). The discussion web: A graphic aid for learning across the curriculum. *The Reading Teacher, 45*(2), 92–99.

Buehl, D. (1995). *Classroom strategies for interactive learning.* Madison: Wisconsin State Reading Association.

Buehl, D. (2011). *Developing readers in the academic disciplines.* Newark, DE: International Reading Association.

Double-Entry Diaries

Consider texts that you might choose to read, such as a magazine cover story on women and heart disease. As you read, you encounter a wealth of important information: startling statistics, extensive scientific studies, suggested precautions, and recommended actions. Although the article mentions details that you already know, much is new knowledge, some of which may even surprise you or change what you had believed about this topic.

You engage in reading experiences like this many times a day. Somehow, often without thinking about it, you move along with an author, picking out salient elements and sorting them into a meaningful condensation of the message. As you read, you concentrate on making sense of the author, double-check your understanding, and pull your thoughts together—summarizing the gist of the passage; drawing some conclusions; and generalizing about themes, ideas, and implications.

This process of synthesizing meaning involves your mind operating on parallel tracks while reading. You are most aware of the *what* of reading: what this text is about, what is most important, what you should remember, and what you should do with the information. Yet, your mind is also involved in the *how* of reading: the ongoing thinking you must do to get at the *what*. You think of how this text extends your previous knowledge on a topic. You think of questions sparked by your reading that are not yet answered. You think about things that are not expressly stated as you make inferences and predictions. Reading comprehension is, ultimately, the result of the thinking you do when you are engaged with a text.

Students are often unaware of their thinking as they read, especially the thinking that can guide and enhance their comprehension. Strategies that surface this thinking and encourage students to notice how they are reading can strengthen their comprehension abilities as they tackle the various complex texts for disciplinary learning.

Using the Strategy

Double-Entry Diaries (Tovani, 2000) use reader responses to prompt essential comprehension processes, such as making connections to background knowledge, creating mental images, posing questions,

making inferences, and clarifying confusions when thinking about classroom texts. Double-Entry Diaries are a version of two-column (or Cornell) note-taking and are tailored for students to analyze their thinking about a text. This strategy is an excellent option for materials that cannot be marked, such as textbooks or class sets of novels, and are a natural component of interactive notebooks.

1 Ask students to create a T-chart by folding a sheet of paper in half lengthwise into two vertical columns. The left-hand column can be used for recording specific items from a reading, such as text segments, paraphrased notes, "need to know" information, or a summary. The right-hand column accords space for written responses that correspond to the text material selected for the left side. The result is a back-and-forth series of important textual references and the students' personal thoughts and ideas.

For example, a history teacher might use some segments from the textbook to model this process with students. The teacher might record this passage on the left: "Immigrant workers trapped on the upper floors during the Triangle Shirtwaist fire jumped to certain deaths rather than remaining in the flaming factory." On the right, the teacher records her thinking: "I am reminded of the 9/11 tragedy at the World Trade Center in New York City, when people also leaped to their deaths to escape the fire." The teacher is modeling how her background knowledge has connected to a textbook account of a historical event and how her knowledge helps her understand this historical event, which makes it more meaningful. During this interaction with students, emphasize that proficient readers constantly seek to

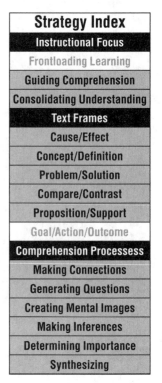

Strategy Index
Instructional Focus
Frontloading Learning
Guiding Comprehension
Consolidating Understanding
Text Frames
Cause/Effect
Concept/Definition
Problem/Solution
Compare/Contrast
Proposition/Support
Goal/Action/Outcome
Comprehension Processess
Making Connections
Generating Questions
Creating Mental Images
Making Inferences
Determining Importance
Synthesizing

draw on their personal knowledge to make sense of new information.

2 During the initial stages of using Double-Entry Diaries, focus on a single comprehension process in the right-hand column. The example in step 1 models asking students to consider how relevant prior knowledge might relate to new information. For this activity, the teacher could instruct students to label the right-hand column "My Knowledge Connections." In addition, students should verbalize how what they already knew contributed to a greater understanding of a passage, through sharing their entries with partners or in collaborative groups.

Other comprehension processes that could form the focus for the right-hand column of a Double-Entry Diary could include the following:

- My Questions: I'm Wondering...

- My Ideas: I'm Thinking That...

- Inferences: The Author May Be Saying...

- Implications: What This Means Is...

- Importance: This Is Important Because...

- Importance: We Need to Know This Because...

For example, a biology teacher might use a Double-Entry Diary to guide students to determine importance by asking them to fill in the right-hand column with the prompt "This is important because..." (see the Double-Entry Diary on Bacteria). Again, all of the preceding prompts prepare students to share their thinking with partners or in collaborative groups after completing their Double-Entry Diary entries.

3 After sufficient practice, students can track multiple comprehension processes using Content/Process Double-Entry Diaries (Harvey & Goudvis, 2007). Content/Process Notes are a natural extension of Text Coding (see the Text Coding strategy pages), which involves students in marking texts to track their comprehension by noticing their thinking processes as they read:

R = The reader was reminded of background knowledge that connects to the text.

Q = A question the reader was wondering about at a given point in the text

V = A spot where the reader could especially visualize what was being described

I = An inference as the reader adds to meaning based on hints provided by the author

? = A point of confusion

Content/Process Notes follow the split-page format of a T-chart: the left-hand side for important content from a selection and the right-hand side for the process, or the thinking noticed during reading. For students, these two columns can be labeled "What I Learned" (content) and "What I Was Thinking" (process). Walk students through this note-taking process by modeling entries in both columns as you extract key information for the left-hand side, and recognize what you were thinking in the right-hand side. As you think aloud about the passage, it is likely that you will alternate from one column to the other, at times emphasizing the content of the text and then registering your thoughts about the material.

The "What I Learned" (content) column focuses on the author: What did I learn from the author that I felt was important? In contrast, the "What I Was Thinking" (process) column focuses on the reader: What thoughts occurred to me that helped my understanding of this text? Although the content column will likely feature similar information recorded by students, entries in the process column will be highly varied and will illustrate the vast breadth of possible thinking that occurs to individual readers.

4 Content/Process Notes are especially advantageous for complex texts that will challenge students. Using the content/process note-taking system, students can keep track of what they judge to be key ideas and information while logging some of their thinking. For example, students in a science course might read a section from their textbooks on hurricanes and tropical storms and use Content/Process Notes to examine

---

Double-Entry Diary on Bacteria

Text Passage and Page Number	This Is Important Because...
p. 325: "Heterotrophic bacteria are unable to make their own food, so they feed on plant and animal matter."	These bacteria get rid of waste, like dead plants and animals. Bacteria recycle unneeded stuff that would otherwise pile up on earth.

Note. From "Double, Double Your Learning," by D. Buehl, 2001, *OnWEAC, 2*(2), p. 13. Copyright © 2001 by Doug Buehl.

Content/Process Notes on Hurricanes

What I Learned	What I Was Thinking
• A hurricane is a low-pressure area with strong winds and heavy rain.	R: I remember watching scenes on the news when Hurricane Sandy did all that damage in New York and New Jersey.
• The winds can blow 120 kilometers per hour or more.	Q: I wonder what that speed would be in miles?
• The greatest damage is from currents called storm surges, which push walls of water inland.	V: I can really see this happening, the waves smashing on the shore, knocking over trees and buildings.
• Hurricanes are similar to cyclones, with the wind spiraling toward the center.	I: It seems the author is saying that hurricanes are like ocean tornadoes.
• The center is called the eye of the storm, where there is no rain and almost no wind.	Q: I wonder why it's called the eye? I: The eye seems like a safe area.

Note. Adapted from "What Were You Thinking?," by D. Buehl, 2003, *OnWEAC*, *3*(9), p. 13. Copyright © 2003 by Doug Buehl.

their understanding (see the Content/Process Notes on Hurricanes). Pair students and ask them to share what they thought was most important and what they were thinking as they read. Ask partners to see if they can clarify any of the confusions that might have emerged during their reading. Elicit from students any ? spots that still remain after their discussions with their peers.

With practice, students can begin to use Double-Entry Diaries as an ongoing method of tracking their thinking. This strategy can be adapted for use with partners or collaborative groups as students work to construct meaning from complex texts. Encourage students to employ this strategy when they struggle with especially challenging material and as a study technique to review for exams.

Advantages

• Students are conditioned to be active thinkers as they read and are reminded of comprehension strategies, such as accessing prior knowledge, raising interesting and clarifying questions, and considering what information is most significant.

• Students are mentored to assume personal responsibility for their comprehension and develop facility with a variety of essential strategies for making sense of classroom materials.

• Students have written records of their thinking, which they can rely on during class discussions, when reviewing for exams, and when seeking clarification from the teacher and their classmates.

• This strategy reinforces that comprehension is a dynamic process that combines what an author offers with what a reader brings to a text.

Meets the Standards

Double-Entry Diaries promote careful reading of an author's message (R.1), discerning main ideas and summarizing (R.2), examining interrelationships of details or ideas (R.3), analyzing text structure (R.5), tracking the author's perspective and purpose (R.6), integrating ideas into visual representations (R.7), supporting argumentation through text-based evidence (R.8), comparing and contrasting with other sources of knowledge (R.9), and mentoring the reading of complex literary and informational texts (R.10). In addition, the collaborative conversations develop expressing and defending thinking with supporting evidence (SL.1, SL.3). Follow-up writing tasks can provide practice in using text-based evidence in arguing (W.1) or explaining (W.2) and drawing evidence from texts for analysis and reflection (W.9). Attention to word relationships (i.e., cause/effect language) addresses vocabulary development (L.5).

References

Buehl, D. (2001). Double, double your learning. *OnWEAC*, *2*(2), 13.

Buehl, D. (2003). What were you thinking? *OnWEAC*, *3*(9), 13.

Harvey, S., & Goudvis, A. (2007). *Strategies that work: Teaching comprehension for understanding and engagement* (2nd ed.). Portland, ME: Stenhouse.

Tovani, C. (2000). *I read it, but I don't get it: Comprehension strategies for adolescent readers*. Portland, ME: Stenhouse.

First-Person Reading

How many times has this scenario happened to you? You are in the company of another person—a spouse, perhaps, or a friend. This individual is seated near you, increasingly preoccupied by the act of reading. Attempts to initiate a conversation go nowhere. You busy yourself with a solitary activity of your own, and when you look up again, your reading companion has vanished!

Well, your companion has not exactly physically departed but is "gone" nevertheless. Certainly, he or she is no longer sharing this space and time with you. Your companion has become completely lost in a good book and has disappeared into the lines on the pages, at this moment vicariously living the events and experiences being spun by the words of an author.

We have all experienced times when our imaginations were so stimulated by what we were reading that we were mentally transported into the literary terrain we held in our hands. It almost felt like we were there ourselves. Our imaginations are essential to our comprehension of written texts. Cued by the author's language, we create our personalized versions of the people, locations, and events we encounter as readers. And because we are different people, tapping into different life experiences, our imaginations do not lead to identical interpretations of how things look, sound, taste, smell, and feel.

Using the Strategies

Three classroom strategies—Eyewitness Testimony Charts, First Impressions, and You Ought to Be in Pictures—encourage students to "read themselves" into a text.

Eyewitness Testimony Charts

An Eyewitness Testimony Chart is a three-column graphic organizer that prompts students to imagine events in their reading as if they were physically present themselves.

1 Begin with a preplanned live interaction with another person, with your students as witnesses. For example, you might ask a colleague to walk into your classroom and initiate a short but spirited argument with you. After your collaborator leaves, turn to your students and ask them to quickly write down

their eyewitness accounts of what they just observed. Caution them not to share their recollections but to draw exclusively on their personal memories.

2 Ask students to exchange their accounts with a partner, again without conversation. As they read their partners' statements, ask students to be alert for specifics their partners included that they omitted and for any discrepancies between these individual versions of the event. Finally, allow them an opportunity for conversation to clarify with each other what they agree they observed.

3 With the entire class, solicit the elements of a reliable eyewitness account. As they talk about their experiences with this activity, students will likely relate that some witnesses were more discerning and noticed more details. Acknowledge that eyewitnesses might disagree in their interpretations but should agree on the facts of the event. Inform students that accounts that are inconsistent with the facts are deemed unreliable.

4 Have students read a selection, and then distribute three-column Eyewitness Testimony Charts (Buehl, 2008; reproducible available in the Appendix). The first column ("I Was There") identifies the aspects of the selection that form the focus of the eyewitness testimony. The middle column ("The Author's Words") represents the facts that each testimony should be based on. The third column ("My Version") is reserved for how each individual student imagined this part of the author's message.

For example, students reading the classic Edgar Allen Poe (1846/1984) short story "The Cask of Amontillado" might be asked to write their eyewitness accounts of the scene of the

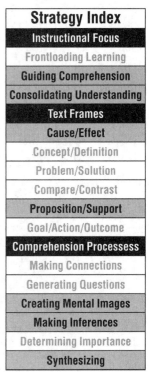

Strategy Index

Instructional Focus
Frontloading Learning
Guiding Comprehension
Consolidating Understanding
Text Frames
Cause/Effect
Concept/Definition
Problem/Solution
Compare/Contrast
Proposition/Support
Goal/Action/Outcome
Comprehension Processes
Making Connections
Generating Questions
Creating Mental Images
Making Inferences
Determining Importance
Synthesizing

crime, drawing on the author's language to create in their imaginations the vaults of the Montresor palazzo (see the Eyewitness Testimony Chart on "The Cask of Amontillado" by Edgar Allan Poe). Imagined personal details, such as "It was so cold that I was shivering" and "It was totally creepy with all those shadows of old skeletons flickering on the stone walls," add uniqueness to these personal eyewitness accounts. Students should write their versions as they imagine it would have been had they been there in person. The "The Author's Words" column prompts students to attend closely to descriptive language and important details so their versions show fidelity to the written text. Ask students to share their versions with partners and also notice points of agreement on the facts of the text (the author's words).

First Impressions

First Impressions (Buehl, 2008) provides a variation of this activity, which again asks students to assume a first-person perspective as they read. This strategy is a good match for tracking a character in literary fiction or developing an interpretation of an author's attitudes and beliefs in expository texts, such as an essay or primary documents in history.

1 Distribute blank First Impressions Charts (reproducible available in the Appendix). As students begin to read a selection, select a place in the text for them to pause and notice their first impressions of a person, place, or event. Students record the author's description under "The Author's Words" and their impressions under "My Version." These are entered in the "First" row at the top of the chart. For example, students could track their impressions of the victim in "The Cask of Amontillado" (see the First Impressions Chart on Fortunato). Like the Eyewitness Testimony Charts strategy, students are accountable for grounding their impressions in the facts of the selection.

2 Students continue reading the selection. As they read further and discover more, their impressions are likely to deepen or perhaps take a different turn. At a second appropriate spot in the text, ask students to pause again and inventory the author's words and to talk once more about their impressions. These are recorded in the "Next" row of the chart.

3 At the end of the selection, students revisit their impressions and add their final comments based on additional information provided by the author. The First Impressions strategy engages students in recording how their impressions of a person, setting, or event evolved as they read. The first reactions represent their initial impressions, and subsequent entries show how their impressions progressed or changed. For the Poe example, students could be asked to track their impressions of the victim, Fortunato, as if they were directly acquainted with the details of the story.

You Ought to Be in Pictures

Remember paging through an old family photo album? As you gazed at pictures of your kinfolk, taken perhaps

---

Eyewitness Testimony Chart on "The Cask of Amontillado" by Edgar Allan Poe[a]

I Was There (and can describe...)	The Author's Words ("The author wrote...")	My Version ("I saw, heard, felt, or experienced...")
The setting of this crime: The ancient vaults of the Montresor family	• Down long and winding staircase • Damp ground of catacombs • Cavern walls • Extensive vaults • Long walls of piled skeletons • Niter hanging like moss • Drops of moisture trickling • Casks and puncheons in recesses • Range of low arches • Kept descending and descending • Deep crypt with foul air • Flames from flambeaux • Bones thrown down on the earth • Walls of solid granite	The Montresor vaults were dug deep into the ground under their mansion. To get there you had to carefully walk down a very long and winding staircase. Soon you were in total darkness except for the torches you carried. Down in the catacombs it was like a cemetery cave, with a dirt floor and stone walls, and skeletons and bones everywhere, some stacked up and some just thrown about. It was cold and very wet, and water dripped down from the ceiling, and the air was horrible to breathe. You kept going down and down, and had to bend down under these arches, and your torch kept shining on all those skulls and bones....

Note. Adapted from "First Person Reading," by D. Buehl, 2008, *On WEAC*, retrieved from www.weac.org/news_and_publications/education_news/2007-2008/readinginroom_first.aspx. Copyright © 2008 by Doug Buehl.
[a]Poe, E.A. (1984). The cask of Amontillado. In *Complete stories and poems of Edgar Allan Poe* (pp. 191–196). New York: Doubleday. (Original work published 1846)

First Impressions Chart on Fortunato

	The Author's Words	My Impressions
First	• Pride in wine knowledge • Carnival season; wore tight-fitting, striped dress, conical cap, and bells • Accosted with excessive warmth; drinking • Insisted check out the amontillado instead of Luchesi, who he said can't tell sherry from amontillado	My first impression was that Fortunato seems like a sort of silly person, and that was how he is dressed, like a jester or clown. He seems to drink a lot and wants others to believe he is a wine expert. He has a very high opinion of himself and talks Luchesi down so he gets the honor of checking the amontillado. Maybe he just wants more drink. He is pretty drunk, loud, pushy, and braggy.
Then	• Gait unsteady; intoxication • Coughed; unable to talk for several minutes • Refused to go back from catacombs • Continued to drink • Called Luchesi an ignoramus	He is very drunk, keeps drinking while in the crypt, and makes rude comments about Luchesi. He seems to have health problems because he has these coughing fits, and I don't think the damp catacombs are good for him, but he won't leave. I think he still wants to show off his wine knowledge (big ego!), but he is also getting more to drink.
Finally	• Stood stupidly bewildered • Too astounded to resist • Low moaning cry after fettered to wall • Loud, shrill screams and then silence • Sad voice; said, "very good joke" • Said, "for the love of God"	He doesn't catch on about what is happening until he is chained and being plastered in. He seems stunned that someone is so angry with him. Then, he loses it and starts moaning and screaming. He seems to panic and then becomes depressed. Finally, he tries to pretend it is a joke. He doesn't beg until the end, though, and he never asks why this is being done. Maybe he has finally figured it out.

Note. Adapted from *Classroom Strategies for Interactive Learning* (3rd ed., p. 84), by D. Buehl, 2009, Newark, DE: International Reading Association. Copyright © 2009 by the International Reading Association.

---

a century or more ago, you probably found yourself pausing periodically and imagining what life was like for those people. What were the daily conditions like for those growing up on a cattle ranch in New Mexico in 1896? How has the landscape changed since then? What was the country like for your great-grandparents who emigrated to North America in the 1880s? Who in a particular photo is most like you?

Photographs can evoke a sense of mood and convey meaningful information that communicates far beyond written description. The old adage "a picture is worth a thousand words" explains why textbook editors undertake the expense of including many photographs and other visuals in the layout of a chapter. Unfortunately, students taking the "quick trip" through a textbook section—endeavoring to rapidly finish the reading and complete the assignment—may overlook these rich sources of insight on the content. In addition, students may regard the textbook as personally uninviting and distant, as merely paragraphs of dense information. Taking time to guide students through a thoughtful examination of photographs can help them connect to concepts and successfully tackle learning new material, especially given the wealth of photographs available online. You Ought to Be in Pictures (Buehl, 2000) is a strategy that encourages students to imagine themselves within the context of a photograph.

1 Look for vivid photographs that connect with your curriculum. Some outstanding photographs already may be provided in the textbook students are reading. Check online as well as in other texts, reference sources, newspapers, and magazines. Search for photographs to which your students can make a personal connection. Project photographs on your classroom screen so students may examine them in detail.

2 Select a photograph that will introduce or extend important ideas or concepts for a unit of study. Guide students in their viewing of the photograph by stimulating their mental imagery and suggesting a personal connection to events portrayed in the picture. For example, to prepare students in a history course for studying the Great Depression of the 1930s in the United States, identify a photograph that illustrates some key themes of the time period, such as a Dorothea Lange photograph (see Photograph From the Great Depression). Using the photograph, take students through the following guided imagery exercise (see the Guided Imagery strategy pages).

> During the period of the Great Depression, many people, especially farmers, lost their land and were forced out on the road. You are looking at a Library of Congress photograph of a homeless family in Oklahoma in 1938.

Photograph From the Great Depression[a]

[a]Lange, D. (1938). *Family walking on highway, five children.* Washington, DC: Library of Congress.

First, examine the location of the photograph and note as many details as possible. What do you observe about the countryside, the land, the plants and vegetation, and the road? What time of year might it be? What does the climate appear to be like? What time of day does it seem to be?

Now, focus closely on each person in the photograph. Pay particular attention to what each person is wearing. Look at how the family members carry themselves: their posture and their facial expressions.

Next, choose one individual in the photograph and imagine that you are this person. What might you have been thinking while this event was happening? Describe what you might have been feeling, what emotions you might have been experiencing. What has the day been like for you? Imagine what might have happened before the scene presented in the photo. What do you see happening later during this day and the following days?

3 Guided imagery using photographs provides an excellent opportunity for students to record their observations and thoughts in writing. Using the Great Depression example, give students the following writing prompt:

It is now many years later. You are showing this photograph of your family to a grandchild. What would you tell this child about your memories of that day? As an entry in your notebook, write what you would share.

Students' writing needs to be grounded in text-based evidence from their learning. Direct students to specifically relate this imagined experience to specifics and details from their reading and class study. After students respond in writing, have them first share their observations with a partner. Then, ask for volunteers to read their entries to the class. Students who have chosen the same individual with whom to identify will hear and compare classmates' musings about that individual during that difficult time. Students will delve into the Great Depression unit with much more empathy for the great personal dramas of the time and more personal involvement in the material. Here is a possible example:

I remember I was so small that Papa plunked me in the wagon. At first, I thought it was a great, long wagon ride, and I would giggle and shriek every time we went over a bump. It was really hot, but I only had one set of clothes to wear. If we happened past a farm with vegetables, we would try to snatch something to eat, but Papa wouldn't eat with us. He used to say, "The bank didn't take my dignity."

This strategy can be adapted for use with photographs that do not feature people. For example, with science pictures, suggest that students are personally witnessing what is portrayed in the photo and guide them through noticing details as if they were actually viewing the scene in person.

Advantages

- "First-person" comprehension strategies stimulate students to fire up their imaginations as if they were actually participating in the events described in a written text.
- Students become accustomed to paying closer attention to author details that can trigger sensory responses.
- Students develop personal interpretations of people, locations, and events that they encounter in their reading; they add their personality to the author's words.
- Students encounter key ideas through pictures before reading, which increases their motivation to learn more about the topic and primes them to learn from text materials that may otherwise be regarded as cold and impersonal.

Meets the Standards

First-Person Reading strategies promote careful reading of an author's message (R.1); discerning main ideas and summarizing (R.2); examining interrelationships of details or ideas (R.3); interpreting word meaning, especially use of figurative language (R4); tracking the author's perspective and purpose (R.6); integrating ideas with visual representations (R.7); supporting argumentation through text-based evidence (R.8); comparing and contrasting with other sources of knowledge (R.9); and mentoring the reading of complex literary and informational texts (R.10). In addition, the collaborative conversations develop expressing and defending thinking with supporting evidence, including evaluating visual media (SL.1, SL.2, SL.3, SL.4). Follow-up writing tasks provide practice in using text-based evidence in arguing (W.1) or explaining (W.2) and drawing evidence from texts for analysis and reflection (W.9). Attention to word relationships (i.e., cause/effect language) addresses vocabulary development (L.5).

References

Buehl, D. (2000). You ought to be in pictures: Using photos to help students understand past. *WEAC News & Views, 35*(8), 14.

Buehl, D. (2008). First person reading. *On WEAC.* Retrieved from www.weac.org/news_and_publications/education_news/2007-2008/readinginroom_first.aspx

Buehl, D. (2009). *Classroom strategies for interactive learning* (3rd ed.). Newark, DE: International Reading Association.

Literature and Art Cited

Lange, D. (1938). *Family walking on highway, five children.* Washington, DC: Library of Congress. Retrieved August 5, 2008, from memory.loc.gov

Poe, E.A. (1984). The cask of amontillado. In *Complete stories and poems of Edgar Allan Poe* (pp. 191–196). New York: Doubleday. (Original work published 1846)

Follow the Characters

Students encounter stories as an ongoing facet of their education. From their earliest years in school, as beginning readers, through high school and beyond, students transition into reading longer and more complex works of literature. Although they are often held accountable for relating what exactly transpired in a story, students often scratch their heads and think to themselves, Why are you telling me this? What are we to make of this story? What does this story mean to the author? What might this story mean to us? What's the point of this story? Providing students with tools that help them crack open literary prose is essential for improving their comprehension of this genre of complex text.

Change and conflict are two constants of life that underlie fictional literature. Literary fiction examines conflict of some dimension: within a character, between characters, or in conjunction with larger forces, such as a struggle against some aspect of nature. Understanding literary fiction necessitates tracking how these conflicts unfold and are resolved. Furthermore, the dynamics among characters are very important for readers to perceive: how the characters feel about one another, how they interact, and whether these feelings and interactions change in any way.

Tracking the emotional content of a text is a particularly effective strategy for examining how characters handle change and conflict. Developing sensitivity to emotional subcurrents—what a character is feeling and thinking and how this affects the actions of and responses from others—can spark inferential thinking and help students develop insight into an author's point of view and articulate possible themes explored in the work.

Using the Strategy

Follow the Characters (Buehl, 1994) is a strategy that cues students to understand stories through character analysis. Students organize key information about a character into a visual outline that can help them develop an interpretation of the author's theme or message. The strategy is appropriate for both short stories and longer works of fictional literature and can be adapted for biographies, autobiographies, and other nonfiction works that feature story lines of individuals.

1 Begin by differentiating between stories that are narrative nonfiction and those that are literary fiction. Narrative nonfiction, such as biographies, autobiographies, and historical recountings, share many elements with literary fiction: characters, actions, and a flow of events. However, narrative nonfiction generally presents a straightforward story line, perhaps interspersed with author commentary, interpretation, and conclusions. Literary fiction, in contrast, may feature story lines that are less open and obvious. Authors of literary fiction tend to rely on the reader to make interpretations and draw conclusions, to construct a meaning of their message that is more implicit rather than explicitly stated.

A key difference, then, is author intent. Authors of narrative nonfiction usually attempt to directly tell what happened in a clearly outlined narration, often to support an interpretation of what these events mean to them. Authors of literary fiction create stories from their imagination that can help readers reflect on and understand their lives in some way. But authors of literary fiction typically do not reveal everything; readers may need to infer some of what is going on in the story. As a result, readers are expected to develop their own interpretations of what a story might mean, both to the author and especially to themselves.

2 Use the role of detective as a metaphor to help students conceptualize the process of character analysis. Ask them how a detective goes about solving a mystery, and they will likely answer that a detective looks for clues and investigates people. Emphasize the detective frame of mind as a way to discover the theme of the story. For clues about an author's viewpoint in a story, students should "follow the

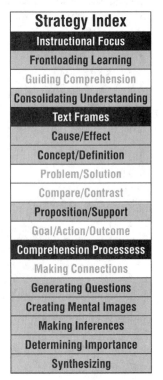

Strategy Index

Strategy Index
Instructional Focus
Frontloading Learning
Guiding Comprehension
Consolidating Understanding
Text Frames
Cause/Effect
Concept/Definition
Problem/Solution
Compare/Contrast
Proposition/Support
Goal/Action/Outcome
Comprehension Processess
Making Connections
Generating Questions
Creating Mental Images
Making Inferences
Determining Importance
Synthesizing

characters" by tuning in to what a character does or says and what others do or say about the character. Students should pay special attention to the role of the character in the story's conflict and whether this role changes the character in any way. Note that focusing questioning on character behavior and development is represented on the understanding level of the Self-Questioning Taxonomy for Literary Fiction (see Chapter 4).

3 Project a blank Character Analysis Grid (reproducible available in the Appendix) and model with students using a familiar story, such as a fairy tale or a selection students have read previously. For example, most students can relate to the classic story of Cinderella, which has appeared in various guises in a number of recent movies. They may know that the major conflict in this fairy tale is between Cinderella and her stepmother and stepsisters. Elicit information about Cinderella from the students to fill in the grid. Record her actions (works hard, scrubs floor, doesn't complain), record her thoughts and words (asks to go to the prince's ball, wishes she could attend, does not tell the prince who she is), record others' views of her (is treated like servant, is told she is less worthy than her stepsisters, is denied a chance to go to the ball, is treated like a princess by her fairy godmother and the prince), and record the changes she undergoes during the story (she begins to believe in herself, she starts to stand up for herself). Help students articulate a theme for the story, such as "Hard work and honesty will ultimately be rewarded."

4 Students are now ready to apply the Character Analysis Grid to a work of literature. For example, students in an English language arts class who read the dramatization of the classic novella *A Christmas Carol* by Charles Dickens (Horovitz, 1979) would analyze the major character, Ebenezer Scrooge, who is visited by a series of spirits who convince him to see the mistakes of his life (see the Character Analysis Grid for *A Christmas Carol* by Charles Dickens). After students read the play, have them work with partners to complete the conflict ring and first three quadrants: "What does the character do?" "What does the character say or think?" and "How do others feel about the character?" Note that "others" might also include the author, the story's narrator, and other characters in the story.

5 Team each pair of students with a second set of partners, forming collaborative groups of four, to work on the fourth quadrant: "How does the character change?" Students should use the information recorded in the first three quadrants to formulate the changes experienced by the character and list them as before-and-after comparisons. Emphasize that authors communicate important insights to readers through

the ways in which characters change. As students examine Scrooge's actions and thoughts, they will find that his internal conflict about how he has lived his life changes him: He is gradually transformed from a nasty, ill-tempered, greedy miser into a charitable and outgoing benefactor of others. Have each group write their version of the theme of the story based on their analysis of the character's changes. Students might express the theme of *A Christmas Carol* as "A person's wealth is measured in friendships and good deeds, instead of merely money."

6 Ask students to complete multiple Character Analysis Grids for fictional works such as novels, which feature more than one major character. These can be compared to analyze the way an author treats different characters and what this might signal about the author's ideas and themes. Students can use their completed grids to write explanations of character development and develop support for their interpretations of the author's themes.

Advantages

- Students are provided with a systematic way to analyze a story to help them articulate meaningful interpretations and determine possible themes explored by the author.

- Students learn to recognize the central roles that conflict and change play in character development.

- Students develop a visual outline of major elements in a story that can help them articulate the author's theme or point of view.

Meets the Standards

Follow the Characters promotes careful reading and rereading of an author's message (R.1), discerning main ideas and summarizing (R.2), examining interrelationships of details or ideas (R.3), analyzing text structure (R.5), tracking the author's perspective and purpose (R.6), integrating ideas into visual representations (R.7), supporting argumentation (R.8), and mentoring the reading of complex literary and informational texts (R.10). In addition, the collaborative conversations develop expressing and defending thinking using visual displays (SL.1, SL.2, SL.4). Follow-up writing provides practice in using text-based evidence in supporting arguments (W.1), summarizing and explaining (W.2), and drawing evidence from texts for analysis and reflection (W.9). Vocabulary development includes attention to word relationships (L.5).

References

Buehl, D. (1994). Persona: Character analysis sheds light on story's meaning. *WEAC News & Views, 29*(10), 21.

Character Analysis Grid for *A Christmas Carol* by Charles Dickens[a]

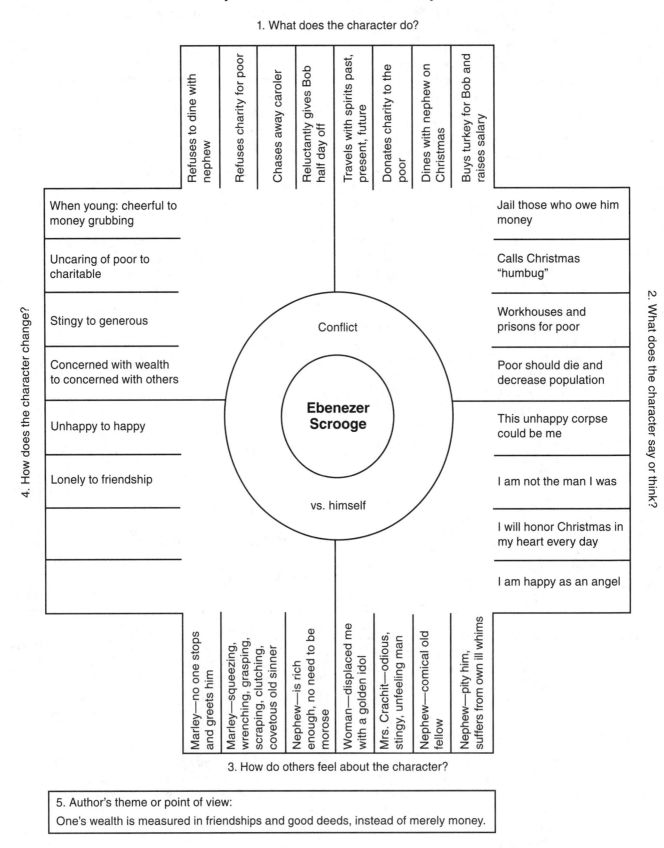

1. What does the character do?

Refuses to dine with nephew

Refuses charity for poor

Chases away caroler

Reluctantly gives Bob half day off

Travels with spirits past, present, future

Donates charity to the poor

Dines with nephew on Christmas

Buys turkey for Bob and raises salary

4. How does the character change?

When young: cheerful to money grubbing

Uncaring of poor to charitable

Stingy to generous

Concerned with wealth to concerned with others

Unhappy to happy

Lonely to friendship

Conflict

Ebenezer Scrooge

vs. himself

2. What does the character say or think?

Jail those who owe him money

Calls Christmas "humbug"

Workhouses and prisons for poor

Poor should die and decrease population

This unhappy corpse could be me

I am not the man I was

I will honor Christmas in my heart every day

I am happy as an angel

3. How do others feel about the character?

Marley—no one stops and greets him

Marley—squeezing, wrenching, grasping, scraping, clutching, covetous old sinner

Nephew—is rich enough, no need to be morose

Woman—displaced me with a golden idol

Mrs. Crachit—odious, stingy, unfeeling man

Nephew—comical old fellow

Nephew—pity him, suffers from own ill whims

5. Author's theme or point of view:
One's wealth is measured in friendships and good deeds, instead of merely money.

Note. Adapted from *Classroom Strategies for Interactive Learning* (3rd ed., p. 88), by D. Buehl, 2009, Newark, DE: International Reading Association. Copyright © 2009 by the International Reading Association.
[a]Horovitz, I. (1979). A Christmas carol: Scrooge and Marley. In *Prentice Hall literature, grade 7* (pp. 740–806). Boston: Pearson Prentice Hall.

Buehl, D. (2009). *Classroom strategies for interactive learning* (3rd ed.). Newark, DE: International Reading Association.

Literature Cited

Horovitz, I. (1979). A Christmas carol: Scrooge and Marley. In *Prentice Hall literature, grade 7* (pp. 740–806). Boston: Pearson Prentice Hall.

Suggested Reading

Beck, I.L., & McKeown, M.G. (1981). Developing questions that promote comprehension: The story map. *Language Arts, 58*(8), 913–918.

Guided Imagery

You weren't there, in the logging camps of the Northwest in the 1870s, to hear the crack of axes against towering pines; to witness the trudging draft horses as they snaked 16-foot logs along forest trails; to inhale the steamy, rich aromas of a camp dining hall's platters of roast beef and baked chicken, baskets of biscuits, and rows of fruit pies. You weren't there, embedded as a miniature visitor in the stalks of slender sprouts of corn, as they continued their growth from a seed into a mature plant, to observe firsthand the life cycle of a plant as it eventually produced its own seeds to perpetuate the species for another season. You weren't there, in the fervently inventive mind of author J.K. Rowling, as she conjured up an entire world and culture, populated with a host of compelling characters and sinister villains, and spun an unfolding story line of intrigue and adventure.

You weren't there, but sometimes it seemed like you were. As readers, we do far more than decipher words on a page. Ultimately, reading triggers a vicarious reality, as we re-create for ourselves how things are, or were, or could be, even though we are not actually experiencing them in the moment. Sometimes we even transcend the physical act we call reading—that conscious awareness that our eyes are processing lines of print—and we are transported in our minds to somewhere else, as if we are immersed in a live event. That bionic DVD player in our heads kicks in, and we feel as if we are there.

It is our imaginations that take us beyond those abstract symbols arrayed as visual information by someone who is employing language to help us get it—a story, an idea, an explanation, a depiction. It is as if authors are saying, "You weren't there, but if you follow what I am telling you, you can almost see it, hear it, smell it, taste it, and feel it." Yet, if you ask many of our students, What do you see when you read, they will respond as if this was a trick question. "Words, of course," they will answer. Many students regard reading as mostly a word identification exercise, and as a result, their comprehension suffers. They struggle with picturing in their imaginations what an author is using language to convey. Comprehension involves animating the abstract language of written texts with life experiences.

Using the Strategy

Guided Imagery (Gambrell, Kapinus, & Wilson, 1987) is a strategy that triggers visualization for students as they read and learn. Guided Imagery can be used either to prepare students for a reading or to deepen their understanding after they have read. For example, this strategy could be used to introduce a history passage by helping students visualize hardships experienced by settlers traveling west across the Great Plains in North America. Or students in a science class may first need to examine a passage on photosynthesis to acquire some basic knowledge before they can successfully visualize the process inside a plant.

1 Start with a variety of imagination tune-ups. Wilhelm (2004) recommends a progression of visualization activities. First, encourage students to become precise observers. Bring in an interesting object, preferably related to the curriculum, and ask students to examine it carefully, to handle it, to notice everything they can about it. A unique item might be especially effective. Cue students to inspect the item from the perspective of a reporter, a person who perceives something with enough detail so he or she can reliably describe it to others even though the item is no longer present. After sufficient viewing time, have students close their eyes and imagine the item, with as much specificity as they can. Students can then be asked to describe the item to a partner or quickly sketch the item from memory. A variation of this activity involves pairing students and providing a different item for each partner to examine. Partners would not see each other's items. Each student then attempts to

Strategy Index
Instructional Focus
Frontloading Learning
Guiding Comprehension
Consolidating Understanding
Text Frames
Cause/Effect
Concept/Definition
Problem/Solution
Compare/Contrast
Proposition/Support
Goal/Action/Outcome
Comprehension Processess
Making Connections
Generating Questions
Creating Mental Images
Making Inferences
Determining Importance
Synthesizing

assist his or her partner in imagining the unseen item by capitalizing on their powers of observation.

Next, have students transition to imagining objects that are not physically present but are commonplace elements of their lives. For example, you might ask students to imagine they are each standing in a room in their homes. What one object captures their attention? Instruct them to zero in on that object and try to perceive it in great detail. Again, have students practice with a partner translating their images into descriptive language.

Extend practice from an emphasis on imagining particular objects to the unfolding of scenes in our mind's eye. Ask students to run action sequences in their imaginations, with all of their senses alert. For example, ask students to imagine a basketball, then the basketball being dribbled, and hearing the sounds it makes while noticing how the basketball feels on their hands each time it bounces up to them. Then, ask them to replay in their imaginations a short series of events on a basketball court, involving people in movement.

2 Select imagery-rich short texts or excerpts and couple them with evocative images—photographs, illustrations, artwork, and the like. Ask students to switch into imagination mode as you do an introductory read-aloud. For example, this excerpt from *National Geographic* is a superb candidate for an imagination read-aloud:

> Breathe in. Feel the air pass through your nostrils and move into your nose. Your diaphragm contracts, pulling the air deep into your chest. Oxygen floods into tiny cavities in your lungs and travels into your capillaries, ready to fuel every cell in your body. You're alive.
>
> So is that breath you just took. When we inhale, our nostrils capture millions of invisible particles: dust, pollen, sea spray, volcanic ash, plant spores. These specks in turn host a teeming community of bacteria and viruses. A few types may trigger allergies or asthma. Far more rare are inhaled pathogens that are themselves the agents of diseases, such as SARS, tuberculosis, and influenza. (Wolfe, 2013, p. 138)

The passage has the additional advantage of first-person elements, inviting the students to interject themselves into the scenario (see the First-Person Reading strategy pages). At this point, project a visual image (photograph or illustration) that relates to the text and ask students to study it as you continue your read-aloud of additional pertinent text excerpts.

3 Have students undertake a visual preview of a reading selection. Classroom texts often strike students as an endless parade of terms and facts. The visual preview alerts students to pay special attention to pictures, drawings, or graphics included with the text. This is especially important for science and social studies texts, which typically feature a number of visual elements that enhance information. As students notice these elements, they begin to anticipate what the material is about. You also may wish to use other sources for pictures that will stimulate the students' imaginations.

Select an image for more intense examination and conduct a Guided Imagery exercise that builds knowledge as students inspect the image (see the discussion of You Ought to Be in Pictures in the First-Person Reading strategy pages). For example, before biology students tackle the dense textual prose, the teacher can take them through a short Guided Imagery exercise on fungi as they view a photograph in their textbook (see the Guided Imagery for Science example). Their imaginations engaged, students are then better prepared to work the technical language that describes these organisms.

4 Introduce Guided Imagery activities independent of your use of visual images. Tell students to close their eyes and turn on their imaginations. Prepare a Guided Imagery exercise by giving them some background on the situation they will be visualizing. Encourage them to make use of all of their senses as

---

Guided Imagery for Science

Fungi

Imagine the air moving through the room. As the air slowly circulates, imagine you can see that on these air currents are carried thousands of microscopic, round, beadlike spores.

These spores are looking for an opportunity to grow. They are like tiny, little seeds, searching for a food source that will enable them to grow and live. If they locate a food source with enough moisture, they can grow.

As you imagine them drifting by, notice that loaf of bread on the counter. The plastic bread bag has been left open.

The drifting spores get closer and closer. Some of them begin to land on a slice of bread.

Watch carefully as tiny, little strings of cells begin to grow from a spore. More and more cells grow out, farther and farther from the spore.

Soon there are so many of them that they appear to be a tangled mass of little strings; these are growing denser and denser as they feed off the bread. Imagine you see some of them have little hooks that attach to the bread fibers. They continue to wind outward and outward.

You can now start to see with the unaided eye a velvety fuzz appearing on the surface of the bread. What colors do you see now?

they imagine: sight, sound, smell, physical sensation, taste, and emotion. Suggest an image to students one sentence at a time and pause for several seconds after each sentence to allow them time to process what you are saying and to visualize the picture. To prepare students for a reading about the rigors of farming in the Great Plains of North America during the 1880s (see the Guided Imagery for Social Studies example), begin with the following: "Imagine being a homesteader on the Great Plains in the late 19th century. You are alone, and you see the prairie much the way it was before the settlers came."

Ask students to share their reflections about what they were imagining during the exercise. What did they notice with their imaginations? Do they have any questions about what they were attempting to visualize? This would be an excellent opportunity to have students write about what they visualized to summarize their insights (see the Quick-Writes strategy pages).

Guided Imagery for Social Studies

The Great Plains

Imagine you are in Nebraska. It is the summer of 1867, and you are standing amid rolling prairie for as far as you can see in all directions.

Look around and see that no trees, buildings, or other human beings are in sight.

Notice the wind gently swaying the two-foot-tall prairie grasses back and forth.

Feel the 90-degree heat from the hot noon sun as it beats down on you.

Breathe in the dust and pollen from the grasses around you and imagine wiping the grimy sweat from your forehead.

Notice the tired ox standing next to your single-bladed steel plow.

See yourself trudging over to the plow and placing your hands on its rough wooden handles.

Watch the hard-packed, deep-black prairie soil turn over from your plow blade as you struggle along behind the ox.

Feel the blisters on your hands as they grip the plow handles.

Imagine the strain in your back muscles and in your arms and legs as the plow jerks you along.

Labor your way over a small hill and notice the small hut made with thick squares of prairie sod in the distance.

Leave the plow and slowly make your way closer to the hut, noticing it in greater and greater detail.

Bend your head as you enter the dark, dank sod hut, and slowly pace around on the hard dirt floor.

Note. Adapted from *Classroom Strategies for Interactive Learning* (2nd ed., p. 60), by D. Buehl, 2001, Newark, DE: International Reading Association. Copyright © 2001 by the International Reading Association.

5 Provide frequent opportunities for students to experiment with responding to author language to trigger mental images. Wilhelm (2004) suggests frequent use of imagery-rich texts as short read-alouds to develop sensitivity to author language. Read a vividly written selection to your students and pause periodically to comment on how you are imagining what the author is relaying in words. These think-alouds underscore that an author relies on readers to fire up their imaginations to breathe life into the words on the page. After modeling, continue to pause but now prompt students to generate their own mental images.

Occasionally, encourage students to quick-sketch images that come to mind or to elaborate what they are imagining to a partner. Quick-sketches are just that—quick—not carefully drawn artistic renditions. Some students find it advantageous to portray their thinking nonverbally in addition to talking about what they imagine. The DVD Scene Selection (reproducible available in the Appendix) is a graphic organizer that mirrors the visual display on DVDs that portray key scene images (see the DVD Scene Selection for Yellowstone example). This strategy is especially effective for helping students visualize and summarize key stages or steps in sequential, goal/action/outcome or cause/effect text frame materials. Students quick-sketch each stage or step in the six panels and provide a caption that captures key language for each panel. For example, science students who read a selection about the impact of the reintroduction of wolves in Yellowstone National Park capture the cause/effect dynamics that lead to enhanced water quality in a DVD quick-sketch.

6 As students gain practice in visualizing, have them create their own Guided Imagery exercises in cooperative groups or with partners, taking turns describing what they visualized. Or ask students to use a movie clip strategy, making decisions from the perspective of a movie director and selecting a segment of text that is rich in mental imagery. The student directors then pitch to their "studio" how this material would appear if it were filmed.

In addition, lead students in discussions of text visuals provided by an author to supplement comprehension. Authors recognize that telling may not be sufficient at times, and readers would be better able to use their imaginations if pictures, drawings, charts, or other visual displays are included. With texts lacking visuals, ask students to suggest the visuals they feel would aid readers in accessing their imaginations. Students can be asked to draw these visual extensions on sticky notes to be affixed to the page next to the appropriate text.

1. Wolves reintroduced to Yellowstone

2. Wolves worry elk, who keep moving & eat less of the aspen trees

3. Healthy aspen trees attract beavers

4. Beavers chew down trees & form dams on streams

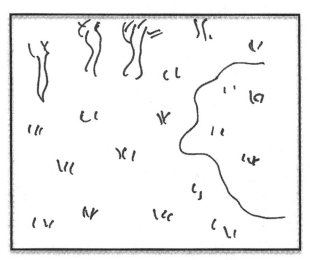

5. Swamplands are formed because of dams

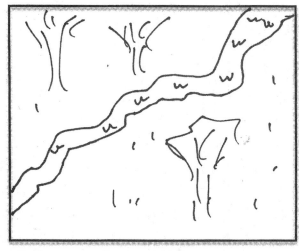

6. Swamps purify water & Yellowstone River is much cleaner & healthier

Advantages

- Imagination activities nurture readers who use visual, auditory, and other sensory connections to fashion personal mental images of an author's message.

- Students who place inordinate attention on reading the words are prompted to enliven their reading by unleashing their imaginations.

- Students develop an eye for evocative language, which stimulates the development of increasingly more sophisticated mental images.

- Students read with a deeper engagement with a text and personalize their reading through individual interpretations of how things might appear if they experienced them.

- Students create vivid mental images of ideas and concepts that help them remember information longer.

Meets the Standards

Guided Imagery promotes careful reading and rereading of an author's message (R.1), discerning main ideas (R.2), examining interrelationships of details or ideas (R.3), interpreting word meaning (R.4), analyzing text structure (R.5), examining and integrating ideas into visual representations (R.7), comparing and contrasting with other sources of knowledge (R.9), and mentoring the reading of complex literary and informational texts (R.10). In addition, the collaborative conversations develop skills for interpreting and creating visual displays (SL.1, SL.2, SL.4). Follow-up writing provides practice in summarizing and explaining (W.2) and drawing evidence from texts for analysis and reflection (W.9). Vocabulary development includes attention to word relationships (L.5) and acquiring domain-specific vocabulary (L.6).

References

Buehl, D. (2001). *Classroom strategies for interactive learning* (2nd ed.). Newark, DE: International Reading Association.

Gambrell, L.B., Kapinus, B.A., & Wilson, R.M. (1987). Using mental imagery and summarization to achieve independence in comprehension. *Journal of Reading, 30*(7), 638–642.

Wilhelm, J.D. (2004). *Reading is seeing: Learning to visualize scenes, characters, ideas, and text worlds to improve comprehension and reflective reading.* New York: Scholastic.

Literature Cited

Wolfe, N. (2013). Small, small world. *National Geographic, 223*(1), 136–147.

Suggested Reading

Lazear, D. (2003). *Eight ways of teaching: The artistry of teaching with multiple intelligences* (4th ed.). Thousand Oaks, CA: Corwin.

Hands-On Reading

And now, the moment of truth: You've lugged the box in from the car, unpacked the contents, and arrayed the obligatory hodgepodge of tools around you. A do-it-yourself project, long overdue, is finally scheduled to be tackled. Another installment in home improvement is imminent. So, where do you start? Ah, yes, the directions. From amid the clutter of bubble wrap and obscure-looking unassembled parts, you snatch the product booklet. Inevitably, your blood pressure starts to head northward.

Hmm, assembly and instructions, turn-of-the-century ceiling fan, canopy and down rod, slot of hanger ball snapped into chip of bracket, the motor blue wire and tangerine wire attached to...wait! Tangerine wire? Goes where? Whoever heard of tangerine wire?!

Welcome to the do-it-yourself nightmare: You are poised to undertake a project, and the enthusiasm you kindled begins to fizzle as you are confronted with the inevitable set of incomprehensible directions and perplexing illustrations. You wonder, Who writes this stuff anyway?

Imagine for a moment the author who wrote these guidelines for installing a ceiling fan. Who does this writer think will be reading these? What does the writer think readers will already know? What expectations does the writer apparently have about readers' abilities to make sense of this document? What could the writer have done to make the writing more accessible? Is it any wonder that after reading directions such as these, many readers might toss the directions aside and try to wing it through their project?

Eventually, the task described above is satisfactorily accomplished, but most of us would likely encounter frustrations along the way. We realize that for our efforts to be successful, we have to engage in a special kind of reading—technical reading—that contrasts with the reading routines we follow when we bury ourselves in a pleasurable novel, study a textbook, or peruse magazine articles. Technical reading is undertaken for a very pragmatic purpose: step-by-step guidance for how-to tasks. Hands-on projects require hands-on reading.

As adults, we recognize the need for technical reading strategies in a variety of daily contexts. Directions for filling out tax forms, care and maintenance instructions in product manuals, help sites for computer software, and the like all mandate reading for pragmatic purposes. Students encounter technical reading demands frequently in school, and like adults, students often find them challenging. Steps to follow in a classroom procedure, such as a science lab, involve technical reading. So does much of the reading in applied technology, computers, business education, family and consumer education, and health and fitness courses. Technical texts are a hallmark of career and workplace literacy and are prioritized in the Common Core's literacy standards.

Using the Strategy

Hands-On Reading (Buehl, 2002) focuses students on coping with the particular demands of complex technical texts. Because readers frequently find themselves overwhelmed by dense, functional writing, this strategy anticipates the need for problem solving while reading. The strategy draws on questioning for working a text through a technical lens (see Table 11 in Chapter 4).

1 Introduce technical nonfiction as a special text genre that tends to exhibit the following characteristics:

- Technical texts are usually very terse. Because it is assumed that an individual is reading only to act on the information, little background is provided. Technical texts generally follow a "just the facts" approach.

- Technical texts usually follow a goal/action/outcome text organization. That is, the reader is usually provided with a clear goal for reading (e.g., to bake a lemon meringue pie, to integrate visuals into a webpage document, to build a cedar

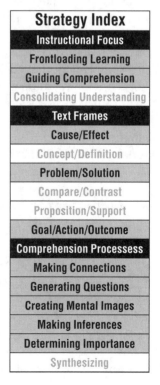

Strategy Index

| Instructional Focus |
| Frontloading Learning |
| Guiding Comprehension |
| Consolidating Understanding |
| Text Frames |
| Cause/Effect |
| Concept/Definition |
| Problem/Solution |
| Compare/Contrast |
| Proposition/Support |
| Goal/Action/Outcome |
| Comprehension Processess |
| Making Connections |
| Generating Questions |
| Creating Mental Images |
| Making Inferences |
| Determining Importance |
| Synthesizing |

chest). The reader is then presented a sequence of steps to follow. Typically, some description or illustration of the expected outcome is also included.

- Technical texts are usually laden with disciplinary-specific vocabulary. Because these texts are very direct and concise, terminology may be used without definitions or explanations. Authors of technical texts expect that the reader will already be familiar with much of the vocabulary and perhaps experienced with the procedures being outlined.

- Technical texts tend to be highly visual. Diagrams and illustrations frequently accompany the written information. Readers may have to infer meanings and functions of some of the technical vocabulary by examining labeled pictorials. Information presented visually may not be adequately repeated in written form.

- Technical texts rarely give any consideration to motivating or entertaining the reader. They are viewed only as a means toward an end. Readers consult them only to the extent necessary to satisfactorily accomplish a task. Language is chosen to be as precise and straightforward as possible. As a result, technical texts strike readers as dry, impersonal, and blunt.

2 Given the nature of complex technical texts, readers need to adopt reading strategies especially tailored for comprehension of technical material. Begin by brainstorming with students problems that readers typically experience with complex technical texts. Students will likely comment that the texts are difficult to understand, they make extensive use of terms that are not well known, they are not clearly written, the visuals are hard to decipher, and they do not provide enough useful information. Like adults, students will probably lament that such texts do not use "friendly" English. Finally, students may comment that they despair of making sense from some of these documents, so they may be tempted to toss the text aside and attempt to complete the project by relying on their personal background knowledge and common sense.

Unfortunately, proceeding without reading can be a hit-or-miss proposition. The task may be done improperly, it may take longer than necessary, or the student may become discouraged and give up on the project.

3 Outline Hands-On Reading as a strategy for reading complex technical texts. Hands-On Reading assumes that readers will be doing while they are reading, manipulating or examining objects when these items are featured in the text. Hands-On Reading follows a "start again, stop again" approach to a written text, as readers set documents aside to attempt

to translate instructions into action, returning to the text to confirm their understandings or to transition into the next stage. Emphasize the following steps for Hands-On Reading of technical texts (see the Hands-On Reading Bookmark; reproducible available in the Appendix):

- *Size up the task:* Start by surveying the text to obtain a general sense of what needs to be done and what the final outcome should look like. What exactly does it appear the reader needs to do with

---

Hands-On Reading Bookmark

1. Size up the task...
  a. to figure out what you will need to do.
  b. to determine what the final outcome should be.
  c. to inventory items or tools needed for the task.

2. Clarify vocabulary...
  a. to review terms you have previously learned.
  b. to identify and explain new terms.

3. Scan the visuals...
  a. to compare the illustrations with any physical items you will be using.
  b. to help imagine what you should be doing at each phase.
  c. to identify items or objects you will be handling.

4. Look out for cautions...
  a. to avoid common errors.
  b. to avoid harmful or dangerous mistakes.

5. Read and apply...
  a. to make sure each sentence makes sense.
  b. to clear up things you don't understand.
  c. to connect the directions to the illustrations.

6. Collaborate...
  a. to work out understandings with your partner.
  b. to reread and confirm your understandings.
  c. to complete each step of the task.

this information? What does the process seem to entail from start to finish? What items or tools will the reader need for the task?

- *Clarify vocabulary:* What key terms are used in the text? Which of these terms are already known, and which are unfamiliar? What aids does the text provide to assist a reader with key terms? What can a reader do if the text does not adequately elaborate critical vocabulary?

- *Scan the visuals:* Examine any visual information provided in the text. The diagrams and drawings should help the reader visualize the process to be followed in completing the task. Compare the visual information to the actual objects with which you will be working.

- *Look out for cautions:* Some projects will be ruined if the steps are not followed exactly as prescribed. In other cases, readers may make a serious error, or even expose themselves to danger, if steps are ignored or done in an improper sequence.

- *Read and apply:* Begin reading and undertaking the task in phases. Read the first segment, clarify the message, and apply the information. Hands-On Reading assumes a recursive spiraling through a technical text: Read a segment, apply the information hands on, reread to confirm the actions taken or to clarify misunderstandings, read the next segment, and so forth.

- *Collaborate:* Hands-On Reading usually requires a degree of problem solving. Therefore, a major component of this reading strategy is interaction with fellow learners. Rereading segments and verbalizing understandings with a partner is a natural problem-solving routine for adults grappling with technical nonfiction.

4 Students work with partners to read and apply information from classroom technical material using the protocol outlined previously. The Hands-On Reading protocol is a variation of the Interactive Reading Guides (see the Interactive Reading Guides strategy pages), which involve students collaborating in teams to work their understanding of a complex text. A key expectation is that students work the technical text to figure out what needs to be done without having to depend on the teacher to tell them or show them what to do. Technical reading is the epitome of close reading (see Chapter 1). Partners need to be able to justify to each other what they are expected to do at each step by citing evidence from the text and its illustrations.

Advantages

- Students practice independent routines for learning from complex technical texts rather than overrelying on teachers to provide all the information.

- Students become more flexible in their approach to various text genres, realizing that some texts need to be read and reread in incremental segments rather than straight through.

- This strategy is appropriate for complex technical texts in all disciplines but especially for courses that feature applied reading as central to the curriculum.

Meets the Standards

Hands-On Reading promotes careful reading and rereading of an author's message (R.1), discerning main ideas (R.2), examining interrelationships of details or ideas (R.3), interpreting word meaning (R.4), analyzing text structure (R.5), tracking the author's perspective and purpose (R.6), integrating ideas with visual representations (R.7), using text-based evidence for supporting argumentation (R.8), and mentoring the reading of complex literary and informational texts (R.10). In addition, the collaborative conversations develop expressing and defending thinking using visual displays (SL.1, SL.2, SL.4). Follow-up writing can provide practice in using text-based evidence for summarizing and explaining (W.2) and drawing evidence from texts for analysis and reflection (W.9). Vocabulary development includes determining and clarifying key vocabulary (L.4), attention to word relationships (L.5), and acquiring domain-specific vocabulary (L.6).

Reference

Buehl, D. (2002). Putting it all together. *OnWEAC, 3*(4), 13.

History Change Frame

The Vikings emerged from the Scandinavian Peninsula at the end of 800 A.D. and regularly plundered the inhabitants of northern Europe over the course of the next century. With their high-prowed, shallow-draft vessels, the Vikings created the perfect attack ship, which allowed them to sail long distances under a variety of oceanic conditions. Not only did they pillage monasteries and communities in the British Isles and France, but they also became permanent settlers. The Vikings created the Duchy of Normandy, for example, which eventually evolved into the country of France.

Students reading complex history texts encounter a dizzying and seemingly endless array of factual information: names, dates, places, and events. What is the point? For many, learning about history soon defaults to short-term memorization of isolated facts. The larger context of historical themes and ideas remains murky at best, and any learning becomes highly in danger of being promptly jettisoned after a unit exam.

In contrast, reading through a historian's lens involves searching for connections and relationships among information instead of becoming engulfed by a torrent of disjointed facts. Students make more sense of history when they use facts to help them explain important changes people have experienced and how changes contribute to problems people confront. Examining historical changes helps students better understand human society and our lives today.

The Thinking Like a Historian framework (Mandell & Malone, 2007) focuses history instruction on essential questions related to this change dynamic: What changed, and what remained the same? Who or what made this change happen? What were the effects of the change? Who supported this change, and who did not? Who benefited from the change, and who did not? These questions probe thinking at the analyzing level for students reading through a historian's lens (see Table 5 in Chapter 4).

Using the Strategies

Teaching students to read complex history texts with a problem/solution frame of mind enables them to examine the major changes discussed in a chapter or text. The History Change Frame (Buehl, 1992) guides comprehension by focusing attention on groups of people who confront problems and cope with change. History Memory Bubbles (Buehl, 1998), a related strategy, provides a tool for analyzing important factual information through a historian's lens.

1 Select several time periods to be covered in the curriculum, such as the American Revolution, the Industrial Revolution, and the Vietnam War. In a brainstorming exercise, ask students who they expect will be featured in a reading for each time period. Emphasize that they should think of groups of people, not individuals. As students consider what they know about each of the time periods, their responses might include angry colonists, loyalists, and the British; factory owners, workers, and labor unions; and antiwar protesters, the U.S. Army, the French colonial government, and Communist guerrillas.

2 Model the History Change Frame (reproducible available in the Appendix) with a text that students have previously read. In your discussion, emphasize that the study of history features stories of people who dealt with change and addressed problems. Factual details in a text are presented to flesh out the nature of these changes and problems. Historical story lines describe actions undertaken to resolve these problems. Highlight the six categories of change that underlie historical events:

1. *Population:* Increases or decreases in a geographical area or changes in composition with regard to factors such as age distribution or ethnicity

2. *Technological:* New inventions or other innovations that affect the way things are done in a society

3. *Environmental:* Changes in the physical geography of an area or in the climate

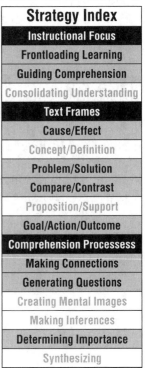

Strategy Index

Instructional Focus
Frontloading Learning
Guiding Comprehension
Consolidating Understanding
Text Frames
Cause/Effect
Concept/Definition
Problem/Solution
Compare/Contrast
Proposition/Support
Goal/Action/Outcome
Comprehension Processess
Making Connections
Generating Questions
Creating Mental Images
Making Inferences
Determining Importance
Synthesizing

4. *Economic:* Changes in how people make a daily living and in their standard of living

5. *Political:* Changes in the type of government, the nature of the leaders, elections, laws, court decisions, treaties, and wars

6. *Cultural:* Changes in customs and what people believe, including religious beliefs, ideas, philosophies, and values

3 Assign students to work as partners to examine a text through use of the History Change Frame graphic organizer. Have them first survey the text to determine the groups that are the focus of this historical period. Model this process by thinking aloud as you examine the title, headings and subheadings, chapter objectives, advance organizers, primary-source excerpts, pictures, and graphics. Determine with students who the key players are in this text. Whose stories are being told? Do not accept individual names during this phase; ask students to generalize groups of people who will be involved in the action. (See the History Change Frame for Prohibition.)

4 Students continue examining as they begin to read, looking for indications of problems that the

groups of people may have encountered: What separate problems did the peasants, the nobles, and the merchants face in feudal Europe? What problems concerned women during the Progressive Era in the United States? How about African Americans and muckrakers? How did the problems of American Indians contrast with those of cattle ranchers and prairie farmers in the 19th-century American West? Interestingly, students will discover that some groups featured in the text may have caused problems that other groups had to deal with: Who experienced problems because of the Crusaders? Who experienced problems because of the kings who believed in divine rights? Who experienced problems because of the dissidents arguing for reformation of the Church? Partners enter problems for each group on their History Change Frames. In our Prohibition example, supporters of prohibiting alcohol consumption (the "drys") both had problems because of and caused problems for opponents of Prohibition (the "wets").

5 As students continue, have them analyze information from the text that describes the changes experienced by each group of people. Students code each change according to the six categories introduced in step 2 and record the changes on their History Change Frame graphic organizers. For example, changes that affected Prohibition supporters in the 19th and early 20th centuries included population (the demographic shift resulting from a huge influx of immigrants, the shift from rural to urban), cultural (more people who brought different cultural practices, the willingness of law-abiding citizens to break the law), economic (the rise of illegal alcohol industries), and political (the passage of the 18th Amendment, which was eventually appealed by the 21st Amendment). Similar changes impacted the wets with different results, leading to conflict between these contrasting camps in the United States.

Finally, students identify actions taken by each group to resolve their problems. Some actions were successful, and others did not achieve the group's desired results.

6 Discuss with students how changes affect people in different ways. Students come to realize that the effects of changes vary depending on the group of people being considered. Sometimes a change benefits one group and causes problems for another. For example, the 18th Amendment, a political change, clearly benefited Prohibition supporters but was detrimental to the lifestyles and livelihoods of Prohibition opponents. Immigration policies opened the floodgates for people coming to the United States with very different cultural practices and beliefs, which caused tensions

History Change Frame for Prohibition

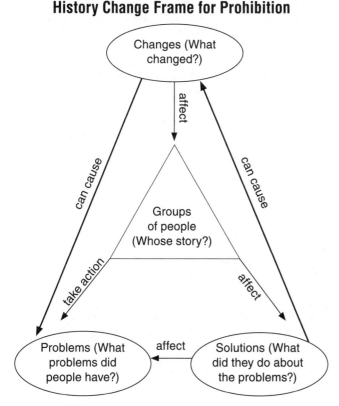

Note. From *Classroom Strategies for Interactive Learning* (p. 57), by D. Buehl, 1995, Newark, DE: Wisconsin State Reading Association. Copyright © 2001 by the International Reading Association.

History Change Frame for Prohibition

Group	What Problems Did They Face?	What Changes Affected These People?	What Did They Do to Solve Their Problems?
Drys	• Cultural values for many Americans supported the drinking of alcohol. • Evidence of crimes, violence, family breakups from alcohol • Men lured by alcohol, wasted wages needed by families • Poor and working-class harmed most by alcohol misuse • Taverns viewed as centers of vice • Need to tame city life • Drinking because of foreign influences • Gangsters and gang violence • Prohibition Bureau lacked agents, money, supplies • Enforcement a losing battle • Objections to governmental interference in personal lives	• *Population:* Rural to urban, immigrants • *Economic:* Alcohol consumption declined, gangsters created multibillion-dollar business, less wages spent on alcohol • *Political:* 18th Amendment banned alcohol use, opposition grew, 21st Amendment repealed • *Cultural:* New traditions, less drinking by poor and ethnic groups, increase in illegal activity by law-abiding people	• Lobbied for Prohibition • Formed advocacy groups (WCTE) • Public demonstrations at bars and taverns • Voted for Prohibition candidates • Passed 18th Amendment • Congress passed the Volstead Act to enforce the ban. • Police enforcement of ban on alcohol • Destroyed illegal alcohol • Closed bars and pubs • Arrested bootleggers
Wets	• Drinking alcohol went against the cultural values of some Americans. • Progressive reformers wanted to ban the use of alcohol. • Perception of crimes, violence, family breakups from alcohol • Nativist prejudice against immigrants • 18th Amendment banned manufacture, sale, transport of alcohol • Violence by gangsters	• *Population:* Rural to urban, immigrants • *Economic:* Alcohol consumption declined, gangsters created multibillion-dollar business, less wages spent on alcohol • *Political:* 18th Amendment banned alcohol use, 21st Amendment repealed • *Cultural:* New traditions, less drinking by poor and ethnic groups, increase in illegal activity by law-abiding people	• Drank less alcohol • Argued Prohibition restricted freedom and bred crime • Argued federal government legislating morality • Called drys "ignorant country bumpkins" • Argued alcohol not sinful, Jesus drank wine • Flouted law, engaged in illegal behavior • Bootlegging, made own alcohol • Got alcohol from Canada • Started speakeasies • Gangsters bribed politicians, judges, police; murdered rivals • Passed 21st Amendment

for Americans uncomfortable with new practices in their midst. Many immigrants resented Prohibition as infringing on their customs, whereas many Prohibition supporters were alarmed by these customs, especially concerning alcohol.

A completed History Change Frame provides an excellent blueprint for writing tasks that engage students in summarizing, developing explanations, and supporting arguments.

History Memory Bubbles

History Memory Bubbles (Buehl, 1998; reproducible available in the Appendix) are a structured variation of concept mapping tailored for thinking like a historian. The strategy emphasizes change dynamics and problem/solution relationships in history.

1 Model key terms or historical facts in terms of their connection to a problem/solution text frame: What is it? What does it have to do with problems discussed in the text? What does it have to do with resolving these problems? What does it have to do with changes highlighted in this text? For example, the term *graft* is a key concept in studying urban politics during the latter half of the 19th century in the United States. Whose story is graft a part of? What does graft have to do with problems during this time? How did people try to solve graft? What changes occurred because of graft?

2 Have students work with a partner to identify key terms or facts from a history selection that they have read. For example, students might earmark the following terms as central to corrupt politics in the post–Civil War era in the United States: *Gilded Age, robber barons, city bosses, political patronage, graft,* and *Civil Service Act.* Ask students to concentrate solely on information that focuses attention on key themes and ideas instead of background detail (see Chapter 3's discussion of Fact Pyramids). Students typically expect to process such terms as isolated historical facts through scanning a text to locate and memorize minimal details associated with each term. Their assignments may resemble disconnected chunks of information, such as "*The Gilded Age* was a book by Mark Twain," "The Tweed Ring was a group of dishonest elected officials in New York City," and "Political patronage was the practice of exchanging political jobs for political support." In contrast, History Memory Bubbles engage students in developing meaningful associations around changes and problems.

Students briefly explain each item in the "Who/What" bubble (see the History Memory Bubbles for City Bosses example).

3 For each selected term or fact, ask partners to complete a History Memory Bubbles graphic organizer. Problems connected to each item are listed in the "Problems" bubble. For *city bosses,* for example, students might list bribes, election fraud, robbing the city treasury, and exchanging jobs and contracts for votes. For the "Solutions" bubble, students might record that city bosses like the Tweed Ring caused reformers to emerge and prosecute these crimes. As a result, a major change was instituted: Civil service reform mandated awarding jobs based on merit, which is entered in the "Changes" bubble.

4 When they finish, invite partners to share their History Memory Bubbles with the entire class. As part of this discussion, students will discover that corresponding information may not be available to fill all four bubbles for every term or fact. After practicing this strategy, students can be asked to self-select key terms and create these graphic organizers independently as they learn new material. Students will begin to perceive interlinking relationships among key terms as they analyze their History Memory Bubbles for a unit of study. Their visual maps provide excellent student-created scaffolds for thorough written explanations and summaries of key terms and information.

History Memory Bubbles for City Bosses

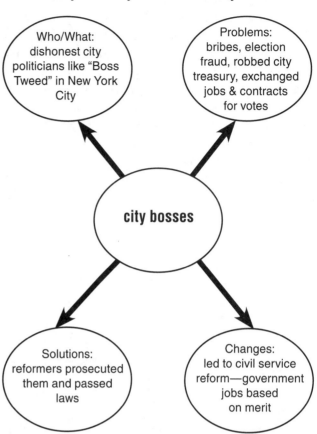

Note. From "Memory Bubbles: They Help Put Information Into Context," by D. Buehl, 1998, *WEAC News & Views, 33*(7), p. 13. Copyright © 1998 by the Wisconsin Education Association Council.

Advantages

- Students are mentored to read and think through a historian's lens.
- Students are provided with visual overviews that help them sort through a wealth of information and recognize important relationships while reading complex history texts.
- Students have a construct that enables them to anticipate patterns in history and to develop a coherent understanding of what history is and why it is studied.
- Students see connections that guide them toward remembering information in the context of larger issues and ideas, and they examine history terms as concepts that involve a number of connecting variables.

Meets the Standards

The History Change Frame and History Memory Bubbles strategies promote careful reading and rereading of an author's message (R.1); discerning main ideas (R.2); examining interrelationships of details or ideas (R.3); interpreting word meaning (R.4); analyzing text structure, especially problem/solution and cause/effect (R.5); integrating ideas into visual representations (R.7); and mentoring the reading of complex literary and informational texts (R.10). In addition, the collaborative conversations develop expressing and defending thinking using visual displays (SL.1, SL.2, SL.4). Summarizing writing provides practice in using text-based evidence in supporting arguments (W.1) and explaining (W.2) and drawing evidence from texts for analysis and reflection (W.9). Attention to word relationships addresses vocabulary development (L.5) and acquiring domain-specific vocabulary (L.6).

References

Buehl, D. (1992). A frame of mind for reading history. *The Exchange, 5*(1), 4–5.

Buehl, D. (1995). *Classroom strategies for interactive learning.* Schofield: Wisconsin State Reading Association.

Buehl, D. (1998). Memory bubbles: They help put information into context. *WEAC News & Views, 33*(7), 13.

Mandell, N., & Malone, B. (2007). *Thinking like a historian: Rethinking history instruction.* Madison: Wisconsin Historical Society Press.

Inquiry Charts

The Etruscans invaded Italy about 600 B.C. They settled in an area by the Tiber River they called Rome. The Etruscans were farmers and also traded with cities like Carthage. They built roads and cultivated the land. The Gauls defeated the Etruscans and sacked Rome in 390 B.C.

Teachers will have no trouble spotting the generic, rote, encyclopedically derived report unfolding in this example. Unfortunately, much student research results in similarly uninspired, "litany of facts" writing, but what about the interesting stuff? What might you really be wondering? What questions might arise about the ancient Etruscans that more research might answer? What was life like in an Etruscan community? What did they believe? What impact did these people have on the succeeding Roman civilization?

Reading to satisfy our curiosity and build our knowledge is an increasing necessity in 21st-century life, and reading for inquiry occupies a special place in the Common Core's writing standards. Inquiry Charts, also known as I-Charts (Hoffman, 1992), emphasize reading for research as a process of inquiry based on a reader's questions, rather than a mere collection of isolated bits of information.

Using the Strategy

An Inquiry Chart prompts the generation of meaningful questions that focus research and organize writing and other projects (see the discussion of essential questions in Chapter 3). Inquiry Charts are suitable for a whole-class, small-group, or individual inquiry.

1 Select a topic studied in the curriculum and brainstorm with students things about this topic that they might be wondering. As you solicit possible questions to explore, look for a mix of thick and thin questions (see the discussion in the B/D/A Questioning Charts strategy pages). Note that although thin questions might be interesting, thick questions are the most promising for further investigation. "Why" questions, in particular, initiate more thoughtful probes for examination. For example, What are some famous jazz pieces? is a thin question. Why is jazz an important genre of music? is a more comprehensive thick question. Ask the class to choose three or four of the most interesting thick questions, which will provide direction for student inquiry.

2 Introduce the Inquiry Chart by modeling how to use this tool to organize information on chart paper or the whiteboard. Also, provide students with individual, blank Inquiry Charts (reproducible available in the Appendix). Record the chosen questions in the boxes along the top. For example, a music teacher wants her musicians to become more knowledgeable about jazz before they begin rehearsing a jazz piece for performance. After an array of questions has been generated, the class chooses four on which to center their inquiry: How did jazz music get started? How is jazz related to other types of music? What are the basic elements of jazz? How has jazz influenced other music? (See the Inquiry Chart for Jazz.)

3 Brainstorm any preexisting knowledge about the topic. Ask students to offer what they know or have heard about jazz and have them indicate which question on the chart this information might answer. Prior knowledge not germane to the questions can be placed in the column labeled "Other Important Information." This process uncovers any misconceptions about a topic that will be confronted as students learn more.

Most music students know that jazz is associated with African American culture and that New Orleans is regarded as a founding city. They may offer that rock music is related to jazz and comment that instruments such as the saxophone, used by performers such as Bruce Springsteen's band, are often regarded as jazz-type instruments. Louis Armstrong and Duke Ellington might be musicians who are known to some students, although others might put forth contemporary artists

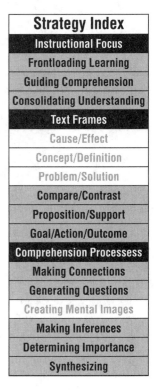

Strategy Index
Instructional Focus
Frontloading Learning
Guiding Comprehension
Consolidating Understanding
Text Frames
Cause/Effect
Concept/Definition
Problem/Solution
Compare/Contrast
Proposition/Support
Goal/Action/Outcome
Comprehension Processess
Making Connections
Generating Questions
Creating Mental Images
Making Inferences
Determining Importance
Synthesizing

Inquiry Chart for Jazz

Topic: Jazz	Question 1: How did jazz music get started?	Question 2: How is jazz related to other types of music?	Question 3: What are the basic elements of jazz?	Question 4: How has jazz influenced other music?	Other Important Information	New Questions
What we know	African Americans in New Orleans	Rock music can have a jazz sound.	Improvisation	*Rock:* Bruce Springsteen's band uses jazz instruments, such as the saxophone.	Jazz clubs in New Orleans, Duke Ellington, Kenny G.	
Book source: *A New History of Jazz*[a]						
Magazine source: *American Heritage*						
Website source: All About Jazz: www.allaboutjazz.com						
Summaries						

Note. Adapted from *Classroom Strategies for Interactive Learning* (2nd ed., p. 68), by D. Buehl, 2001, Newark, DE: International Reading Association. Copyright © 2001 by the International Reading Association.
[a]Shipton, A. (2007). *A new history of jazz* (Rev. ed.). New York: Continuum International.

like Kenny G. and Diana Krall as examples of jazz musicians. Students' awareness of jazz clubs, which does not fit under the target questions, is recorded in the "Other Important Information" column.

4 Provide access to a variety of materials, including websites and newspaper and magazine articles, for students to consult to answer their target questions. Have students work in collaborative groups, with each group consulting a different source. The target questions will guide students as they decide which material in a source is useful and which is extraneous. Have each group record their information on sticky notes,

one fact per note, which are affixed to the chart paper or whiteboard under the appropriate question. Color-coded sticky notes make it easier to identify the source from which the information was taken. As notes are added to the Inquiry Chart, it becomes clear whether enough information has been discovered and whether each question has been answered adequately.

As students consult sources on jazz, they discover a variety of facts and information to address their questions: Blues, a music with which they may be less familiar, is a precursor of jazz, as are work songs and gospel songs. Ragtime is an early form of jazz.

These facts are entered in the "Question 2" column on the Inquiry Chart. Students place information according to the specific source in which they found it, although some information is contained in all sources, which is also indicated on the Inquiry Chart. Students are often surprised to learn that classical music has been influenced by jazz, so they record information about George Gershwin and Leonard Bernstein in the "Question 4" column. As they read about jazz clubs and jazz radio stations, a new question emerges from their research: How popular is jazz today?

5 Ask students to synthesize information from each question into a summary. Sometimes contradictory material is uncovered, which also needs to be acknowledged. Summarization provides a transition from inquiry to writing, as students decide on main idea statements for each question and organize pertinent details.

6 Students are now ready to write about their topic, and they proceed to discuss each question and the information that relates to it. Each vertical column may comprise a paragraph or, with more sophisticated inquiry, a section of a written discussion of the topic. Students also may wish to respond to one or two additional questions that occurred to them as they delved into their sources, which can be added to either the "Other Important Information" or "New Questions" column.

Advantages

- As students become more independent, they can develop individual Inquiry Charts that focus their inquiry and organize their notes.
- Student writing is less likely to be a rambling compendium of facts and more likely to be centered on the significant questions that they had a role in developing.

- Students receive guided practice in synthesizing and summarizing information.
- Students use multiple sources that provide a variety of information as a basis for an inquiry project rather than answering identical questions based on a single source.
- This strategy is especially well suited for Web-based inquiry projects.

Meets the Standards

Inquiry Charts promote careful reading and rereading of an author's message (R.1), discerning main ideas and summarizing (R.2), tracking the author's perspective and purpose (R.6), integrating ideas into visual representations (R.7), supporting argumentation (R.8), comparing and contrasting with other sources of knowledge and using multiple texts (R.9), and mentoring the reading of complex literary and informational texts (R.10). In addition, the collaborative conversations develop expressing and defending thinking using visual displays (SL.1, SL.2, SL.4). Writing that follows the inquiry stage provides practice in using text-based evidence in supporting arguments (W.1), summarizing and explaining (W.2), conducting research based on focus questions (W.7), gathering information from multiple sources (W.8), and drawing evidence from texts for analysis and reflection (W.9). Attention to word relationships addresses vocabulary development (L.5) and acquiring domain-specific vocabulary (L.6).

References

Buehl, D. (2001). *Classroom strategies for interactive learning* (2nd ed.). Newark, DE: International Reading Association.
Hoffman, J.V. (1992). Critical reading/thinking across the curriculum: Using I-charts to support learning. *Language Arts, 69*(2), 121–127.

Literature Cited

Shipton, A. (2007). *A new history of jazz* (Rev. ed.). New York: Continuum International.

Interactive Reading Guides

Align flats on inside of spreader support assembly with flats on end of pivot rod and fasten using long hex bolt and external tooth lockwasher...

Recall a time when you were confronted with a complex technical text that needed to be deciphered before you could undertake a needed project. For most of us, having a collaborator help us work such a problematic text was often a lifesaver. My able collaborator for the above example, instructions for assembling a table saw, was my son Jeremy. The two of us had to navigate a terse, terminology-laden sheet crammed with obscure-looking illustrations, and comprehension was of the essence. You do not want to turn the power on for a table saw that has been improperly assembled!

We worked the text as a team: Jeremy read a step out loud, we deliberated, I sometimes also repeated the read-aloud, we examined the appropriate illustrations, and we sometimes reread the step additional times, always conferring. Eventually we signed off on the step, verbalizing our agreement as to what we were actually expected to do, and then we paused our reading, took up the designated pieces, and assembled what the step entailed. Once accomplished, we moved on to the next step and repeated the process until we were facing the desired result: a ready-to-use table saw. (Our comprehension was successful; the saw works perfectly!)

Teaming to work a complex text can be a critical scaffold for transitioning students from depending on being told information to gradually developing the capacity to access the information themselves as readers. Developing a guide based on Questioning the Author prompts (see the Questioning the Author strategy pages) is a particularly effective method for mentoring a team approach for working texts that could be otherwise overwhelming for many readers.

Using the Strategy

Interactive Reading Guides (Wood, 1988) make it possible for students to learn from complex texts that may be too difficult for independent reading. Unlike typical study guides, which sometimes can be completed by skimming for facts and details, Interactive Reading

Guides are carefully constructed to prompt all of the essential comprehension processes: making connections, generating questions, creating mental images, inferring, determining importance, and synthesizing (see the discussion in Chapter 1). In addition, Interactive Reading Guides assume collaborative problem solving: Students work with partners or in small groups as they read rather than afterward.

1 Preview the reading assignment to determine priorities for learning, and locate possible pitfalls for understanding. Be especially concerned with difficulties struggling readers might have with the material. Notice salient features of the text that students might overlook, such as pictures, charts, and graphs. Determine any mismatch between students and text. Does the author assume knowledge that some students might lack? Does the author introduce ideas and vocabulary without sufficient explanations or examples? Does the author use language or sentence styles that may be difficult for some students? All of these are hallmarks of complex text.

2 Construct an Interactive Reading Guide that provides students with a walk-through for effectively working a complex text. Interactive Reading Guides are just that: students engaging in ongoing conversations with partners or in collaborative groups as they think through the author's message.

Design the guide to cue students to thoughtfully engage in understanding and to support the learning of challenging material. At times, you will want to ask students to inventory their prior knowledge as they consider what an author expects them to already know. In addition, prompt them to raise questions rather than merely answer

Strategy Index
Instructional Focus
Frontloading Learning
Guiding Comprehension
Consolidating Understanding
Text Frames
Cause/Effect
Concept/Definition
Problem/Solution
Compare/Contrast
Proposition/Support
Goal/Action/Outcome
Comprehension Processess
Making Connections
Generating Questions
Creating Mental Images
Making Inferences
Determining Importance
Synthesizing

them. Some tasks should trigger students' imaginations as a tool for understanding what an author is saying. Students should be asked to grapple with implicit as well as explicit elements of comprehension, and the guide should avoid requiring students to respond to "bottom of the Fact Pyramid" items (see Chapter 3). Finally, students should be asked to sum up their understandings and consider conclusions or generalizations that can be drawn from their reading. Explicitly label each comprehension process (see Table 1 in Chapter 1) to reinforce for students the thinking necessary to work a complex text.

3 Divide the passage into segments: those to be read orally by individuals to their group, those to be read silently by each student, and those to be more closely examined and reread. Stipulate when both partners will engage in the same task, when partners have different tasks, and when partners are to collaborate and work together after reading a section. Use the guide to frontload additional background information or encourage students to brainstorm what they already know about the topic. Create items that draw on the appropriate set of disciplinary-specific questions for working a text (see Tables 5–14 in Chapter 4).

For example, in a physical science class, an Interactive Reading Guide helps students manage an otherwise formidable text on rivers (see the Interactive Reading Guide for Physical Science). Notice how the student roles are highlighted in bold, the comprehension processes elicited by each item are underlined before the corresponding text, and the reading is chunked—students read a little and then pause and work over the author's meaning before going on. The items are challenging; none of them can be accomplished by

---

Interactive Reading Guide for Physical Science

1. **Both partners:** Before opening the book, answer the following question individually. Then, talk over your answer with your partner. <u>Inferring:</u> Even though flooding along rivers is potentially harmful, many farms are located near rivers. Why might people build farms along rivers?

2. Turn to page 12. **Partner A:** Read aloud the title of Section 2 and the paragraph underneath. **Partner B:** Read aloud the next paragraph. **Work together:** <u>Creating mental images:</u> What does the author compare rivers to? Why?

3. **Both partners:** Silently read the paragraph under the heading "Deposition in Water." **Work together:** <u>Determining importance:</u> In your own words, explain the following terms:

    deposition:

    sediment:

4. **Partner A:** Read aloud the paragraph under the heading "Placer Deposits" on page 13. **Work together:** <u>Determining importance:</u> In your words, explain your understanding of a placer deposit. <u>Inferring:</u> A river runs down a rapids, eases through a valley for about three miles, and then tumbles down a waterfall into a lake. Where along this path would you most likely find a placer deposit? Explain why you think so.

5. **Work together:** <u>Creating mental images:</u> Examine Figure 2 and describe what it is showing. <u>Making connections:</u> Explain how Figure 2 helps you understand what you have read so far.

6. **Work together:** <u>Making connections:</u> Write down something you know about the California gold rush. OR <u>Questioning:</u> Write one thoughtful question about the California gold rush.

7. **Both partners:** Before reading the rest of the page, read the title of the next section. <u>Making connections:</u> What are some things you already know about the meaning of the term *delta*?

8. **Partner B:** Read the first paragraph under the heading "Delta" out loud. **Work together:** <u>Determining importance:</u> Identify the three cause-and-effect relationships described by the author.

Cause	Effect
1.	1.
2.	2.
3.	3.

Work together: <u>Determining importance:</u> In your own words, explain the term *delta*.

(continued)

Interactive Reading Guide for Physical Science (continued)

9. **Partner A:** Read the last paragraph on page 13 out loud. **Partner B:** Locate the map of the Mississippi River watershed on page 6. **Work together:** <u>Making connections:</u> Review what deltas are made of. <u>Inferring:</u> Then, predict whether or not it would be good to live on the land created by a delta. Explain why you think so.

10. **Partner B:** Read the paragraph under the heading "Deposition on Land" on page 14 out loud. **Partner A:** Read the caption for Figure 4 aloud. **Work together:** <u>Determining importance:</u> In your own words, explain the term *alluvial fan*.

11. **Work individually:** Write characteristics of a delta and an alluvial fan in the appropriate areas of the Venn diagram below:

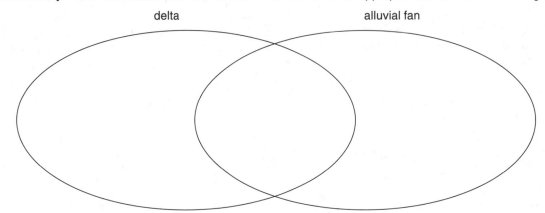

delta   alluvial fan

Work together: Share your ideas from the Venn diagram and discuss any differences. Make changes if necessary.

12. **Partner B:** Read aloud the first paragraph under the heading "Floodplains." **Work together:** <u>Determining importance:</u> Explain the term *floodplain*.

13. **Partner A:** Read aloud the next paragraph. **Work together:** <u>Inferring:</u> Even though flooding along rivers is potentially harmful, many farms are located near rivers. Why do people build farms along rivers? Compare your answer here with your original answer at the beginning of this guide.

14. **Both partners:** Silently read the three paragraphs on page 15. Also, look at Figure 6 and read its caption. Complete the chart below:

Type of Flood Control	Explanations in Your Own Words	How It Helps/Works
Dam		
Levee		
Other: Do you know of any other type of flood control?		

Work together: Share your charts.

15. <u>Summarizing:</u> Talk about three things a person should know based on your understanding from this reading.

Note. Adapted, with permission, from an Interactive Reading Guide by Nancy Duff and Katie Winn, Whitman Middle School, Wauwatosa, WI.

"locate and copy" skimming (see the discussion in Chapter 1). The items reflect text-specific variations for questioning through a scientist's lens (see Table 8 in Chapter 4).

In another example, for a world history class, an Interactive Reading Guide helps students navigate a complex text on medieval Europe (see the Interactive Reading Guide for World History). Items in this guide are crafted from questions that are central to reading through a historian's lens (see Table 5 in Chapter 4). Notice that in both examples, graphic organizers are integrated into the flow of working the texts.

Interactive Reading Guide for World History

1. "Section 2: Medieval Life": **Both partners:** Silently read the introductory paragraph.
   a. <u>Making connections:</u> **Work together:** The author mentions historical information that was discussed earlier in this textbook. List the things you studied before and briefly explain what you remember about each.
   b. <u>Determining importance:</u> An important phrase in this paragraph is *mutual alliance*. **Partner A:** Use a resource to look up definitions for the term *mutual*. **Partner B:** Use a resource to look up definitions for the term *alliance*. **Work together:** <u>Synthesizing:</u> In your own words, explain your understanding of the term *mutual alliance* as it is used in this paragraph.
   c. A central concept in this paragraph is feudalism. **Partner A:** Reread this paragraph out loud. **Work together:** <u>Inferring:</u> Why does the author apparently feel that knowing about feudalism is important in the study of world history?

2. "Feudal Relationships": Paragraph 2 talks about why feudalism got started. **Both partners:** Silently read paragraph 2. **Work together:**
   a. <u>Determining importance:</u> Explain why the king (Charles Martel) found it necessary to start the feudal system.
   b. <u>Making connections:</u> A key term in this paragraph is *fief*. How is a fief like someone owning their own home today?
   c. <u>Making connections:</u> How is a fief different from owning your own home today?

3. The word *noble* is used frequently in this section. **Partner B:** Read paragraph 3 aloud. **Partner A:** As you listen, think about what this word apparently means. **Work together:**
   a. <u>Inferring:</u> Look for clues in the first three paragraphs and use your own words to explain your understanding of what a noble is.
   b. <u>Determining importance:</u> What kinds of powers were granted to nobles under the feudal system?
   c. <u>Determining importance:</u> What did the nobles have to give in return?
   d. <u>Inferring:</u> What does this have to do with mutual alliance?

4. **Partner A:** Read paragraph 4 aloud. **Partner B:** Read paragraph 5 aloud. **Work together:** Apparently, feudalism was a confusing arrangement. The author describes feudalism as a pyramid. <u>Creating mental images:</u> Use evidence from the text and place the following terms in the pyramid below: *king, peasant, noble, vassal, lord,* and *knight*.

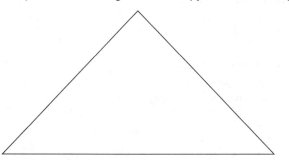

5. "Feudal Obligations": **Both partners:** Silently read this paragraph. **Work together:** <u>Summarizing:</u> What would your life be like if you were a vassal to a lord?

6. "A Time of Warfare and Castles for Defense": **Both partners:** Silently read these paragraphs. **Work together:** <u>Inferring:</u> What seems to be the author's main point in giving you all of this information?

7. **Both partners:** Silently read the rest of this section, from page 264 to 266. These three pages contain a lot of information that contrasts the life of nobles to the life of peasants. <u>Determining importance:</u> As you read, list details in the T-Chart below:

What Life Was Like for Nobles	What Life Was Like for Peasants

Work together: Compare your T-charts and add new details from your discussion.

8. **Work together:** <u>Summarizing:</u> Explain your understanding of feudalism in three sentences using the following key terms: *king, vassal, peasant, fief, warfare, knight, noble, mutual alliance,* and *castle*.

9. **Work together:** <u>Questioning:</u> Write two questions you have about feudalism at this point.

4 Whole-class discussions then capitalize on the completed guides and focus on essential questions, such as, What effects do rivers have on the landscape? and Under feudalism, who got what, and who decided? The completed guides then serve as students' resources for writing summaries, interpretations, or explanations of their understandings. Therefore, during the collaborations, every student completes a guide for future personal reference instead of one student writing responses for the entire group.

Advantages

- Students use partners as collaborators for tackling challenging reading assignments and discussing the material while they read.

- Students are mentored to track their own comprehension processes as they work a complex text.

- Students are conditioned to read materials at different rates for varying purposes, including rereading some sections that warrant closer examination.

- Students gain explicit and guided practice in reading through a disciplinary lens—historical, scientific, literary, technical, artistic, mathematical, and so forth.

- Struggling readers are especially supported by the use of Interactive Reading Guides.

- Completed Interactive Reading Guides serve as organized notes for classroom discussions, written tasks, and follow-up activities and as study guides for exams.

Meets the Standards

Interactive Reading Guides promote careful reading and rereading of an author's message (R.1), discerning main ideas and summarizing (R.2), examining inter-relationships of details or ideas (R.3), interpreting word meaning (R.4), analyzing text structure (R.5), tracking the author's perspective and purpose (R.6), integrating ideas into visual representations (R.7), supporting argumentation (R.8), comparing and contrasting with other sources of knowledge (R.9), and mentoring the reading of complex literary and informational texts (R.10). In addition, the collaborative conversations develop expressing and defending thinking using visual displays (SL.1, SL.2, SL.4). Follow-up writing provides practice in using text-based evidence in supporting arguments (W.1), summarizing and explaining (W.2), and drawing evidence from texts for analysis and reflection (W.9). Vocabulary development includes determining and clarifying key vocabulary (L.4), attention to word relationships (L.5), and acquiring domain-specific vocabulary (L.6).

Reference

Wood, K.D. (1988). Guiding students through informational text. *The Reading Teacher, 41*(9), 912–920.

Suggested Reading

Wood, K.D., Lapp, D., Flood, J., & Taylor, D.B. (2008). *Guiding readers through text: Strategy guides for new times* (2nd ed.). Newark, DE: International Reading Association.

Knowledge/Question/Response Charts

Initially, it is the arresting title that captures your eye as you shuffle through the sections, browsing the daily newspaper: "Hard-Knock Lessons From the Concussion Files" (Brody, 2007). What new information do we need to know about concussions? What "hard-knock" lessons is this author going to tell me about, and what do I need to learn about these problematic clunks on the head?

As you begin digging into the meat of the article, an array of factual information starts popping out of the paragraphs. You discover that 50 out of every 100,000 people in the United States undergo a concussion each year. You wonder how this compares with other kinds of injuries people might encounter. You are startled to read that an ex–NFL player who recently died at age 44 had a brain similar to that of an 85-year-old victim of Alzheimer's. How typical is this condition, you pause to consider, for athletes who once played high-contact sports? You are then stopped at the statement that most concussions are experienced by youngsters between the ages of 5 and 14. You think of your own children, as they bumped and banged their way into adulthood, zipping around on their bicycles, falling off playground equipment, and diving full force into soccer games or other sporting endeavors.

You bubble with questions and ruminate with concerns. It is natural that you interject your own life and perspectives into the thinking sparked by this author. And when you are done, you summarize what you now understand into a few "need to know" realizations about concussions.

Finally, inevitably, you lean toward your spouse to share your new insights. When a text piques your interest and changes the way you think about the world, you invariably want to talk about it. The morning news feed, with two readers sitting side by side immersed in stories, is a daily conversation starter.

Using the Strategy

This opening scenario illustrates that as an accomplished reader, you focus on gleaning only what is most essential from a text, recognizing that the bulk of an article will comprise background details. You activate an inquiring mind-set that constantly surfaces a variety of questions about the topic, and you then probe the text to satisfy your curiosity and need for clarification. You react personally to what you read, considering implications for you and others, weighing your previous understandings that may now need alteration and refinement, and drawing some takeaway conclusions. Knowledge/Question/Response Charts (adapted from Harvey & Goudvis, 2007; reproducible available in the Appendix) guide students through these thinking phases as they construct an understanding of a complex text.

1 The first column is designated for significant knowledge extracted from a text. However, not everything from an article is worthy of being included in the "Knowledge" column. Students may display a tendency to jot down facts that are not of utmost importance, without pondering whether this information is truly significant or merely background details. In a think-aloud, model how to decide on the most transcendent information. Display the opening segment of a complex text. Observe that although the text may be jam-packed with information, most of these details are presented to build a foundation for understanding but are not likely to be long remembered.

Emphasize information that meets a stringent "need to know" qualification: What does this author say that a person would need to know if someone is knowledgeable about the topic? In our concussions example, the author tells us that a concussion is "an immediate and short-lived loss of consciousness accompanied by a brief period of amnesia after a blow to the head" (para. 8). Make the case to your students why you believe this statement qualifies as "need to know" knowledge:

> I thought the part about the two football players with brain damage was

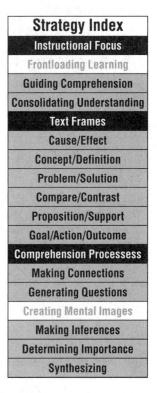

Strategy Index

- Instructional Focus
- Frontloading Learning
- Guiding Comprehension
- Consolidating Understanding
- **Text Frames**
- Cause/Effect
- Concept/Definition
- Problem/Solution
- Compare/Contrast
- Proposition/Support
- Goal/Action/Outcome
- **Comprehension Processes**
- Making Connections
- Generating Questions
- Creating Mental Images
- Making Inferences
- Determining Importance
- Synthesizing

interesting, but these stories were just examples of concussions. This statement explains exactly what a concussion is, with two important characteristics: loss of consciousness and brief amnesia. This information clarifies what we mean by the term *concussion*. I think a person would really need to know exactly what a concussion is.

2 Students read to identify "need to know" knowledge from the rest of the text. Initially, have them track candidates for the "Knowledge" column by placing a light check mark in the margin next to promising statements or by affixing small sticky notes to the page. Students will likely have more than five check marks or sticky notes when they finish reading, which mandates that they revisit the text to prioritize statements.

Next, have students meet with partners or in collaborative groups to negotiate knowledge that a person needs to take away from this reading. This phase involves reasoning and argumentation, as students choose from all their knowledge candidates the five statements that seem most important. Each team must be prepared to justify why they believe each statement warrants inclusion in the "Knowledge" column (see the Knowledge/Question/Response Chart for an Article on Concussions).

Then, solicit statements from partners or groups for whole-class deliberations. Students make their cases for "need to know" items, and the class decides which items should ultimately complete the "Knowledge" column. Students will likely have some disagreement with one another on what is most significant. It is crucial during this phase for students to verbalize their justifications as to why certain information deserves to be remembered.

Notice whether any critical areas of the text are being neglected, which could signal challenging segments that students are overlooking. In such cases, ask students to take another look and reread an ignored segment to evaluate possible "need to know" inclusions. These segments may need to be worked as a class for clarification and understanding.

3 Model some issues you might be wondering about related to the first knowledge item. Perhaps you might wonder if at any time you have personally experienced a concussion. You might wonder how long

Knowledge/Question/Response Chart for an Article on Concussions[a]

Knowledge	Question	Response
A concussion is an immediate and short-lived loss of consciousness, resulting in brief amnesia, caused by a blow to the head.	Have I ever had a concussion?	Being knocked out must be a more serious form of concussion. Boxers are highly at risk for brain injury from concussions.
Even a mild concussion may cause fatigue, irritability, difficulty with concentrating, memory problems, and depression over time.	How many people are suffering these symptoms and are unaware that they have had a concussion?	We need to take concussions much more seriously and more thoroughly monitor people who have experienced them.
Postconcussion syndrome happens when the brain is not given a chance to heal before another head injury occurs.	How can doctors tell whether a brain has been given enough time to heal?	I didn't understand why some athletes took so long to return to playing after a concussion, but I do now!
Concussions occur most frequently with children, in sports and bicycle accidents.	How strong a connection is there between learning disabilities and concussions?	I think of sports announcers laughing and saying a player "got his bell rung." They don't seem to take the dangers of concussions seriously.
Young athletes should wait a month or more to return to their sport, and their school workload should be reduced.	How often is this advice followed in sports for kids? How many teachers are aware of this need for less work?	Because young brains are still growing and are very vulnerable, parents and coaches need to make sure kids are protected.
Prevention of concussions involves properly fitted sports helmets and wearing seat belts in vehicles.	What makes a helmet properly fitted? How can you tell if a helmet is going to be effective for concussions?	I think of all those years of riding my bike without a helmet! I also appreciate workers needing safety helmets for certain jobs.

Note. Adapted from "FQR Chart," by D. Buehl, 2007, *OnWEAC*, retrieved July 10, 2013, from www.weac.org/News/2006–07/march07/readingroommarch07.htm. Copyright © 2007 by Doug Buehl.
[a]Brody, J.E. (2007, February 13). Hard-knock lessons from the concussion files. *The New York Times*, p. 13.

"brief amnesia" lasts—a few seconds, or could it be a minute or more? You might wonder how powerful a blow to the head must be to induce a concussion. These are entered in the "Question" column.

This second phase underscores that knowledge does not exist as stand-alone information. Once we know something, we are likely to have additional questions: If this is true, then what about...?

Students return to collaborating with their partners or groups and continue the conversation by considering questions that emerge for them for each of the knowledge items, which are entered on their charts. The group talks about their questions and speculates on possible answers. Again, solicit questions from the groups for a continuation of the whole-class discussion about the text.

4 The third phase allows readers to weigh in with what's on their minds: What connections might they have to this information, what ideas occur to them, and what is their take on what this means? The "Response" column prompts readers to interject their

experiences and perceptions into the chart and engages them in synthesizing new learning. Model some of your thinking:

> I was thinking about being knocked out, which I now understand is a fairly serious concussion. Most concussions have short-lived loss of consciousness, but being knocked out lasts longer. I also think of boxers who basically are trying to give their opponent a concussion every time they fight. I know some boxers have been knocked out many times, which causes very dangerous damage to the brain.

This last phase is done individually, as each student writes a response to sum up his or her thinking and personal connections. These can then be shared with partners or group members.

5 After experience in applying this strategy, students can be asked to engage in a variation that specifically asks them to evaluate arguments raised by an author (see the Argument/Question/Response Chart for Machiavelli). Argumentation is a decided undercurrent

Argument/Question/Response Chart for Machiavelli

Argument	Question	Response
A leader should want to be considered merciful and not cruel.	Will people be more willing to follow a leader who is not mean or does not treat them cruelly?	I think sometimes leaders need to make tough decisions that might seem harsh or cruel, but most people will respect and follow this leader.
A leader should be both loved and feared.	How can a leader maintain being loved while still being feared?	Leaders who are fair but punish those who break the rules are able to maintain a level of love while still being intimidating.
It is easier for a leader to be feared than loved.	Will people follow a leader who is only feared and not loved?	To a certain degree, people will follow a leader through fear, but in times of controversy, support for the leader will be hard to find.
To keep his subjects united and loyal, a leader ought not to mind the approach of cruelty.	Does cruelty really inspire loyalty, or will people become resentful instead?	To keep subjects united and loyal, a leader has to demonstrate leadership and show stability and power to prove he or she is strong enough to lead.
A leader should earn allies through greatness and nobility of mind rather than by buying friends.	Could a leader really trust followers whose loyalty is to financial advantages and not to the person?	I think a leader would rather have real friends to rely on, because if friends are bought, they were not secured through respect and probably won't be reliable.
A leader should rule the way he or she feels is right and not the way others might want the leader to rule.	Does this mean that the leader doesn't listen to other people's advice on how to do things?	I think if a leader is wise, he or she listens to others but is clear that he or she is the decision maker and always in control. Otherwise, the leader will lose authority.

Note. Adapted, with permission, from an Argument/Question/Response Chart for Machiavelli by Thomas Tourtillott, Rice Lake High School, Rice Lake, WI.

in many texts, as well as the formal structure of writing for essays and advocacy pieces, and receives major emphasis in the Common Core literacy standards.

Advantages

- Students pinpoint statements that truly stand out from the dense background of details.

- Students read to inquire as they entertain personal questions about a text.

- Students are encouraged to personalize their learning by integrating new ideas into previous understandings and by responding to what an author has shared with them.

Meets the Standards

Knowledge/Question/Response Charts promote careful reading and rereading of an author's message (R.1); discerning main ideas and summarizing (R.2); interpreting word meaning, especially use of figurative language (R.4); tracking the author's perspective and purpose (R.6); integrating ideas into visual representations (R.7); supporting argumentation (R.8); comparing and contrasting with other sources of knowledge (R.9); and mentoring the reading of complex literary and informational texts (R.10). In addition, the collaborative conversations develop expressing and defending thinking using visual displays (SL.1, SL.2, SL.4). Summarizing writing provides practice in using text-based evidence in explaining (W.2) and drawing evidence from texts for analysis and reflection (W.9). Attention to word relationships addresses vocabulary development (L.5).

References

Buehl, D. (2007). FQR chart. *OnWEAC*. Retrieved July 10, 2013, from www.weac.org/News/2006-07/march07/readingroom march07.htm

Harvey, S., & Goudvis, A. (2007). *Strategies that work: Teaching comprehension for understanding and engagement* (2nd ed.). Portland, ME: Stenhouse.

Literature Cited

Brody, J.E. (2007, February 13). Hard-knock lessons from the concussion files. *The New York Times*, p. 13.

K–W–L Plus

et's say you are planning a trip to another country. As you prepare your itinerary, you consider what you already know about the country. As you sort through various travel guides, articles, maps, and brochures, you plot activities and designate places to visit. At this point, you probably think to yourself, What don't I know about this country that I would like to learn more about? After you have immersed yourself in resources, you take stock of what you have learned about the destination and act on this knowledge by constructing an itinerary that matches your desires and priorities.

This scenario represents a very purposeful and pragmatic reading event. A persistent challenge for teachers is to encourage students to adopt a similar attitude—to be active thinkers who use the texts they read. Chapter 1 detailed essential characteristics of comprehension, which are exemplified in this travel-planning scenario. Before you started reading, you considered what you already knew about the topic, you generated questions that got you wondering about this topic, and you anticipated what else you might need to know. Then, you used your reading to satisfy your curiosity, answer your questions, and deepen your knowledge. You had a personal agenda for reading, a clear idea of what you were looking for, and when you finished, you could evaluate whether you learned what you were seeking.

The K–W–L Plus strategy (Carr & Ogle, 1987) is a classic instructional practice that prompts all the thinking embedded in comprehension. Using this strategy helps students activate what they already know before they begin a reading assignment. A natural offshoot of this student activity is the generation of questions that they could use their reading to answer. Students use the text to confirm and enhance their knowledge and to satisfy their questions. The strategy also helps students organize what they have learned when they are finished reading, especially as a prelude to writing.

Using the Strategies

K–W–L (Ogle, 1986) is an acronym for what I *k*now, what I *w*ant to know, and what I *l*earned. The strategy involves the use of a three-column graphic organizer that becomes the students' study guide as they read. The graphic organizer is effective as a worksheet and

as a class record displayed on a whiteboard or projected on a screen. The "plus" stage of K–W–L Plus engages students in categorizing and summarizing the work that they have collected in the graphic organizer. The Confirming to Extending Grid (Buehl, 2011) is a more advanced variation of this strategy.

1 Write the main topic of a selection or story at the top of the K–W–L grid (see the K–W–L Plus Grid for Pythons). Start with prior knowledge brainstorming (see the Brainstorming Prior Knowledge strategy pages). First, allow students a designated time to generate a list of things that they have heard or might know about the topic. Point out that some of the things we hear may not be accurate, so we use reliable texts to confirm or revise our understandings. Students can do this prior knowledge brainstorming individually, with partners, or in collaborative groups. Record student contributions in the column "K (*k*now)." Students preparing to read a science selection about pythons might contribute the following: squeeze victims to death, eat animals whole, and live wild in Florida Everglades. A story about sled dogs might elicit huskies, live in the far north, harnessed as teams, transportation on snow and ice, and Iditarod.

2 Next, ask students what they are wondering about the topic. Again, students can engage in this phase individually, with partners, or in cooperative groups. In addition to wondering whether specific items recorded in the "W (*w*ant to know)" column might be true, students will likely be curious about a variety of other things about the topic. Solicit these questions and record them in the column "W (*w*ant to know)." For instance, students studying pythons may have these questions: Are pythons poisonous?

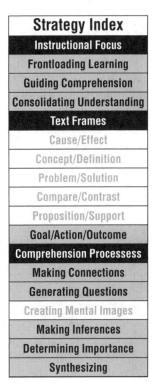

Strategy Index

Instructional Focus
Frontloading Learning
Guiding Comprehension
Consolidating Understanding
Text Frames
Cause/Effect
Concept/Definition
Problem/Solution
Compare/Contrast
Proposition/Support
Goal/Action/Outcome
Comprehension Processess
Making Connections
Generating Questions
Creating Mental Images
Making Inferences
Determining Importance
Synthesizing

K–W–L Plus Grid for Pythons

K (*know*)	W (*want to know*)	L (*learned*)
✓ • They squeeze things to death with their powerful coils. ✓ • They eat animals whole by swallowing them. • They can eat ~~cows and~~ humans. ✓ • There are a lot of them in the wild in Florida. • ~~They live in sewers in large cities.~~ ✓ • People keep them as pets. ✓ • The wild ones were once pets that people released. ✓ • They were originally from Africa.	• Do they bite as well as squeeze?	A—Kill by grasping the victim with their sharp teeth, coiling their bodies around the animal, and squeezing until it suffocates D—A type of constrictor D—May only need to eat four or five times a year
	• Are any of them poisonous?	NA
	• What do they look like?	D—Have beautifully colored skin D—Skin made into boots and shoes D—Reproduce rapidly D—Can reach 23 feet long and 200 pounds
	• What do they eat?	A—Eat mammals, birds, and even alligators A—Swallow their prey whole after squeezing to death
	• How many of them are there in the United States?	L—More than 1,800 removed from Everglades Park
	• Where are most of them in the United States? • Do they really live in sewers? • How dangerous are they?	L—Native to Africa, India, Indochina, and Indonesia L—Not likely to survive north of lower Florida E—Are seriously impacting the ecosystem in the Everglades E—May attack people when feeling threatened, although this rarely happens E—Hunt dogs, cats, and livestock (pigs, goats, and chickens) when near people D—Live on ground or in trees, excellent swimmers A—Young are hatched from eggs

Categories of information: A = abilities (what they do). D = description (how they look). E = effect (what effect(s) they have). L = location (where they live). NA = not answered.

How dangerous are they to humans? Do they bite as well as squeeze? (See the "W (*want to know*)" column in the K–W–L Plus Grid for Pythons example.)

3 Students read the selection or story. As they read, ask them to put a check mark next to any item in the "K (*know*)" column confirmed by the author and to put a line through any item contradicted by the author. In addition, students jot down answers to questions in the "W (*want to know*)" column that they discovered in the text. These can be recorded on their personal worksheets in the "L (*learned*)" column. Students note where in the text they obtained this information.

4 When students have completed their reading, focus their attention on the "L (*learned*)" column. Some items written in this column will represent information that answers questions in the "W (*want to know*)" column. In addition, ask students to offer new information they discovered in the reading and record this on the grid.

One variation is to create a graphic organizer that features an additional column. For this version of the strategy, reserve the "L (*learned*)" column for answers that were learned to the questions in the "W (*want to know*)" column. The new fourth column is labeled "N

(*new* learning)." Information that students deem important, but it did not surface in the "K (*know*)" or "L (*learned*)" column, is added here as new learning.

5 Guide students in categorizing their knowledge. (This is the "plus" stage of the strategy.) With partners or in groups, ask students to sort all information in the "K (*know*)" and "L (*learned*)" columns (and "N (*new* learning)" column if this variation is used) by deciding what items might meaningfully be placed with others. They then decide on a label for each grouping. Categories for pythons might include where they live (location), what they do (abilities), how they look (description), and their effects on an area (effect). Experienced students may complete this step independently, but many students will need guidance and direction in organizing the new information.

6 When the K–W–L Plus Grid is complete, create a Concept Map that brings together all the information under each category, designed by either the whole class or by students working in pairs or groups (see the Concept Map for Pythons). This synthesizing step organizes the information so students can express their understandings in writing assignments or other projects. Questions from the "W (*want to know*)" column that

Concept Map for Pythons

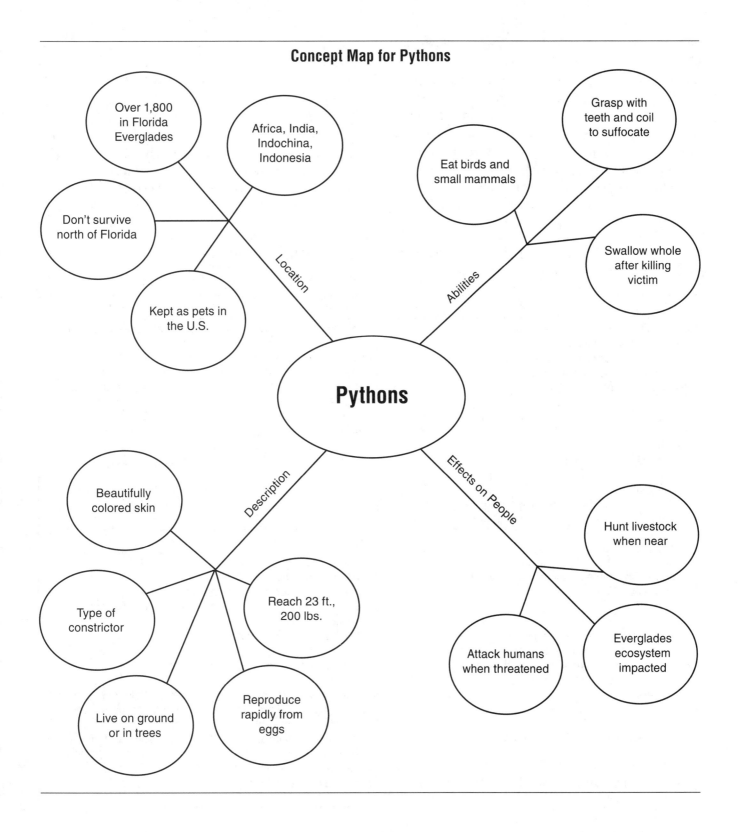

are not answered by the reading are regarded as hanging questions—questions we inevitably have after a learning episode that may provide the basis for future investigation and reading. Their Concept Maps and K–W–L Plus Grids provide organized notes for summarization and explanatory writing tasks.

Confirming to Extending Grid

The Confirming to Extending Grid (Buehl, 2011; reproducible available in the Appendix), a more advanced variation, guides students in examining a selection in phases, from brainstorming and questioning through reading and rereading.

1 Provide students with two to three minutes to generate their lists of what they have heard or might know about the topic. Then, students expand their lists with the Give One, Get One strategy (Schoenbach, Greenleaf, & Murphy, 2012). At this time, they circulate the room and share with three or four classmates, offering an item from their list that a classmate may not have and adding an item to their own list from the same classmate. Next, solicit items from the whole class, which are recorded in the "Confirming" box (see the Confirming to Extending Grid for Health and Fitness). These items are regarded as tentative, subject to confirmation by the author of the text(s) to be read.

2 Students next work with a partner, again for about three minutes, to generate two questions about the topic that a person might want answered. Solicit a question from each set of partners and enter these in the "Inquiring" box. Students do the same on their personal grids, so in effect the entire class has developed a questioning guide to be resolved by their reading.

Confirming to Extending Grid for Health and Fitness

Performance-Enhancing Drugs (PEDs)

Confirming	Revising

✓ • They help you build up your muscles.
✓ • You become much stronger.
✓ • You have more endurance and quickness.
✓ • There are a lot of ways for athletes to cheat today.
✓ • You can beat the testing process.
? • It seems like you will eventually get caught.
✓ • Many athletes believe it's worth the gamble of getting caught.
   • ~~They prevent injuries.~~
? • You get an unfair advantage.
   • Lance Armstrong and Alex Rodriguez were users.
✓ • Science is always coming up with new ways.
✓ • It's illegal, so you need to find a supplier.
✓ • You could have out-of-control "roid rage."
	• Steroids build muscle mass and strength because they are synthetic testosterone.
	• Diuretics are used as a masking agent to dilute urine.
	• "Designer steroids" are undetectable with current tests.
	• The competitive drive to win is fierce for serious athletes.
	• You can recover faster from injuries and also from tough workouts, so you can train harder, longer, and more frequently without damage.
	• PEDs are sold on the black market.
	• Aggressive behaviors, rage, violence, depression

Inquiring	**Resolving**
• How many athletes are guilty of using PEDs these days? • Can we ever come up with foolproof testing? • How many different types are there? • If some athletes are already benefiting from them, why not just permit everyone to use them legally? • Has anyone ever died from using them? • How dangerous are they to use? • What are the long-term risks? • How many kids are using PEDs? • Are other sports erasing records of athletes guilty of cheating, like in the Olympics and in cycling?	• "Doping" is increasingly common. • Not answered by the author • Anabolic steroids, androstendeione, human growth hormone, erythropoietin, diuretics, creatine, and stimulants are mentioned. • Not answered by the author • Suicides are related to depression from steroid use. • Males: breast growth, shrunken testicles, baldness; females: more body hair, infrequent periods, baldness; both: acne, liver damage, high blood pressure, heart problems • *Journal of Pediatrics* study: Nearly 40% of boys in middle and high school said they used protein supplements, and nearly 6% said they experimented with steroids. • Not answered by the author
Extending	
• Steroids can be taken as pills, through injections with needles, or as creams or lotions that are spread on. • Long-term studies of effects of high-dose usage hard to do; unethical to design such studies • Can stunt growth and development and cause future problems for teenage users • Because they're illegal, many made in other countries and smuggled in; no safety standards; could be impure • Steroids can increase bad cholesterol (LDL) and decrease good cholesterol (HDL). • Creatine a food supplement; related to short bursts of power; high dose could damage liver and kidneys • Human growth hormone only available by prescription; taken to improve muscle mass and performance	

3 Students read the text for the first time and confirm or refine the items in the "Confirming" box. As they read, students code places in the text (see the Text Coding strategy pages):

✓: Confirms what you knew or heard

X: Contradicts what you knew or heard

+: adds to what you knew or heard

Students then meet with partners to analyze the statements in the "Confirming" box and to evaluate the evidence from the text that they have identified. The intention during this phase is for students to be able to argue whether or not their statements were consistent with the author's. Statements that were confirmed can be checked off. Inconsistent statements need to be revised and entered in the adjoining "Revising" box. Additional information that elaborates on the statements (the + items) is also entered in the "Revising" box. As a class, solicit arguments and evidence for the "Confirming" items, and have the class draw a line through items contradicted by the author to note them as inaccurate. Finally, identify which items were neither confirmed nor disconfirmed because the author did not mention them.

4 Partners now team to reread and resolve the questions that surfaced for the class in the "Inquiring" box. Questions that can be resolved are answered in the "Resolving" box. Again, partners need to be prepared to cite specific evidence from the text to justify their answers. Invariably, some questions will not be resolved because they were not mentioned or satisfactorily dealt with by the author.

5 The final dynamic shifts to the last phase, the "Extending" box. Some of what the author has told readers will likely not have been anticipated in either the "Confirming" or "Inquiring" boxes. Partners undertake a third examination of the text to inventory additional items that seem significant and are not yet represented in their grids. These are entered in the "Extending" box as new learning. Again, solicit sharing from the whole class to wrap up the careful consideration of the author's message. Students can use their grids for summarizing, writing explanations, and developing supported arguments.

Advantages

- Teachers are provided with an inventory of students' background knowledge about a topic, and students remind themselves of what they already know about a topic.

- Class prior knowledge is pooled because students who know less about a topic are included in interactive conversations with students who bring more knowledge to the reading.

- Students are prompted to take an inquiring mindset toward reading, to use a text to address their questions, and to confirm and refine their previous understandings.

- Students are guided into meaningful organization of new information to synthesize their understandings.

- Student misconceptions about the topic are revealed and addressed during instruction.

- These strategies are appropriate for topics in social studies, science, and other curricular areas.

Meets the Standards

K–W–L Plus and the Confirming to Extending Grid promote careful reading and rereading of an author's message (R.1), discerning main ideas and summarizing (R.2), examining interrelationships of details or ideas (R.3), tracking the author's perspective and purpose (R.6), integrating ideas into visual representations (R.7), supporting argumentation (R.8), comparing and contrasting with other sources of knowledge and multiple texts (R.9), and mentoring the reading of complex literary and informational texts (R.10). In addition, the collaborative conversations develop expressing and defending thinking using visual displays (SL.1, SL.2, SL.4). Follow-up writing provides practice in using text-based evidence in supporting arguments (W.1), summarizing and explaining (W.2), and drawing evidence from texts for analysis and reflection (W.9). Vocabulary development includes attention to word relationships (L.5) and acquiring domain-specific vocabulary (L.6).

References

Buehl, D. (2011). *Developing readers in the academic disciplines*. Newark, DE: International Reading Association.

Carr, E., & Ogle, D. (1987). K–W–L Plus: A strategy for comprehension and summarization. *Journal of Reading, 30*(7), 626–631.

Ogle, D.M. (1986). K–W–L: A teaching model that develops active reading of expository text. *The Reading Teacher, 39*(6), 564–570. doi:10.1598/RT.39.6.11

Schoenbach, R., Greenleaf, C., & Murphy, L. (2012). *Reading for understanding: How reading apprenticeship improves disciplinary learning in secondary and college classrooms* (2nd ed.). San Francisco: Jossey-Bass.

Magnet Summaries

Imagine a team of scientists sifting through mounds of data from a host of experiments. What sense could be made out of such a formidable body of information? Amid this wealth of material, the group of researchers must decide what all of this means. Eventually, after carefully examining and analyzing their data, they will be able to develop an interpretation, a theory, or an explanation of the big picture that emerges from all the disparate slivers of detail. These scientists, like proficient readers, are able to synthesize.

As adults, on the job as well as in other aspects of daily life, we are bombarded by information that needs to be condensed to be understood. As readers, we constantly rely on synthesizing—the distillations by various experts, analysts, writers, and of course, ourselves—to render a bulk of information manageable for understanding.

Synthesizing takes place when a reader steps back from a text; sums up what is important; and goes on to make a generalization, create an interpretation, draw a conclusion, or posit an explanation. When proficient readers talk about a piece of meaningful text—a discussion about a news article, for example, or a book club chat about a novel—they do not just repeat what the text said. In addition, they offer their personal take on a selection: "That's not the way I read it." "I think the author was getting at…." "I think the character acted this way because…." In essence, proficient readers pause periodically to reflect and ponder the meaning of a text, and then eventually exclaim, "Aha! I get it!"

One key component of synthesizing is summarizing. Students often have a difficult time with summarizing what they read. Typically, students may produce a string of disconnected pieces of information or segments of a story but overlook the major themes or main ideas. Synthesizing combines summarizing—the ability to focus on the most important ideas and information—with a reader's perspective.

Using the Strategy

Magnet Summaries (Buehl, 1993) is a strategy that helps students rise above the details and construct meaningful summaries in their own words. Magnet Summaries involve the identification of key terms or concepts—magnet words—from a reading, which students use to organize important information into a summary.

1 To summarize, a reader must identify the most important ideas and omit details of lesser significance. An effective summary also includes paraphrasing—reinterpreting what was read in the reader's own words. As a prelude to summarizing, ask students to retell what they have read. Initial retellings, especially with younger students or struggling readers, can take on a rambling quality, which is a clear indicator that the teller has not yet developed the facility to cut to the chase. Likewise, some retellings may be unduly terse; too much is left out.

To help students focus during retellings, emphasize that all important elements or ideas need to be included and that smaller, less important details can be left out. When students are done, their retelling should make sense to the listener. They may also splice in personal commentary and reflections so their summaries begin to incorporate other aspects of synthesis. Paired reviews can be an excellent classroom vehicle for retellings (see the Paired Reviews strategy pages). Have partners take turns retelling what they have been reading (or watching in a video or listening to during a classroom presentation).

Oral paraphrasing practice can help students become comfortable with composing written summaries. Asking students to express their thinking in writing is a critical step in teaching them to summarize. Writing helps students realize what they have learned and provides them with a visual record of their thinking. Writing also allows students to refine their thinking as they

Strategy Index
Instructional Focus
Frontloading Learning
Guiding Comprehension
Consolidating Understanding
Text Frames
Cause/Effect
Concept/Definition
Problem/Solution
Compare/Contrast
Proposition/Support
Goal/Action/Outcome
Comprehension Processess
Making Connections
Generating Questions
Creating Mental Images
Making Inferences
Determining Importance
Synthesizing

revisit their thoughts, clarifying and expanding their understandings. Learning Logs provide an excellent transition into written summaries (see the discussion of Learning Logs in the Quick-Writes strategy pages). Classroom journaling encourages students to be more preoccupied with the dynamics of summarizing than the mechanics of writing.

2 Introduce the idea of magnet words to students by inquiring what effect a magnet has on certain metals. Just as magnets attract those metals, magnet words attract information. To illustrate, ask students to read a short portion of their text assignment, looking for a key term or concept to which the details in the passage seem to connect. After students finish reading, solicit from them possible magnet words, pointing out that these "attract" information in the passage. Note that magnet words frequently appear in titles and headings and may be highlighted in boldface or italic print, but caution students that not all boldface or italicized words are necessarily magnet words.

Write the magnet word on the whiteboard and ask students to recall important words or phrases from the passage that are connected to the magnet word. As you write these details around the magnet word, have students follow the same procedure on an index card. Allow them a second look at the passage so they can include any important details that they may have missed.

History students studying 19th-century Mexicano culture in the American Southwest may decide on the magnet term *cattle ranching* for one segment of the text. Key details surrounding this concept might include rancheros, longhorns, and huge tracts of land (see the Magnet Summaries for History).

3 Ask students to reread the passage and decide on three or four additional magnet words. Have students work with partners to negotiate what the remaining magnet words should be as they determine the main ideas of each text segment. Distribute additional index cards for recording magnet words decided on by each set of partners. For younger students, target text of a more modest length and indicate that they should identify a magnet word for each paragraph or section following a heading. Next, have partners generate the important terms or details for each magnet word, which are recorded on the front of the card. When the teams are finished, each student will have four or five cards, each with a magnet word and key related information.

4 Model for students how the information on one card can be organized and combined into a sentence that sums up the passage. The magnet word should occupy a central place in the sentence. Omit any unimportant details from the sentence.

Have students continue to work with partners to construct sentences that summarize each of their remaining cards. Urge students to combine information into one sentence, although it may be necessary to construct two sentences for a particular card. They may decide to omit some details if they judge them to be of secondary importance. Have students write their sentences on scratch paper first. Then, instruct them to put the final version of each sentence on the back of the appropriate card and underline the magnet words. For example, the card for *cattle ranching* might be summarized as follows:

> Many Mexicanos were rancheros who needed huge tracts of land for their <u>cattle ranching</u> because their longhorn cattle were left on the range to graze, which is why the cattle needed to be branded.

5 Direct students to arrange the sentences in the order they wish their summary to read. At this point, the sentences will need to be altered so they flow smoothly from one to the other. Model inserting connectives and other language that integrate the sentences into a summary. At this point, students should also judge whether all the important ideas have been included and whether anything further can be deleted. Students can then test their summaries by listening to how they sound when they are read aloud. The following example is a Magnet Summary for a history passage on Mexicano life in the Southwest:

> Many Mexicanos were rancheros who needed huge tracts of land for their cattle ranching because their longhorn cattle were left on the range to graze. This is why the cattle needed to be branded. Vaqueros, who wore sombreros for protection from the hot sun and invented the western saddle, were Mexicano cowboys who worked on the ranches. Vaqueros were skilled in roping the cattle with lariats during rodeos, which was when they had roundups of the longhorn cattle. Mexicanos lived in homes with thick walls, made from bricks called adobe, and tile roofs. These homes were necessary because of the hot, dry climate of the Southwest. Many Mexicano homes had courtyards called patios where people could spend time. Mexicanos started food traditions that combined Old World foods such as corn, which they made into tortillas, and beans, which they made into chili, with New World foods such as oranges and lemons, which they grew using irrigation because of the lack of water.

Advantages

- Students learn to prioritize what they need to remember, and they develop facility in separating main ideas from supporting details.

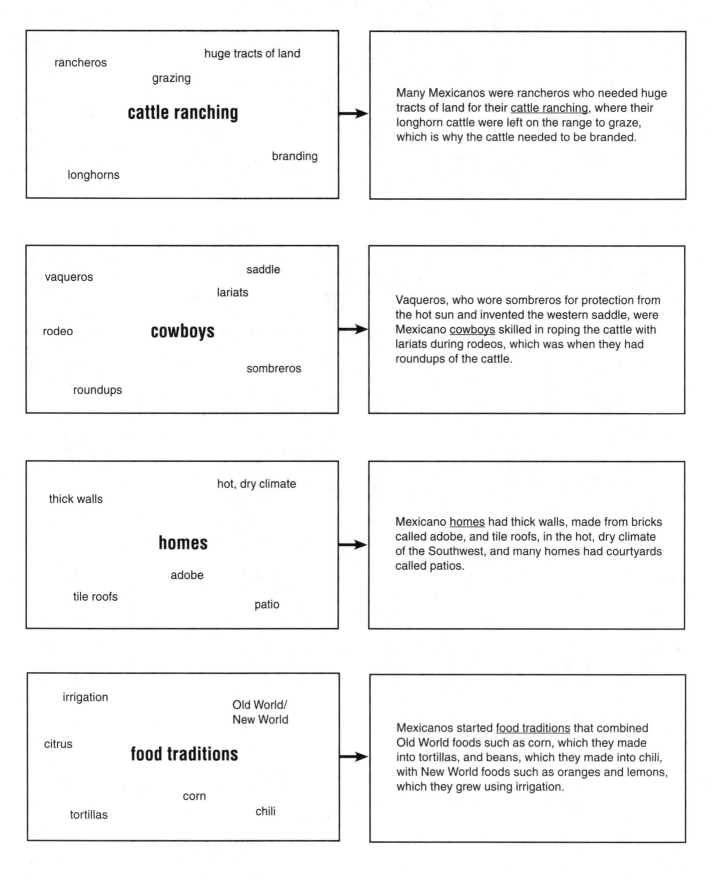

rancheros

huge tracts of land

grazing

cattle ranching

branding

longhorns

Many Mexicanos were rancheros who needed huge tracts of land for their <u>cattle ranching</u>, where their longhorn cattle were left on the range to graze, which is why the cattle needed to be branded.

vaqueros

saddle

lariats

rodeo

cowboys

sombreros

roundups

Vaqueros, who wore sombreros for protection from the hot sun and invented the western saddle, were Mexicano <u>cowboys</u> skilled in roping the cattle with lariats during rodeos, which was when they had roundups of the cattle.

thick walls

hot, dry climate

homes

adobe

tile roofs

patio

Mexicano <u>homes</u> had thick walls, made from bricks called adobe, and tile roofs, in the hot, dry climate of the Southwest, and many homes had courtyards called patios.

irrigation

Old World/ New World

citrus

food traditions

corn

tortillas

chili

Mexicanos started <u>food traditions</u> that combined Old World foods such as corn, which they made into tortillas, and beans, which they made into chili, with New World foods such as oranges and lemons, which they grew using irrigation.

- Students flesh out their understandings of key vocabulary and ideas.
- Students gain practice in reducing texts to their most essential elements, allowing them to reflect on their personal understandings of what a text means.

Meets the Standards

Magnet Summaries promote careful reading and re-reading of an author's message (R.1), discerning main ideas and summarizing (R.2), examining interrelationships of details or ideas (R.3), interpreting word meanings (R.4), analyzing text structure (R.5), and mentoring the reading of complex literary and informational texts (R.10). In addition, the collaborative conversations develop expressing and defending thinking (SL.1, SL.3, SL.4). The writing phase provides practice in using text-based evidence in summarizing and explaining (W.2) and drawing evidence from texts for analysis and reflection (W.9). Vocabulary development includes determining and clarifying key vocabulary (L.4), attention to word relationships (L.5), and acquiring domain-specific vocabulary (L.6).

Reference

Buehl, D. (1993). Magnetized: Students are drawn to technique that identifies key words. *WEAC News & Views, 29*(4), 13.

Suggested Readings

Hayes, D.A. (1989). Helping students GRASP the knack of writing summaries. *Journal of Reading, 33*(2), 96–101.

Vacca, R.T., Vacca, J.A.L., & Mraz, M.E. (2010). *Content area reading: Literacy and learning across the curriculum* (10th ed.). Boston: Pearson.

Math Reading Keys

An angle ∠ is formed by two rays with the same endpoint. The rays are the sides of the angle. The endpoint is the vertex of the angle. One way to measure an angle is in degrees. To indicate the size or degree measure of an angle, write a lowercase *m* in front of the angle symbol, as in *m*∠A = 62. (adapted from Charles et al., 2012, pp. 27–28)

Hmmm, let's see here. An angle is formed when two rays, which are straight lines, come together and touch. The parts of the angle are the rays, which are the sides, and the vertex, which is the point where they touch. The size, or how big the angle is, is indicated by degrees. I wonder how degrees in angles compare with degrees in temperature.

Increasingly, the Common Core's mathematics standards and assessments expect students to develop the capacity to access mathematics knowledge through reading. But as the geometry example illustrates, math texts present special challenges for students. Mathematics language is very precise and compact; each sentence conveys a heavy load of conceptual information. Mathematics authors emphasize previous learning; readers are expected to bring a great deal of prior knowledge to their reading of complex mathematics texts. In particular, readers are assumed to be fluent in using the discourse of math vocabulary. In addition, many students bring a mind-set that math is only the manipulation of numbers, an overemphasis on procedural knowledge. They glide over the conceptual passages that explain the mathematical relationships in an attempt to jump right into solving problems. Consequently, students become dependent on the teacher to clear up misunderstandings.

Readers of mathematics texts must integrate knowledge that is communicated in three platforms: the succinct, terminology-dense prose sections; the symbolic notation displaying numerical relationships; and graphic representations. Readers must also transition from thinking about the logic and relationships of conceptual knowledge to applying these understandings to procedural knowledge (see Tables 9 and 10 in Chapter 4). Hence, students must take a decidedly different approach to reading math texts compared with social studies, science, or literature.

Using the Strategies

The Math Reading Keys strategy (Buehl, 1998) provides a protocol for helping students navigate the unique features of complex mathematics texts as readers and learners. Math Reading Keys is a variation of Interactive Reading Guides, which involves students collaborating in teams to work their understanding of a complex text (see the Interactive Reading Guides strategy pages). Review/New Charts (Buehl, 2011) is a related strategy that facilitates revisiting and verbalizing mathematics concepts and vocabulary.

1 Use Questioning the Author to introduce math reading strategies (see the Questioning the Author strategy pages). There are two especially significant questions for math: What does the author assume I already know? and What previous math concepts does this author expect me to remember? Students need to approach math text with careful deliberation and constantly confirm their understandings, especially of math terminology. Close reading, which mandates rereading, is a necessity for comprehension of complex math texts.

2 Model how to read a challenging section of text. Project a short section from a text and have students follow along as you think aloud. Highlight hidden knowledge—spots where the author thinks readers have sufficient knowledge and therefore need no further explanation. For example, a passage on absolute value in a pre-algebra text states,

> Integers are the set of whole numbers, including 0, and their opposites. The sum of two opposite integers is 0. One way to add integers is to use absolute value. The absolute value of a number is its distance from 0. The absolute value

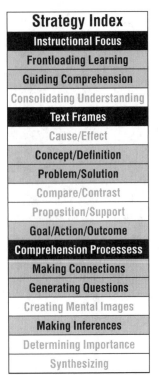

Strategy Index

Instructional Focus
Frontloading Learning
Guiding Comprehension
Consolidating Understanding
Text Frames
Cause/Effect
Concept/Definition
Problem/Solution
Compare/Contrast
Proposition/Support
Goal/Action/Outcome
Comprehension Processess
Making Connections
Generating Questions
Creating Mental Images
Making Inferences
Determining Importance
Synthesizing

of −4, written as |−4| is 4, and the absolute value of 5 is 5. If the signs are the same, find the sum of the absolute values. Use the same sign as the integers. If the signs are different, find the difference of the absolute values. Use the sign of the integer with the larger absolute value. (adapted from Bennett et al., 2008, p. 60)

Your think-aloud on this passage might unfold as follows:

> Integers—the authors tell me what these are, whole numbers and their opposites. The authors must think I know what whole numbers are because they don't define them. They give examples (0, 4, −4, and 5), and I remember that *whole number* means it's not a fraction or decimal. Absolute value seems a key idea here, and this seems a little confusing, so I better reread this part carefully: "distance from 0." I know a number can go either way from 0, positive or negative, so absolute value seems to be the number of places from 0. Absolute value looks like it will always be expressed as a positive number because it reflects how many places from 0.

3 Hand out copies of the Math Reading Keys Bookmark (see the example; reproducible available in the Appendix) and point out how your think-aloud followed the steps on the bookmark. Use an analogy such as reading the operating manual for a piece of equipment or reading instructions for assembling an item. Often these documents are frustrating to read, so it is tempting to discard them and figure out what to do on your own, running the risk of making an important or costly error. Instead, it may be necessary to read the material several times, consult with another person, or eventually translate the confusing instructions into something you can understand.

4 Pair students with partners to read portions of a math text together during class time. Typically, such reading is assigned as independent work, and many students skip it and attempt to solve problems by following examples in the text. Or students are not even asked to read the text, and instruction focuses solely on the teacher telling and showing what students need to know. As students follow the Math Reading Keys and reach points of confusion, they check with their peers and practice verbalizing their understandings.

5 Encourage students to compile their own explanations of key terms in an interactive notebook or on index cards. Students often discover that terms not sufficiently explained in a chapter are equally unclear in the book's glossary. For example, the precise glossary definition of *scientific notation*—a streamlined way of representing extremely large or small numbers—can be explained in a more student-friendly way (see the Translating Math Terms Into Student-Friendly

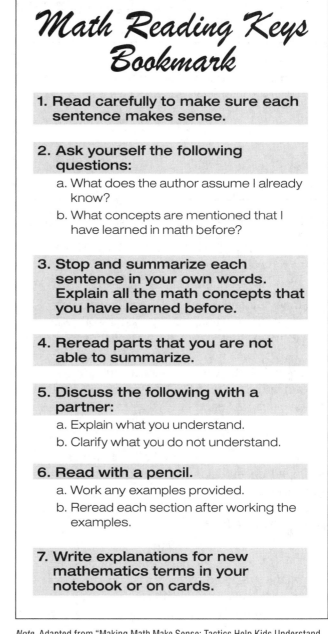

Math Reading Keys Bookmark

1. **Read carefully to make sure each sentence makes sense.**

2. **Ask yourself the following questions:**
   a. What does the author assume I already know?
   b. What concepts are mentioned that I have learned in math before?

3. **Stop and summarize each sentence in your own words. Explain all the math concepts that you have learned before.**

4. **Reread parts that you are not able to summarize.**

5. **Discuss the following with a partner:**
   a. Explain what you understand.
   b. Clarify what you do not understand.

6. **Read with a pencil.**
   a. Work any examples provided.
   b. Reread each section after working the examples.

7. **Write explanations for new mathematics terms in your notebook or on cards.**

Note. Adapted from "Making Math Make Sense: Tactics Help Kids Understand Math Language," by D. Buehl, 1998, *WEAC News & Views, 34*(3), p. 17. Copyright © 1998 by Doug Buehl.

Explanations example and the Student-Friendly Vocabulary Explanations strategy pages). Urge students to treat difficult math language the same way they would a foreign language. For example, once they translate a sentence from Spanish into English, it makes more sense. They must also get into the habit of translating "math talk" into English so it, too, is personally meaningful. This step combines the precision of math vocabulary, which is essential, with synthesizing personal understanding, which is necessary for comprehension.

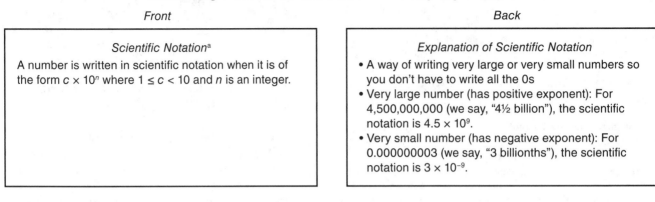

Translating Math Terms Into Student-Friendly Explanations

Front

Scientific Notation[a]

A number is written in scientific notation when it is of the form $c \times 10^n$ where $1 \leq c < 10$ and n is an integer.

Back

Explanation of Scientific Notation

- A way of writing very large or very small numbers so you don't have to write all the 0s
- Very large number (has positive exponent): For 4,500,000,000 (we say, "4½ billion"), the scientific notation is 4.5×10^9.
- Very small number (has negative exponent): For 0.000000003 (we say, "3 billionths"), the scientific notation is 3×10^{-9}.

Note. Adapted from *Classroom Strategies for Interactive Learning* (3rd ed., p. 117), by D. Buehl, 2009, Newark, DE: International Reading Association. Copyright © 2009 by the International Reading Association.
[a]Definition from *Algebra 1* (p. 512), by R. Larson, L. Boswell, T.D. Kanold, and L. Stiff, 2009, Evanston, IL: McDougall Littell. Copyright © 2009 by McDougall Littell.

---

6 Have students create a classroom dictionary of key math terms. Then, have students work with partners to write student-friendly explanations that can be voted on by the entire class. The explanations for each term voted as the easiest to understand are placed on a word wall as the official classroom dictionary. An option is to fold sheets of letter-sized card-stock paper in half to form individual flip charts, which are tacked to the word wall. The math term with its precise definition is placed on the front. When the card is flipped up, students will find their student-friendly explanation.

Review/New Charts

The Review/New Charts strategy (Buehl, 2011) guides students in creating a graphic display of conceptual knowledge triggered by math vocabulary in a section of text. Students assume the responsibility for working a math text to establish understanding of new concepts.

1 Initially, it is desirable to permit students to highlight a portion of math text as they read. Provide them with a photocopied section from the currently used math text. Hand each student two highlighters of different colors (e.g., one yellow, one pink). Instruct students to be consistent in their color coding:

- Highlight in yellow all math terms encountered previously (the author assumes I already know this).

- Highlight in pink all new math terms learned in this lesson (the author is introducing new math concepts and procedures).

2 Organize students into collaborative groups to compare their highlighting choices. Invariably, students will perceive that most of the text will be highlighted in yellow because math language heavily relies on explanations of new concepts using the terminology acquired from previous math learning. The group then records all terms in yellow in the "Review" column of a Review/New Chart (reproducible available in the Appendix). These review terms represent math vocabulary that students should be comfortable using, although many will recognize the terms but will not be sufficiently practiced in verbalizing their understandings. For example, students embarking on a study of polynomials will confront a great deal of review terms in the opening section of this math concept (see the Review/New Chart for Polynomials).

The group then rehearses explaining each review item. The expectation is that each member of the group is prepared to adequately explain all of the review items. It is the group's responsibility to ensure that all members are confident in elaborating all items under review. Hence, the group needs to be engaged in sufficient conversation, and all members are expected to participate in depth.

3 The group then repeats the process for all new items, highlighted in pink, which are entered in the "New" column of the Review/New Chart. The explanations of review terms have laid the groundwork for explaining all new terms presented in the lesson. Again, each member needs to feel sufficiently prepped to be called on to explain any new item from the chart.

4 Call on individual members to offer their explanations of review items during whole-class sharing. Ask, Is this explanation complete, or does something more need to be added to our understanding of this concept? Continue with the discussion about the new math terms.

Review/New Chart for Polynomials

Review	New
expression	monomial
real number	polynomial
variable	binomial
product	trinomial
whole number	
exponent	
degree	
constant	
term	
like term	
sum	
standard form	

Note. Developed from a strategy by Rita Crotty, Hempstead High School, Dubuque, IA.

Advantages

- Students learn strategies that can aid them in understanding conceptually dense texts.

- Students are encouraged to consider how effectively an author has communicated information and to solve problems when things are not clear.

- Students learn to translate text into more personal and understandable language and to make connections to prior knowledge.

- Students learn to collaborate as problem solvers of challenging texts rather than merely relying on the teacher to tell them the information.

Meets the Standards

Math Reading Keys and Review/New Charts promote careful reading and rereading of an author's message (R.1), discerning main ideas and summarizing (R.2), examining interrelationships of details or ideas (R.3), interpreting word meaning (R.4), analyzing text structure (R.5), tracking the author's perspective and purpose (R.6), integrating ideas with visual representations (R.7), using text-based evidence for supporting argumentation (R.8), comparing and contrasting with other sources of knowledge (R.9), and mentoring the reading of complex literary and informational texts (R.10). In addition, the collaborative conversations develop expressing and defending thinking using visual displays (SL.1, SL.2, SL.4). Follow-up writing can provide practice in using text-based evidence for supporting justifications for problem solving (W.1), summarizing and explaining (W.2), and drawing evidence from texts for analysis and reflection (W.9). Vocabulary development includes determining and clarifying key vocabulary (L.4), attention to word relationships (L.5), and acquiring domain-specific vocabulary (L.6).

References

Buehl, D. (1998). Making math make sense: Tactics help kids understand math language. *WEAC News & Views, 34*(3), 17.

Buehl, D. (2009). *Classroom strategies for interactive learning* (3rd ed.). Newark, DE: International Reading Association.

Buehl, D. (2011). *Developing readers in the academic disciplines.* Newark, DE: International Reading Association.

Literature Cited

Bennett, J.M., Chard, D.J., Jackson, A., Milgram, J., Scheer, J.K., & Waits, B.K. (2008). *Pre-algebra.* Austin, TX: Holt, Rinehart and Winston.

Charles, R.I., Hall, B., Kennedy, D., Bass, L.E., Johnson, A., Murphy, S.J., & Wiggins, G. (2012). *Geometry: Vol. 2. Common Core.* Boston: Pearson.

Larson, R., Boswell, L., Kanold, T.D., & Stiff, L. (2009). *Algebra 1.* Evanston, IL: McDougal Littell.

Suggested Reading

Beck, I.L., McKeown, M.G., Hamilton, R.L., & Kucan, L. (1997). *Questioning the author: An approach for enhancing student engagement with text.* Newark, DE: International Reading Association.

Mind Mapping

Drive down Leonardo Street for about 10 blocks until you come to the second set of lights. Turn left onto Raphael and go about three blocks until you see a Supermart. Continue another 1/2 block and take the first right. You're now on Botticelli Boulevard, which winds through a subdivision and then along a heavily wooded park. When you come to the railroad intersection, go about 1/4 mile until you see the Lutheran church. Take a sharp left on Van Gogh and...

What we really need here is a map! Even in the verbal environment of these GPS-guided times, we still rely on these visual representations that are designed to guide us to our destinations. Maps allow us to perceive how the necessary information is connected within the context of the larger picture. They let us see where we are going, and alert us to important signposts along the way. Likewise, students find that visual representations, such as maps, displaying major concepts and their relationships can make journeys through a complex text more navigable. Buzan (1991) describes visual representations, or graphic organizers, that demonstrate connections among key concepts and ideas as Mind Maps.

Using the Strategy

Mind Maps are structured outlines that can effectively introduce new material to students (Barron, 1969; Tierney & Readence, 2004).

1 Analyze a passage that students will read in terms of the important ideas and concepts. Next, identify key facts and vocabulary from the reading that students will use for developing an understanding of these concepts. Ignore any difficult terms in the text that are not essential to learning the central ideas so students do not get sidetracked by terms that are only of secondary importance when they read (see the discussion of Fact Pyramids in Chapter 3). For example, as a science teacher peruses a chapter on soil in an earth science textbook, she decides on the following central concepts:

- Soil consists of particles of weathered rock, decayed organic matter, air, and water.

- Soil is layered into topsoil, subsoil, and a dense bottom layer, each of which contains different soil combinations.

- Soil has four variations of structure, ranging from small, loosely connected particles that are advantageous for growing plants to very dense, compact forms.

Key academic vocabulary for this chapter might be Tier 3 words, such as *topsoil*, *subsoil*, *humus*, *leaching*, *granular*, *platy*, *blocky*, *prismatic*, and *weathering*, and Tier 2 words, such as *infiltration* and *horizon* (see the discussion of Tier 2 and Tier 3 words in the Student-Friendly Vocabulary Explanations strategy pages).

2 Organize key concepts and vocabulary into a Mind Map that shows relationships and connections among the terms (see the Mind Map for Science). Include visual elements, such as arrows, boxes, circles, and pictorial representations, or other creative touches to make the Mind Map more vivid and memorable. In addition to specific vocabulary featured in the reading, include relevant terms that students already know. These familiar verbal landmarks will help students recognize how the material fits into their current background knowledge of the subject. In the soil example, add references to plants, topsoil, and the relationship of earthworms and small animals in developing soil conditions.

3 Present the map to the class to frontload learning the new material. Project the Mind Map to the entire class or provide students with individual copies to discuss as a collaborative group activity. Encourage students to speculate on the meanings of new vocabulary terms and the nature of the

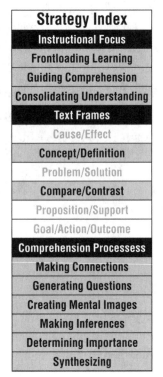

Mind Map for Science

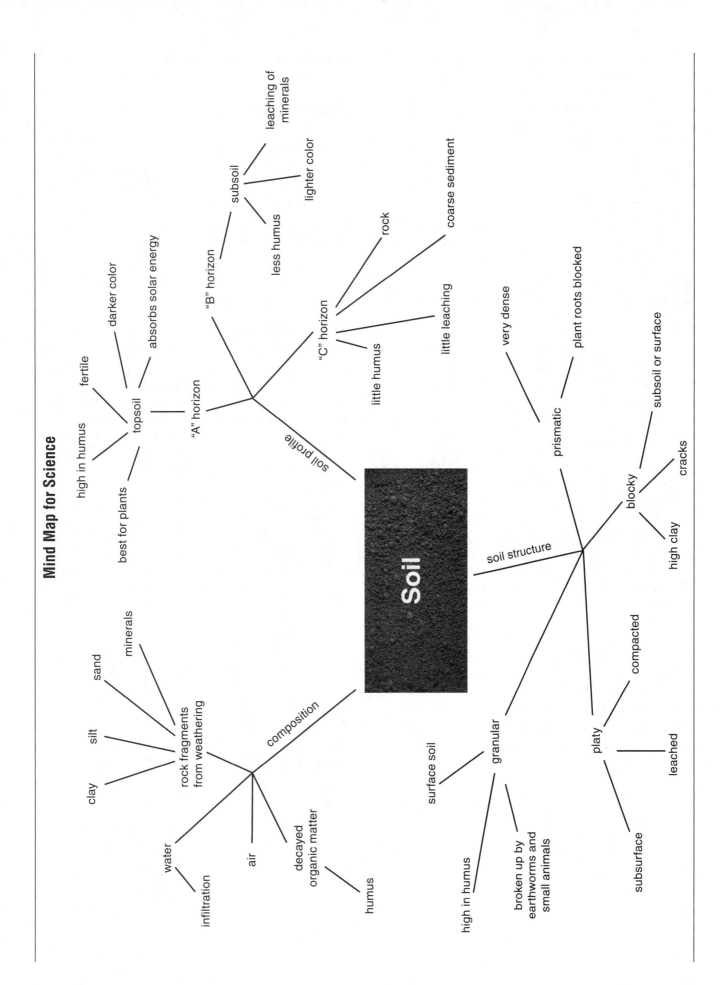

Soil

soil profile
- "A" horizon
  - topsoil
    - fertile
      - darker color
      - absorbs solar energy
    - high in humus
    - best for plants
- "B" horizon
  - subsoil
    - leaching of minerals
    - lighter color
    - less humus
- "C" horizon
  - rock
  - coarse sediment
  - little leaching
  - little humus

composition
- rock fragments from weathering
  - minerals
  - sand
  - silt
  - clay
- water
  - infiltration
- air
- decayed organic matter
  - humus

soil structure
- prismatic
  - very dense
  - plant roots blocked
- blocky
  - subsoil or surface
  - cracks
  - high clay
- platy
  - compacted
  - leached
  - subsurface
- granular
  - surface soil
  - high in humus
  - broken up by earthworms and small animals

relationships among concepts. Stimulate discussions with open-ended questions, such as, What can you tell me by looking at this overview?

One effective method for encouraging investigation of the Mind Map is the Expert/Novice variation of the Think/Pair/Share strategy (see the Paired Reviews strategy pages). Have students work as partners, with one student designated as the "expert" and the other as the "novice." When both have had ample opportunity to examine the map, the expert describes what the topic is about by systematically going through the Mind Map, and the novice talks about elements that remain confusing and will need to be clarified by the reading.

4 Recommend to students that they should consult their Mind Maps while reading the new selection. To prompt the use of these Mind Maps as guides, ask students to add new terminology, both from the text and from their experiences, as they make connections while reading. After reading, have students return to their collaborative groups to incorporate any additional important ideas and terms into the maps.

5 After students have practice with Mind Maps, they can use the strategy in a variety of ways:

- Students can add illustrations to represent key terms, and color code each offshoot of information from the central concept with highlighters.

- Students can create their own Mind Maps by using a list of important concepts and terms. This is especially effective for helping students see relationships within material they have just read and can be done both individually and in small groups (see the discussion of Concept Maps in the K–W–L Plus strategy pages).

- Students can select their own list of important concepts and terms from a passage and create a Mind Map that represents their understanding of the relationships. In addition, they can add information to their maps from their background knowledge.

- Students can be assigned to map a text and present the overview to fellow students as a way to introduce a new reading.

- Students can use their Mind Maps to write a summary of the material to synthesize their understanding.

Advantages

- Students see a visual display of the whole picture of an informational text.

- Students are provided with an outline of major ideas and relationships among important pieces of information in a text to guide them as they read.

- Students encounter and discuss new vocabulary before reading a challenging passage.

- Students are encouraged to consider how their prior knowledge fits into the new material that they will be studying.

Meets the Standards

Mind Mapping promotes careful reading and rereading of an author's message (R.1), discerning main ideas and summarizing (R.2), examining interrelationships of details or ideas (R.3), interpreting word meaning (R.4), analyzing text structure (R.5), interpreting visual representations (R.7), and mentoring the reading of complex literary and informational texts (R.10). In addition, the collaborative conversations develop expressing and defending thinking using visual displays (SL.1, SL.2, SL.4). Follow-up writing provides practice in using text-based evidence in summarizing and explaining (W.2) and drawing evidence from texts for analysis and reflection (W.9). Vocabulary development includes determining and clarifying key vocabulary (L.4), attention to word relationships (L.5), and acquiring domain-specific vocabulary (L.6).

References

Barron, R.F. (1969). The use of vocabulary as an advance organizer. In H.L. Herber & P.L. Sanders (Eds.), *Research in reading in the content areas: First year report* (pp. 29–39). Syracuse, NY: Reading and Language Arts Center, Syracuse University.

Buzan, T. (1991). *Use both sides of your brain* (3rd ed.). New York: Plume.

Tierney, R.J., & Readence, J.E. (2004). *Reading strategies and practices: A compendium* (6th ed.). Boston: Allyn & Bacon.

Paired Reviews

"Time out!" In the middle of a frantically paced basketball game, a player's hands signal a *T*. At a crucial juncture during a football game, a coach wants the clock stopped. Often during athletic competitions, coaches and players need to pause the proceedings to take stock of events and plot adjustments necessary for a successful outcome.

Students, too, can benefit from a pause in the action. At times during the flow of new learning, students need to signal for a time-out so they can collect their thoughts and reflect on their understandings. Like athletes, students may need to catch up, raise questions, clear up confusions, and set their minds for what will happen next.

Proficient readers know that understanding is not a one-step process. Often, we need to revisit what is being learned to make sure we understand. Therefore, a momentary pause clears up uncertainties and helps us mentally reconstruct material so it makes sense. Reflecting, clarifying, and paraphrasing are automatic responses during learning.

However, many students cling to the habit of reading new material only once, whether they truly understand it or not. They may become preoccupied with completing an assignment rather than pondering the meaning of a passage. As a result, students' reading becomes a race to get done and close the book, and they retain only a vague notion of what was read. Classroom strategies that encourage rereading, review, and reflection are a necessary step for synthesizing students' understandings.

Paired Reviews strategies enhance clarifying and paraphrasing skills and establish regular patterns of brief interruptions, which allow students to process what they are learning.

Using the Strategies

Steps for using five different Paired Reviews strategies—3-Minute Pause (McTighe, as discussed in Marzano et al., 1992), Paired Verbal Fluency (Costa, 1997), Think/Pair/Share (McTighe & Lyman, 1988), Reflect/Reflect/Reflect (Costa, 1997), and Line-Up Reviews (Buehl, 2003)—are outlined in this section.

3-Minute Pause

During 3-Minute Pause, students engage in the following three modes of thinking:

1. Summarizing what they have learned
2. Identifying interesting aspects or making connections to what they already know
3. Questioning what they find confusing or do not understand

1 Introduce 3-Minute Pause by asking students to imagine themselves working for an extended period at a computer, perhaps writing an essay or working on a project. Then, without saving their work, they turn off the computer. Students will likely gasp and blurt out that all that work is gone forever. Some may offer instances when they neglected to save and irretrievably lost work that they had labored over and subsequently had to redo. Recount personal instances when you were lax in saving and lost your work. Computer experts recommend that you save frequently so unexpected problems do not wipe out your work.

Extend the analogy to classroom learning. If you do not pause every few minutes to think about what you are hearing, viewing, or reading, then you are not saving or retaining the information. New information may be stored in memory banks for a limited period, but much of it will be heard, seen, or experienced and then forgotten soon afterward. By pausing every 10 or 15 minutes to think through new material, emphasize that you are in effect beginning to save it in your memory.

2 Have students work with partners for a lesson or unit. Each pair decides who is Partner A and Partner B. When a 3-Minute Pause is called, either A or B is selected to

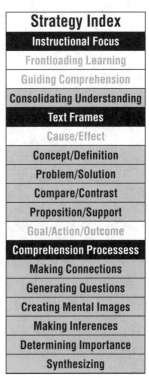

Strategy Index

Strategy Index
Instructional Focus
Frontloading Learning
Guiding Comprehension
Consolidating Understanding
Text Frames
Cause/Effect
Concept/Definition
Problem/Solution
Compare/Contrast
Proposition/Support
Goal/Action/Outcome
Comprehension Processess
Making Connections
Generating Questions
Creating Mental Images
Making Inferences
Determining Importance
Synthesizing

summarize, question, and identify interesting information for his or her partner. Project a timer (e.g., www.online-stopwatch.com) to accentuate the urgency of moving directly to task to complete the duties within the specified time period. For example, in a history class viewing a film clip on Mahatma Gandhi's non-violent protests, pause the film after a few minutes for reflection.

3 During the pause, Partner A summarizes key points, and Partner B comments on both familiar and confusing material. At the next pause, reverse these roles.

Paired Verbal Fluency

Paired Verbal Fluency is a similar strategy that provides practice in summing up what has been read or learned. Students take turns reviewing with a partner what they learned from a reading, video, class presentation, or discussion. Emphasize the concept of airtime from television and radio: When broadcasting live, you need to completely fill your allotted airtime to avoid a silent stretch of dead air. Again, using a timer is imperative.

1 Pair students as Partner A and Partner B. Partner A begins by recounting something memorable or interesting in the material and talks steadily for 60 seconds while Partner B listens. Then, tell the partners to switch and change roles. Partner B starts talking and cannot repeat anything recalled by Partner A.

2 When Partner B has talked for 60 seconds, tell the partners to switch again. Now, Partner A has 40 seconds to continue the review. Again, stipulate that nothing stated by either partner can be repeated. Announce another switch in which Partner B gets a 40-second turn.

3 Follow the same pattern, allowing each partner 20 seconds to recap. This strategy is a fast-paced way for students to summarize their learning. The no-repeat rule forces partners to dig deeper into the information and listen carefully during the review rather than mentally rehearsing what to say when roles switch. The lengths of each time period can be adjusted to fit the needs of the students, and when the activity is completed, confusions or questions that surfaced during the review can be addressed. Allowing students access to their notes or textbook during the review is optional.

Think/Pair/Share

This strategy is an extended version of the 3-Minute Pause strategy.

1 Provide students with a specific question or issue to consider, allowing them a short wait time to ponder their thinking individually. A Quick-Write (see the Quick-Writes strategy pages) can also provide individual students this time for processing thinking.

2 Have students discuss the topic in pairs. In addition to discussion, ask students to engage in other types of thinking during this phase, such as reaching a consensus on an issue, solving a problem, or arguing an opposing position.

3 As a variation of Think/Pair/Share, have one partner assume the role of "expert," as though he or she were explaining new content to the "novice," his or her partner. The expert must talk about material so a person unfamiliar with the information can understand it. Concepts and vocabulary unknown to a novice must be translated so they make sense. The novice asks clarifying questions and repeats what is understood about the content to the expert, who verifies whether the novice understood correctly and clears up any misunderstandings.

As students become more independent, have them practice the expert role with people outside of class. For example, a student studying chemistry might explain the day's concepts to a parent or sibling. The challenge is to translate the technical language of chemistry into layman's terms. If the listener understands, then the student knows that the content has been successfully paraphrased.

Reflect/Reflect/Reflect

As students become more comfortable with retelling what they learned, engage them in Reflect/Reflect/Reflect, a more sophisticated strategy for paraphrasing and clarifying. The strategy involves dividing students into groups of three. Each member of the triad, Partners A, B, and C, takes a turn assuming the roles of authority, reporter, and observer (see the Reflect/Reflect/Reflect Outline). To help students understand the roles, ask them to imagine a news program in which a reporter interacts with an authority about a topic (or show a short film clip of such an interaction). Ask students to notice how the authority presents information and personal thoughts about the topic; the reporter at times summarizes the authority's words and asks clarifying questions, or delves into the authority's attitudes and emotions; and the observer (the TV viewer) takes stock of what the authority is saying and what the reporter is summarizing and clarifying. At times, the observer may want to declaim at the screen, "But what about...?" or "That's not exactly right!"

1 Allow the authority two minutes to talk about a part of the reading material that was interesting,

Reflect/Reflect/Reflect Outline

Step 1: Partner A (authority) presents information and personal thoughts about information. Partner B (reporter) summarizes information presented by the authority ("I heard you say..."). Partner C (observer) comments on the presentation and summary (Was anything missed or incorrectly stated? Is anything still unclear?).

Step 2: Switch roles. Partner B (authority) presents information and personal thoughts about the information. Partner C (reporter) summarizes the information presented by the authority ("I heard you say...") and asks questions to clarify or get more information ("I was wondering..."). Partner A (observer) comments on the presentation and summary (Was anything missed or incorrectly stated? Is anything still unclear?).

Step 3: Switch roles again. Partner C (authority) presents information and personal thoughts about the information. Partner A (reporter) summarizes the information presented by the authority ("I heard you say..."), asks questions to clarify or get more information ("I was wondering..."), and notes the authority's emotions ("You seem to feel..."). Partner B (observer) comments on the reporter's presentation and summary (Was anything missed or incorrectly stated? Is anything still unclear?).

Note. Adapted from *Classroom Strategies for Interactive Learning* (2nd ed., p. 90), by D. Buehl, 2001, Newark, DE: International Reading Association. Copyright © 2001 by the International Reading Association.

---

familiar, confusing, or perhaps difficult to learn. Assign the reporter the task of paraphrasing what the authority says. Ask the observer to comment on the accuracy of the reporter's paraphrasing and note whether any important information was omitted.

2 Students read the next passage. Partners switch to different roles and proceed as they did in step 1. But this time, the reporter must not only paraphrase the authority's remarks but also clarify them by asking questions. The observer evaluates the paraphrasing and comments on whether questions were clarified.

3 Students read the next portion of text. Partners now assume their remaining roles, with the authority continuing as before. This time, the reporter does three things: paraphrases; asks questions to clarify; and identifies emotions exhibited by the authority, such as excitement, frustration, confusion, or disagreement. This step brings empathy with a fellow learner into the interaction. The observer completes the activity as before, commenting on the paraphrasing, clarifying, and empathizing.

Line-Up Reviews

Line-Up Reviews (Buehl, 2003) is an especially effective strategy for exam review. Students can be asked to predict a specific piece of information they think might appear on an exam, explain it, and note on an index card why it is important to know. To avoid the same material appearing on the cards, you can assign different sections of a unit or chapter to groups of students. The Line-Up (students lined up, facing a progression of different review partners) allows them a chance to revisit a number of important concepts and engages students in summing up their understandings.

1 Students respond to a particular prompt on an index card, which will then be shared with their peers. As a result, students should be cautioned to write clearly and legibly because others will also be reading their cards. For example, students may be asked to describe something important that they have learned or read that they think many people may not know. On the back of the card, students write why they believe this item is of particular significance. (See the Quick-Writes strategy pages for ideas for prompts for the review cards.)

2 When they have completed their cards, students form two lines of equal numbers so each person is facing a partner. The students in line A proceed first, sharing their cards with their partners in line B. After the students in line A have discussed the item on their card for one minute, the roles are reversed, and the students in line B share their cards for one minute. Again, use a timer to monitor responses.

3 After both students have talked, the partners swap their cards, and everyone in line B moves down to the next student to their left (of course, the person on the far end of Line B must circle back to the head of the line to link up with a new partner in line A). Each student now has a new card to share and a new partner. After this second round of one-minute sharing, partners swap cards again, and line B shifts to the left one more time. In this way, students have an opportunity to verbalize a number of concepts and ideas with several of their peers. Line B can keep shifting to the left until students have had perhaps eight to 10 different partners and cards to review.

Line-Up Reviews promote careful listening because students realize that they will soon be repeating what their partners tell them to another student. Therefore, they are also encouraged to clarify what their partners tell them, to ask questions if they are confused about any details, and to assist a partner who is struggling with understanding a card. The strategy has the additional advantage of coordinated movement because students get to talk on their feet, which can provide a welcome active transition between class activities.

Advantages

- Students come to realize that learning does not happen all in one step, so they need to revisit new material several times as they continue to explore it.

- Students are reminded that merely hearing, viewing, or reading is not enough; they also must pause periodically to think about what they are experiencing.

- Students become comfortable with verbalizing their understandings to others and to themselves.

- Students are encouraged to use classmates as collaborators to help construct personal meaning from important content, as well as to clarify and remember new information.

- Students receive continued practice in reducing what they are learning to meaningful summaries, which emphasize key ideas rather than an accumulation of information.

- These strategies also can be used for eliciting students' prior knowledge about a topic before introducing a new lesson.

Meets the Standards

The Paired Reviews strategies promote careful reading and rereading of an author's message (R.1), discerning main ideas and summarizing (R.2), examining interrelationships of details or ideas (R.3), interpreting word meaning (R.4), analyzing text structure (R.5), tracking the author's perspective and purpose (R.6), supporting argumentation (R.8), comparing and contrasting with other sources of knowledge (R.9), and mentoring the reading of complex literary and informational texts (R.10). Strategies employing Quick-Writes provide practice in using text-based evidence in summarizing and explaining (W.2) and drawing evidence from texts for analysis and reflection (W.9). The collaborative conversations develop expressing and defending thinking (SL.1, SL.3, SL.4). Vocabulary development includes determining and clarifying key vocabulary (L.4), attention to word relationships (L.5), and acquiring domain-specific vocabulary (L.6).

References

Buehl, D. (2003). Wait. Let me think about that. *OnWEAC*, *3*(10), 13.

Costa, A.L. (1997). *Teaching for intelligent behavior*. Davis, CA: Search Models Unlimited.

Marzano, R.J., Pickering, D.J. Arredondo, D.E., Blackburn, G.J., Brandt, R.S., & Moffett, C.A. (1992). *Dimensions of learning: Teacher's manual*. Alexandria, VA: Association of Supervision and Curriculum Development.

McTighe, J., & Lyman, F.T., Jr. (1988). Cueing thinking in the classroom: The promise of theory-embedded tools. *Educational Leadership, 45*(7), 18–24.

Power Notes

Imagine that you are in the market for a new automobile. Your mind immediately begins to sort and categorize information relevant to your decision. As you consider vehicles you would like to own, the first mental sorting divides vehicles into cars you can afford and cars you cannot afford. Next, you might group the affordable cars into subcategories, perhaps based on design, vehicle size, or fuel efficiency. Finally, within these clusters, you might list the makes of vehicles that are potential purchases.

Classifying and subdividing information is a natural mental activity and an essential process in classroom learning. As a proficient reader, you can separate the wheat from the chaff. For example, as you peruse the daily newspaper, you delve into a complex article about the stock market that is full of market terms: *Dow, drop of 32 points, day traders, NASDAQ, corporate downsizing, Federal Reserve Board, outsourcing, Internet overvaluing, yen, prime rate.* As you read, however, you dwell less on specific details and instead organize your thinking around main ideas, such as causes of current global economic shifts and the possible impact on employees and consumers.

Many students struggle with perceiving integral relationships in their reading. As a result, they have difficulty distinguishing attributes, examples, and details from main ideas. Power Notes (Santa, 1988; Santa, Havens, Franciosi, & Valdes, 2012) provides a systematic way to help students organize information for their reading, writing, and studying.

Using the Strategies

Power Notes are a streamlined form of outlining that is easy to introduce to students. Power Notes can also be combined with Concept Mapping to further enhance students' comprehension and synthesize their learning.

Power Notes involves assigning various components of a text a different power rating, which helps students differentiate more global concepts from specific information. Main ideas or categories are assigned a power 1 rating. Attributes, details, or examples are assigned power 2, 3, or 4 ratings.

1 Start by modeling Power Notes using categories that are familiar to students. Point out how the powers relate to one another. For example, power 1 is a main idea or concept, such as fruit. Power 2s are examples or elaborations of power 1, such as bananas, peaches, grapes, pears, and apples. Power 3s are examples or elaboration of a power 2. For example, some power 3 examples for apples (power 2) would be varieties, such as Macintosh, Yellow Delicious, and Honeycrisp. For power 4s, students might offer characteristics, such as red-skinned, great for pies, and keeps a long time.

2 Provide students with practice in using Power Notes to categorize information and relationships found in factual material. Select a number of power 1, 2, and 3 terms from a unit of study and write them on separate index cards. Distribute sets of cards to students working in collaborative groups. As students group the cards, have them determine what power each term represents and then arrange the cards according to powers and corresponding relationships. For example, cards for a U.S. history unit on the beginning of the reform era in the 19th century would include a power 1 (*reformers*), power 2s (*Populists, unions, Progressives*), and power 3s (*NAACP, Farmer's Alliance,* etc.). Students might arrange the cards as follows:

1. reformers
   2. Populists
      3. National Grange
      3. Farmer's Alliance
      3. Populist Party
   2. unions
      3. The Knights of Labor
      3. American Federation of Labor
      3. Industrial Workers of the World
   2. Progressives
      3. muckrakers
      3. NAACP
      3. Progressive Party

This activity is an excellent review exercise. As

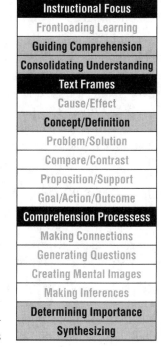

Strategy Index
Instructional Focus
Frontloading Learning
Guiding Comprehension
Consolidating Understanding
Text Frames
Cause/Effect
Concept/Definition
Problem/Solution
Compare/Contrast
Proposition/Support
Goal/Action/Outcome
Comprehension Processess
Making Connections
Generating Questions
Creating Mental Images
Making Inferences
Determining Importance
Synthesizing

an additional study technique, provide students with blank cards so they can add descriptive power 4 items to power 3 cards or add other items to the outline.

3 To help students organize their writing, have them use a simple 1–2–2–2 outline to construct a well-organized paragraph, such as in the following example:

1. Healthy methods to lose weight
    2. Set realistic goals.
    2. Eat fewer calories.
    2. Develop a regular exercise program.

> You should follow healthy methods if you want to lose weight. First, you should set realistic weight-loss goals. Next, you should plan a diet that involves eating fewer calories. Finally, you should develop a regular program of exercise in addition to your diet.

Students can further elaborate each point by adding power 3 and power 4 details to their outline. Power Notes gives students a means to analyze their writing in terms of structure and development of ideas.

Power Notes and Concept Maps

After students understand the concept of Power Notes, the strategy can be expanded to enhance comprehension and learning. Power Notes work well with Concept Mapping activities (see the Concept Map for Pythons example in the K–W–L Plus strategy pages). Concept Maps (visual webs of information that illustrate important relationships within material) are sometimes constructed by students without a sense of superordinate and subordinate information. Their maps may be only a haphazard mishmash of facts. Combining Power Notes and Concept Maps creates highly organized visual resources for summarizing and further study.

1 Model Concept Mapping using Power Notes with students. Reserve the center of the map for the topic being developed. Stress that only power 1 ideas can emanate from the center. Each power 1 idea is further defined with power 2s, and power 3s elaborate on the power 2s on the map. For example, students reading a textbook segment about the role of fat in our diets determine three power 1s: importance of fat to our diet, kinds of fats, and proper amounts of fat in our diet (see the Power Notes Concept Map of the Role of Fat in Human Diets). Each category is developed with power 2 and power 3 details. The completed map is a strong visual representation of key information, with corresponding relationships clearly defined.

2 Have students work with partners to create Concept Maps from a new selection. Students can share their maps by projecting them for the whole class, or they can be posted for a gallery walk by their classmates, especially if the maps are created on chart paper.

Advantages

- Students become tuned into text structure as they read and write.
- This is an easy-to-understand strategy for classifying information.
- Students learn to read actively and to reread to prioritize main ideas from supportive details as they study.
- Students are prompted to look for relationships within material being studied.
- Power relationships can guide students in taking coherent notes from textbooks or classroom presentations.
- Power Notes can be integrated with a number of other strategies to help students perceive how information is interconnected.

Meets the Standards

Power Notes promotes careful reading and rereading of an author's message (R.1), discerning main ideas and summarizing (R.2), examining interrelationships of details or ideas (R.3), analyzing text structure (R.5), integrating ideas into visual representations (R.7), supporting argumentation (R.8), and mentoring the reading of complex literary and informational texts (R.10). In addition, the collaborative conversations develop expressing and defending thinking using visual displays (SL.1, SL.2, SL.4). Follow-up writing provides practice in using text-based evidence in supporting arguments (W.1), summarizing and explaining (W.2), and drawing evidence from texts for analysis and reflection (W.9). Vocabulary development includes attention to word relationships (L.5) and acquiring domain-specific vocabulary (L.6).

References

Santa, C.M. (with Havens, L., Nelson, M., Danner, M., Scalf, L., & Scalf, J.). (1988). *Content reading including study systems: Reading, writing and studying across the curriculum.* Dubuque, IA: Kendall/Hunt.

Santa, C., Havens, L., Franciosi, D., & Valdes, B. (2012). *Project CRISS: Helping teachers teach and learners learn* (4th ed.). Kalispell, MT: Lifelong Learning.

Literature Cited

Foss Science. (2005). *Food and nutrition.* Berkeley, CA: Delta Education.

Power Notes Concept Map of the Role of Fat in Human Diets

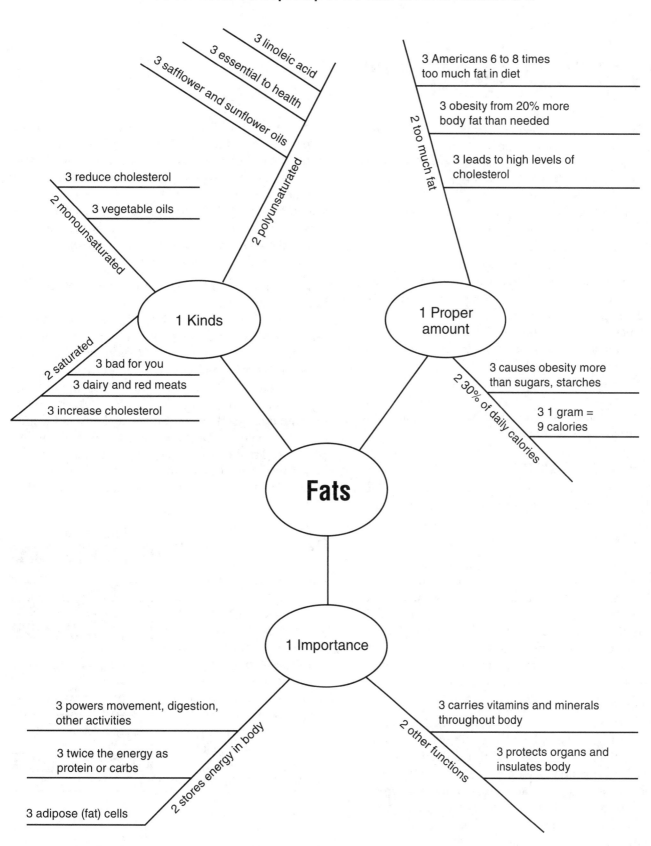

Note. Developed for *Food and Nutrition* (pp. 1–4), by Foss Science, 2005, Berkeley, CA: Delta Education. Copyright © 2005 by Delta Education. Adapted from *Classroom Strategies for Interactive Learning* (p. 126), by D. Buehl, 2009, Newark, DE: International Reading Association. Copyright © 2009 by the International Reading Association.

Pyramid Diagram

Visualize the following setting: the conference room of a major corporation with a table surrounded by executives, each responsible for delivering a report. What follows is a parade of statistics, an array of colorful charts and computer graphics, and a pile of data. Clearly, the point of the meeting is to understand the implications of the information so important decisions can be made. But what sense is to be made from all of this information?

As a critical part of their daily reading demands, students also need to sort through a considerable wealth of information to draw conclusions, develop interpretations, and make generalizations. Yet, many state and national assessments consistently indicate that students have much more difficulty with making inferences and summarizing understandings than identifying facts. In particular, Common Core Reading Anchor Standard 2 targets articulating main ideas and summarizing as major emphases.

Using the Strategy

The Pyramid Diagram strategy (Solon, 1980) guides students in selecting appropriate information from a reading to be analyzed and helps them consider possible implications of this material.

1 Provide students with a focusing question that will help them select relevant information from a text. For example, a focusing question for students reading a social studies selection about Benjamin Franklin might be, What were Franklin's most significant accomplishments? A focusing question for students reading a passage on tropical storms might be, What are the problems caused by tropical storms?

2 Distribute index cards to students and have them read a selection. As they read, they should write on the cards information that deals with the focusing question. One piece of information is recorded on each card. Students looking for Franklin's achievements might write "invented the lightning rod" on one card and "was ambassador to France" on a second card. Students continue making cards until they finish reading the passage.

3 Model the process of categorizing the selected information from the reading by soliciting student responses from the cards. Write each response on an index card and line the cards along the whiteboard tray in the order given. Next, ask students to work with partners to decide which of the cards can be grouped together. With the whole class, continue the discussion, recognizing disagreements as students determine how the cards might be categorized. Move the cards to reflect the class consensus, thus forming the foundation layer of the Pyramid Diagram.

4 Ask partners to brainstorm category headings for each grouping of cards. Again, continue with a whole-class discussion and help the class reach a consensus. Write the headings selected for each group as a second layer of boxes you create on the whiteboard above the corresponding categories. For example, students might decide on statesman, politician, or leader for cards detailing Franklin's roles as a delegate to the Constitutional Convention and a diplomat to France (see the Pyramid Diagram for Benjamin Franklin). Several of Franklin's other accomplishments could fall under the categories of inventor, writer, or scientist after students consider the information on the other cards.

5 On the whiteboard, draw two rectangles representing the top two layers of the pyramid. Ask students to determine an appropriate title for the pyramid, which should reflect the overall topic area of the selection and the focusing question. The title is placed in the top rectangle. "Benjamin Franklin's Accomplishments" might be offered as a potential title for our social studies example. Then, using the title, category labels, and details from the reading, have students collaborate with their partners to write a one-sentence statement that summarizes the information

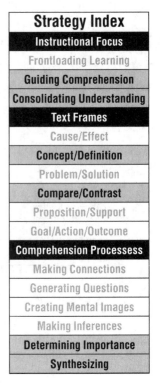

Strategy Index

Instructional Focus

Frontloading Learning

Guiding Comprehension

Consolidating Understanding

Text Frames

Cause/Effect

Concept/Definition

Problem/Solution

Compare/Contrast

Proposition/Support

Goal/Action/Outcome

Comprehension Processes

Making Connections

Generating Questions

Creating Mental Images

Making Inferences

Determining Importance

Synthesizing

Pyramid Diagram for Benjamin Franklin

	Benjamin Franklin's Accomplishments						
	Ben Franklin's accomplishments in writing, science, and government show that he was a man of many talents and interests.						
	Writer		Inventor		Scientist		Statesman
Published *Poor Richard's Almanack*	Wrote an autobiography	Invented the lightning rod	Devised the Franklin stove	Conducted experiments on electricity	Studied weather patterns	Delegate to the Constitutional Convention	Diplomat to France during the Revolutionary War

Note. From *Classroom Strategies for Interactive Learning* (p. 85), by D. Buehl, 1995, Madison: Wisconsin State Reading Association. Copyright © 2001 by the International Reading Association.

represented in the pyramid. For example, after constructing a Ben Franklin pyramid, a pair of students might conclude, "Ben Franklin's accomplishments in writing, science, and government show that he was a man of many talents and interests."

6 Partners now write a one-paragraph conclusion that addresses the focusing question. The second layer of the pyramid provides them with a topic sentence. The third layer suggests subsequent sentences that will expand on the topic sentence. The bottom layer identifies appropriate details that may be used to illustrate each of these examples. The following paragraph illustrates how students might combine the information in each layer of the Pyramid Diagram for Benjamin Franklin:

> Benjamin Franklin's accomplishments in writing, science, and government show that he was a man of many talents and interests. Franklin was a well-known writer who published the popular *Poor Richard's Almanack* and wrote an autobiography. He was an inventor, bringing us the lightning rod and Franklin stove, for example. He also was a scientist who conducted experiments on electricity and studied weather patterns. Finally, Franklin was an important statesman who served as a delegate to the Constitutional Convention and as a diplomat to France during the Revolutionary War.

Once students have become comfortable with using Pyramid Diagrams, these steps may be accomplished with less teacher guidance as students work collaboratively and, eventually, independently. Students first read the selection and complete their cards on their own and then meet to construct the rest of the pyramid as a group. Students could then write their one-paragraph conclusions as individuals or as a team.

Advantages

- Students construct a visual representation of how important details are used to draw conclusions and make observations.

- Students are directive in their reading so they actively search for appropriate information from a text. The strategy is also a perfect task for rereading a selection with a more analytical eye.

- Students gain practice in writing well-organized summaries of text.

Meets the Standards

The Pyramid Diagram strategy promotes careful reading and rereading of an author's message (R.1), discerning main ideas and summarizing (R.2), examining interrelationships of details or ideas (R.3), analyzing text structure (R.5), tracking the author's perspective and purpose (R.6), integrating ideas into visual representations (R.7), supporting argumentation (R.8), and mentoring the reading of complex literary and informational texts (R.10). In addition, the collaborative conversations develop expressing and defending thinking using visual displays (SL.1, SL.2, SL.3, SL.4). The writing phase provides practice in using text-based evidence in summarizing and explaining (W.2) and drawing evidence from texts for analysis and reflection (W.9). Vocabulary development includes attention to word relationships (L.5) and acquiring domain-specific vocabulary (L.6).

References

Buehl, D. (1995). *Classroom strategies for interactive learning.* Madison: Wisconsin State Reading Association.

Solon, C. (1980). The pyramid diagram: A college study skills tool. *Journal of Reading, 23*(7), 594–597.

Suggested Reading

Kinkead, D., Thompson, R., Wright, C., & Gutierrez, C. (1992). Pyramiding: Reading and writing to learn social studies. *The Exchange, 5*(2), 3.

Questioning the Author

"Are you talking to me?" We exist as individuals amid a daily buzz of language, and much of this linguistic hum may seem impersonal—generic jabbering, indiscriminately targeted, everyone talking to everyone else. Yet, at times, it becomes apparent that a speaker is singling you out as an audience, a flow of discourse directed toward you personally: a joke, a comment, a criticism, a threat, a compliment, a confidence, a sharing, or a solicitation. Someone wants *your* attention. Someone is talking to you.

In our daily lives, we are ever aware of others talking to us. In print, these communications assume a variety of forms: a set of directives delivered in a memo at work, an editorial in the newspaper, an appeal mailed to our homes, a request appearing on our computer screens via e-mail, a speech by a political leader televised in our living rooms. But we also tune in to other voices reaching out to us: a novelist, perhaps dead for a century or more, speaking to us through a work of literature; a reporter, from across the globe, chronicling events in a distant land; a historian, looking back on a lifetime of study, constructing an analysis of a past civilization; or a scientist, steeped in research data, describing new insights on some physical phenomenon. As mature readers, we recognize that every time we pick up a piece of print, someone is talking to us.

This ability to perceive the person behind the message is a hallmark of proficient reading, a prerequisite for critical thinking. For many of our students, however, the voice of an author becomes lost behind a din of words. In particular, texts that students read in school may seem particularly authorless. Students may become so immersed in grappling with information that they lose sight of the writer, thereby bypassing the author's intentions, viewpoints, assumptions, and perspectives. They read just to get the facts and miss the larger scope of a piece of text. They read as if no one is talking to them.

Beck, McKeown, Hamilton, and Kucan (1997) argue that a mental posture of "questioning the author" is an especially powerful strategy to help students adopt an inquiring orientation to texts. Questioning the Author (QtA) focuses on a series of questions that one might naturally pose about any message we might receive, in any form: Who is talking to me? Why are you telling me this? What is the point of your message? What do you expect of me as a reader of your message? What do you think I can (or should) do with your message? These are questions we would ask another human being, but this time they are directed to the author.

Using the Strategies

In contrast to most of the questions that typify students' experiences, a QtA disposition moves students beyond merely identifying information to engaging them in considering the person writing to them and what that person has attempted to offer them. Extensions to this strategy, Question–Answer Relationships and Elaborative Interrogation, provide additional questioning tools for working a text to deepen comprehension.

Teaching this strategy to students requires frequent modeling and reinforcement during classroom routines.

1 Initially, QtA involves a subtle but significant shift in classroom language. Rather than talking about "what the book says" or "what it said in the story," recalibrate the classroom discourse to focus on authorship: "What did the author say?" Emphasize that "books don't talk, authors do." This underscores that reading is an act of communication between an author and the readers. Have students personalize the authors by identifying these individuals by name and locating available biographical information that provides insight on their identity: What perspective or authority do they bring to the text? (This is the evaluating-level focus question in the Self-Questioning Taxonomy strategy.)

Select a passage from classroom materials and model examination of the

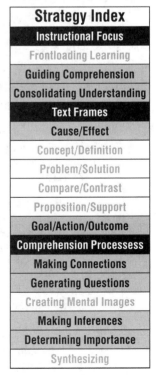

Strategy Index

Strategy Index
Instructional Focus
Frontloading Learning
Guiding Comprehension
Consolidating Understanding
Text Frames
Cause/Effect
Concept/Definition
Problem/Solution
Compare/Contrast
Proposition/Support
Goal/Action/Outcome
Comprehension Processess
Making Connections
Generating Questions
Creating Mental Images
Making Inferences
Determining Importance
Synthesizing

authorship with students: What does the author expect students to already know? What could the authors add or change to make the passage more understandable? Emphasize that authors have viewpoints and make decisions about what to put in their writing, and although authors may be very knowledgeable about the material, sometimes they may not express their ideas in ways that are clear to all readers.

Note that the intent of the modeling is not to condemn classroom texts as poorly written but to underscore the natural tension that occurs between readers and writers. Writers have a responsibility to clearly communicate their ideas to the target audience, and readers have a responsibility to size up what an author provides and what they must do to make sense of a text. (As mentioned in Chapter 1, some texts are more considerate of readers than others in the way they present information and ideas.)

2 Introduce the standard QtA queries to students, either as individual handouts or posted in the classroom (see the Questioning the Author Bookmark; reproducible available in the Appendix). Students need to see the questions you are working from during this modeling phase. Stress that QtA represents those questions that are central to working challenging texts. Emphasize that proficient readers do not need questions provided to them by someone else; they know what questions to ask to make sense of a text. Model QtA with a short and intriguing complex disciplinary text. Project the text for students to follow as you display your questioning of that text as a think-aloud. At this stage, you are modeling; the students are not participating but observing an expert reader at work. For example, the following is a portion of a transcript of a science teacher's QtA think-aloud:

> Here is an article that recently caught my eye: "That Cuddly Kitty Is Deadlier Than You Think" [Angier, 2013]. Immediately, I turn to one of the QtA questions and rephrase it for this text: What is this author going to be telling me about cats? I notice two extreme contrasts in this title, *cuddly kitty* and *deadlier*. I am wondering, Deadlier to what? Other animals? Other cats? Humans? I'll read on.

> "For all the adorable images of cats that play the piano, flush the toilet, mew melodiously and find their way back home over hundreds of miles, scientists have identified a shocking new truth: cats are far deadlier than anyone realized." [Angier, 2013, p. A19]

> This is a good spot to stop and examine some more. The QtA question that immediately comes to mind is, How does what the author tells me connect with my previous knowledge or experience? I think the author expects me to imagine all of those cute cat videos that we see on the Internet.

Questioning the Author Bookmark

- **What is the author telling you?**

- **What does the author assume you already know?**

- **Why is the author telling you this?**

- **What is the point of the author's message?**

- **What does the author want you to understand?**

- **What does the author apparently think is most important?**

- **How does the author signal what is most important?**

- **How does this follow with what the author has told you before?**

- **How does what the author tells you connect with your previous knowledge or experience?**

- **What does the author say that you need to clarify?**

- **What can you do to clarify what the author says?**

- **Does the author explain why something is so?**

Note. Adapted from *Questioning the Author: An Approach for Enhancing Student Engagement With Text*, by I.L. Beck, M.G. McKeown, R.L. Hamilton, and L. Kucan, 1997, Newark, DE: International Reading Association. Copyright © 1997 by the International Reading Association.

Another QtA question that seems to fit here is, What point is the author making? The author starts with these cutesy cat images, but again she uses very contrasting language: *adorable* and *mew melodiously* with *shocking* and *deadlier*. The author uses a colon to punctuate the phrase "cats are far deadlier than anyone realized" to make that statement really stand out. So, I think the point is that maybe our knowledge of cats has now changed in an important way. Let's see what comes next.

"In a report that scaled up local surveys and pilot studies to national dimensions, scientists from the Smithsonian Conservation Biology Institute and the

Fish and Wildlife Service estimated that domestic cats in the United States—both the pet Fluffies that spend part of the day outdoors and the unnamed strays and ferals that never leave it—kill a median of 2.4 billion birds and 12.3 billion mammals a year, most of them native mammals like shrews, chipmunks and voles rather than introduced pests like the Norway rat." [Angier, 2013, p. A19]

What does the author assume I already know here? The author refers to local surveys and pilot studies but doesn't explain them, so I'll have to draw on my background knowledge to come up with hunches about what these scientific methods entail. The author doesn't tell us what domestic cats are, but later she refers to pets and strays, so that helps me figure out that domestic cats are the small housecat breeds, not larger cats like a lynx or cougar. The author assumes that I know what *feral* means. Because the author groups strays and ferals together as cats that never leave the outdoors, I think these must be wild, untamed cats.

I'm also going to ask, What does the author apparently think is important? She uses statistics, which often signals that an author wants to make a convincing case for an argument, and these statistics reinforce that cats really are deadly animals. The author also emphasizes that these are scientific studies and not just somebody's opinion and mentions the Smithsonian Biology Institute and the Fish and Wildlife Service, which appear to be very credible sources for this information.

Finally, is there anything the author says that is not clear? The author does not explain what *scaled up* means. That seems important to know because it appears that's how the scientists got these statistics. The author also refers to a "median of" with the statistics; I need to clarify exactly what that means.

3 The next step engages the students as full participants. Preview a selection that will be assigned for reading. Choose places in the text where you will stop students and initiate discussion to clarify key points. Have students work with partners and provide a partner log sheet for them to record their responses during the collaborative interludes (see the Questioning the Author Partner Log on Hurricanes). Unlike most text lessons that involve discussion before or after reading, a QtA activity has the teacher lead discussion *during* reading, at predetermined breaks in the text. Students might read a paragraph or two before a discussion break with their partner, or you might wish to follow a pivotal single sentence with discussion. For example, the following science passage, which is an excerpt from "Hurricanes: Earth's Mightiest Storms" (Lauber, 1996) that is featured as a Common Core exemplar text, has three breaks in this opening paragraph. Each stopping point is indicated by an *. The students read to each stopping point, deliberate with their partner for perhaps a minute and a half to two minutes, continue

---

Questioning the Author Partner Log on Hurricanes

Hurricanes: Earth's Mightiest Storms

QtA 1: What do you predict the author will tell you in this section? Decide on two predictions:

1.

2.

QtA 2: What are some things the author thinks readers might already know? Pick one and write down two things you and your partner know about it:

1.

2.

QtA 3: What does the author think is important to know about these storms? How does the author signal importance?

QtA 4: What major point does it look like the author is making here?

QtA 5: Are you clear on what the author is telling you here? What are some questions you have about high pressure?

QtA 6: Are you clear on what the author is telling you here? What are some questions you have about low pressure? How would you compare what the author says about high pressure and low temperature?

QtA 7: How does the author connect pressure to things she tells you in the first paragraph?

---

on to debrief during whole-class sharing, and then go on to the next segment and repeat the process.

> Great whirling storms roar out of the oceans in many parts of the world. They are called by several names—hurricane, typhoon, and cyclone are the three most familiar ones.* But no matter what they are called, they are all the same sort of storm. They are born in the same way, in tropical waters. They develop the same way, feeding on warm, moist air. And they do the same kind of damage, both ashore and at sea.* Other storms may cover a bigger area or have higher winds, but none can match both the size and the fury of hurricanes. They are earth's mightiest storms.* (Neely, from Lauber, 1996, p. 19)

Focus the discussion during pauses on appropriate author queries, questions that are not about the information but rather about the author's intentions: What is the author trying to say? What is the author's message? Did the author explain clearly? How does this connect with what the author has told us before? Discuss what the author is trying to communicate and continually focus student attention on the text to verify what the author has provided for readers. The strength of these QtA discussions is derived from the modeling of appropriate problem-solving questions that help readers think about their comprehension as they read.

4 As students become comfortable with responding to QtA queries, ask them to generate their own for a selection. With a partner, ask them to lightly pencil in an asterisk or mark with a small sticky note at a few places in the text where they believe a reader should stop and ponder. Have them select one or more of the queries from the Questioning the Author Bookmark (listed on a classroom poster or on their individual copies of the bookmark) that a reader might ask at each of these junctures. For added practice, group two sets of partners together and have them pose their queries to one another.

QtA is a transcendent classroom literacy practice, as it melds a strategy approach to comprehension with the text-based approach envisioned by the Common Core's reading standards. The array of questions trigger all of the comprehension processes articulated in Chapter 1 (see the Comprehension Processes and Questioning the Author chart). QtA makes the previously overlooked actions of the author more visible to students as they attempt to learn from complex texts. Many of the strategies in this book use QtA as a foundation for student thinking.

Question–Answer Relationships

Question–Answer Relationships (QARs; Raphael, 1982, 1986) mentor students on the relationships authors establish with readers. QARs alert students to balance what an author tells them with what the author expects them to already know when questioning a text.

1 Introduce QARs with a short text that can be used to distinguish between author-centered and reader-centered QARs (see the Question–Answer Relationships chart). For example, a history teacher might select a short excerpt from a text on the early 19th-century explorers Meriwether Lewis and William Clark to illustrate these different questioning relationships:

> Lewis and Clark followed the Missouri River for several hundred miles as they moved westward in the spring of 1804. Along with their goal of mapping the new territory, the two explorers were also instructed to keep careful records of their journey. As they traveled, the explorers gained a great deal of information through the difficult process of trying to communicate with the American Indians they met. Their journals were filled with words, such as *skunk*, *hickory*, *squash*, *raccoon*, and *opossum*, that are American Indian terms for plants and animals. After their return in September 1806, Lewis and Clark reported to President Thomas Jefferson, and their journals were eventually published.

Comprehension Processes and Questioning the Author

Comprehension Process	Questioning the Author
Make connections	• What does the author assume you already know? • How does what the author is telling you connect with your previous knowledge or experience?
Generate questions	• All
Create mental images	• Why is the author giving you this description or example or showing you this visual?
Make inferences	• What does the author want you to understand? • Why is the author telling you this? • Does the author explain why something is so?
Determine importance	• What does the author want you to understand? • What is the point of the author's message? • What does the author apparently think is most important? • How does the author signal what is most important?
Synthesize	• What does the author want you to understand? • How does this follow with what the author has told you before?
Monitor reading	• What does the author say that you need to clarify? • What can you do to clarify what the author says?

Question–Answer Relationships

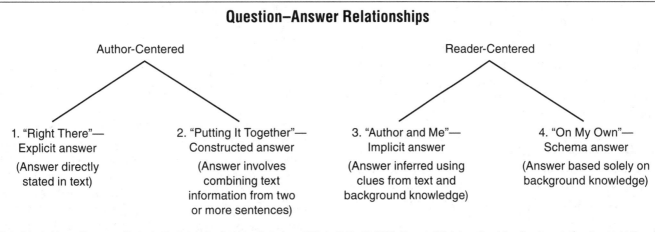

Author-Centered

1. "Right There"—
Explicit answer

(Answer directly
stated in text)

2. "Putting It Together"—
Constructed answer

(Answer involves
combining text
information from two
or more sentences)

Reader-Centered

3. "Author and Me"—
Implicit answer

(Answer inferred using
clues from text and
background knowledge)

4. "On My Own"—
Schema answer

(Answer based solely on
background knowledge)

Note. Adapted from *Classroom Strategies for Interactive Learning* (3rd ed., p. 134), by D. Buehl, 2009, Newark, DE: International Reading Association. Copyright © 2009 by the International Reading Association.

First, model author-centered QARs. Start with clarifying questions that double-check something directly stated in the passage, such as, What river did Lewis and Clark follow in the spring of 1804? It would be useful for readers to clarify where exactly this expedition took place. Students will perceive that this question accesses information (the Missouri River) that the author felt compelled to explicitly impart to the reader. Readers pondering questions with a "right there" relationship can locate a specific place in the text where the author directly provides a satisfactory answer. "Right there" QARs are a version of the question, What is the author telling you?

Again, using the passage, model how some author-centered QARs require more thinking than others. For example, the question, How long did it take Lewis and Clark to complete their explorations? requires readers to synthesize information from more than one part of the passage. The answer, about two and a half years, can be obtained only after combining two pieces of information together: the dates mentioned in the first and last sentences. "Putting it together" questions (the length of their trip) work differently from "right there" questions (the river they followed) in that the author provides sufficient information for both answers, but "putting it together" questions involve constructing answers using several pieces of information. "Putting it together" relationships mandate the examination of more than one sentence to connect facts and draw conclusions.

Another way to describe these two QARs is that "right there" relationships are already preassembled, waiting for you to find them. In contrast, "putting it together" relationships have all the necessary pieces in the text, but the reader has to locate each piece and assemble the pieces to arrive at a satisfactory understanding.

"Putting it together" QARs require more interaction between the reader and the author to establish what the author is telling you.

2 Demonstrate that although some questions are anticipated by authors, who either directly or indirectly provide what they feel readers need to know, other questions require additional information not provided by authors, referred to as "hidden knowledge" in Chapter 2. This second type of questioning relationship, reader-centered QARs, can be exemplified by the question, Why was trying to communicate with the American Indians a difficult process for Lewis and Clark? The author expects readers to figure this out without having to be told directly. Readers need to access clues from the author (e.g., noticing that American Indian terms appeared in the explorers' journals) combined with the readers' personal knowledge base (e.g., realizing that these peoples spoke different languages) to develop a satisfactory understanding. This inferential relationship is an "author and me" QAR—a mental collaboration between authors and readers derived from the questions, What does the author assume you already know? and How does what the author tells you connect with your previous knowledge or experience?

The second type of reader-centered QAR, "on my own," relies almost solely on the reader's personal knowledge. The question, How did American Indians react to the Lewis and Clark expedition? could lead to important considerations regarding the changing dynamic in the American West. The author does not really deal with this critical issue other than to imply cooperation between the explorers and the peoples they encountered. But discussion that extends from the reading of this text through a historian's lens would raise questions about the impact of change on these people. "On my own" QARs are an outgrowth of the question, Does the author explain why something is so?

3 Refer to QAR author–reader interactions as students use QtA to work complex disciplinary texts. This strategy can be an essential step in weaning students away from fixating on only literal-level, "right there" questioning.

Elaborative Interrogation

The QtA query, Does the author explain why something is so? is especially significant for comprehension of complex texts. Elaborative Interrogation (Pressley, Symons, McDaniel, Snyder, & Turnure, 1988; Wood, Pressley, & Winne, 1990) prompts students to ask probing *why* questions of the author, which guides readers in their working of complex texts:

• Closely examine a text for what an author states or implies.

• Activate your relevant prior knowledge that might help explain why something might be so.

1 Model for students appropriate *why* questions about the material that the class is studying. Initially, it might be helpful to provide students with important factual statements from the text or story, which will guide them on the types of information worthy of consideration. For example, the following excerpt from a history textbook dealing with the invention of the printing press could be modeled as an Elaborative Interrogation exercise:

> The European invention of printing appears to have been independent of the Chinese process. Scholars believe that in about 1450, Johannes Gutenberg of Mainz, Germany, became the first European to use movable type to print books. Gutenberg used his printing press to print copies of the Bible. Not all Europeans were enthusiastic about Gutenberg's invention. Some complained that books printed on paper would not last long. Others noted that hand-copied manuscripts were far more beautiful than printed books. Scribes, who made a living by hand-copying manuscripts, realized that the printing press threatened their profession. The impact of Gutenberg's work was economical as well as social and technological. (Holt, Rinehart and Winston, 2003, p. 359)

After students review the statements, ask a series of why questions to focus student attention on implied cause-and-effect relationships in the material: Why would the Chinese and European developments be independent of each other? Why would the author say "scholars believe" Gutenberg was the first? Why would Gutenberg start with printing the Bible? Why were some people not enthusiastic about this invention? Why would the author say the impact was economical, social, and technological? and so forth. As students ponder possible responses, emphasize that the author may give hints to the answers, but that they must also consider things they might know (see the Question–Answer Relationships section). Clearly, this passage contains a great deal of hidden knowledge (see Chapter 2).

Students may express frustration that they do not know enough or are not told enough to come up with plausible answers to some of these why questions. Reassure them that they will not always be able to determine unambiguous or exact answers to why questions they might pose. The strength of the Elaborative Interrogation strategy lies in the process of close analysis of what an author says for possible relationships. By asking why, students are engaged in a much deeper level of processing than if they merely read over the material; they are making connections and drawing possible conclusions.

2 As students study new information, have them work with partners to generate why questions about the material and to brainstorm possible responses to their questions. When students become practiced in asking good why questions, they can create their own for their classmates. Pair students and have them create a series of why questions for one section of a passage. Then, have them exchange their questions with those of another student pair, who developed questions on a different section. Each pair will then reread the appropriate sections to hypothesize answers to their classmates' questions. The Elaborative Interrogation strategy can work just as successfully with fiction as with nonfiction.

Advantages

• Students are engaged in a more active form of questioning, which goes beyond questions that target a literal level of understanding.

• Students are less likely to be frustrated by complex texts as they realize that part of the responsibility for a passage making sense belongs to the author.

• Students are taught to be metacognitive—readers who actively monitor their comprehension during reading.

• Students become deeply engaged with reading, as issues and problems are addressed while they learn rather than afterward.

• Students learn to internalize a self-questioning process that proficient readers use to monitor and enhance their comprehension.

• QtA discussions can be used to introduce selections that students will read independently, perhaps as homework. They are especially helpful when students may need some assistance in coping with difficult but important segments of a chapter.

- QtA discussions are valuable as a comprehension-building strategy for struggling readers.
- QtA lessons may be developed in all content areas and can be tailored for young students as well as adolescent learners.

Meets the Standards

QtA and variations of the strategy promote careful reading and rereading of an author's message (R.1), discerning main ideas (R.2), examining interrelationships of details or ideas (R.3), interpreting word meaning (R.4), analyzing text structure (R.5), tracking the author's perspective and purpose (R.6), interpreting visual representations (R.7), supporting argumentation (R.8), comparing and contrasting with other sources of knowledge (R.9), and mentoring the reading of complex literary and informational texts (R.10). In addition, the collaborative conversations develop expressing and defending thinking (SL.1, SL.3, SL.4). Follow-up writing provides practice in using text-based evidence in supporting arguments (W.1), summarizing and explaining (W.2), and drawing evidence from texts for analysis and reflection (W.9). Vocabulary development includes determining and clarifying key vocabulary (L.4), attention to word relationships (L.5), and acquiring domain-specific vocabulary (L.6).

References

Beck, I.L., McKeown, M.G., Hamilton, R.L., & Kucan, L. (1997). *Questioning the author: An approach for enhancing student engagement with text*. Newark, DE: International Reading Association.

Buehl, D. (2009). *Classroom strategies for interactive learning* (3rd ed.). Newark, DE: International Reading Association.

Pressley, M., Symons, S., McDaniel, M.A., Snyder, B.L., & Turnure, J.E. (1988). Elaborative interrogation facilitates acquisition of confusing facts. *Journal of Educational Psychology*, *80*(3), 268–278. doi:10.1037/0022-0663.80.3.268

Raphael, T.E. (1982). Question-answering strategies for children. *The Reading Teacher*, *36*(2), 186–190.

Raphael, T.E. (1986). Teaching question answer relationships, revisited. *The Reading Teacher*, *39*(6), 516–522.

Wood, E., Pressley, M., & Winne, P.H. (1990). Elaborative interrogation effects on children's learning of factual content. *Journal of Educational Psychology*, *82*(4), 741–748. doi:10.1037/0022-0663.82.4.741

Literature Cited

Angier, N. (2013, January 29). That cuddly kitty is deadlier than you think. *The New York Times*, p. A19.

Holt, Rinehart and Winston. (2003). *World history: The human journey*. Austin, TX: Author.

Lauber, P. (1996). *Hurricanes: Earth's mightiest storms*. New York: Scholastic.

Suggested Reading

Raphael, T.E., Highfield, K., & Au, K.H. (2006). *QAR now: Question answer relationships*. New York: Scholastic.

Quick-Writes

"Could you run that by me again?" Sometimes, once is not quite enough when we are trying to understand. Often, we will interject, "Wait! Did I hear you say...?" as we listen to a speaker, rephrasing the message to ensure that it makes sense to us. Or we reach for the replay button on our remote as we view a video, needing to absorb a scene a second time and mull over what we saw. Most especially, as we read, we periodically need to pause, a thumb holding our place in the book while we ponder and consider, perhaps sneaking another look at a crucial passage to verify what we think we read.

As learners, we frequently discover that we need multiple opportunities for further deliberation, to double-check our understandings and clarify our thinking. This essential component of comprehension, synthesizing, involves processing a message so it has personal meaning. Students need ongoing practice in reformulating what they learn into their own words. Expressing understandings in writing is a particularly important stage in synthesizing learning.

Quick-Writes, advocated by Rief (1998), are planned interludes during class for students to respond to their learning. As they verbalize their thoughts and understandings in these rapidly written brief reflections, students make personal connections to a text and become increasingly comfortable with integrating new vocabulary into their talk about key ideas and concepts.

Using the Strategies

With Quick-Writes, students are allocated a prescribed period of time to quickly gather their thoughts about some aspect of a course of study. Quick-Writes represent informal writing, not polished or edited composition. Learning Logs (Fulwiler, 1980) are an extension of Quick-Writes, in that students record their thoughts and ideas while learning as a way to explore and evaluate what they have learned. An additional extension of Quick-Writes is Admit and Exit Slips, which also encourage students to reflect on their learning. A more structured adaptation is Template Frames.

1 Establish with students the purpose of this strategy in your curriculum. Quick-Writes might be collected as part of a class learning log or included as classroom journal entries; they can be an integral component of interactive notebooks. The ground rules for a Quick-Write are as follows:

- Students are informed of time parameters (usually a set time ranging from one to three minutes).
- Students are expected to begin writing immediately and use the entire (albeit short) time period.
- Students quickly capture thoughts that occur to them as they respond to the writing prompt.
- Students should not be overly concerned about writing form (the intent of a Quick-Write is fluency of expression rather than careful writing).
- Students may be asked to share their Quick-Writes with a partner.

A timer with a buzzer is an especially useful tool during Quick-Writes (e.g., online-stopwatch.com) to reinforce that students need to transition directly into their thinking and that extended writing is not an expectation. An appropriate time reserved for a Quick-Write depends on the students and the nature of the topic. Rief (1998) frequently uses one-minute writes to involve students very quickly in casual thinking about a topic. With a short period of time to work in, students cannot ponder and procrastinate before they commence writing. Instead, when they hear, "Go!" everybody starts writing.

2 Consider using a stimulus to introduce a Quick-Write. A stimulus is intended to jump-start students' thinking about some important aspect of a unit of study and to provide some focus for their personal musings. A read-aloud of a minute or two can suffice in igniting student thinking about a topic. A striking quote or a read-aloud from

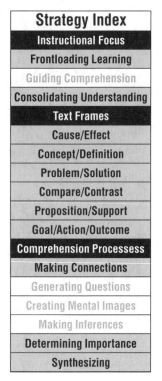

Strategy Index

Instructional Focus
Frontloading Learning
Guiding Comprehension
Consolidating Understanding
Text Frames
Cause/Effect
Concept/Definition
Problem/Solution
Compare/Contrast
Proposition/Support
Goal/Action/Outcome
Comprehension Processess
Making Connections
Generating Questions
Creating Mental Images
Making Inferences
Determining Importance
Synthesizing

a portion of a class text can be highly effective in sparking a Quick-Write. As students listen, they have a chance to rehearse their thinking about the material. For example, students studying the Vietnam War protests in the 1960s listen to the teacher read a couple paragraphs from a first-person account describing student demonstrations on college campuses. Then, students produce a one-minute Quick-Write about what they were thinking, such as in the following example:

> I was wondering if the protests about Iraq in recent years were anything like the 1960s. It seems that the anti–Vietnam War protests were happening all over the country, and they were frequently violent. I wonder if I would have been involved if I had been in a college like Kent State.

Quick-Write prompts are an excellent opportunity to bring in quality short passages to be shared. The excerpt below from *National Geographic* provides science students learning about volcanoes with vivid mental imagery of these destructive natural forces:

> In the first seconds of the eruption, the collapsing north face of St. Helens sends juggernauts of ice tumbling down into the hot ash. Quickly the ice melts, and an estimated 46 billion gallons of water create the combination of mudflow and flood that geologists had feared....Like a science-fiction monster, the debris eats the river, the roads, the downed trees, the logging trucks, a few cars and campers. (Findley, 1981, p. 35)

3 A Quick-Write may, of course, be open ended, allowing students to pen whatever is on their minds as they respond to a stimulus. However, Quick-Writes can also be constructed to elicit specific types of thinking. Teachers can indicate a stem that students can use to frame their thinking, such as the following:

- "This reminds me of..." (to emphasize making connections between the curriculum and personal knowledge and experiences)
- "I wonder what/if/why/whether..." and so on (to stimulate questions that occur to students about the topic)
- "What seems especially important is..." (to help students narrow into key concepts and ideas)
- "I was interested in..." or "I feel that..." (to engage students in examining personal responses to a topic)
- "I think that..." (to encourage conclusions or generalizations about the material)

A host of other prompt variations are of course possible (see the Quick-Write Prompts).

4 Quick-Writes can be expanded or applied in additional ways to take students deeper into their learning of disciplinary content. Quick-Writes provide

Quick-Write Prompts

- I learned...
- I remember that...
- I already knew that...
- I was wrong to think...
- I realized...
- I would explain...
- I would describe...
- Something confusing was...
- This helped me understand...
- What made sense to me was...
- A person should know...
- A key term about this topic is...because...
- Something that surprised me was...
- Something that impressed me was...
- Something I should share about this is...
- Something that people get wrong about...is...
- I want to know more about...
- My learning answered my questions about...
- Since then, one thing I have thought about...is...
- One thing I understand now is...
- I changed my thinking about...
- A brief summary of...should include...

an excellent opportunity for students to explore new vocabulary. For example, students in a geometry class could be instructed, "Write down what comes to mind when you hear the term *symmetrical*," or students in a science class may be asked to use the terms *precipitation*, *evaporation*, and *transpiration* in a Quick-Write summarizing the water cycle. Students may also use Quick-Writes to summarize their reading. A seven-minute write, for example, allows students to talk about what they have read, describe what they found interesting or important, and interject other personal sentiments about the material.

Learning Logs

Learning Logs are a systematic way to integrate more extended, informal reflective writing into the curriculum (Fulwiler, 1980). These logs can become a journal component of a class notebook assignment.

1 Emphasize to students that Learning Logs are a mechanism for recording their thoughts and ideas while learning, which is also a time for evaluating learning. Ask your students to reserve a separate section of their class notebook for a Learning Log. In some cases, it may make more sense to follow a thematic approach and have students integrate their reflections along with other homework and assignments recorded in their notebooks.

Establish with students the role this strategy will play in monitoring their learning. Learning Logs can have a number of applications in the classroom (Santa & Havens, 1991). This strategy can be especially useful as an introductory exercise to initiate class or collaborative-group discussions. Learning Logs provide students with the opportunity to explore their thinking before being called on to communicate their ideas to others. Here are some other applications:

- Reflecting on a unit of study to prepare for exams

- Predicting results of experiments or situations

- Expressing personal viewpoints related to what is being studied

- Explaining why something happened

- Summarizing understandings of a previous lesson

- Clarifying points of confusion and raising questions about material that is not yet clearly understood

- Recording observations, such as during a science experiment or the viewing of a video

- Comparing how ideas have changed after learning or how misconceptions have been corrected

2 Highlight the importance of Learning Logs in the classroom because they tend to be most effective if students use them frequently: Two or three times a week is ideal. Students may be given two to 10 minutes to record their entries. Establish that Learning Logs are informal writing—the recording of reflections—not polished, edited writing, and that the focus is more on thinking and less on the writing form. Note that entries will be collected periodically, read, and perhaps responded to by the teacher, thus creating a written dialogue between teacher and students.

3 Use Learning Logs as an integral part of the routine for learning in your classroom. You might have students write an entry to prepare for learning new material. For example, before a group of fifth graders reads a science passage on glaciers, ask them to write about some of the things they already know about this topic, such as in the following example:

> Glaciers are made of ice. I know we had them in Canada because of a camping trip our family took. We hiked along hills the glacier made. All of these glaciers must have melted, but I don't know why.

Reflective writing is also appropriate after students have read a selection. For example, the following is an entry by a ninth grader reading a U.S. history passage on the Progressive Era:

> I was especially upset that the Progressives were doing these reforms and that they were ignoring African Americans. I agree that they did a lot of good things like the child labor laws, but they mostly left racism alone. I didn't know that the NAACP was started then, but I can see that the NAACP was the Progressives who wanted to fight racism.

Admit and Exit Slips

Admit and Exit Slips is an additional Quick-Write strategy that encourages summarizing and personal reflection. Students jot down their thoughts, questions, confusions, or key ideas on index cards or small slips of paper, which are collected as they enter the room at the beginning of class or as they leave at the end of a period.

1 Admit Slips can be assigned as a homework component, which students are expected to hand to the teacher when they arrive in class (the slip acts as a ticket to enter the room). Exit Slips are perfect for the last few minutes of class to ask students to engage in some synthesizing when ideas are still fresh in their minds (this time, the slip serves as a ticket to leave the room). Students might be provided with a variety of prompts that encourage revisiting their learning:

- Write one significant thing you learned today on the front of the card and one question you have about the material on the back.

- If you shared one thing you learned in our class today, what would it be, and why does it strike you as that important?

- Write one "I didn't know that..." statement on the card and briefly describe what it is.

- Write one thing in particular about today's reading or lesson that you think might be confusing to a lot of people (even yourself) and comment on what might make it confusing.

- Select a quote from your reading that you feel is worthy of some discussion and, on the back of the card, briefly mention why.

2 Admit and Exit Slips also provide the teacher with feedback on points needing further clarification or discussion. The teacher can read from selected cards to start a class period and refocus the previous day's learning. At times, you may wish to have the slips be anonymous to encourage honest responses to confusions or questions that remain, and at other times, you may decide to have the students include their names on their slips.

Template Frames

A template provides students with more extended prompting. Templates are essentially mental structures for guiding increased elaboration in student writing, ranging from five to 10 minutes, or even short essay responses. Template Frames transition Quick-Writes into written responses that emphasize well-structured formats.

1 Share with students exemplary models, either created or collected, of the kind of writing you expect. Well-written examples will exhibit a clear text frame organization, such as cause/effect, compare/contrast, proposition/support, problem/solution, or concept/definition (see Chapter 3). To reveal the structure of the template, underline key elements of the writing, such as topic sentence, text frame language, transitions, and summary or conclusion. This will make the template explicit for students. For example, the answer in the following example illustrates a cause/effect template for students studying weathering in science:

> Explain the causes of mechanical weathering and describe its effects on rocks.
>
> Mechanical weathering is caused by water, by plants, and by animals. First, water causes weathering in two ways: by freezing and by wetting and drying. Freezing water forms ice in cracks of rocks, which splits them apart. Water also causes weathering because when some rocks get wet, they expand, and when they dry, they shrink. This leads to rocks breaking up. Second, plants cause weathering when their roots grow into cracks in rocks and then break them up. Third, animals dig holes in the ground, which expose rocks to water, which weathers them. As a result of mechanical weathering, rocks are broken into smaller pieces but keep their same chemical composition.

2 Provide students with a template containing the key elements of a paragraph to use as an outline for a writing task. This will guide them in constructing an organized written response. Keywords that forecast the text organization of the paragraph are emphasized, as in the following examples:

- Comparison: *similarly, likewise, in a like manner*
- Contrast: *but, yet, however, on the one hand/on the other hand, on the contrary*
- Concept/definition: *for example, furthermore, such as*
- Problem/solution: *for this reason, therefore, instead of*
- Proposition/support: *in conclusion, if, indicate, suggest*
- Cause/effect: *because, consequently, since, if/then, as a result*
- Goal/action/outcome: *steps, first, second, next, finally*

The following is a Template Frame for students responding to a history prompt:

> What problems did the women's suffrage movement encounter, and what did they do to solve their problems?

> The women's suffrage movement encountered a number of problems that made winning voting rights very difficult. First ___. Another problem ___. ___ was a third challenge they had to face because ___. One action followed by leaders of the suffrage movement was ___. They also ___. Finally, ___.

Emphasize to students that they should not treat the Template Frame as a fill-in-the-blank exercise. Instead, instruct them to use the cues provided in the template as a guide to rewriting answers in a paragraph format. Some students will customize the template to fit their ideas and writing style. Encourage them to expand their paragraphs with additional sentences and information. The purpose of the template is not to render students' writing as mechanical and formalistic but to model constructing coherent and expanded written responses. Students learn how to craft well-written responses that can be personalized as they become more sophisticated writers.

Template Frames can be used to structure the writing of lab reports in science, character analyses in language arts, book critiques, position papers, and other types of student writing.

Advantages

- Students are encouraged to reflect on their learning, and they receive practice in using writing to internalize what they are studying.
- Students come to realize that learning does not happen all in one step but that they need to return several times to new material to continue to explore it.
- Students receive regular prompts to express their learning in their own words.
- Students receive continued practice in reducing what they are learning to meaningful summaries, which emphasize key ideas rather than merely an accumulation of information.
- Teachers are provided with direct feedback and insight on how their students are understanding the curriculum and what difficulties are being encountered.

Meets the Standards

The various versions of Quick-Writes promote careful reading and rereading of an author's message (R.1), discerning main ideas and summarizing (R.2), examining interrelationships of details or ideas (R.3), interpreting word meaning (R.4), analyzing text structure (R.5), tracking the author's perspective and purpose (R.6), supporting argumentation (R.8), comparing and contrasting with other sources of knowledge (R.9), and mentoring the reading of complex literary and informational texts (R.10). In addition, ensuing collaborative conversations develop expressing and defending thinking (SL.1, SL.3, SL.4). Writing practice emphasizes supporting arguments (W.1), summarizing and explaining (W.2), drawing evidence from texts for analysis and reflection (W.9), and developing writing fluency (W.10). Vocabulary development can include attention to word relationships (L.5) and acquiring domain-specific vocabulary (L.6).

References

Fulwiler, T. (1980). Journals across the disciplines. *English Journal, 69*(9), 14–19. doi:10.2307/816370

Rief, L. (1998). *Vision and voice: Extending the literacy spectrum*. Portsmouth, NH: Heinemann.

Santa, C.M., & Havens, L.T. (1991). Learning through writing. In C.M. Santa & D.E. Alvermann (Eds.), *Science learning: Processes and applications* (pp. 122–133). Newark, DE: International Reading Association.

Literature Cited

Findley, R. (1981). In the path of destruction. *National Geographic, 159*(1), 35–49.

Suggested Reading

Santa, C., Havens, L., Franciosi, D., & Valdes, B. (2012). *Project CRISS: Helping teachers teach and learners learn* (4th ed.). Kalispell, MT: Lifelong Learning.

RAFT

Who do you imagine yourself to be as you read? As you drift through a novel, such as F. Scott Fitzgerald's *The Great Gatsby*, who are you? Do you identify with the tragic Jay Gatsby or the unhappy Daisy? Maybe Tom, the aggrieved but inadequate husband, or the narrator, Nick Carraway, observing the unfolding story as an increasingly involved outsider? Or perhaps Daisy's friend, Jordan Baker? As you become engaged in the story and emotionally attached to the characters, you splice yourself into the action. You indulge yourself in the delicious experience of living other people's lives vicariously, through print.

The ability to interject ourselves into our reading deepens our comprehension and broadens our learning as we begin to develop empathy for the situations of others and perceive perspectives that are not necessarily our own. Encouraging students to adopt this mental role-playing frame of mind can help them improve their reading of complex disciplinary texts and provide focus to their writing assignments.

We know, in particular, that writing is an effective way to help students synthesize their understandings. But often teachers are frustrated with the quality of writing completed by students—writing that is too brief, lacking in detail, poorly organized, bereft of imagination, or carelessly thrown together. Students tend to view writing as a laborious task in which they have no personal investment. As a result, the purpose of using writing as a tool for learning is sometimes defeated.

The RAFT strategy (Santa, 1988; Santa, Havens, Franciosi, & Valdes, 2012) addresses these teacher concerns with student writing. A RAFT activity infuses a writing assignment with imagination, creativity, and motivation. The strategy involves writing from a viewpoint other than that of a student, to an audience other than the teacher, and in a form other than a standard assignment or written answers to questions.

Using the Strategy

RAFT is an acronym:

R: Role of the writer ("Who are you?")

A: Audience for the writing ("To whom are you writing?")

F: Format of the writing ("What form will your writing assume?")

T: Topic to be addressed in the writing ("What are you writing about?")

1 Analyze the important ideas or information that you want students to learn from a story, a textbook passage, or other appropriate text. Consider how a writing assignment will help consolidate this learning. How might writing help students remember the stages of the digestive system, understand the frustrations of North American colonists, or empathize with the emotions of a character in a story? This establishes the topic for the writing.

2 Brainstorm possible roles that students could assume in their writing (see the Examples of RAFT Assignments). For example, students studying the Colonial period in a U.S. history class could assume the role of a colonist upset with the lack of self-government. Students reading Roald Dahl's book *James and the Giant Peach* in a language arts class could assume the role of James, who needs to tell somebody about how his malevolent aunts are treating him. Students in a science class could personify a french fry, describing the physical changes experienced during each stage of the digestive process.

Decide who the audience will be for this communication and determine the format for the writing. For example, the colonist could be writing in the form of a petition intended for other outraged colonists. James could be writing a letter to state adoption authorities to complain about his ill treatment. The french fry could be writing in the format of a travel journal, to be read by other french fries headed toward the digestive system.

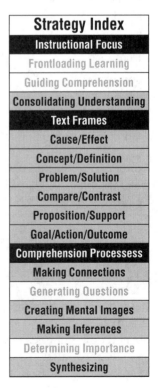

Strategy Index

Instructional Focus
Frontloading Learning
Guiding Comprehension
Consolidating Understanding
Text Frames
Cause/Effect
Concept/Definition
Problem/Solution
Compare/Contrast
Proposition/Support
Goal/Action/Outcome
Comprehension Processess
Making Connections
Generating Questions
Creating Mental Images
Making Inferences
Determining Importance
Synthesizing

Examples of RAFT Assignments

Role	Audience	Format	Topic
Newspaper reporter	Readers in the 1870s	Obituary	Qualities of Crazy Horse
Lawyer	U.S. Supreme Court	Appeal speech	Dred Scott case decision
Abolitionist	American public	Blog entries	Frustrations with ending slavery
Susan B. Anthony	Television viewers	Talk show	Women's suffrage in the early 20th century
Frontier woman	Self	Diary	Hardships in 1700s United States
Constituent	U.S. senator	Letter	Need for civil rights legislation in the 1950s
Public relations agent	Public	News release	How coal is formed
Chemist	Chemical company	Instructions	Dangerous combinations to avoid
Astronaut	Future travelers	Travel guide	Surface of Jupiter
Plant	Sun	Thank-you note	Sun's role in the plant's growth
Scientist	General public	Memo	Need to correct a misconception
Square root	Whole number	Love letter	Explanation of the relationship
Repeating decimal	Set of rational numbers	Petition	Proof that you belong to this set
Chef	Other chefs	Recipe	Revolution
Tour guide	Museum visitors	Script	Understanding Impressionism
Doctor's association	Future parents	Webpage	Proper prenatal nutrition
Advertiser	Television audience	Public-service announcement	Fruits and vegetables in diet
Lungs	Cigarettes	Complaint	Effects of smoking
Huck Finn	Jim	Telephone conversation	What I learned on the raft
Joseph Stalin	George Orwell	Book review	Reactions to *Animal Farm*
Comma	Ninth-grade students	Job description	Use in sentences
Trout	Environmental Protection Agency	E-mail	Climate change effects on a lake
Mozart	Prospective employer	Résumé	Qualifications as a composer

Note. Adapted from *Classroom Strategies for Interactive Learning* (3rd ed., p. 145), by D. Buehl, 2009, Newark, DE: International Reading Association. Copyright © 2009 by the International Reading Association.

3 After students complete the reading assignment, write, "RAFT," on the chalkboard and list the role, audience, format, and topic for their writing. You can assign all students the same role for the writing or offer several different roles from which students can choose. For instance, after reading a passage on soil erosion, they could write from the perspective of a farmer, a fish in a nearby stream, a corn plant, or a worm in the topsoil. Students could be given the choice of several characters from a story to represent their role for writing.

Before students begin writing the RAFT, engage them in developing a deeper understanding of their roles (Shearer, 1998). Some students will be confused and uncertain about how they should react to the topic in their role. Place students with the same role in a collaborative group and have them brainstorm critical elements of that role. Suggest the following questions for the group to consider:

- What perspective would I, in my role, have on the assigned topic?
- Why do I care about this particular topic?
- Where would I look to find out more about this perspective?
- What information (or parts of the story) do I need to examine carefully for my role?
- What should I be particularly concerned about within this topic?
- What emotions might I be feeling as I think about this topic?
- Is this a role that might lead me to be in favor of or against something related to this topic?
- Could a person in my role have a choice of several viewpoints on this topic? Which viewpoint might appeal to me the most?
- How can I give my role some personality?
- How can I ensure that what I say about the topic in my role is accurate?
- What information or details must I mention to show that I am really knowledgeable about the topic?

To provide a visual framework for this brainstorming phase, provide each student with a three-column RAFT Role Definition Chart (reproducible available in the Appendix), which will prompt them to write down pertinent thoughts as they probe their role in their groups. The chart can serve as a guide for their writing. For example, students in a music performance class can use the chart to brainstorm the role 12-Bar Blues to create a Facebook page for this "individual" (see the RAFT Role Definition Chart for 12-Bar Blues). The chart guides them in exploring their knowledge of this form of music more deeply.

4 Make available sample authentic examples for a specific RAFT project for students to consult as they plan their writing. For example, if they are creating a television script, supply examples to help them visualize what to include in their versions. If they are writing an obituary of a famous composer, bring in actual obituaries of musical figures as models for specifics to be included and to show the form and tone of this type of text. By consulting actual examples, students can rely on a measure of reality to give them ideas for how to proceed with their personal RAFTs. As students become comfortable with writing in the guise of various roles, they eventually can be expected to define their own RAFT assignments. Students can devise an appropriate role for a unit of study, designate a relevant audience, and consider possible formats for communicating their thoughts.

Although RAFT assignments offer students a chance to display creativity and imagination, it is important to stress that their writing must demonstrate the targeted learning and needs to be grounded in

RAFT Role Definition Chart for 12-Bar Blues

Personality: Who am I, and what are some aspects of my character?	*Attitude:* What are my feelings, beliefs, ideas, and/or concerns?	*Information:* What do I know that I need to share in my writing?
I am a type of music, a specific form of the blues.	Sometimes I'm really down in the dumps.	Started in the South and moved all over the world
Jazz is my first cousin.	My music helps me get by.	African American roots
I like to take my time; I can be pretty laid-back.	There's comfort and security in my repetition.	Basic pattern found in a wide range of music, including rock
I can also be spontaneous sometimes.	My predictability makes it possible to risk improvising.	Examples include some Delta blues and Chicago blues.
I repeat myself a lot (I need to tell people how I'm feeling).	I'm flattered that so many writers use me in their music.	A repeating chord progression (uses only three chords: I, IV, and V) and blue notes (lower third, fifth, and seventh of the scale)
I'm very predictable.	I'm proud to be an American.	

Note. Adapted from *Classroom Strategies for Interactive Learning* (3rd ed., p. 146), by D. Buehl, 2009, Newark, DE: International Reading Association. Copyright © 2009 by the International Reading Association.

text-based evidence. The goal of the writing is that a reader should find their RAFTs informative and sufficiently detailed. Otherwise, students may stray in their flights of fancy from a key purpose of the writing: a novel way of synthesizing understanding.

Advantages

- Students offer more thoughtful and often more extensive written responses as they demonstrate their learning.

- Students are actively involved in processing information rather than merely writing answers to questions.

- Students are given a clear structure for their writing; they know what point of view to assume, and they are provided with an organizational scheme. Furthermore, the purpose of the writing is outlined clearly.

- Students are more motivated to undertake a writing assignment because the task involves them personally and allows for more creative responses to learning the material.

- Students are encouraged to reread to examine a text from perspectives other than their own and to gain insights on concepts and ideas that may not have occurred to them during the initial reading of an assignment.

- RAFT is an adaptable strategy for all content areas, including science, social studies, and math.

Meets the Standards

The RAFT strategy promotes careful reading and rereading of an author's message (R.1), discerning main ideas and summarizing (R.2), examining interrelationships of details or ideas (R.3), analyzing text structure (R.5), tracking the author's perspective and purpose (R.6), supporting argumentation (R.8), comparing and contrasting with other sources of knowledge (R.9), and mentoring the reading of complex literary and informational texts (R.10). In addition, the collaborative conversations develop expressing and defending thinking using visual displays (SL.1, SL.2, SL.4). Writing development includes practice in using text-based evidence in supporting arguments (W.1), summarizing and explaining (W.2), drawing evidence from texts for analysis and reflection (W.9), and developing writing fluency (W.10). Vocabulary development includes attention to word relationships (L.5) and acquiring domain-specific vocabulary (L.6).

References

Santa, C.M. (with Havens, L., Nelson, M., Danner, M., Scalf, L., & Scalf, J.). (1988). *Content reading including study systems: Reading, writing and studying across the curriculum.* Dubuque, IA: Kendall/Hunt.

Santa, C.M., Havens, L., Franciosi, D., & Valdes, B. (2012). *Project CRISS: Helping teachers teach and learners learn* (4th ed.). Kalispell, MT: Lifelong Learning.

Shearer, B. (1998, February). *Student directed and focused inquiry.* Paper presented at the annual meeting of the Wisconsin State Reading Association, Milwaukee.

Role-Playing as Readers

"What do you think about...?" We live in an age when people's points of view are being solicited almost continuously. Public opinion polls, radio call-in shows, newspaper sound-off columns, man-in-the-street interviews, telephone surveys, blogs—all are attempts to find out what we think.

Consider a recent election barrage of debates, press interactions, talk show appearances, and public forums. One candidate after another responded to a gamut of questions put to them by reporters, media hosts, panels of experts, or even fellow citizens—but probably not by you. As you watched these events, you may have thought to yourself, "I wish I were interviewing those candidates. I know what questions I would ask so the candidates reveal themselves, so they represent who they really are."

Role-playing reading strategies capitalize on this interest in examining the perspectives of others. Students read a selection not as themselves but while imagining they are someone involved in the events being described. The process of reading becomes more personalized as students bring insights related to a role into their understanding of the text.

Using the Strategies

Role-Playing as Readers can be constructed for a wide variety of material, including literature, social studies, and science selections. Three variations of this strategy are included: Point-of-View Study Guides, Vocabulary Interviews, and Readers Theatre.

Point-of-View Study Guides

A Point-of-View Study Guide (Wood, 1988) follows an interview format and encourages students to respond in their own words to the ideas and information in the reading. By asking a series of well-chosen questions, an interviewer can gain valuable insight into who a person is, what that person believes, and what he or she might do.

1 Identify an appropriate role or character from a selection that students have already read. Model the strategy for students by assuming this role yourself. Ask students to interview you by having them generate meaningful questions that could be answered

by information in the text. For example, following the reading of a textbook passage about explorers in the Americas, you could be interviewed as an Aztec farmer of that time. Or following a selection on endangered species, you could be interviewed as a whale. Slip into a character during your modeling, showing how your reading of the material is affected by the perspective you bring. Demonstrate that your attitudes might diverge from the point of view of the author in the textbook or novel. Students will notice that you are connected to the material more emotionally than they are because you are talking about things that affect you and that you really care about.

2 Choose a role or character from a new selection. Create a series of interview questions that will help students focus on the important elements of the text. Distribute these questions as the study guide for the selection. For example, students reading the novel *The Hunger Games* by Suzanne Collins could be asked to comment on events from the perspective of Katniss, the girl who narrates the story, or from the perspective of other characters, such as Peeta or Rue. Students reading a history passage on life in the United States during World War II could be asked to read from the perspective of a 16-year-old Japanese American girl sent to an internment camp (see the Point-of-View Study Guide for Social Studies). Students reading a science selection on the nature of the earth's atmosphere could answer interview questions from the perspective of our atmosphere (see the Point-of-View Study Guide for Science).

3 As students read, have them look for information that will enable them to respond to interview questions. Interview

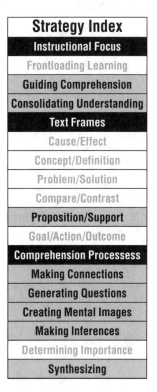

Strategy Index
Instructional Focus
Frontloading Learning
Guiding Comprehension
Consolidating Understanding
Text Frames
Cause/Effect
Concept/Definition
Problem/Solution
Compare/Contrast
Proposition/Support
Goal/Action/Outcome
Comprehension Processess
Making Connections
Generating Questions
Creating Mental Images
Making Inferences
Determining Importance
Synthesizing

Point-of-View Study Guide for Social Studies

You are about to be interviewed as if you were a 16-year-old Japanese American girl living in the United States during World War II. Respond to the following interview questions from her perspective.

1. Why were you and people like you sent to these internment camps?

2. Can you describe in some detail what happened to you and your family when President Franklin Roosevelt issued Executive Order 9066?

3. What kind of losses did your family suffer because of these actions by the government?

4. In what kind of places were these internment camps located? What were the conditions like?

5. What was life like for you and your family in these camps?

6. Why do you think only Japanese people were rounded up, when the United States was also at war with Germany and Italy and had many people of those nationalities living here?

7. When the war ended and the camps were discontinued, what was life like for you and your family?

Point-of-View Study Guide for Science

You are about to be interviewed as if you were the earth's atmosphere. Respond to the following questions based on your knowledge as the atmosphere.

1. Where would we find you? Could you describe your location in some detail?

2. It seems like we can see right through you as if you were made up of nothing. Can you provide some detailed specifics as to what you actually are?

3. I've heard you described as a "column of air," but you seem quite different depending on where in the column one is. Please describe your different layers.

4. Could you talk more about the layer we humans are most familiar with?

5. Do we blame you for the weather? What exactly do you have to do with the weather?

6. We sometimes hear about ozone when people talk about you. Can you clarify your relationship with ozone?

7. You have been around a long time. Is anything changing for you? Why?

8. To clear up an argument that we've been having, are you supposed to take care of humans, or are we supposed to take care of you?

responses should be written in the first person and should elaborate on material from the reading. The responses should read as dialogue, not as typical answers to questions in the text. For example, the following is a student response to a question asked of an Italian immigrant regarding the difficulties of life in the United States:

> We have not been accepted by many Americans. We have encountered prejudice because of our different language and customs. We also have had to work in jobs with long hours and low wages, and some of us have experienced acts of violence. Some of us are accused of being anarchists or socialists, and we are treated as if we are a threat to the government.

An even more intriguing use of Point-of-View Study Guides involves assigning groups of students different characters with different sets of questions relevant to each role. For example, in addition to being interviewed as an Italian immigrant, students might assume the role of a native-born factory worker, an African American sharecropper, a U.S. senator, or a New York City social activist. After reading, have each group conduct their interview for the entire class. The multiplicity of viewpoints will significantly enhance students' understanding of and insight into the material.

4 As students become familiar with Point-of-View Study Guides, have them create their own interview questions. Assign a role and have students work in pairs. Have one student read the selection as the character, and have his or her partner read as the interviewer. The interviewer's task is to formulate questions to be posed to the character. Following the reading, have students participate in a mock interview or answer the questions as a writing exercise (see the RAFT strategy pages).

Vocabulary Interviews

A Vocabulary Interview engages students in posing questions to clarify, expand, or explore key ideas. Pavlik (2000) recommends using the Vocabulary Interview as a strategy to help students develop meaningful understandings of important curricular concepts.

1 To initiate the practice of asking revealing questions, model the process with a version of the old game 20 Questions. Select a relevant concept from a unit of study and solicit questions from students that will lead them toward identifying that key term. Model the questioning with more concrete or tangible concepts. For example, in a biology class, the teacher might choose *chloroplast*: "I am necessary to the growth of green plants. Who am I?" Students will soon discover that starting with general questions gains them more information than specific questions, which can be hit or miss. Hence, "Are you part of a plant?" helps them narrow the range of possibilities much more than, "Are you the sun?" which would only eliminate one of many possible correct answers.

2 Students are now ready to apply this questioning technique to more abstract concepts and vocabulary. In this phase, however, students are informed of the identity of whom they are interviewing. Provide students with a partial list of potential questions and recruit individual students to pose them to you as you model the strategy. For example, in a world history class, the students interview the teacher, who is portraying the concept of "revolution," by starting with questions such as these:

- Where were you born? When?
- Where do you come from?
- How would we be able to recognize you?
- How do you choose where to appear?
- What must you have to come alive?
- Why are you needed?
- What was one of your best days?
- In what ways are you accepted or controversial? Why?
- What actions are associated with you?
- Where do you exist today?
- Who are some of your brothers and sisters?

The interview responses from the teacher might unfold as follows:

> I was born in dissatisfaction, in times before recorded history. I come from desires to alter the balance of power in society. You would recognize me in social ferment, increasing frustration and discontent. Some of my best days were in the United States in the 1770s, France in the 1790s, Russia in the 1900s, and Iran in the 1970s. You see me throughout Middle Eastern countries today, such as Egypt and Syria. My younger siblings are protest, public unrest, civil disobedience, terrorism, and revolt. Sometimes I am violent, but not everyone knows me this way. My enemy is the status quo, and I have no faith in the ballot box.

Students should be encouraged to interject their own questions as the interview unfolds. Queries such as, "What is your favorite movie?" "What music do you like to listen to, and why?" "What are your heroes?" and "What was your greatest failure?" allow students to playfully assume the role of interviewer and provide the teacher opportunity to further elaborate the concept. Students will also enjoy the anthromorphological nature of the activity as they make meaningful connections between a key concept and broader ideas in the curriculum as well as to their own experiences.

3 After sufficient modeling, students can be asked to conduct the interviews themselves with partners or in collaborative groups. Initially, provide them with seed interview questions that can be expanded ad hoc by the students. With experience, students can be expected to develop their own interviews of key disciplinary concepts. The partners reread relevant text portions to prepare for the interviews. The interviewer looks for ideas for promising questions, and the role player reinforces main ideas about the concept. Again, certain generic questions such as those listed previously can be provided to jump-start the process, but students should be expected to customize it with additional questions of their own devising. Have students keep track of those questions that stump the role player. These questions are then aired during a general debriefing of the role with the entire class, and students postulate how these tough questions might be answered.

As students become practiced with this interview strategy, emphasize that they should ask questions as if they were a party host trying to find out more about a guest. These natural questions can help them flesh out a more expansive sense of who the "guest" is and help them become acquainted with this new visitor.

4 Students write character profiles like the example created for *revolution*, which display their understandings of the concept and fold in information derived from the interviews.

Readers Theatre

Reformatting a text segment into a Readers Theatre script is another interactive option for engaging students in Role-Playing as Readers.

1 Preview materials to identify passages that could be modified for Readers Theatre with little editing after scanning them onto your computer. Create a script for a group of four or five students who can take turns reading lines. If necessary, rework any material to fit the Readers Theatre format and change the language from third person to first person (e.g., *he* and *they* become *I* and *we*). Therefore, a descriptive passage becomes a personal narrative when delivered by the Readers Theatre group. For example, a U.S. history textbook passage describing a pivotal event during the Progressive Era provides an excellent framework for a quick reworking into a Readers Theatre script (see the Readers Theatre for Social Studies).

2 Students read their parts as if they were assuming these roles. Ask students to imagine how someone with their roles would speak the lines. Readers Theatre read-alouds need not be elaborate productions. However, allow students the opportunity to

Readers Theatre for Social Studies

The Triangle Fire

Readers A and B are news reporters. Readers C and D are immigrant workers. Reader E is Rose Schneiderman.

Reader A: A gruesome disaster in New York in 1911 galvanized Progressives to fight for safety in the workplace.

Reader B: About 500 young women,

Reader A: most of them young Jewish or Italian immigrant women,

Reader B: worked for New York City's Triangle Shirtwaist Company, a high-rise factory that made women's blouses.

Reader A: One Saturday, just as these young workers were ending their six-day workweek,

Reader C: A fire erupted, probably from a discarded match.

Reader D: Within moments the eighth floor was ablaze, and the fire quickly spread to two other floors.

Reader C: Escape was nearly impossible.

Reader D: Many doors were locked to prevent theft.

Reader C: The flimsy fire escape broke under the weight of us panic-stricken people,

Reader D: Sending us victims tumbling to our deaths.

Reader C: With flames at our backs, dozens of us workers leaped from the windows.

Reader D: More than 140 of us men and women died in the Triangle Shirtwaist Company fire.

Reader A: Union organizer Rose Schneiderman commented on the senseless tragedy.

Reader E: This is not the only time girls have been burned alive in the city. Each week I must learn of the untimely death of one of my sister workers. Every year thousands of us are maimed. The lives of men and women are so cheap and property is so sacred. There are so many of us for one job it matters little if 143 of us are burned to death.[a]

Reader B: The Triangle Shirtwaist fire was a turning point for reform.

Reader A: With the efforts of Schneiderman and others,

Reader B: New York State passed the toughest fire safety laws in the country.

Note. Adapted from *American Anthem: Modern American History*, by E. Ayers, R. Schulzinger, J. de la Teja, and D. White, 2007, Austin, TX: Holt, Rinehart and Winston. Copyright © 2007 by Holt, Rinehart and Winston.
[a]This is a quote from the source above, p. 256.

---

review and briefly rehearse their lines so the parts can be read aloud with polish for the entire class.

3 Students can be asked to work with partners to create their own Readers Theatre excerpts from a classroom text. The activity also provides an impetus for summary writing, as students explain their roles, actions, and events from a RAFT perspective (see the RAFT strategy pages).

Advantages

- Students use their imaginations to become more personally engaged in their reading, which helps bring material to life.

- Students gain practice in translating the language of text into their own words and are involved in a more in-depth synthesis of the material.

- Students are encouraged to draw from their own experiences to understand events in text and are asked to elaborate on information in a meaningful way.

- Students develop sensitivity to different perspectives of events and ideas.

- Students adopt a questioning frame of mind for reading and learning, which causes them to think about key ideas rather than merely attempting to memorize isolated information.

Meets the Standards

Role-Playing as Readers strategies promote careful reading and rereading of an author's message (R.1), discerning main ideas (R.2), examining interrelationships of details or ideas (R.3), interpreting word meaning (R.4), analyzing text structure (R.5), tracking the author's perspective and purpose (R.6), supporting argumentation (R.8), comparing and contrasting with other sources of knowledge (R.9), and mentoring the reading of complex literary and informational texts (R.10). In addition, the collaborative conversations develop expressing and defending thinking textual support (SL.1, SL.3, SL.4). Follow-up writing provides practice in using text-based evidence in supporting arguments (W.1), summarizing and explaining (W.2), and drawing evidence from texts for analysis and reflection (W.9). Vocabulary development includes determining and clarifying key vocabulary (L.4), attention to word relationships (L.5), and acquiring domain-specific vocabulary (L.6).

References

Pavlik, R. (2000, June 9). *Questions to host learning*. Paper presented at the Madison Metropolitan School District Literacy Institute, Madison, WI.

Wood, K.D. (1988). Guiding students through informational text. *The Reading Teacher, 41*(9), 912–920.

Literature Cited

Ayers, E.L., Schulzinger, R.D., de la Teja, J.F., & White, D.G. (2007). *American anthem: Modern American history*. Austin, TX: Holt, Rinehart and Winston.

Suggested Readings

Flynn, R.M. (2007). *Dramatizing the content with curriculum-based Readers Theatre, grades 6–12*. Newark, DE: International Reading Association.

Wood, K.D., Lapp, D., Flood, J., & Taylor, D.B. (2008). *Guiding readers through text: Strategy guides for new times* (2nd ed.). Newark, DE: International Reading Association.

Save the Last Word for Me

Think back on various point–counterpoint news programs that you have watched. Sometimes you witness a verbal free-for-all, with a news correspondent desperately mediating between two or more individuals who have diverging viewpoints that they are eager to express. Each wants to capture airtime to tell you, the public, what "it really means." And each wants the last word.

Wouldn't it be refreshing if your students also wanted the last word about what they are learning in class? Instead, usually only a handful of students venture thoughts about what they found interesting in class reading assignments. The rest of the class is often hard-pressed to verbalize what the reading really means to them.

For many students, *reading* translates to a quick, superficial trip through a text for the sole purpose of answering assigned questions. Unfortunately, these students often never achieve more than a cursory, literal idea of what they have read, and such an approach is antithetical to the close reading described in Chapter 1. Classroom discussions that encourage students to think about their reading tend to sputter as a result because students do not engage in a reflective interaction with an author.

Instructional activities that stimulate students to reflect on what they read develop active and thoughtful readers. Save the Last Word for Me (Burke & Harste, as described in Vaughan & Estes, 1986) prompts students to actively engage with a complex text and provides a collaborative format for the subsequent class discussion.

Using the Strategy

Save the Last Word for Me is an excellent strategy to use with complex texts that may elicit differing reactions or multiple interpretations. The strategy's discussion format is controlled by the students rather than directed by the teacher (see the Save the Last Word for Me Instructions). The collaborative group setting is more inviting to students who are reluctant to talk in front of an entire class and, in addition, gives them time to rehearse their comments by writing their initial thoughts on index cards as preparation for conversation.

1 Assign a selection, passage, or story to be read. After reading, have students return to the text to locate five statements that they find interesting or would like to comment on. The statements could be ones with which they agree or disagree or that contradict something they thought they knew. They could also be statements that particularly surprised, excited, or intrigued them. When reading literature, students also could select revealing statements or actions made by characters in a story. Have students place a light pencil mark or affix a small sticky note next to their five chosen statements.

2 Distribute five index cards to each student, a card for each selected statement. Have students write one statement on the front side of a card. On the reverse side, have them write comments about the statement (see the Quick-Writes strategy pages). For example, a student reading an informational selection about wolves as an endangered species might select the following statement for the front of a card: "Wolves are sometimes illegally shot by ranchers who fear that their livestock will be attacked." On the reverse side, the student may write the following comment: "Ranchers ought to have a right to protect their animals from dangerous predators like wolves."

3 Divide the class into collaborative groups of four or five members. Display the Save the Last Word for Me instructions or provide them as a handout. All students in each group take turns sharing one of their five text statements with their group members. The first student reads a statement to the group and helps members locate the statement in the text. However, the student is not allowed to make any comments on the statement until all other members of the

Strategy Index
Instructional Focus
Frontloading Learning
Guiding Comprehension
Consolidating Understanding
Text Frames
Cause/Effect
Concept/Definition
Problem/Solution
Compare/Contrast
Proposition/Support
Goal/Action/Outcome
Comprehension Processess
Making Connections
Generating Questions
Creating Mental Images
Making Inferences
Determining Importance
Synthesizing

Save the Last Word for Me Instructions

1. As you read, make a light check mark (✓) in pencil or place a sticky note next to five statements that you
   - agree or disagree with.
   - already know something about.
   - are wondering something about.
   - found interesting.
   - want to say something about.
2. After you finish reading, write each statement on the front of a separate index card.
3. On the back of each card, write the comment that you would like to share with your group about each statement.
4. When you meet in your group, take the following steps:
   - Select a group member to go first.
   - The selected member reads the statement from the front of one of his or her cards but is *not* allowed to make any comments.
   - All other group member talk about the statement and make comments.
   - When everyone is done commenting, the member who wrote the statement makes comments.
   - A second group member is selected, and the process is repeated until all cards are shared.

Note. Adapted from *Classroom Strategies for Interactive Learning* (3rd ed., p. 152), by D. Buehl, 2009, Newark, DE: International Reading Association. Copyright © 2009 by the International Reading Association.

group weigh in with their reactions or responses. In effect, the student gets the last word in the discussion of the statement. For example, a student might share the following statement: "Wolves naturally try to avoid contact with humans." But the student does not discuss his or her comments—that people's fears of wolves are exaggerated, especially because of the way wolves are treated in fairy tales—until other group members have commented about the statement. The attitude during this phase is, Here is a statement that interested me. You tell me what you think, and then I will tell you what I think.

4 Have students continue the process until everyone in the group has shared one statement and provided the last word in the discussion. Begin another round with students sharing another of their cards.

Advantages

- Students are mentored to adopt a more reflective stance as they read.
- Students are encouraged to talk about things in the reading that they personally connect to, and they all have an equal opportunity (and expectation) to participate in a discussion on the reading.
- Students are able to hear classmates' views before offering their own, giving them the chance to adjust their comments and reflect on their ideas before expressing them to others.

Meets the Standards

Save the Last Word for Me promotes careful reading and rereading of an author's message (R.1), discerning main ideas and summarizing (R.2), examining interrelationships of details or ideas (R.3), tracking the author's perspective and purpose (R.6), supporting argumentation (R.8), and mentoring the reading of complex literary and informational texts (R.10). The collaborative conversational format develops expressing and defending thinking (SL.1, SL.3, SL.4). The writing of comments on the cards provides practice in using text-based evidence in supporting arguments (W.1), summarizing and explaining (W.2), drawing evidence from texts for analysis and reflection (W.9), and developing writing fluency (W.10). Vocabulary development includes attention to word relationships (L.5).

References

Buehl, D. (2009). *Classroom strategies for interactive learning* (3rd ed.). Newark: DE: International Reading Association.

Vaughan, J.L., & Estes, T.H. (1986). *Reading and reasoning beyond the primary grades*. Boston: Allyn & Bacon.

Science Connection Overview

How does the world around us work? What is in a match head that makes it burst into flame when scratched? Where do rainbows come from? Why do cats purr? How does electricity move through wires? What does aspirin do to your body to make it feel better? Why does our hair turn gray as we become older? Questions—all are part of the process of making sense of the world we live in and making sense of ourselves. We are born into this world observing the phenomena around us, and we spend a lifetime trying to understand it. Humans, as a species, seem determined to know.

This natural curiosity about the workings of the world should form a strong foundation for student learning in science classrooms. Yet, for many students, science does not necessarily appear to be connected to their questions about real-life processes. Instead, science looms as a formidable body of difficult technical information that intimidates and frustrates. For these students, reading science materials is like reading a foreign language. Consider the following biology example:

> Humans as well as most animals are vertebrates. Vertebrates are chordates that have a vertebral column. The first vertebrates evolved from the class of jawless fishes known as agnathans. Agnathans today include the lampreys, whose skeleton is composed mostly of cartilage. Lampreys have a notochord, which functions as their major support column. The gills of these creatures are contained in pouches that branch out from the pharynx. Many lampreys live as external parasites and cause great damage to the host populations of fish.

Whew! Students reading complex science texts may encounter an avalanche of unfamiliar words that have precise meanings in the language of science. Many of these new terms are seen only rarely outside a science context. Students soon become bogged down in this detailed information and lose sight of possible relationships between the science in their books and their understandings of the world around them.

Using the Strategy

Science Connection Overview (Buehl, 1992) is a frontloading strategy that guides students into making connections to their lives and experiences as they study topics in science. The strategy encompasses a student-directed preview of a science chapter or article before reading to link the content with what they already know or have experienced. Before students become immersed in the details of the reading, they gain an overview of the big picture of a chapter and how it relates to the world around them.

1 Introduce the exercise by discussing with students how science helps them understand aspects of their lives or world. Select several examples of science texts and elicit from the class how each can be connected to their lives; for example, a passage on cold and warm fronts and the resulting rain might connect to student questions about why rain occurs when it does or why it is often colder after it rains. For a chapter on microorganisms that live in water, students might make connections by reflecting on why it is unsafe to drink lake or river water. For an article on endangered plants and animals, students might make connections to news stories about the Amazon jungle or dolphins captured in tuna nets. This process emphasizes questioning a text at the applying level of the Self-Questioning Taxonomies for Biological and Physical Science Texts (see Tables 7 and 8 in Chapter 4).

2 Distribute a blank Science Connection Overview (reproducible available in the Appendix) to students and model its use. Tell students to follow along as you skim a portion of a science text, thinking aloud about things in the text that you recognize or with which you are familiar. Intentionally ignore technical terms or information that seems unfamiliar. For example, modeling an overview of a biology chapter on fungi, you would pass over terms such as *basidiomycota, multinucleate,*

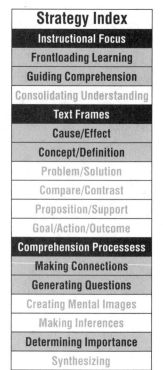

Strategy Index
Instructional Focus
Frontloading Learning
Guiding Comprehension
Consolidating Understanding
Text Frames
Cause/Effect
Concept/Definition
Problem/Solution
Compare/Contrast
Proposition/Support
Goal/Action/Outcome
Comprehension Processess
Making Connections
Generating Questions
Creating Mental Images
Making Inferences
Determining Importance
Synthesizing

and *zygospore*. Instead, focus on familiar terms, such as *mushrooms*, *bread mold*, and *yeast*.

3 Have students work with partners to survey the remainder of the text. First, they complete the "What's familiar?" section of the Science Connection Overview. Emphasize that only familiar, nontechnical information should be gleaned from their survey and skimming of the chapter. Encourage them to use the pictures and graphics in the chapter to assist them in making connections. For example, students doing an overview of the chapter on fungi would likely discover that even though the text contains a heavy load of terminology, there is much that connects to their lives and experiences (see the Science Connection Overview for Fungi). Many students will recognize many of the mushrooms, lichens, and molds featured in chapter photographs and can begin to weave this chapter's materials into their life experiences. In addition, authors of some science texts include features that are intended to help readers make personal connections to the material. Make sure students notice where these features are placed in the text.

Science Connection Overview for Fungi

What's familiar?	What's the connection? Skim and survey the chapter for things that are familiar and that connect with your life or world. List them below: • mushrooms • fungi on rotting plants • mold on spoiled food • lichens • spores • penicillin • yeasts • Dutch Elm disease • plant rusts
What topics are covered?	Read the summary. What topic areas seem to be the most important? • how they look or are structured • how they reproduce • how they feed and stay alive
What are you wondering?	Questions of interest. What questions do you have about this material that may be answered in the chapter? • Why do mushrooms grow in damp places? • Why does food get moldy when it spoils? • Why do they put yeast in bread doughs? • Why are some mushrooms poisonous? • How can you tell which mushrooms are poisonous and which are safe? • What do fungi eat? • Does the medicine penicillin come from a fungus?

What will the author tell you?	Chapter organization: What categories of information are provided in this chapter?
	• structure of fungi
	• nutrition
	• reproduction
	• variety of fungi: molds
	           imperfect
	           yeasts
	           mushrooms
	           lichens

Read and explain.	Enter science words with your explanations into your vocabulary system.

Note. Adapted from "The Connection Overview: A Strategy for Learning in Science," by D. Buehl, 1992, *WSRA Journal, 36*(2), p. 24. Copyright © 1992 by Doug Buehl.

4 If the chapter has a summary, direct students to read it as the next phase of the overview. Ask them to identify key topics that seem to be the focus of the chapter. Although summaries are typically placed at the end of a chapter, students should develop the habit of consulting this study feature *before* becoming immersed in the new information. For example, the summary of the fungi chapter indicates that three general areas appear to be addressed: how fungi are structured, how they reproduce, and how they feed. These items are entered in the "What topics are covered?" section of the overview. This phase emphasizes questioning a text at the remembering and understanding levels of the Self-Questioning Taxonomies for Biological and Physical Science Texts (see Tables 7 and 8 in Chapter 4).

5 Ask students to generate personal questions about the material. Working with partners, encourage them to think about what they know in this topic area and what they might be wondering. These are entered in the "What are you wondering?" section. Initially, you will need to model the kinds of questions that people normally have about science—questions typically not featured in textbooks, which instead tend to emphasize factual details. This phase focuses questioning on the analyzing level of the Self-Questioning Taxonomies for Biological and Physical Science Texts (see Tables 7 and 8 in Chapter 4). Pose more general questions about the material that naturally inquisitive people might raise. For example, questions generated about fungi might be Why do mushrooms grow where they do? Why are some mushrooms poisonous? Why do they put yeast in bread? Why does food get moldy? Are there spores in the air in this room? What happens when you breathe them in? How do we get medicine from fungi?

6 Will students receive answers to their questions in the reading? Have students complete the "What will the author tell you?" portion of the Science Connection Overview by outlining the text's organization. Categories on information are usually signaled by headings or section titles. For example, the fungi chapter was organized into four sections: structure, nutrition, reproduction, and variety. Students have now taken an aggressive and directive survey of the text. They have focused on making connections with the material rather than allowing themselves to become overwhelmed by a mass of challenging new vocabulary.

7 Ask students to read the first segment of the text, with their Science Connection Overview available to consult as they encounter technical terminology and detailed information. As students read, have them develop a vocabulary resource system—use index cards, keep a vocabulary section of their notebooks (see the Double-Entry Diaries strategy pages), or create an electronic vocabulary file—to explain technical science terms (see the Card for Science Vocabulary example). Science terms (referred to as Tier 3 words in the Student-Friendly Vocabulary Explanations strategy pages) are usually featured in easily identifiable ways within the text. Students are adept at locating the definitions and merely copying them as answers to questions; however, they may not really understand what the terms truly mean. Encourage students to treat science vocabulary as they would foreign-language vocabulary: by translating it into more conversational English. Have students use their vocabulary resource system (e.g., cards, Double-Entry Diaries, interactive notebook entries, electronic files) for the same

---

Card for Science Vocabulary

Front	*Back*
# rhizoid (rye bread)	Little fibers that grow out of a mold spore. They are like roots, and they hook the mold onto the bread or other food.

Note. Adapted from *Classroom Strategies for Interactive Learning* (p. 95), by D. Buehl, 1995, Madison: Wisconsin State Reading Association. Copyright © 2001 by the International Reading Association.

purpose: to translate science terms into more understandable language that demonstrates their personal understandings.

8 Integrating memory clues in their vocabulary resource systems is an especially effective technique for helping students become conversant with the new vocabulary (Levin, 1983). A memory clue helps students associate the word with its meaning or explanation (see the Vocabulary Overview Guide strategy pages). For example, the memory clue *rye bread* for the term *rhizoid* may trigger remembering that rhizoids are the little hooks that attach mold to what it is growing on. The clue is suggested by the pronunciation of the word, which triggers a connection between rhizoids and their later appearance on a slice of rye bread. Encourage students to use their imaginations when developing these memory clues for different vocabulary.

Advantages

- Students make meaningful connections with science texts before they are asked to comprehend unfamiliar information.

- Students perceive relationships that bind the information together, and they build a mental construct for making sense of what they read.

- Students develop the habit of questioning a complex science text through a scientific lens.

- Students are provided with a system for translating academic science vocabulary into meaningful understandings.

Meets the Standards

The Science Connection Overview promotes careful reading and rereading of an author's message (R.1), discerning main ideas (R.2), examining interrelationships of details or ideas (R.3), interpreting word meaning (R.4), analyzing text structure (R.5), tracking the author's perspective and purpose (R.6), integrating ideas into visual representations and examining visual displays (R.7), and mentoring the reading of complex literary and informational texts (R.10). In addition, the collaborative conversations develop expressing and defending thinking using visual displays (SL.1, SL.2, SL.4). Writing centers on summarizing and explaining academic vocabulary (W.2) and drawing evidence from texts for analysis and reflection (W.9). Vocabulary development includes determining and clarifying key vocabulary (L.4), attention to word relationships (L.5), and acquiring domain-specific vocabulary (L.6).

References

Buehl, D. (1992). The connection overview: A strategy for learning in science. *WSRA Journal, 36*(2), 21–30.

Buehl, D. (1995). *Classroom strategies for interactive learning.* Madison: Wisconsin State Reading Association.

Levin, J.R. (1983). Pictorial strategies for school learning: Practical illustrations. In M. Pressley & J.R. Levin (Eds.), *Cognitive strategy research: Educational applications* (pp. 213–237). New York: Springer-Verlag. doi:10.1007/978-1-4612-5519-2_8

Self-Questioning Taxonomy

I wonder. I wonder how much rain these threatening clouds are promising. I wonder what response my proposal will elicit. I wonder why these tomato plants seem so droopy. I wonder if this traffic delay will cause me to arrive late. I wonder whether it makes any difference if I substitute honey for sugar in this recipe. I wonder where I misplaced my car keys again. When we wonder, we are posing questions to ourselves.

Questions provide the scripts of our daily internal dialogues with ourselves. We ask questions to speculate and to guide us. We ask questions to kindle our curiosity and to clarify our confusions. We realize that self-questioning is an essential component of critical thinking, decision making, problem solving, and constructing sense from our experiences. Self-questioning is also a hallmark of comprehension. Studies of proficient readers reveal that they spontaneously formulate their own questions before, during, and after reading a piece of text (see the discussion in Chapter 3). Questioning helps readers focus, make inferences, read critically, and draw conclusions.

However, self-questioning is a reading strategy that many of our students employ sporadically or unsuccessfully. Self-questioning assumes an inquisitiveness about a text, an expectation that something in a passage will connect to a reader's experiences and background knowledge, an optimism that the act of reading will result in meaningful ends. Instead, many of our students appear programmed to routinely answer only questions provided to them by someone else. They become overly dependent on textbook editors, worksheet activities, and teacher-led discussions for discovering relevant questions that can be asked about a specific text.

Unfortunately, literal, fact-level questions are disproportionately represented in textbook and worksheet activities. Students know how such questions work. Often, they merely need to undertake minimal surface sampling of a text to derive an acceptable answer. Students can answer these "locate and copy" items rather quickly, and even struggling readers can frequently get through them with little assistance. Researchers have long cautioned us that many of these questions can be answered even if a student is confused about a text's meaning. In other words,

questions asked ostensibly to help students get the facts rarely help students construct an understanding of an author's message. Students can find answers, but they miss the important questions—the questions they should pose to themselves to guide their reading and learning. Instead of searching for answers, students need to be asking questions.

Using the Strategy

Most educators are well versed with Bloom's Taxonomy of Educational Objectives, which posits that teachers need to prompt more complex thinking from their students (Bloom, Engelhart, Furst, Hill, & Krathwohl, 1956). Often, the taxonomy is employed to help teachers ask better and deeper questions, but the other side of this dynamic is for teachers to model self-questioning strategies so students themselves begin to generate increasingly more sophisticated questions as they engage with complex texts. Bloom's Taxonomy, updated by Anderson and Krathwohl in 2001, presents an excellent framework for guiding comprehension instruction as students read and learn during classroom lessons.

1 Walk students through the different levels of thinking in the revised taxonomy. Notice that the revised version emphasizes strong verbs as cues for thinking: *remembering, understanding, applying, analyzing, evaluating,* and *creating* (see the levels of thinking in the Taxonomy of Self-Questioning Chart). Introduce the Taxonomy of Self-Questioning Chart (Buehl, 2007) and model as a think-aloud how these different levels of thinking influence your comprehension. For example, the following think-aloud based on an article on the Great Wall of China demonstrates these levels:

Strategy Index
Instructional Focus
Frontloading Learning
Guiding Comprehension
Consolidating Understanding
Text Frames
Cause/Effect
Concept/Definition
Problem/Solution
Compare/Contrast
Proposition/Support
Goal/Action/Outcome
Comprehension Processess
Making Connections
Generating Questions
Creating Mental Images
Making Inferences
Determining Importance
Synthesizing

Taxonomy of Self-Questioning Chart

Level of Thinking	Comprehension Self-Assessment	Focusing Question	Comprehension Process	Common Core Anchor Standards for Reading
Creating	I have created new knowledge.	How has the author changed what I understand?	• Synthesizing • Creating mental images	2: Main ideas 6: Author's purpose/ perspective 10: Text complexity
Evaluating	I can critically examine the author's message.	What perspective or authority does the author bring to what he or she is telling me?	• Inferring	1: Explicit/implicit meanings 3: Text relationships 4: Vocabulary 6: Author's purpose/ perspective 8: Argument and support 9: Multiple texts 10: Text complexity
Analyzing	I can explore deeper relationships within the author's message.	How is this similar to (or different from) what I've heard or read before?	• Making connections • Determining importance	3: Text relationships 5: Text structure 7: Visual literacy/technology 9: Multiple texts 10: Text complexity
Applying	I can use my understanding in a meaningful way.	How can I connect what the author is telling me to understand something better?	• Making connections • Inferring	1: Explicit/implicit meanings 4: Vocabulary 7: Visual literacy/technology 9: Multiple texts 10: Text complexity
Understanding	I can understand what the author is telling me.	What does the author want me to understand?	• Determining importance • Inferring • Creating mental images	1: Explicit/implicit meanings 2: Main ideas 6: Author's purpose/ perspective 10: Text complexity
Remembering	I can recall specific details, information, and ideas from the text.	What do I need to remember to make sense of this text?	• Determining importance	1: Explicit/implicit meanings 2: Main ideas 10: Text complexity

Note. Adapted from "Modeling Self-Questioning on Bloom's Taxonomy," by D. Buehl, 2007, *OnWEAC*, retrieved July 15, 2013, from www.weac.org/news_and _publications/education_news/2007-2008/readiingroom_modeling.aspx. Copyright © 2007 by Doug Buehl.

Hmm, what does this author want me to understand about the Great Wall of China? Large sections are being eroded by sandstorms. Why does the author argue this is happening? Let's see...farming practices that have drained underground reservoirs have led to ecological change, leading to sandstorms, which cause the wall to crumble. What crucial information should I remember? Predictions are that parts of the wall will disappear in only 20 years. How can I use this knowledge? Perhaps we need to be more careful in how we use natural resources, or we may suffer similar climate changes that can destroy features that have lasted for centuries. Does this information seem reliable? The author supports these conclusions with lots of convincing data and quotes an esteemed museum director. How has my understanding changed? I realize that even long-standing treasures like the Great Wall can quickly fall victim to climatic change.

2 Relate each level of thinking to a statement that a reader can make to self-assess comprehension of a text (see the Taxonomy of Self-Questioning Chart). Emphasize that a thorough understanding, rather than surface-level sampling, will include comprehending at all six of these levels. For example, the evaluating level asks a reader to view a text through a critical lens: "I can critically examine this author's message." Each statement reflects an expectation of a level of thinking that a reader should factor in to construct an in-depth comprehension of a text. In addition, walk students through how the comprehension processes of proficient readers (see Chapter 1) are also cued by the thinking at each level.

3 Each statement of the taxonomy is aligned with a focus question. Emphasize that proficient readers constantly check their comprehension through self-questioning. For example, when readers ask themselves, What perspective or authority does the author bring to what he or she tells me? they are evaluating a message. These focus questions should be modeled extensively with a variety of materials so they become a habit of mind for students as readers. Notice that each focus question is cross-referenced with the Common Core's Anchor Standards for Reading that emphasize working a text at that level of thinking. Each focus question is also derived from the Questioning the Author strategy (see the Questioning the Author strategy pages). Developing a wall poster or bookmarks of the Taxonomy of Self-Questioning Chart can serve as a daily reminder of this array of questions to guide students' comprehension.

4 After sufficient modeling, have students work with partners following their reading of a complex text, using the Taxonomy of Self-Questioning Chart as a graphic organizer for their responses. Partners examine their comprehension by deliberating the questions at each of the six levels of thinking. Some of the questions will necessitate rereading segments of the text. The chart prompts students to weigh in at all levels of complexity as they consider their understandings.

For example, students reading a health and fitness article about physical activity might respond to the focus question, "How can I connect what this author is telling me to understand something better?" at the applying level by stating:

> The author recommends getting up and walking around frequently. But how about students in classrooms? Look at how much sitting they have to do. Kids need to get up and move around, too.

(See the Self-Questioning Chart for Health and Fitness; blank reproducible available in the Appendix.)

Self-Questioning Chart for Health and Fitness

Level of Thinking	Focusing Question	Comprehension Statement
Creating	How has this author changed what I understand?	I thought exercise could balance physical inactivity, but the research says that although exercise is very important, it does not undo the damage done from prolonged time spent in sedentary behaviors like sitting. Exercise *and* limit all of that sitting around!
Evaluating	What perspective or authority does the author bring to what he or she is telling me?	The author is a journalist for *The New York Times*, and this article was in the Science Times section, both credible sources. The author cites findings from several research studies, including one by the American Cancer Society. The author quotes a couple of doctors who have researched this issue.
Analyzing	How is this similar to (or different from) what I've heard or read before?	I've heard about harmful effects, like blood clots, when one sits a long time on airplanes or in cars. You always hear people saying, "Get up and be active," and this article really reinforces that. I knew inactivity was related to being overweight, but the other effects surprised me.
Applying	How can I connect what this author is telling me to understand something better?	I do a lot of sitting during long stretches of the day, especially when working at the computer. The author recommends getting up and walking around frequently. But how about students in classrooms? Look at how much sitting they have to do. Kids need to get up and move around, too.
Understanding	What does the author want me to understand?	There is a relationship between the amount of time a person spends in sedentary inactivity, like sitting, and a variety of very harmful physical effects that can lead to a shorter life.
Remembering	What do I need to remember to make sense of this text?	Sedentary inactivity leads to negative effects on our metabolism, calorie burning drops dramatically, electrical activity in our muscle groups drop, good cholesterol levels fall because of lower enzyme action, and risks of Type 2 diabetes and obesity rise.

5 As students become practiced with eliciting focusing questions on their own, they can be given additional examples. Analyzing could also include questions like, How does the author support these ideas? Companion questions for evaluating might be, Does the author adequately support the viewpoints or conclusions? Is the argument convincing? and Did the author omit or overlook other possible arguments or evidence?

6 The Self-Questioning Taxonomy provides the foundation for more disciplinary-specific versions that mentor students in how to engage in questioning as they work complex texts for understanding through a disciplinary lens (see Tables 5–14 in Chapter 4). These more intensive disciplinary questions need to be modeled similarly to the above steps, and students need continual practice in using these questions to guide their thinking and develop their comprehension.

Advantages

- Students use focusing questions that cue them to use increasingly more sophisticated thinking as they become more accomplished readers and learners.

- Students internalize high-value questions that can be posed to authors rather than expecting to respond to questions developed by someone else.

- Students' comprehension of a text factors in both their reading of what an author is saying and their personal interpretations of the meaning of a work.

Meets the Standards

The Self-Questioning Taxonomy promotes careful reading and rereading of an author's message (R.1), discerning main ideas and summarizing (R.2), examining interrelationships of details or ideas (R.3), interpreting word meaning (R.4), analyzing text structure (R.5), tracking the author's perspective and purpose (R.6), integrating ideas into visual representations (R.7), supporting argumentation (R.8), comparing and contrasting with other sources of knowledge (R.9), and mentoring the reading of complex literary and informational texts (R.10). In addition, the collaborative conversations develop expressing and defending thinking using visual displays (SL.1, SL.2, SL.4). Follow-up writing provides practice in using text-based evidence in supporting arguments (W.1), summarizing and explaining (W.2), and drawing evidence from texts for analysis and reflection (W.9). Vocabulary development includes attention to word relationships (L.5) and acquiring domain-specific vocabulary (L.6).

References

Anderson, L.W., & Krathwohl, D.R. (Eds.). (2001). *A taxonomy for learning, teaching, and assessing: A revision of Bloom's taxonomy of educational objectives*. New York: Longman.

Bloom, B.S., Engelhart, M.D., Furst, E.J., Hill, W.H., & Krathwohl, D.R. (Eds.). (1956). *Taxonomy of educational objectives: The classification of educational goals: Handbook 1. Cognitive domain*. New York: Longman.

Buehl, D. (2007). Modeling self-questioning on Bloom's taxonomy. *OnWEAC*. Retrieved July 15, 2008, from www.weac.org/news_and_publications/education_news/2007-2008/readiingroom_modeling.aspx

Story Impressions

Teen athletes...concussions...soccer, football, volleyball...susceptible...head injury...62,800...headaches,
sleep disorders...high risk...learning disabilities.

Can you piece together the story line implied
by the preceding chain of keywords excerpted
from a recent news article? In all likelihood, by
connecting these terms and drawing from what you
already know about them, you can successfully infer
the focus of this public health report.

As you probably surmised, the article raises cautions about concussions suffered by teen athletes, especially those participating in sports such as soccer,
football, and volleyball. Adolescents are more susceptible to head injuries from concussions, and a recent
study estimated that 62,800 adolescents receive at least
mild sports-related concussions each year. Symptoms
of a concussion include headaches and sleep disorders, and students with learning disabilities are especially at risk for lingering brain injuries resulting from
concussions.

The chain of keywords prompted you to access what
you know about sports concussions, and perhaps your
curiosity was piqued about what the article would say
about dangers for teen athletes. You were able to form
an impression of the text before you actually read it.

Using the Strategy

Story Impressions (McGinley & Denner, 1987) is a
frontloading strategy that introduces significant terms
and concepts to students before they encounter them
in an assignment. The strategy can later be extended
to provide a template for summary writing.

1 Preview a text that students will read, and identify
a series of words and two- or three-word phrases
related to significant information or plot events. List the
words and phrases in the order students will encounter them while reading the text. Include both familiar
words and vocabulary that will reflect new learning
for many students, especially Tier 3 words (see the
discussion of Tier 2 and Tier 3 words in the Student-
Friendly Vocabulary Explanations strategy pages). This
vocabulary listing cues students about the sequence
of events or cause/effect relationships. Create a Story
Impressions chart with the terms arranged in a vertical

column, connected by arrows to indicate the order.
For example, to prepare students for a science textbook passage on geysers, select a chain of words and
phrases that emphasize how volcanic activity leads
to the heating of groundwater, which can sometimes
create geysers (see the Story Impressions for Earth
Science).

2 Have students work with partners to brainstorm
possible connections to the chain of clues on
their Story Impression sheets. Using what they might
know about some of the terms, encourage them to
make predictions about both the content of the text
and the meanings of unfamiliar keywords. In the earth
science example, students can tap their knowledge of
how volcanic activity generates heat and brainstorm
possible connections to geysers. Some students will
realize that heated water builds up pressure, which explains the phenomena of geysers such as Old Faithful
in Yellowstone National Park. Students may also need
to form conjectures of the meanings of Tier 2 terms
(e.g., *pent-up* and *constricted*) and Tier 3 terms (e.g.,
igneous and *fissure*) as they work on their predictions.

3 Have partners draft a
plausible impression
of what a text might con-
tain. First, inform them of
the context for the terms:
textbook passage, news article, biographical excerpt,
short story, informational
webpage, or other specific
genre. Ask students to create a possible version of
this text based on their
knowledge of the key terms
and their hunches about
unknown items. In the
box adjacent to the word
chains, have students write
a paragraph representing
their prediction of the text
in the appropriate style of
the original material (textbook passage, news article,
webpage, story, and so

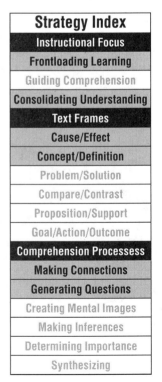

Strategy Index

Instructional Focus

Frontloading Learning

Guiding Comprehension

Consolidating Understanding

Text Frames

Cause/Effect

Concept/Definition

Problem/Solution

Compare/Contrast

Proposition/Support

Goal/Action/Outcome

Comprehension Processes

Making Connections

Generating Questions

Creating Mental Images

Making Inferences

Determining Importance

Synthesizing

Story Impressions for Earth Science

Write a paragraph using the chain words in order.

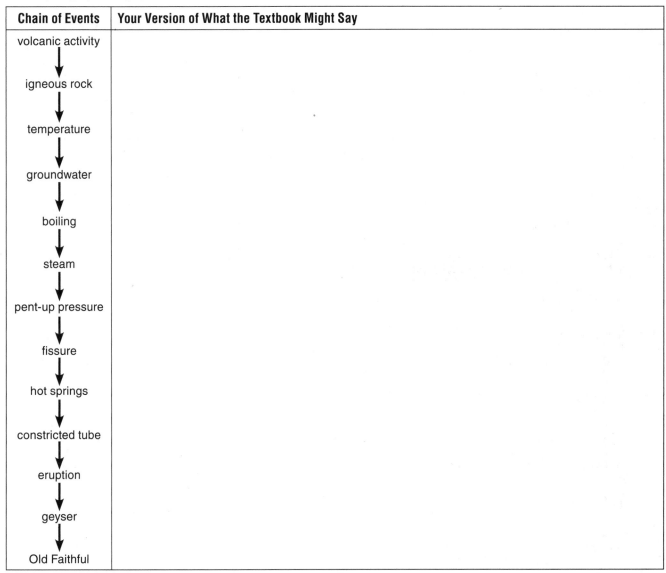

Chain of Events	Your Version of What the Textbook Might Say
volcanic activity	
igneous rock	
temperature	
groundwater	
boiling	
steam	
pent-up pressure	
fissure	
hot springs	
constricted tube	
eruption	
geyser	
Old Faithful	

Note. Adapted from *Classroom Strategies for Interactive Learning* (2nd ed., p. 133), by D. Buehl, 2001, Newark, DE: International Reading Association. Copyright © 2001 by the International Reading Association.

forth). All terms from the chain must be used in this paragraph, and students should integrate them in their writing in the order that they appear on the list. Have partners share their prediction paragraphs with the entire class. For example, a pair of earth science students might use their partial knowledge of terms to record the following impression:

> Volcanic activity pushes igneous rocks out of the center of the earth. The high temperature there heats groundwater to the boiling point, and it becomes steam. This steam has pent-up pressure that causes it to fissure and then change to hot springs. The hot springs come out of the ground in a constricted tube with an eruption. This is called a geyser, like Old Faithful in Yellowstone National Park.

4 Now that students have encountered key terms and concepts, activated relevant prior knowledge, and entertained predictions about the material, have them test their impressions by reading the actual text. As they read, have them check off the terms in the chain that they used accurately in their prediction paragraphs. To solidify new learning, have students follow up by writing a new paragraph(s), again using all the terms in the order they are represented in the chain, which summarizes what they have read and corrects their predictions. Our earth science students will discover that some of their original Story Impression was confirmed by the text, but other parts now need to be revised to be accurate.

As another example, students studying early 20th-century U.S. history were given a Story Impression for an article on the Harlem Renaissance, a time of intense creative activity in the African American community in New York City. After reading the text, students revisited these key terms to explain significant cultural changes resulting from these actions, which represent two key areas of thinking like a historian (change and cause/effect; see Table 5 in Chapter 4). As a result, their writing shifts to developing an explanatory summary paragraph that demonstrates their understanding of the article (see the Story Impressions for History).

Story Impressions for History

The Harlem Renaissance

Key terms summary: After reading the article on the Harlem Renaissance, write a paragraph explaining the significant changes represented by this period of U.S. history, using the terms below in the order they appear. Talk about three of the following people in your explanation: Claude McKay, Duke Ellington, Zora Neale Hurston, Langston Hughes, James Weldon Johnson, Paul Robeson. Place them in the list where you feel their contributions would best fit.

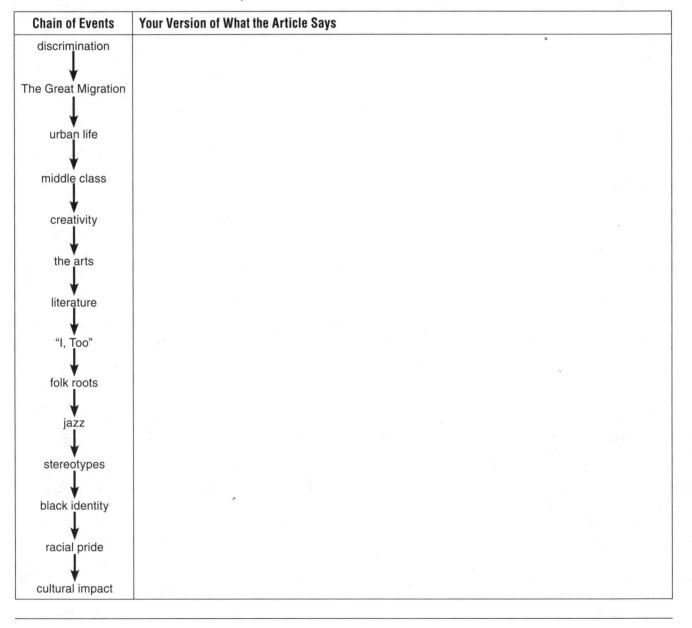

Chain of Events	Your Version of What the Article Says
discrimination ↓ The Great Migration ↓ urban life ↓ middle class ↓ creativity ↓ the arts ↓ literature ↓ "I, Too" ↓ folk roots ↓ jazz ↓ stereotypes ↓ black identity ↓ racial pride ↓ cultural impact	

A Story Impressions chain can make an excellent template for essay exams. Students can be asked to synthesize their learning by linking key information into explanations and summaries of the material from a unit of study. Furthermore, students gain practice in applying important new academic vocabulary in a meaningful discussion of their understandings rather than merely responding to isolated facts in multiple-choice or matching items.

Advantages

- Students are introduced to essential terminology and information before they become immersed in reading.

- Students marshal what they know about a topic and brainstorm possible connections to the new material.

- Students receive guidance in two comprehension tasks that are often difficult: determining importance and summarizing.

- Students verbalize their learning in writing and contrast what they knew before reading to what they know now.

- After sufficient practice, students can be asked to create their own chains of key terms—as a comprehension activity and for use as a Story Impressions chart to prepare their classmates for a new selection.

Meets the Standards

Story Impressions promotes careful reading and rereading of an author's message (R.1), discerning main ideas and summarizing (R.2), examining interrelationships of details or ideas (R.3), interpreting word meaning (R.4), analyzing text structure (R.5), tracking the author's perspective and purpose (R.6), comparing and contrasting with other sources of knowledge (R.9), and mentoring the reading of complex literary and informational texts (R.10). In addition, the collaborative conversations develop expressing and defending thinking (SL.1, SL.3, SL.4). The writing phases provide practice in using text-based evidence in summarizing and explaining (W.2) and drawing evidence from texts for analysis and reflection (W.9). Vocabulary development includes determining and clarifying key vocabulary (L.4), attention to word relationships (L.5), and acquiring domain-specific vocabulary (L.6).

References

Buehl, D. (2001). *Classroom strategies for interactive learning* (2nd ed.). Newark, DE: International Reading Association.

McGinley, W.J., & Denner, P.R. (1987). Story impressions: A prereading/writing activity. *Journal of Reading, 31*(3), 248–253.

Story Mapping

"What's the point of this story?" We have all been afflicted with the tedious experience of being ensnared by a rambling storyteller who persists with trudging us through a wearisome litany of events and details that apparently have no guiding focus and, ultimately, no real meaning for us: "Then, she said...and he couldn't find...so the two of them...just yesterday...they decided to..." and so on. Usually, we listen politely, resolving to quickly change the subject when the opportunity presents itself or perhaps even positioning ourselves for a quick exit. All the while, we are thinking, Why are you telling me this? Students have similar experiences with stories they read in our curricula; events unfold, but the point of the story remains elusive.

Stories—we grew up hearing them as children. We read them throughout our schooling. We relax while enjoying them in novels that we read for pleasure. We experience them on television and in movie theaters, and we tell them to our friends. Much of the way we view the world around us is organized into stories. In addition, stories are also a timeless method of sharing ideas, insights, and understandings with one another. A well-told story can illustrate a truth, prompt reflection and introspection, challenge our preconceptions, stimulate discussion and refinement of our thinking, inspire us and move us to action, or change the way we understand ourselves and our world. Stories are a powerful way of communicating things we need to know. And literary fiction, as the philosopher George Santayana observed, offers readers imaginary rehearsals for living.

Stories are also predominantly an indirect method of delivering messages; as listeners and readers, it is generally up to us to figure out just what an author is saying through the guise of story. Although we often turn to stories for relaxation and entertainment, literary fiction offers readers more, and sometimes we have to grapple with what a story might mean—to the author and to us as readers.

Using the Strategy

Children encounter narrative text very early in their lives and begin to internalize the common elements found in most stories. Story Mapping (Beck & McKeown, 1981) helps students track their knowledge of narrative structure to analyze stories. Story Maps feature graphic representations of key story elements to help students build a coherent framework for examining a story. Story Maps can be created for both short stories and longer works of fiction, such as novels.

1 Reinforce with students the key elements of a story. Suggest, for example, that they want to find out more about a work of fiction a friend has enjoyed: "What might you want to know about this story?" Students would likely comment that they want to know who the story is about, where it takes place, what happens, and how the story ends. Emphasize that our natural curiosity about an unfolding story line reflects the basic elements of a story: *who* refers to characters, *where* and *when* involve setting and mood, *what* details events of the plot, and *how* involves the resolution of the story's conflict. Refer to the questions at the remembering level of the Self-Questioning Taxonomy for Literacy Fiction (see Table 6 in Chapter 4), which concern establishing the basic story line of a work of fiction.

Why questions, however, engage readers in delving deeper into a literary work: Why did this character behave this way? Why did certain events happen? Why did the author make certain choices or employ certain literary techniques? Such questions reach beyond following a story line and trigger questions at the higher levels of the Self-Questioning Taxonomy for Literary Fiction.

2 Model using a story selected for its clear illustration of story structure. Have students fill in the key elements from the story on a blank Story Map (reproducible available in the Appendix). Stress recording only major events—those

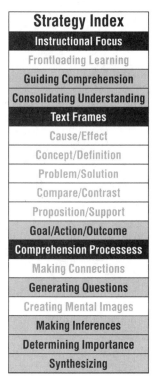

Strategy Index
Instructional Focus
Frontloading Learning
Guiding Comprehension
Consolidating Understanding
Text Frames
Cause/Effect
Concept/Definition
Problem/Solution
Compare/Contrast
Proposition/Support
Goal/Action/Outcome
Comprehension Processess
Making Connections
Generating Questions
Creating Mental Images
Making Inferences
Determining Importance
Synthesizing

that move the plot along—and establish the initiating event that sets the story into motion. (Instruct students to circle the number of this event on their maps.) Students expect a story to feature some sort of conflict, and how that conflict gets resolved is what makes a story interesting. As part of the modeling, review the basic kinds of conflict that are inherent in fictional literature:

- *Within a person:* A character is struggling within himself or herself, trying to figure out what to do.

- *Between people:* A character has some sort of problem with others that needs to be addressed.

- *Between people and nature:* A character is presented with a difficult natural situation that he or she must overcome, such as threatening animals, treacherous weather, a dangerous environment, or a disaster such as a fire.

Story Mapping becomes a valuable strategy for navigating complex fictional texts that are told in unconventional ways, out of sequence, by multiple or even unreliable narrators, or in a manner in which what happens is implicit rather than explicitly stated.

For example, eighth graders reading the short story version of Daniel Keyes's (1987) classic *Flowers for Algernon* encounter a narrative told through diary form, which means they have to extrapolate the story structure from the progression of entries. First, students identify the characters (Charlie, the doctors, Miss Kinnian, factory workers) and the setting (a laboratory in the 1950s). Students note that the action is initiated by Charlie's acceptance for the experimental operation, and they record the other major events leading to the climax, such as when the mouse Algernon becomes violent and loses his intelligence. Subsequent action includes Charlie's desperate attempt to use his intelligence to forestall a similar fate, and then his eventual reversion to the character met at the beginning of the story. Students identify the conflict as Charlie versus nature because he confronts changes in his own nature as a person, and they observe that this conflict is resolved by Charlie losing his intelligence and again becoming the person he used to be (see the Story Map for *Flowers for Algernon*).

3 Model with students how to use the organized information in the Story Map to develop an interpretation of an author's theme. Emphasize that the conflict and the way it is resolved provide a great deal of insight on possible points the author may have wished to communicate through the story. Students will recognize in *Flowers for Algernon* that a good-faith action, an experiment to improve one's intelligence, has unintended consequences and ends up hurting people.

The reader must grapple with a moral dilemma that surfaces in the story.

4 Point out that significant questions that can be asked about a story arise from the structure displayed in the Story Map. Certainly, we read stories to find out what happens, but we use what happens to ponder meaningful insights and ideas. Significant questions can relate to character development, events of the plot, the conflict and its resolution, and the author's possible themes. Questions may also focus on the author's craft, such as the use of language and literary devices used to develop the story's components. For example, questions for *Flowers for Algernon* might highlight the irony of a formerly cognitively disabled person becoming smarter than the scientists and actually becoming engaged in investigating his own experimental procedure. Students may raise questions about whether it is right to manipulate a person like this for scientific knowledge and the ethics of experimenting with human subjects, especially those who do not understand what will transpire. Students may ponder whether Charlie was better off having been granted superior intelligence, even if he lost it eventually.

5 Have students use the Story Map to analyze complex fictional texts that they read independently. After reading, have partners negotiate key elements that need to be included to clearly represent story structure. This collaboration is an especially important scaffold for examining complex literary texts in which some elements of the story line are implicit or not obvious, and thus will be missed by many readers. Solicit possible statements from the whole group about the possible themes that can be defended by evidence from the text, and discuss the rationale for plausible interpretations.

Advantages

- Students are provided with a visual framework for understanding and analyzing stories, and their knowledge of story structure is reinforced as a foundation for the successful interpretation of complex literary fiction.

- Discussion questions that are derived from the elements of story structure lead to more coherent and integrated comprehension by students. They improve their ability to predict probable questions for a particular story.

- Students become practiced in using story structure to determine and summarize critical story elements to explore possible themes and insights into human behavior.

Story Map for *Flowers for Algernon*[a]

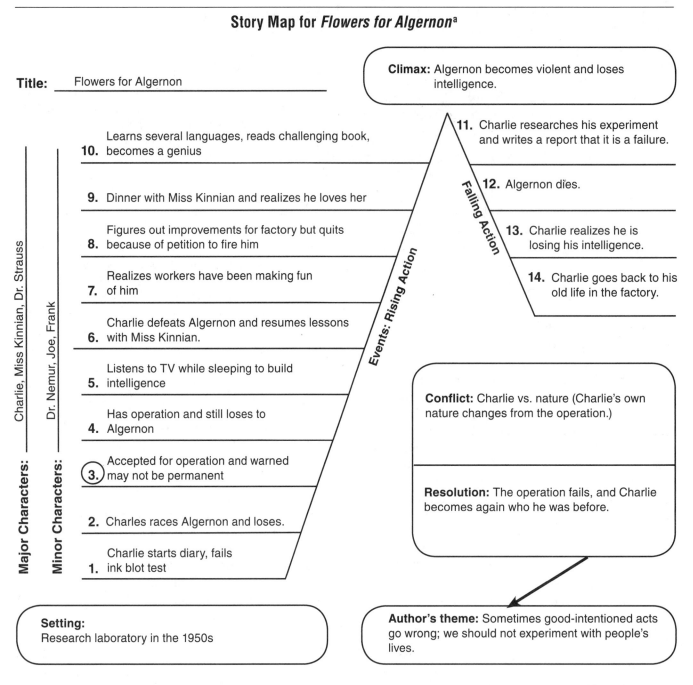

Title: Flowers for Algernon

Major Characters: Charlie, Miss Kinnian, Dr. Strauss

Minor Characters: Dr. Nemur, Joe, Frank

Events: Rising Action

10. Learns several languages, reads challenging book, becomes a genius

9. Dinner with Miss Kinnian and realizes he loves her

8. Figures out improvements for factory but quits because of petition to fire him

7. Realizes workers have been making fun of him

6. Charlie defeats Algernon and resumes lessons with Miss Kinnian.

5. Listens to TV while sleeping to build intelligence

4. Has operation and still loses to Algernon

3. Accepted for operation and warned may not be permanent

2. Charles races Algernon and loses.

1. Charlie starts diary, fails ink blot test

Climax: Algernon becomes violent and loses intelligence.

Falling Action

11. Charlie researches his experiment and writes a report that it is a failure.

12. Algernon dies.

13. Charlie realizes he is losing his intelligence.

14. Charlie goes back to his old life in the factory.

Conflict: Charlie vs. nature (Charlie's own nature changes from the operation.)

Resolution: The operation fails, and Charlie becomes again who he was before.

Setting: Research laboratory in the 1950s

Author's theme: Sometimes good-intentioned acts go wrong; we should not experiment with people's lives.

Note. Adapted from *Classroom Strategies for Interactive Learning* (3rd ed., p. 168), by D. Buehl, 2009, Newark, DE: International Reading Association. Copyright © 2009 by the International Reading Association.
[a]Keyes, D. (1987). *Flowers for Algernon.* Orlando, FL: Harcourt Brace.

- This strategy is appropriate for most narrative texts. It can also be modified for use with some types of expository material, such as biographies and autobiographies.

Meets the Standards

Story Mapping promotes careful reading and rereading of an author's message (R.1), discerning main ideas and themes (R.2), examining interrelationships of details or ideas (R.3), interpreting word meaning (R.4), analyzing text structure (R.5), tracking the author's perspective and purpose (R.6), integrating ideas into visual representations (R.7), supporting argumentation (R.8), and mentoring the reading of complex literary and informational texts (R.10). In addition, the collaborative conversations develop expressing and defending thinking using visual displays (SL.1, SL.2, SL.4). Follow-up writing provides practice in using text-based evidence in supporting arguments (W.1), summarizing and explaining (W.2), and drawing evidence from texts for analysis and reflection (W.9). Vocabulary development includes attention to word relationships (L.5).

Reference

Beck, I.L., & McKeown, M.G. (1981). Developing questions that promote comprehension: The story map. *Language Arts*, *58*(8), 913–918.

Literature Cited

Keyes, D. (1987). *Flowers for Algernon*. Orlando, FL: Harcourt Brace.

Structured Note-Taking

A workshop on how to set up a webpage. A genealogical investigation of vital records at a county courthouse. Your grandmother's recipe for au gratin potatoes. The directions to a track meet in a neighboring city. A plan of action being developed by the school literacy committee.

What do all of these situations have in common? They all involve note-taking. As you recall instances when you have taken notes, you will notice that your note-taking had a very pragmatic emphasis. You took notes because you needed a written record of information that you could refer to and use. Sometimes your notes serve a particular function and are then discarded. Other notes are kept as a reference for years.

Yet, teachers are frequently disappointed with the results of student note-taking. "Make sure you take notes on this!" is an oft-heard directive delivered by teachers almost daily to students. Teachers know that note-taking is a prerequisite for remembering and learning and that it is an essential study strategy, but student notes are often disorganized and lack important information. Students are frequently confused as to what to write down and what to leave out. Some students associate note-taking with mindlessly copying material verbatim from a book, the whiteboard, or a PowerPoint presentation. The result may be a student notebook that contains quite a bit of writing but is ineffective as a resource for understanding.

Structured Note-Taking (Smith & Tompkins, 1988) is a strategy that guides students toward taking more effective notes. The strategy makes use of graphic organizers, a powerful means of representing ideas and information. Graphic organizers provide students with a visual framework for making decisions about what should be included in their notes and impose a structure on student notes that makes them useful for future deliberations. Structured Note-Taking is an excellent strategy to use in all aspects of classroom learning in which note-taking is desirable—whether from print materials, video, Web-based inquiries, teacher presentations, or class or group discussions.

Using the Strategies

Structured Note-Taking provides an effective alternative to worksheets and provides students with a well-organized visual display of important information. This strategy engages students in the crucial comprehension processes of determining importance and synthesizing their understanding. Proposition/Support Outlines and Pyramid Notes, variations of Structured Note-Taking, are also presented.

1 Preview the content that students will be learning and identify the organizational structure that is best represented in the material. The following six text frames address common ways that information is organized: problem/solution, compare/contrast, cause/effect, proposition/support, goal/action/outcome, and concept/definition (see Chapter 3).

2 Create a graphic organizer using boxes, circles, arrows, and other visual structures that emphasize a particular text frame(s). It is essential to label the graphic with frame language, such as causes/effects, similarities/differences, or problem/causes of problem/possible solutions. This is an indispensable first step because graphic organizers are not merely sheets with random geometric figures for students to fill with minutia. You are instead creating structured notes to spotlight relationships among information. In addition, graphic organizers should focus on disciplinary thinking. A graphic should draw readers toward resolving questions that are central to thinking through a disciplinary lens (see Tables 5–14 in Chapter 4).

Distribute this graphic organizer to students as a note-taking study guide. They will take notes by recording relevant information in the appropriate spaces in the graphic outline. Highlight the type of text frame being used each time you provide structured notes so students recognize the various types of text frames and internalize

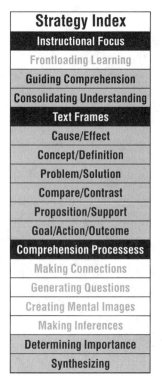

their use. Students need to be aware that boxes and circles are not aimlessly placed on a page but that each graphic organizer is devised to help them perceive meaningful connections.

For example, a Structured Note-Taking graphic organizer for a U.S. history article about the Great Migration helps students analyze the decisions of African Americans to move from the rural, southern states to northern cities in the early 20th century (see the Structured Notes for History). The graphic organizer highlights text frames for both cause/effect relationships (factors that led to the migration, and

---

Structured Notes for History

The Great Migration

Explain Why
African Americans left their homes in the southern United States and relocated to cities in the North in the early 1900s.

Causes: Push Factors	Causes: Pull Factors
• Life in the South was very hard for African Americans. • Many were poor sharecroppers and lived in shacks. • Few jobs, especially for African Americans • Wages were very low. • Frequently had barely enough to eat • Experienced violence and discrimination • Forced to live in segregated communities • Jim Crow laws; not allowed to use same facilities as white Southerners • Denied adequate education; poor schools • Were denied the right to vote and hold office • Were harassed by the Ku Klux Klan; often lived in fear • Had second-class status; had to know their "place" • Lynchings and other attacks increasing • Little protection from the courts and the law • Boll weevil ruined cotton crops; wrecked economy and ability to support themselves	• Many job opportunities in the North • Industrialization; factories hiring workers • New laws were restricting immigration from other countries; factories needed workers. • Factories recruited them to come North. • World War I caused a labor shortage. • World War I industries brought new jobs and new factories. • Agents were sent South to encourage African Americans to move North. • Sometimes provided with free transportation on the railroads • Black newspapers like *The Chicago Defender* argued that African Americans should come North. • Many African Americans had family and friends who had relocated in the North. • Family and friends in the North wrote letters of how their lives were better.

Explain the Changes

Historical changes that led to the Great Migration:
• *Population:* Fewer immigrants to work in factories; explosion of African Americans living in the North
• *Technological:* New industries leading to new factories
• *Environmental:* Boll weevil destroying crops
• *Economic:* New jobs in the North with better wages; transportation on railroads to the North provided
• *Political:* World War I led to a need for workers; white males drafted into the army; rise of the Ku Klux Klan
• *Cultural:* Increased violence against African Americans in the South; encouraged to move to the North by black newspapers, factory owners, and family and friends living in the North

Results of These Changes

• Also segregation in the North; creation of African American communities in cities
• Wages were low, and many still lived in poverty.
• Housing shortages; many lived together; many lived in crowded ghetto areas
• Competed for jobs with returning soldiers and other white workers
• The Great Depression after World War I led to many workers being out of work.
• African Americans were "last hired, first fired."
• Increased racial tensions in many northern cities
• Race riots in some cities; bombings, killings, and other violence against African Americans
• Southern black culture, such as blues, jazz, and food traditions, spread throughout the country.
• African American culture flourished; in music, arts, food, churches, literature
• African American city leaders and business leaders emerged.
• African American middle class expanded in northern cities.
• African Americans increasingly became a political voice in cities.

the resulting effects of that movement north) and compare/contrast relationships (negative factors that pushed African Americans out of the South versus positive factors that pulled them to northern cities). The Structured Notes are intentionally created to reflect reading through a historian's lens and emphasize two key questioning focuses of that discipline: What happened, and what caused it to happen? and What changed, why did these changes occur, and how did the changes impact people? (See Table 5 in Chapter 4.) Therefore, students are prompted to also analyze the changes that precipitated this population movement by connecting the text to the six types of change examined by historians (see the History Change Frame strategy pages).

3 Structured Note-Taking provides a number of opportunities for students to collaborate. When introducing the strategy, have students work in pairs while reading, or rereading, a passage and justify to their partners their decisions on what to select and where to place it in the graphic outline. Students could also compare notes from their reading with classmates to develop a more thorough set of Structured Notes. Another variation is to solicit items from partners to create exemplary notes for the entire class as part of a follow-up discussion dynamic.

4 Ask students to use their Structured Notes as a guide for verbalizing their understandings. Although much of the specific information contained in the notes will be forgotten (see the discussion of Fact Pyramids in Chapter 3), they should prove invaluable in holding information so students can synthesize their understandings—summarize key ideas, draw conclusions, develop interpretations, and make generalizations. Information in Structured Notes represents text-based evidence that is then employed for written syntheses of new learning—summaries, explanations, and arguments.

5 As students gain practice in using Structured Notes, they will begin to develop their own graphic organizers to structure their notes (Jones, Pierce, & Hunter, 1988). At first, help students identify the most appropriate text frame for their notes, a task that they will become increasingly able to accomplish independently.

Proposition/Support Outlines

Proposition/Support Outlines (Buehl, 1992) are a variation of Structured Note-Taking for texts that present viewpoints, positions, debatable assertions, theories, hypotheses, or any sort of argumentation. Proposition/Support Outlines supply students with a framework for analyzing the types of justification an author uses to support an interpretation, conclusion, or generalization.

1 Initiate a discussion with students about the distinction between argumentation and opinion. Brainstorm definitions of each and generate a list of examples. Arguments are supportable statements; they can be defended by the marshaling of an array of factual information. Opinions tend to be viewpoints that primarily draw on personal beliefs and experiences, or perhaps a very narrow sampling of a few facts. All of us are equally entitled to our opinions, but that does not make our opinions equal. When students offer opinions that they cannot support beyond their personal beliefs and experiences, they may maintain, "Well, it's just my opinion, and we disagree," which is an acknowledgment that they cannot make a justifiable defense of their position. The emphasis in the Common Core's literacy standards is argumentation—interpretations, conclusions, generalizations, or explanations that can be adequately buttressed by text-based evidence and support. The bar is considerably higher for making arguments than for stating opinions.

"Abraham Lincoln assumed the presidency of the United States in 1861" is a fact statement; it is either accurate or inaccurate, but it is not arguable. "Lincoln's election precipitated the American Civil War" is an argument; it is an interpretation that can be either supported or not supported by facts that comprise the historical record. Historians debate such assertions but must offer convincing factual evidence to make their case. "Lincoln looked more presidential with his beard than without it" is an opinion—in this case based on personal preferences—that really cannot be supported by facts that extend beyond personal tastes or beliefs.

Emphasize that fact statements can be proven right or wrong and that facts form the basis for arguments, which are either accepted or not accepted. Clearly, some arguments are more defensible than others because they are better supported by known facts. Opinions cannot be proven, and opinions that have little basis in fact are termed *unfounded*.

2 Introduce the term *proposition*—a statement that can be argued as true. Provide students with several possible propositions, such as the following:

• Today's movies are too violent.

• Drug testing is necessary for all professional athletes.

• Dogs make the best pets.

Divide students into collaborative groups and assign each group the task of generating several arguments that could support one of these propositions. Introduce a blank Proposition/Support Outline (reproducible available in the Appendix) and model for students how various supports for a proposition can be categorized in five ways: as facts, research and statistics, examples, expert authority, or logic and reasoning.

3 Assign students a proposition/support text selection and have them work with partners to complete the outline as they analyze the author's arguments. Select for students a text that features a clear proposition. For example, students in a social studies class read an article detailing how the loss of the world's rain forests portends global environmental disaster. After ascertaining this proposition, they complete the outline to categorize arguments supporting the global catastrophe scenario. In this case, the rain forest article contained information and arguments reflected in all five support categories (see the Proposition/Support Outline for Rain Forests).

4 Analyze with students the type of support presented. How convincing is it? Does the author rely solely on logic, reasoning, and examples, neglecting to use statistics or other facts? Is only a single expert authority cited? How reliable are the statistics? (For example, public survey results are statistics but are volatile and change frequently.) Do the examples seem to be

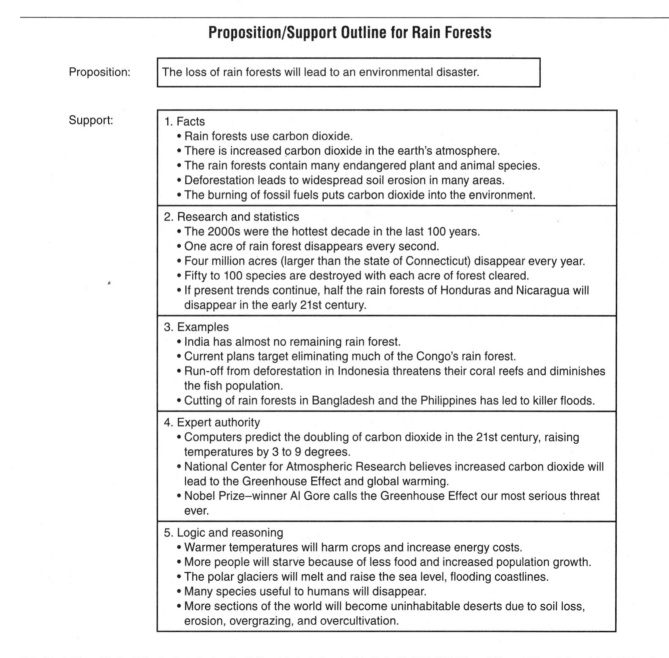

Proposition/Support Outline for Rain Forests

Proposition: | The loss of rain forests will lead to an environmental disaster.

Support:

1. Facts
   - Rain forests use carbon dioxide.
   - There is increased carbon dioxide in the earth's atmosphere.
   - The rain forests contain many endangered plant and animal species.
   - Deforestation leads to widespread soil erosion in many areas.
   - The burning of fossil fuels puts carbon dioxide into the environment.

2. Research and statistics
   - The 2000s were the hottest decade in the last 100 years.
   - One acre of rain forest disappears every second.
   - Four million acres (larger than the state of Connecticut) disappear every year.
   - Fifty to 100 species are destroyed with each acre of forest cleared.
   - If present trends continue, half the rain forests of Honduras and Nicaragua will disappear in the early 21st century.

3. Examples
   - India has almost no remaining rain forest.
   - Current plans target eliminating much of the Congo's rain forest.
   - Run-off from deforestation in Indonesia threatens their coral reefs and diminishes the fish population.
   - Cutting of rain forests in Bangladesh and the Philippines has led to killer floods.

4. Expert authority
   - Computers predict the doubling of carbon dioxide in the 21st century, raising temperatures by 3 to 9 degrees.
   - National Center for Atmospheric Research believes increased carbon dioxide will lead to the Greenhouse Effect and global warming.
   - Nobel Prize–winner Al Gore calls the Greenhouse Effect our most serious threat ever.

5. Logic and reasoning
   - Warmer temperatures will harm crops and increase energy costs.
   - More people will starve because of less food and increased population growth.
   - The polar glaciers will melt and raise the sea level, flooding coastlines.
   - Many species useful to humans will disappear.
   - More sections of the world will become uninhabitable deserts due to soil loss, erosion, overgrazing, and overcultivation.

Note. Adapted from "Outline Helps Students Analyze Credibility of Author's Premise," by D. Buehl, 1992, *WEAC News & Views, 28*(1), p. 8. Copyright © 1992 by Doug Buehl.

typical or atypical? Has important counteracting information been omitted from the discussion? As the rain forest outline is discussed, students will make a judgment about the case presented by the author—whether to accept or reject the author's proposition.

The Proposition/Support Outline is also an excellent guide for independent inquiry because it provides students with a framework for scrutinizing websites and reference materials for relevant information and arguments. For example, students assigned the task of writing a position paper on a topic or preparing for a debate will find that the strategy is an excellent prompt for examining sources and organizing writing.

Pyramid Notes

Pyramid Notes (Burke, 2002) are a variation of Structured Note-Taking that uses graphic elements to perceive and outline superordinate and subordinate textual information.

1 Develop a Pyramid Note-Taking template that follows the textual organization of a text that students will be reading. This strategy can be especially valuable in guiding student examination of textbook sections or chapters. The template should mirror features such as chapter, section, headings, and subheadings as they are presented in the text (see the Pyramid Notes for Health and Fitness).

2 Model using the pyramid diagram for note-taking, especially in deciding which supporting details and developing details warrant attention. Read a segment aloud, or have students work with partners, to determine which details seem most worthy for summarizing key ideas. Emphasize that not everything stated by an author is sufficiently significant to be included in the pyramid outline.

3 Have students work with partners to complete the Pyramid Notes for a section of text that they have previously read.

Pyramid Notes provide a valuable option to worksheet assignments, as students create a visual display of key ideas and supportive detail that can be used for writing summaries and explanations and for further study.

Advantages

- Students are able to see relationships between ideas as they take notes; they realize that note-taking is more than writing down isolated pieces of information.

- Students can take notes that are coherent and easy to use for synthesizing their understandings in subsequent discussions and writing activities.

- Structured Notes emphasize visual representation of information, which facilitates memory of the material.

- Proposition/Support Outlines provide students with practice in developing critical reading skills as they become adept at noticing an author's viewpoint.

Meets the Standards

Structured Note-Taking promotes careful reading and rereading of an author's message (R.1), discerning main ideas and summarizing (R.2), examining interrelationships of details or ideas (R.3), analyzing text structure (R.5), tracking the author's perspective and purpose (R.6), integrating ideas into visual representations (R.7), supporting argumentation (R.8), and mentoring the reading of complex literary and informational texts (R.10). In addition, the collaborative conversations develop expressing and defending thinking using visual displays (SL.1, SL.2, SL.4). Follow-up writing provides practice in using text-based evidence in supporting arguments (W.1), summarizing and explaining (W.2), and drawing evidence from texts for analysis and reflection (W.9). Vocabulary development includes attention to word relationships (L.5) and acquiring domain-specific vocabulary (L.6).

References

Buehl, D. (1992). Outline helps students analyze credibility of author's premise. *WEAC News & Views, 28*(1), 8.

Burke, J. (2002). *Tools for thought: Graphic organizers for your classroom.* Portsmouth, NH: Heinemann.

Jones, B.F., Pierce, J., & Hunter, B. (1988). Teaching students to construct graphic representations. *Educational Leadership, 46*(4), 20–25.

Smith, P.L., & Tompkins, G.E. (1988). Structured note-taking: A new strategy for content area readers. *Journal of Reading, 32*(1), 46–53.

Literature Cited

Bronson, M.H. (2011). *Glencoe health.* Columbus, OH: Glencoe/McGraw-Hill.

Suggested Reading

Armbruster, B.B., & Anderson, T.H. (1982). *Idea-mapping: The technique and its use in the classroom or simulating the "ups" and "downs" of reading comprehension* (Reading Education Report No. 36). Urbana: Center for the Study of Reading, University of Illinois at Urbana-Champaign.

Pyramid Notes for Health and Fitness

Chapter Title	Managing Stress and Coping With Loss
Section Title	Understanding Stress

Main Idea (Find on the first page of the section.)	Stress can affect you in both positive and negative ways.

	1. What Is Stress?	**2. Causes of Stress**	**3. Response to Stress**	**4. Stress and Your Health**
Supporting Details (Write the headings on the lines and summarize the introductory paragraphs.)	Stress is the reaction of the body and mind to the challenges and demands of daily life. Stress is natural, and we can't avoid the situations in life that can cause it.	Stressors are explained as anything that causes stress for a person. Stressors are different for different people and groups. What can be stressful for some people or groups might not be stressful for others.	Your body automatically activates a stress response when you face a stressful situation. Your body's nervous system and some hormones are triggered without any thought on your part.	Physical changes in the body can have a negative impact. A psychosomatic response is a negative impact on your body caused by stress and not injury or illness.
Developing Details (Use the subheadings to explain the supporting details listed above.)	Perception is related to stress: • If your perception is negative, then your stress may interfere with your ability to perform; you may feel overwhelmed, frustrated, or angry. • If your perception is positive, then your stress may motivate and inspire you to perform well.	Stressors for teens: • Life situations: School, problems with friends, bullying, family and peer pressure • Environmental: Living in an unsafe neighborhood, media messages, natural disasters • Biological: Body changes, illness, injury • Thinking: poor self-esteem, appearance, not fitting in • Behavioral: Busy life, relationship issues, smoking, alcohol, drugs	• Stage 1 is alarm, "fight or flight" as body prepares to defend itself. • Stage 2 is resistance as the body adapts and reacts; you may perform at a higher level. • Stage 3 is fatigue as the body tires and loses the ability to adapt because of prolonged stress.	Physical effects of stress: • Headaches • Weakened immune system • High blood pressure • Clenched jaw, teeth grinding • Digestive disorders Mental effects of stress: • Difficulty concentrating • Irritability • Mood swings

Note. Developed for *Glencoe Health* (pp. 92–95), by M.H. Bronson, 2011, Columbus, OH: Glencoe/McGraw-Hill. Copyright © 2011 by Glencoe/McGraw-Hill.

Student-Friendly Vocabulary Explanations

How comfortable are you with the following words: *inclined, abnormal, privy, unsought, feigned, preoccupation, levity, intimate, revelation, quivering, horizon, plagiaristic, marred, suppressions, infinite, snobbishly, fundamental,* and *parceled?* Very likely, some of these words surface occasionally in your speech and writing. Others are easily recognizable as words you can confidently understand when you are reading or listening. Perhaps there is even a word or two in this list that you are not necessarily sure of. What do these words have in common? Each is an example of a Tier 2 word—a word encountered predominantly through written texts but heard less frequently in spoken language (Beck, McKeown, & Kucan, 2013).

In addition to being Tier 2 words, each of the words in the list share another similarity: Imagine them appearing together in a paragraph. What might this paragraph be about? How might these words be related to one another? Each can be sighted in the third paragraph of the opening page of F. Scott Fitzgerald's classic novel *The Great Gatsby.* Like many authors, Fitzgerald expected his readers to be able to navigate prose packed with vocabulary that extends beyond the normal discourse of spoken language.

As teachers, we are frequently asked what a word means. What students are generally expecting from us is a definition, a word or short phrase that can be conveniently inserted as a substitution for the unknown word. Yet, researchers are pessimistic about the effectiveness of definitions in building one's knowledge about vocabulary. Various studies have shown that about two thirds of the sentences created by students to use new words based on definitions did not make sense. Without truly having a feel for the new word, students tend to swap unknown words into familiar contexts, resulting in sentences that are awkward, odd, or nonsensical.

Using the Strategy

Concerned that students equate copying definitions from a dictionary with vocabulary development, Beck and her colleagues (2013) recommend Student-Friendly Vocabulary Explanations, a strategy for constructing word knowledge as networks of personal connections and useful associations. To gain facility with a new word, students learn multiple facets of the word's meaning, practice using the word in a variety of acceptable contexts, and integrate the word into their existing background knowledge.

1 Determine which words are most worthy of instructional time by considering three levels of utility. Beck and her associates (2013) categorize words as falling into three tiers (see the Three Tiers of Vocabulary). Words targeted for instruction will include a mix of Tier 2 and Tier 3 words.

Feldman and Kinsella (2005) caution, however, that many words highlighted in textbooks or listed in a teacher's manual do not deserve instructional attention, and other mainline and essential words are left for students to infer their meanings. Feldman and Kinsella offer the following types of words to serve as guidelines for teachers who want to select high-utility vocabulary for instruction:

- *Big idea words:* Tier 3 words that are the core of the academic language of an academic discipline. These would include key conceptual science terms, social studies terms, math terms, language arts terms, and so forth. Words such as *seismic, feudalism, equation,* and *symbolism* fall under the category of big idea words.

- *Academic tool kit words:* Tier 2 words that students will meet again and again across academic disciplines. Words such as *contrast, function, environment,* and *perspective* pop up continually in written texts, yet these words are typically not taught. As a result, students develop hazy or imprecise meanings of highly crucial and recurring vocabulary.

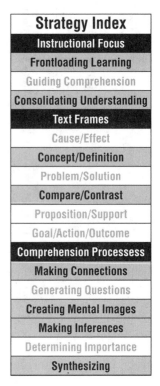

Strategy Index

Instructional Focus
Frontloading Learning
Guiding Comprehension
Consolidating Understanding
Text Frames
Cause/Effect
Concept/Definition
Problem/Solution
Compare/Contrast
Proposition/Support
Goal/Action/Outcome
Comprehension Processess
Making Connections
Generating Questions
Creating Mental Images
Making Inferences
Determining Importance
Synthesizing

Three Tiers of Vocabulary

Tier 1 Words	Tier 2 Words	Tier 3 Words
Basic words that commonly appear in spoken language	The more sophisticated vocabulary of written texts	Words central to building knowledge and conceptual understanding within the various academic disciplines and which are integral to instruction of content
Because they are heard frequently, in numerous contexts, and in consort with a great deal of nonverbal communication, Tier 1 words rarely require explicit instruction in school. English learners, of course, must first develop this conversational language as a foundation for further vocabulary growth.	Mature language users employ such words with regularity, but students encounter them less frequently as listeners. As a result, these words are unknown to many of our learners. Because of their lack of redundancy in oral language, Tier 2 words present challenges to students who primarily meet them in print.	Medical terms, legal terms, biology terms, and mathematics terms are all examples of Tier 3 words. These words surface relatively rarely in general vocabulary usage, but students must master them as they study the various content disciplines. All content areas feature their own distinct Tier 3 words that need explicit instruction.

Note. Adapted from *Classroom Strategies for Interactive Learning* (3rd ed., p. 176), by D. Buehl, 2009, Newark, DE: International Reading Association. Copyright © 2009 by the International Reading Association.

- *Disciplinary tool kit words:* Tier 2 words common to the study of an academic discipline that are used frequently in the discourse of a subject area. Terms such as *alliance* and *policy* in social studies and *hypothesis* and *dilute* in science are words that students may have to figure out totally on their own and, as a result, accrue only indistinct meanings for them.

- *Polysemous words:* Words that have multiple meanings and often very specific meanings in an academic discipline. *Matter* has a distinct meaning in science that contrasts a great deal to its general usage; *mean* in mathematics does not *mean* anything close to the second usage of the word in this sentence. In these examples, both *matter* and *mean* qualify as Tier 3 words that should receive explicit instruction.

For example, a history teacher might choose big idea terms like *segregation, integration,* and *Jim Crow laws* when studying the U.S. Civil Rights movement of the 1950s and 1960s. But academic tool kit words, such as those related to argumentation—*contention, proposition,* and *counteract*—would also be useful to discussions of people's beliefs and justifications for actions. Disciplinary tool kit words might include *discriminate, boycott,* and *martyr.*

2 Model for students how to explain a word rather than seeking a definition. A Student-Friendly Vocabulary Explanation should include the following components:

- The word is described in everyday language rather than dictionary-speak.

- The word is explained in connected language, not with isolated single-word or short-phrase definitions.

- The explanation exemplifies multiple contexts that feature the word in action.

- The explanation includes *you, something,* or *someone* to help students ground the new word in familiar situations.

For example, a teacher modeling an explanation of the word *belligerent* might say,

> If you are belligerent with someone, you are showing a lot of hostility to that person. Someone who is belligerent with you is threatening to you, and you feel like you are being attacked. Someone who has a belligerent attitude will likely get into a lot of fights. Two countries that are at war are called belligerents.

Notice how an explanation reaches far beyond the provision of a simple one-word definition or synonym.

3 Solicit students to provide their own examples of the word in action. Students need guided opportunities to playfully experiment with contexts that might feature the new word. Usually, the individual in the classroom who gets the most practice in saying a keyword is the teacher; instead, students need to begin the process of moving the word into their spoken vocabulary: "My cat is very belligerent to other cats. It always snarls and hisses at them." "The Al-Qaeda terrorists have been extremely belligerent toward the United States." As students explore appropriate usages of the word, encourage them to continue to refine their understanding by venturing into possible uses that do not exactly parallel your examples. As a result, students are less likely to narrowly trap the word into the original context where they first encountered it.

This experimentation phase can also clear up misunderstandings or misconceptions about a word's usage. For example, the student who offers "The approaching thunderstorm was very <u>belligerent</u> to me" has overgeneralized the connection between *belligerent* and *threatening*. A clarification that *belligerent* is a threatening attitude shown by people or animals can be added to the explanation at this time.

4 Prompt students to consider the question, Who would use this word? Ask them to imagine the kinds of people who would likely be regular users of the new word and to create sentences that reflect what these people might say, such as the following (see also the Word Family Trees strategy pages):

- A police officer: "The violence in the community was caused by a <u>belligerent</u> confrontation between two gangs."
- A school principal: "If you don't stop being <u>belligerent</u> to those boys, you will be suspended!"

Be conscious of regular modeling of Tier 2 and Tier 3 words in your oral language. Students will incrementally gain a grasp of a new word as a result of these ongoing repetitions in a variety of appropriate contexts.

5 Have students keep records in their class notebooks of the new words you devote to explicit instruction. Feldman and Kinsella (2005) recommend a word study guide that features a graphic organizer that tracks facets of a word's meaning (see the Word Study Guide for *Boycott*). Students record the initial context for where the word was sighted, which offers them an appropriate model for its usage. They then fashion their Student-Friendly Vocabulary Explanation of the word and practice putting it in play themselves

with an example or two. Visual representations of a new word can be especially powerful mnemonics. Ask students to quickly sketch an image that crystallizes their understanding of the word or some key aspect of it. Students can be expected to add words that they are taught as an integral class assignment.

6 Create vocabulary exercises that effectively reinforce students experimenting with putting targeted words in play. Beck, McKeown, and Kucan (2008) advocate several high-quality options for fostering vocabulary usage. For example, reinforcement activities that enhance knowledge of *privy*, one of our opening examples from *The Great Gatsby*, could include the following:

- Examples/nonexamples

  Which of the following would be examples of being <u>privy</u> to something? Explain your thinking.

  1. Your best friend tells you a secret.
  2. You read about an international event in this morning's newspaper.
  3. You witness a person doing something that he doesn't want others to know about.
  4. Your sister tells the family she's getting married.
  5. Something happened to you that no other person is aware of.

- Word associations

  What associations do you have with the word *privy* that can help you remember it?

  "I think of President Obama for the word *privy* because he is privy to lots of classified information that hardly anyone is permitted to see."

- Generating situations, contexts, and examples
  - What might someone say to you if she made you <u>privy</u> to some embarrassing information?
  - Make a list of advantages you might have if you were <u>privy</u> to something.
  - Make a list of disadvantages you might have if you were <u>privy</u> to something.

Word Study Guide for *Boycott*

Word	Found in This Sentence	Explanation	Examples	Visual Image[a]
boycott	The Montgomery bus boycott in 1955 protested the practice of racial segregation in the public transit system.	When you boycott something, you avoid having anything to do with it.	• My sister had an argument with our parents, and now she boycotts family gatherings. • Because the store owner is rude to young people, all the kids now boycott shopping there.	

Note. Adapted from *Classroom Strategies for Interactive Learning* (3rd ed., p. 177), by D. Buehl, 2009, Newark, DE: International Reading Association. Copyright © 2009 by the International Reading Association.
[a]Students draw a visual representation of the word here.

- Word relationships: Explore relationships between targeted words rather than learning them in isolation:
  - Decide how the words *privy* and *feigned* could be meaningfully connected.
  - Demonstrate your connection of these two words by using them together in a sentence.
- Personal connections

  Talk about a time when you were <u>privy</u> to something, or someone was privy to something about you. Make sure you use the word *privy* in your writing.
- Writing: Sentence stems
  - The company's competitors wanted to be <u>privy</u>...
  - Overhearing the phone conversation made me <u>privy</u>...
- Embedded word study (examples from *The Great Gatsby*)
  - Explain how the word *privy* relates to an understanding of Nick Carraway.
  - Explain how the word *feigned* relates to the character of Jay Gatsby.

Advantages

- Students receive assistance in how to meld understandings of new words with their existing background knowledge.
- Students learn many facets about a new word instead of fixating on a single definition.
- Students associate vocabulary learning with practicing using new words in their speaking and writing rather than merely memory work.

- Students gradually build their academic vocabulary, making them better prepared to read complex disciplinary texts and to learn academic subjects.
- This strategy may be used with students from elementary through secondary levels.

Meets the Standards

The Student-Friendly Vocabulary Explanations strategy promotes interpreting word meaning (R.4), integrating ideas into visual representations (R.7), and mentoring the reading of complex literary and informational texts (R.10). In addition, collaborative conversations develop expressing and defending thinking (SL.1, SL.3, SL.4). Follow-up writing provides practice in summarizing and explaining (W.2) and drawing evidence from texts for analysis and reflection (W.9). Vocabulary development includes determining and clarifying key vocabulary (L.4), attention to word relationships (L.5), and acquiring domain-specific vocabulary (L.6).

References

Beck, I.L., McKeown, M.G., & Kucan, L. (2008). *Creating robust vocabulary: Frequently asked questions and extended examples*. New York: Guilford.

Beck, I.L., McKeown, M.G., & Kucan, L. (2013). *Bringing words to life: Robust vocabulary instruction* (2nd ed.). New York: Guilford.

Buehl, D. (2009). *Classroom strategies for interactive learning* (3rd ed.). Newark, DE: International Reading Association.

Feldman, K., & Kinsella, K. (2005). *Narrowing the language gap: The case for explicit vocabulary instruction*. New York: Scholastic.

Text Coding

Imagine that you are lying in bed, about to drift off to sleep after an eventful day jam-packed with activity. Your mind is still percolating with thoughts as you relax, and suddenly you realize that you have chanced upon an excellent idea for tomorrow's lesson. "I should click on the light and write this down" flickers through your consciousness, but instead, inevitably, you continue to relax and soon are fast asleep. Sure enough, the next morning you awaken with the knowledge that a great idea occurred to you the night before, but of course, you cannot recall it.

This scenario is a frequent happening in our lives. As we are engaged in a variety of routines—driving a car, jogging, eating lunch—valuable thoughts pop into our minds, but because they are ephemeral, and our mind moves on to other territory, we soon lose them. We need a system for tracking our thinking.

This also holds true for reading comprehension. A text triggers a host of useful connections and associations as we read along, but if we have no system for processing them, these insights may not be available to us when we reflect back on the passage and decide how to make sense of it. Struggling readers in particular have difficulty with harnessing their thinking as they negotiate the terrain of a complex text. As a result, they may conclude their reading with only a hazy outline of disjointed facts.

Proficient readers carry on an internal monologue while they read. It is as though these readers operate with a split personality. One personality is hard at work with the task at hand, such as reading a textbook chapter. The second personality works in the background, directing and evaluating all the cognitive activities needed to learn successfully—making meaningful connections, posing questions about the author's message, determining what is important in the chapter, and synthesizing understanding. This personality represents that inner voice that issues commands during reading: "Slow down! This is pretty tough going!" "Hold it here! This doesn't make any sense. Better reread." or "This stuff doesn't look very important. I'll just skim over it quickly and get into the next section." Proficient readers talk to themselves.

Researchers call this internal monologue metacognition—the ability to think about thinking and monitor comprehension (see the Metacognitive Conversations section in the introduction to Section 2). Metacognition reflects an ability to switch gears and try something else when learning breaks down, such as when a reading passage is proving particularly difficult, rather than continuing to plow ahead even if nothing is making sense. All readers can be taught how to activate the control center in their mind that directs their learning.

Using the Strategy

Text Coding (Harvey & Goudvis, 2007; Tovani, 2000) represents an annotation system for students to track their thinking while reading. As students catch themselves in the act of a specific comprehension process, they can apply the following codes to the texts they read:

R: "This *r*eminds me of..." to signify a connection to background knowledge or experiences

V: "I can picture this..." to signify *v*isualizing and creating mental images

E: "This makes me feel..." to signify an *e*motional response to the text

Q: "I wonder..." to signify a *q*uestion that occurred during reading

I: "I figured out that..." to signify making an *i*nference, such as a prediction or an interpretation

?: "I don't understand this..." to signify a segment that is confusing or does not make sense

!: "This is interesting..." to signify something that particularly intrigued you

1 Model how readers "talk to themselves" and "talk back to the author" with a text projected on your whiteboard. Think aloud as you read, jotting comments in the margins and underlining key

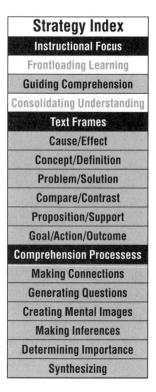

Strategy Index

Instructional Focus
Frontloading Learning
Guiding Comprehension
Consolidating Understanding

Text Frames
Cause/Effect
Concept/Definition
Problem/Solution
Compare/Contrast
Proposition/Support
Goal/Action/Outcome

Comprehension Processess
Making Connections
Generating Questions
Creating Mental Images
Making Inferences
Determining Importance
Synthesizing

segments or terms. Select a short piece of challenging text and introduce the selection to the class by noting that even excellent readers occasionally encounter problematic complex texts. Short pieces that contain confusing segments, ambiguities, unfamiliar vocabulary, or technical subject matter make excellent choices for these think-alouds.

Read the passage aloud as students follow along. Pause periodically to illustrate what you are thinking. For example, you can demonstrate predicting by saying, "I think this author is going to talk about...," and making connections by saying, "This reminds me of...." You can model creating images by saying, "I can picture that the author is describing...," and posing questions by saying, "I wonder why/how/what/who/where...." Clarifying can be demonstrated by saying, "This doesn't make sense to me. I think I should try...."

For example, the following short passage about rugby, a game unfamiliar to most students, could serve as an excellent think-aloud:

> Rugby is a type of football that is popular in the United Kingdom. Rugby matches consist of two 40-minute periods of play, with a five-minute halftime break. A match begins with a kickoff, from the center of the halfway line, of an oval-shaped ball somewhat larger than a U.S. football. Each team, which consists of eight forwards and seven backs, attempts to ground the ball in the opposing team's goal area. Action is generally continuous, although after a penalty, play is resumed by a scrummage. In a tight scrummage, a player rolls the ball into a tunnel formed by the opposing team's forwards, who are linked together with their arms around one another's waists. As they push, both teams attempt to heel the ball.

Parts of this passage will probably make sense, but at other points, a pause is needed so you can record a question mark to highlight material that needs clarification. After reading the entire passage, model to students how to paraphrase material in words that make sense to them. For example, you might say, "I wonder if in rugby the kickoff is like placekicking in American football or if it is more like the goalie kicking the ball in soccer." In this case, you are demonstrating both self-questioning and making connections to your personal experiences and knowledge.

2 After students have experienced several teacher think-alouds, have them practice the process themselves with partners as they tackle potentially difficult complex disciplinary texts. The partners take turns reading a segment aloud, pausing to share their thinking and strategies as they go along (see the Say Something Read-Aloud discussion in the Author Says/I Say strategy pages).

3 Prepare students to track their thinking through text coding. Coding a text involves two elements: highlighting or marking a spot in a paragraph, and then jotting a symbol in the margin to indicate the kind of thinking that was elicited at this point. Notice how these text codes parallel the comprehension processes outlined in Chapter 1.

As a variation for use with texts that cannot be marked, provide students with packs of small sticky notes, which can be affixed to the margin with a text code. An advantage of sticky notes is that students can make annotations that relate to the text code. In addition, Tovani (2000) recommends using Double-Entry Diaries (see the Double-Entry Diaries strategy pages). The left side of the paper is reserved for phrases that are lifted from the text; on the right side, students mark the code and jot down thoughts they had at that point in the reading.

4 Have students confer with partners and talk about places in the text where they have marked a code. Emphasize that these are particularly interesting spots because they represent something the author said that triggered deeper thinking on their part as readers.

During partner shares, ask students to pay special attention to ? codes—places where they experienced confusion or needed clarification. The Self-Monitoring Approach to Reading and Thinking (SMART) strategy (Vaughan & Estes, 1986) emphasizes problem solving these glitches in understanding (see the SMART Strategy Steps). The steps of the SMART strategy could be projected for students or displayed on a classroom chart.

Ask partners to brainstorm what could be done to make sense of those parts. Observe that some parts of the reading coded with question marks may have made sense after the entire passage was read. Partners should collaborate to specify the source of their problem (e.g., an unfamiliar word, an unclear sentence, a need for more examples) and explain how they tried to resolve their lack of understanding.

5 Text Graffiti (Buehl, 2004) is a method of annotating a text that expands on Text Coding by including marginal commentary. As learners, we have all highlighted, underlined, and annotated texts to impose our priorities on someone else's words. It is this conception of graffiti that can be employed as a classroom strategy—personalizing learning through activities that prompt students to put their face onto texts created by others.

Model and solicit from students their contributions for marginal graffiti. Emphasize that readers can begin to own a text by intertwining their ideas with those of the author's. Provide them with a photocopy of the

SMART Strategy Steps

1. Read a section of the text. Using a pencil, lightly add a "?" next to each paragraph that contains something you do not understand.
2. Self-translate. At the end of each section, stop and explain to yourself, in your own words, what you read. Look back at the text as you go over the material.
3. Troubleshoot. Go back to each "?." Reread the trouble spot to see if it now makes sense. If it still does not make sense:
   a. Pinpoint a problem by figuring out why you are having trouble:
      • Is it a difficult word or unfamiliar vocabulary?
      • Is it a difficult sentence or confusing language?
      • Does the author expect you to know something that you do not know?
   b. Try a fix-up strategy:
      • Use vocabulary resources, such as a glossary, a dictionary, or the Internet.
      • Use visual information, such as pictures and other graphics.
      • Use other parts of the chapter, such as a summary, a review section, diagrams, or other features.
      • Use online resources to clarify unknown information.
   c. Explain to yourself exactly what you do not understand or what confuses you.
   d. Collaborate and develop an interpretation of what the text might mean.

Note. Adapted from *Reading and Reasoning Beyond the Primary Grades* (pp. 143–144), by J.L. Vaughan and T.H. Estes, 1986, Boston: Allyn & Bacon. Copyright © 1986 by Allyn & Bacon.

---

text that allows wide margins on both the right and left sides to facilitate their graffiti. An alternative is to provide students with pads of sticky notes to affix their comments to a text that cannot be reproduced. Point out the usefulness of the following annotations:

• Enumerate ideas and information by writing numbers and keywords for each item in the margin (e.g., three reasons for..., two results of..., four events that...).

• List significant examples, both those presented in a text and those that occur to the reader.

• Integrate additional information on charts or other graphic organizers to make it more understandable and to connect visual information to what is discussed in a passage.

• Create a marginal glossary of key terms and definitions.

• Use margins to posit possible meanings of key terms if definitions are not directly stated.

• Indicate areas of agreement (A) or disagreement (D) with the author, or positives (+) and negatives (–), and briefly register reasons why.

• Jot down gist statements that sum up key segments in the reader's words, not the author's.

Color felt-tip pens are an excellent resource for annotating texts. Some estimates are that consistent use of color for coding (e.g., red for main points, blue for details or examples) can enhance memory of a text up to 20%. Students can achieve the same effect by using different-colored pads of sticky notes if they are attaching their comments to a textbook chapter or the pages of a novel. As students begin writing their graffiti on the text, reiterate that this activity asks them to go public with their thinking as they read and allows them to place their personal stamp on an author's message.

As a variation, Wilhelm, Baker, and Dube (2001) propose formatting a text as a Double-Entry Diary (see the Double-Entry Diaries strategy pages). The selection or story is flowed into the left-hand column, and the right side is left blank, offering students space for their marginal graffiti. This option is especially useful with presenting texts obtained from digital sources.

Advantages

• Text Coding while reading is a powerful strategy that helps students retain their thinking and create a personal understanding of an author's message.

• Students come to realize that comprehension is the result of the interplay between an author's words and a reader's thinking.

• Students become accustomed to listening to their inner dialogue about a text as they read.

• Students are provided with a system to verbalize their problem solving through difficult texts, and are encouraged to attempt fix-up strategies rather than give up or accept partial comprehension of a passage.

• Students become involved in summarizing a text in their own words, thus helping them remember as well as understand.

Meets the Standards

Text Coding promotes careful reading and rereading of an author's message (R.1), discerning main ideas and summarizing (R.2), examining interrelationships of details or ideas (R.3), interpreting word meaning (R.4), analyzing text structure (R.5), tracking the author's perspective and purpose (R.6), examining visual representations (R.7), supporting argumentation (R.8), and mentoring the reading of complex literary and informational texts (R.10). In addition, the collaborative conversations develop expressing and defending thinking (SL.1, SL.3, SL.4). Follow-up writing based on the coding can provide practice in using text-based evidence in supporting arguments (W.1), summarizing and explaining (W.2), and drawing evidence from texts for analysis and reflection (W.9). Vocabulary development includes determining and clarifying key vocabulary (L.4), attention to word relationships (L.5), and acquiring domain-specific vocabulary (L.6).

References

Buehl, D. (2004). Using graffiti as a reading tool. *OnWEAC*, *4*(8), 13.

Harvey, S., & Goudvis, A. (2007). *Strategies that work: Teaching comprehension for understanding and engagement* (2nd ed.). Portland, ME: Stenhouse.

Tovani, C. (2000). *I read it, but I don't get it: Comprehension strategies for adolescent readers*. Portland, ME: Stenhouse.

Vaughan, J.L., & Estes, T.H. (1986). *Reading and reasoning beyond the primary grades*. Boston: Allyn & Bacon.

Wilhelm, J.D., Baker, T.N., & Dube, J. (2001). *Strategic reading: Guiding students to lifelong literacy, 6–12*. Portsmouth, NH: Heinemann.

Suggested Reading

Simpson, M.L., & Nist, S.L. (1990). Textbook annotation: An effective and efficient study strategy for college students. *Journal of Reading, 34*(2), 122–129.

Three-Level Reading Guides

How often have we encountered, or even used, the phrase "I'm hearing you say..."? But we don't then proceed by merely parroting what we heard; instead, we convey our version of what we think we heard. We extend beyond exact statements to get at the nuances of the message. What are you saying that you aren't quite saying?

Of course, we recognize that communications operate at different levels. Some of what we receive we can accept at face value, and some needs further exploration beneath the surface. We need to interpret so we truly understand. This expectation also drives our thinking when we interact with authors. As proficient readers, we seamlessly shift our thinking about a text into deeper and more sophisticated levels. Of course, we want to be clear that we understood exactly what an author said—a literal comprehension of the text. In addition, however, we know that much of what authors tell us is implicit because they expect us to figure out some things—an inferential comprehension of the text. Finally, authors leave it to us to draw conclusions about the message, to consider implications and develop our take on the topic—an application of our comprehension of a text.

Common Core Reading Anchor Standard 1 encapsulates thinking at these levels and provides the foundation for comprehension of complex texts: "Read closely to determine what the text says explicitly and to make logical inferences from it; cite specific textual evidence when writing or speaking to support conclusions drawn from the text" (NGACBP & CCSSO, 2010, p. 10).

Using the Strategy

The Three-Level Reading Guide is a strategy that prompts students to engage in all three levels of thinking when they interact with written texts. Wilhelm (2007) typifies these three levels as on the line, between the lines, and beyond the lines.

1 Preview a selection to identify the particulars that should be highlighted in a Three-Level Reading Guide. First, focus on clarifying what the author is saying. Locate five or six main ideas that are central to understanding the author's message. Rephrase your statements so some represent what the author is saying, and some misrepresent what the author is saying. Use somewhat different language in your guide than the words chosen by the author so students must carefully evaluate each statement in terms of whether "the author said it." You are emphasizing "putting it together" Question–Answer Relationships that involve students constructing an answer (see the discussion of Question–Answer Relationships in the Questioning the Author strategy pages). You want to avoid "right there" Question–Answer Relationships at this level. Otherwise, many students will endeavor to complete this phase of the strategy through "locate and copy" skimming rather than careful reading and rereading. (See the "on the line" examples in the Three-Level Reading Guide for Social Studies).

The "on the line" statements should be verifiable; readers should be able to ascertain whether the author in effect said it.

2 Next, consider possible inferences that might be drawn from a reading of the text. In this case, the focus begins to shift to how the author is saying it. Students will be asked to locate clues in the text that signal something the author might be implying but does not directly state. Again, target inferences that are central to the author's message. Some of these inferred statements that you create should be consistent with author clues; others should be inconsistent or perhaps unfounded; and still others could be ambiguous, arguable either way, given what the author has provided. (See the "between the lines" examples in the Three-Level Reading Guide for Social Studies.)

You are stressing "author and me" Question–Answer Relationships at this second level, as students must combine the

Strategy Index
Instructional Focus
Frontloading Learning
Guiding Comprehension
Consolidating Understanding
Text Frames
Cause/Effect
Concept/Definition
Problem/Solution
Compare/Contrast
Proposition/Support
Goal/Action/Outcome
Comprehension Processess
Making Connections
Generating Questions
Creating Mental Images
Making Inferences
Determining Importance
Synthesizing

Three-Level Reading Guide for Social Studies

The Roaring Twenties

On the Line

Did the author say it? Check the statements below that represent what the author said in the article. *Note:* The statement will not be in the exact words used by the author. Locate the places in the text where "the author said it."

____ 1. Affordable automobiles were a major cause of social change in the United States.

____ 2. As people moved to cities, they tended to become more religious.

____ 3. City dwellers had more opportunities to experience new things.

____ 4. Things were very different in the United States after World War I as compared with before.

____ 5. Mass media—magazines, radio, movies—were primary defenders of "American values."

Between the Lines

Did the author imply it? Check the statements below that you believe are implied by the author. You will have to connect what the author says to information from your knowledge or experiences, to other texts that you have read, or to your general understandings about this topic. Locate the places in the text where the author provides you with clues about implied meanings.

____ 6. People in rural areas were out of step with the future.

____ 7. There was a lot more "sinning" going on in the cities.

____ 8. Young people sometimes really went too far with their newfound freedoms.

____ 9. Change may be unsettling sometimes, but you can't turn back the clock.

____ 10. Traditionalists and modernists really didn't understand each other.

Beyond the Lines

Check the statements below that you could agree with. You will need to think about what the author said in the text and your own knowledge to support your ideas.

____ 11. Society breaks down when people stray from established customs.

____ 12. It is healthy to break with traditions and seek new ways.

---

author's implications with their background knowledge to arrive at inferred answers. Three types of author implications can be included in the statements at this level:

1. *Expected inference:* The author expects readers to make these inferences, based on presumed reader background knowledge. Therefore, the author refers to or makes an allusion to something that readers are expected to add to from their personal knowledge to comprehend what the author is saying.

2. *Positioned inference:* The author positions readers to make these inferences, which readers may do without necessarily realizing it. The weight of the evidence provided, the language the author uses, the choice of examples, the handling of counterarguments—all can be means for authors to position readers to arrive at certain inferences.

3. *Revealed inference:* The author reveals personal beliefs, values, attitudes, or perspectives, perhaps not necessarily intentionally, that readers pick up on through inference. Author perspectives can greatly influence the way the author presents a message,

and this third category prompts students to notice the person behind the communication.

The "between the lines" statements should be arguable; readers may or may not be able to categorically resolve whether the author implied them. The key during this phase is text-based evidence that supports the argumentation. It is important to emphasize that the dynamic during this stage is not to establish whether the students themselves agree with the statements but to determine whether they can cite evidence that the author apparently agrees with the statements.

3 Finally, consider the article as a conversation starter: What larger issues are provoked by a reading of this text? What are you thinking now that you have read this text? What might be some conclusions or implications of the author's message? The emphasis at this stage is on the meaning we can take away from this author's message. Decide on two or three ideas that will prompt students to apply their thinking in a more global way. You are moving to "on my own" Question–Answer Relationships at this level. These statements will be open ended in the sense that the author does not resolve them in the text, and different perspectives might lead to a range of varying interpretations and positions. These applied statements should be worthy of debate and discussion and should flow naturally from the initial treatment of the topic by the author. (See the "beyond the lines" examples in the Three-Level Reading Guide for Social Studies.)

4 Construct the Three-Level Reading Guide to be completed by students in three stages. It is advisable to format the guide so students only receive one level at a time. Otherwise, they may be tempted to complete all three levels in one read, which negates the intentionality of rereading and returning to the text for fresh purposes. Initially, students read the text and respond individually to the "on the line" statements. As they double-check the author's message, students annotate the text by placing the number of each statement next to places in the selection that verify that the author did (or did not) say it. They then meet with a partner to come to a consensus regarding which statements were actually consistent with what the author said.

The second stage is intended to be done collaboratively, with students working with their partners to unearth implicit meanings. Again, students are asked to annotate the text, this time by placing the statement number next to spots where they detect clues from the author that would confirm (or disconfirm) the statement. This stage necessitates rereading and closer examination of segments of the text, and consensus may not be possible because partners may have valid reasons for disagreeing. The need for text-based evidence to support their arguments is paramount at this stage.

The third stage emphasizes "What does all this mean?" and is an excellent activity for collaborative group deliberations. Combine partners into groups of four and ask them to seek an understanding of the "beyond the lines" statements. For each statement, you may wish to ask a group recorder to list arguments for and arguments against as a prelude for a whole-class discussion of these ideas. Students should include references to statements made by the author and make connections to their relevant background experiences and knowledge as they construct and defend their arguments.

5 The Three-Level Reading Guide serves as an excellent prelude for either argumentative or explanatory writing. Students are prepared to cite textual statements as they expand on statements from either the level 2 or level 3 phases.

Advantages

- Students are engaged in a progressively deeper and more sophisticated reading and rereading of a text.
- Students clarify the literal message of an author to ensure that they understood what the author is telling them.
- Students become increasingly sensitive to implicit meanings and receive practice in making and justifying inferences.
- Students are asked to synthesize their understandings by considering "if this, then…" thinking, which requires drawing conclusions and applying their learning to larger ideas and themes.
- Students receive practice in close examination of a text and citing text-based evidence to support their interpretations.

Meets the Standards

The Three-Level Reading Guides strategy promotes careful reading and rereading of an author's message (R.1), discerning main ideas and summarizing (R.2), examining interrelationships of details or ideas (R.3), interpreting word meaning (R.4), analyzing text structure (R.5), tracking the author's perspective and purpose (R.6), supporting argumentation (R.8), comparing and contrasting with other sources of knowledge (R.9), and mentoring the reading of complex literary and informational texts (R.10). In addition, the collaborative conversations develop expressing and defending thinking (SL.1, SL.3, SL.4). Follow-up writing provides practice in using text-based evidence in supporting arguments (W.1), summarizing and explaining (W.2), and drawing evidence from texts for analysis and reflection (W.9). Vocabulary development includes determining and clarifying key vocabulary (L.4) and attention to word relationships (L.5).

References

National Governors Association Center for Best Practices & Council of Chief State School Officers. (2010). *Common Core State Standards for English language arts and literacy in history/social studies, science, and technical subjects.* Washington, DC: Authors.

Wilhelm, J.D. (2007). *Engaging readers and writers with inquiry: Promoting deep understandings in language arts and the content areas with guiding questions.* New York: Scholastic.

Suggested Reading

Manzo, A.V. (1969). The ReQuest procedure. *Journal of Reading, 13*(2), 123–126.

Vocabulary Overview Guide

The vagaries of Andrew's life before he returned to Oregon and joined the family business are rarely mentioned these days.

Vagaries? Can you recollect seeing this word before? Could you offer a hunch as to its meaning? Would you feel confident using this word in your speaking and writing? For many people, a word such as *vagaries* lies on the periphery of their vocabulary. The word may be somewhat familiar, perhaps encountered infrequently during reading, but most people have never had the urge to look it up in a dictionary.

Instead, they develop an increasingly meaningful concept of this word through context. Initially, proficient readers would look at the word for possible etymological connections: Does *vagary* fit with *vague*, or is *vagrant* a better match? How about *vagabond?* Then, they would track subsequent sightings of *vagary* and begin to construct a working definition based on its appearance in multiple contexts, such as "The vagaries of government policy toward the homeless..." or "The vagaries of his jokes until they hit the punch line...." Eventually, readers would refine their understandings that *vagary* refers to aimless and unpredictable wandering or actions.

As teachers, we know that vocabulary development is a critical component of reading comprehension and is highly emphasized throughout the Common Core's literacy standards. But many of the activities we use with students to improve their vocabularies are not as successful as they need to be. Students who are given lists of words to look up and study admit that they forget most of them once the test is over. Instead, vocabulary study that is embedded in discussions of complex texts is particularly valuable.

Using the Strategy

A Vocabulary Overview Guide (Carr, 1985) is a graphic organizer that includes a meaningful clue in addition to rich contextual information. This strategy conditions students to be sensitive to Tier 2 words (encountered predominantly in written texts and infrequently in spoken language) and Tier 3 words (used to communicate key concepts in specific academic disciplines) as they read (see the Student-Friendly Vocabulary Explanations strategy pages). The strategy also provides a system for studying words so students can retain their meanings over time.

1 Select vocabulary words from material that students are reading in class, and be sure to select words that are connected to key themes or ideas in the text. Traditionally, teachers often identify difficult words from a text, ask students to ascertain the meanings of these words, and then quiz them in some fashion, perhaps asking for definitions and demonstrations of usage in sentences. However, Beck, McKeown, and Kucan (2013) caution against this practice. They argue that many students merely copy a simplistic definition from the dictionary without really gaining a solid understanding for the new word.

Therefore, Tier 2 and Tier 3 words that are related to key themes and ideas represent the most meaningful vocabulary to highlight for instruction because they naturally coincide with class activities and discussions about the text selection. As a result, these words become part of the discourse of learning while students explore a complex disciplinary text.

2 Rather than sending students to the dictionary, start with a knowledge rating activity (Blachowicz & Fisher, 2010). Ask students to evaluate their current level of knowledge about each selected word:

K: I know it.

H: I have a hunch about what it means.

S: I've seen it, but I don't know what it means.

N: I've never seen it before today.

Next, display from the selection the actual contexts for each of these target words. Researchers

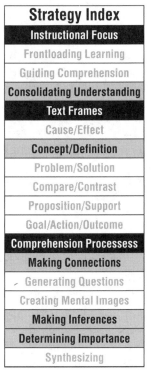

Strategy Index

Instructional Focus
Frontloading Learning
Guiding Comprehension
Consolidating Understanding
Text Frames
Cause/Effect
Concept/Definition
Problem/Solution
Compare/Contrast
Proposition/Support
Goal/Action/Outcome
Comprehension Processess
Making Connections
Generating Questions
Creating Mental Images
Making Inferences
Determining Importance
Synthesizing

argue that relying on context alone is often inadequate because students may misread contextual clues, or the specific context may be open to several varied interpretations of a word's possible meaning. Therefore, to help students react to a word in a variety of contexts, provide multiple instances of the word in action. For example, students in a social studies class might initially see the word *chide* in a newspaper article that says, "Critics chided the government for the slow response to requests for disaster aid." In addition to this contextual example of *chide*, ask students to examine the following additional examples:

- Jeremy was tired of his parents constantly chiding him for the messy state of his room.
- Her friends chided Mandi into apologizing for the rude remark.
- The principal chided the students for their noisy behavior in the hallway.

Ask students to determine the tone of the context: Does it seem to be positive, negative, or neutral? Does *chide* seem like something you would like someone to do to you? Next, ask them to try to substitute a word or phrase that seems to work within the general parameters of the context. For example, what word might critics use to tell the government that it was responding too slowly to disaster aid requests? How about *criticize, condemn, blame,* or *scold*? Which word fits best in all contexts? As students explore each context, they will realize that although all their guesses might work with the first context, the subsequent sentences cause them to narrow and refine their working definitions and come up with the closest synonym: *scold*—to goad someone into action. They develop a much richer and more complex understanding of a useful word than if they had merely attempted to memorize a possibly obscure dictionary definition.

3 Students read the selection, again paying special attention to the broader contexts of the target words, as well as other unfamiliar words they encounter.

4 Now that students have taken stock of their own level of knowledge of the target words and have been provided with further information about each word with examples of usage, ask them to begin to explain each word in terms of what they know or think they might know. Emphasize that you are not seeking a tidy definition but instead an articulation of useful associations and various facets of a word's meaning (see the Student-Friendly Vocabulary Explanations strategy pages). In these discussions, encourage students to verbalize hunches they had about the words and how these hunches were confirmed, or not confirmed, by

the contextual information. What contexts do they associate with these words?

Distribute Vocabulary Overview Guides (reproducible available in the Appendix) to students as a strategy for recording their developing understandings of these words. For example, target words in the classic Shirley Jackson short story "Charles" might include *insolently, swagger, reformation, warily, incredulously,* and *haggard*. Discuss with students the main topic or theme of the selection and note how the words selected connect to this topic or theme. Students enter these target words on the guide (see the Vocabulary Overview Guide for "Charles").

Encourage students to develop a strong association between new words and mnemonic clues that trigger a sense of the words' meanings. These clues help link new words to background knowledge. For example, students may decide that *insolently* means acting in a way that one would find insulting. *Insult* becomes their meaningful clue for remembering this word. Likewise, *beware* reminds students of their meaning for *wary*—to be very cautious about something. Encourage students to personalize their clues because a clue that works for one student may not connect for another. For example, some students might connect *swagger* to the way a particular actor walks in a movie, but students who have not seen this movie will need a different clue to remember *swagger*. As students study new words with their Vocabulary Overview Guides, ask them to cover the explanations to see if their clues are sufficient to help them recall the words' meanings.

5 Embed these target words in classroom activities and purposefully interject them into ongoing discussions of the text so students are hearing them as well as reading them (Beck, McKeown, & Kucan, 2008). Provide students with multiple opportunities to test-drive these Tier 2 words as they talk and write about the book, story, or selection. In particular, include the words in assessments, not as separate vocabulary items but for students to demonstrate word knowledge by using the words to discuss their understandings: "Describe why the word *insolently* would be a good way to describe the way the main character acts in his kindergarten classroom. What would be some examples of his insolence?"

6 Gradually move students toward accepting more responsibility for selecting and explaining words they deem important in a reading. Transition to assigning these tasks in small groups or with student pairs. Finally, have individual students construct their own Vocabulary Overview Guides based on a reading assignment.

Vocabulary Overview Guide for "Charles"[a]

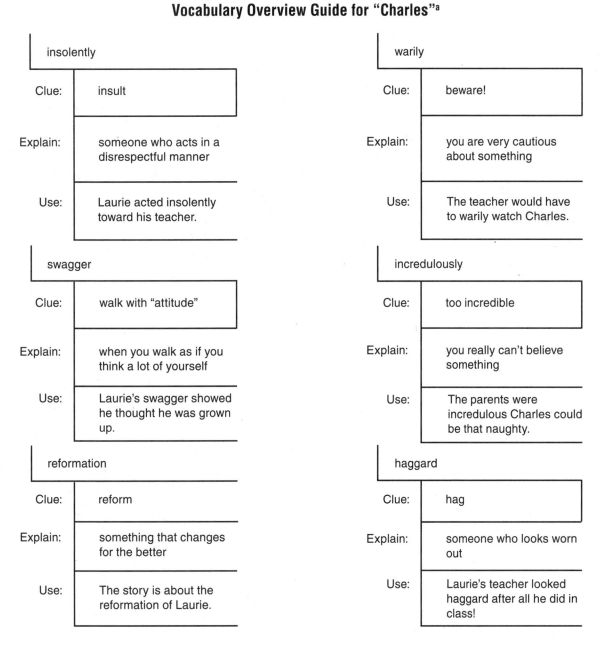

insolently

Clue:	insult
Explain:	someone who acts in a disrespectful manner
Use:	Laurie acted insolently toward his teacher.

swagger

Clue:	walk with "attitude"
Explain:	when you walk as if you think a lot of yourself
Use:	Laurie's swagger showed he thought he was grown up.

reformation

Clue:	reform
Explain:	something that changes for the better
Use:	The story is about the reformation of Laurie.

warily

Clue:	beware!
Explain:	you are very cautious about something
Use:	The teacher would have to warily watch Charles.

incredulously

Clue:	too incredible
Explain:	you really can't believe something
Use:	The parents were incredulous Charles could be that naughty.

haggard

Clue:	hag
Explain:	someone who looks worn out
Use:	Laurie's teacher looked haggard after all he did in class!

Note. From *Classroom Strategies for Interactive Learning* (p. 185), by D. Buehl, 2009, Newark, DE: International Reading Association. Copyright © 2009 by the International Reading Association.
[a]Jackson, S. (1990). *Charles.* Logan, IA: Perfection Learning.

Advantages

- Students come to regard vocabulary learning as more than looking up definitions in a dictionary because they develop ownership of new words that they encounter and use.
- Students have the opportunity to incrementally build their knowledge of new words as they connect to ideas in their reading and practice using them in their speaking and writing.

- Students are provided with a well-organized structure for keeping track of and studying important words.
- Students approach vocabulary learning thoughtfully and come to realize that word knowledge is gained gradually, through repeated exposures and uses in a variety of contexts.
- Students are more motivated to learn words that they have personally selected from a reading.

Meets the Standards

The Vocabulary Overview Guide strategy promotes careful reading and rereading of an author's message (R.1), discerning main ideas (R.2), examining interrelationships of details or ideas (R.3), interpreting word meaning (R.4), integrating ideas into visual representations (R.7), comparing and contrasting with other sources of knowledge (R.9), and mentoring the reading of complex literary and informational texts (R.10). In addition, collaborative conversations develop expressing and defending thinking using visual displays (SL.1, SL.2, SL.4). Writing elements provide practice in using text-based evidence in summarizing and explaining (W.2) and drawing evidence from texts for analysis and reflection (W.9). Vocabulary development includes determining and clarifying key vocabulary (L.4), attention to word relationships (L.5), and acquiring domain-specific vocabulary (L.6).

References

Beck, I.L., McKeown, M.G., & Kucan, L. (2008). *Creating robust vocabulary: Frequently asked questions and extended examples*. New York: Guilford.

Beck, I.L., McKeown, M.G., & Kucan, L. (2013). *Bringing words to life: Robust vocabulary instruction* (2nd ed.). New York: Guilford.

Blachowicz, C., & Fisher, P.J. (2010). *Teaching vocabulary in all classrooms* (4th ed.). Boston: Pearson.

Carr, E.M. (1985). The vocabulary overview guide: A metacognitive strategy to improve vocabulary comprehension and retention. *Journal of Reading, 28*(8), 684–689.

Literature Cited

Jackson, S. (1990). *Charles*. Logan, IA: Perfection Learning.

Word Family Trees

Can you guess this word? It once referred to a scrap of food given to someone less fortunate. Initially a Latin term, the word was later adopted by the French in medieval times to signify a lump of bread or other leavings of a meal provided to a beggar. The English expanded the word's usage from a gift begged to a present. Along the way, the word has taken on a decidedly negative connotation. The modern meaning is to offer a gift, sometimes substantial, to influence someone's behavior.

What is the word? *Bribe*. What an interesting etymological journey—from a small gesture of generosity to a calculating act of corruption. One can almost speculate the circumstances that led the word *bribe* to be associated today with a different type of beggar.

Clearly, a word such as *bribe* has a deep and involved meaning. We understand the word far beyond any terse dictionary definition. All sorts of connections may come to mind: a parent who offers a child candy to quell a tantrum, a favor from a sibling for keeping quiet about a family rule infraction, a payment made to a decision maker to influence the awarding of a contract, or a campaign contribution handed to a politician to further a group's political (or financial) agenda. *Bribe* is a rich concept with many layers of meaning; it is not a mere vocabulary word.

Students, however, often view vocabulary learning in a very narrow sense. They look up a new word in a dictionary, perhaps obtaining only a foggy notion of its meaning or grasping quickly at a possible synonym. If they must master the word for a vocabulary quiz, they memorize it as an act of short-term learning, forgetting it soon afterward and never incorporating it into their speaking and writing. Students often attempt to learn vocabulary words as facts (definitions) rather than concepts. Encouraging students to be word browsers, to become playfully engaged with new vocabulary, can help reinforce that true vocabulary acquisition involves more than quick trips to a dictionary.

Using the Strategy

The Word Family Tree (Buehl, 1999) is strategy that involves students in connecting a key term to its origins, to related words that share a common root, to words that serve a similar function, and to situations in which one might expect the word to be used.

1 Introduce the Word Family Tree graphic organizer (reproducible available in the Appendix) as a means of vocabulary study. As an analogy, refer to genealogical family trees to prepare students for this activity. Family trees list an individual's ancestors, direct descendants, and other relatives, such as cousins, aunts, and uncles, whereas the Word Family Tree lists the relatives of a word.

2 Teaching vocabulary strategies that help students detect meaningful word parts is referred to as generative vocabulary instruction; students become skilled in generating possible meanings of a string of new words based on their knowledge of roots and affixes. Start with the basic premise that if you learn one word, you actually learn 10 (Templeton, Johnston, Bear, & Invernizzi, 2010). When students learn the word *convert*, they have in effect also learned *converts, converted, converting, converter, converters,* and *unconverted,* a natural by-product of encountering these forms of the word while reading. However, other, less familiar forms may be overlooked by students and should also be displayed when they are learning a useful base word like *convert: convertible, convertibility, convertibleness, inconvertible, inconvertibility, unconvertible, reconvert, reconvertible.* If the teacher does not intentionally include these words in conversations about *convert,* then many students will not notice the relationship to a word they have come to know. As a result, students are more likely to skip the word as too hard when they encounter *reconvert* in a text, even though they have constructed sufficient knowledge about the base word *convert* to successfully hypothesize a probable meaning. (Online resources such as OneLook are invaluable for this stage: www.onelook.com.)

As students examine the variations of how *convert* might appear in a larger word, ask them to apply their knowledge of suffixes and prefixes to speculate on possible meanings of these more sophisticated forms. In addition, use the opportunity to teach the root in the base word—in this case, *vert*, which means to turn. So, if *convert* means to turn something into something else, then *convertible* can be explained as something that is capable of being turned into something else.

3 Model using the Word Family Tree by using an important term from a disciplinary text. For example, *dominion* is a Tier 3 word encountered by students in a history text (see the Student-Friendly Vocabulary Explanations strategy pages for more discussion on tiered words). Show how the word is linked to a meaningful root to help them gain insight on likely contexts where the new word might appear (see the Word Family Tree for *Dominion*).

Word Family Tree for *Dominion*

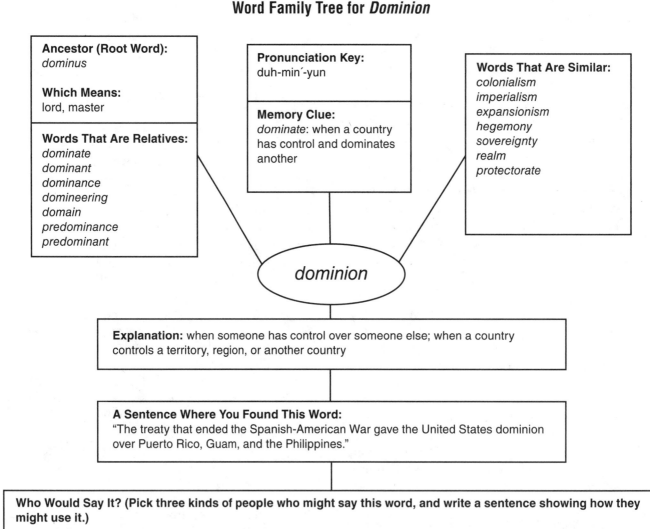

Ancestor (Root Word):
dominus

Which Means:
lord, master

Words That Are Relatives:
dominate
dominant
dominance
domineering
domain
predominance
predominant

Pronunciation Key:
duh-min´-yun

Memory Clue:
dominate: when a country has control and dominates another

Words That Are Similar:
colonialism
imperialism
expansionism
hegemony
sovereignty
realm
protectorate

dominion

Explanation: when someone has control over someone else; when a country controls a territory, region, or another country

A Sentence Where You Found This Word:
"The treaty that ended the Spanish-American War gave the United States dominion over Puerto Rico, Guam, and the Philippines."

Who Would Say It? (Pick three kinds of people who might say this word, and write a sentence showing how they might use it.)

a king	a native leader	an imperialist politician
As king, I have dominion over all the people in my country; all of my subjects must submit to my rule.	We must not allow another country to have dominion over us; we must fight to preserve our freedom!	For our country to thrive and be a great nation, we must expand our dominion over regions that are rich in the natural resources we need for our industries.

4 Select a group of target Tier 2 and Tier 3 words for students to investigate. These could be pivotal words in a short story, key terms in a unit of study, or generally useful academic vocabulary words. For example, key terms in a biology unit might include *genetics, mutation, recessive, inherited,* and *dominant.* Although students will encounter other biological terminology, selected words should represent essential concepts to be learned. The history passage that included *dominion* might also feature words such as *imperialism, exploitation, diplomacy, treaty,* and *colonialism.* Have students work with partners or in collaborative groups to complete Word Family Trees for target words, using appropriate resources such as textbooks, a thesaurus, a dictionary, online vocabulary sites, or other vocabulary-rich sources. Part of the activity involves brainstorming to determine what kinds of people might be heard using the word, and devising possible sentences for those contexts. Ask students to brainstorm possible mnemonic clues to help them remember the meaning of each word. In the biology example, students investigating the Word Family Tree for *genetics* may uncover a rich array of relatives all derived from the same origin: *gene, genealogy, gender, genius,* and *generate.*

Allow time for students to share their Word Family Trees with classmates to discover other related words, possible synonyms, and useful contexts where the word might make an appearance. For example, a music teacher may ask, "Can you remember the difference between a sonata and a concerto?" The word *concerto* is derived from the same Latin root *concertare* (to organize or arrange) as in *concert* (to act together, to work in harmony): "It will take the concerted effort of our entire community to revitalize the downtown area." "A *concerto* is a composition that requires the soloist(s) to work together with a symphony orchestra to produce music." Students creating a family tree for *sonata* will discover that the ancestor is the root *sonare*—to sound. Close relatives that share this origin are *sound, sonar, sonic, sonnet,* and *sonorous.* Similar words include *solo* and *recital.*

5 Next, take frequent opportunities to model vocabulary problem solving using knowledge of a key base word and its root. Here is another example of a potentially difficult word for students: "The negotiations finally were called to a halt because both sides proved to be <u>intractable</u>." (Templeton et al., 2010) recommend modeling a four-step analysis procedure for tackling new words like *intractable*:

- First, ask yourself if there are any prefixes or suffixes (parts added to the beginnings and ends of words). If you find some, take them off (erase *in* and *able*).

- Second, notice what is left. In this case, the long word is built around the root *tract.* Ask yourself what you know about this base word or root. Where have you seen it before?

- Third, think of a familiar keyword that contains that word part: *tract.* How about *tractor?* You know that a tractor is a machine that pulls things.

- Fourth, put the affixes back on—the suffix and the prefix. Develop your hunch about the word's meaning and see if the sentence makes sense. Sometimes, you may need to study more than just the sentence; you may need to read the entire paragraph or think about the topic or main idea of the whole passage. In this case, *intractable* seems to be a word that has something to do with not being pulled, which makes sense because the negotiations were stopped, so it seems that neither side could be pulled into an agreement.

As an integral component of generative vocabulary instruction, be constantly on the lookout for meaningful keywords, already known to students, to be used as automatic problem-solving prompts. For example, notice how the meaningful keyword *fracture* (to break) can be used as a tool to problem solve these more sophisticated forms: *fractionate, fractious, refraction, fracas,* and *infraction.* Notice that Tier 3 words with meaningful parts appear as key vocabulary in a wide variety of subject areas. *Fractionate* (as in a country *fractionating*) may surface in social studies texts. *Refraction* is a science concept, *fraction* a math concept, and *infraction* a physical education concept, and *fractious* could be employed to describe a character in a short story or novel. It is therefore incumbent on all teachers to take advantage of the daily opportunities for generative vocabulary instruction in their curriculum.

Advantages

- Students develop a thorough understanding of important vocabulary.

- Students come to see the organic nature of vocabulary, as word meanings have grown and changed over the years.

- Students begin to identify useful word roots and notice connections among words derived from similar origins.

- Students are more likely to remember new words and feel confident in using them when they write and talk.

- Students are encouraged to raise questions of their own about possible word backgrounds and to consult sources other than abridged dictionaries to enrich their vocabulary understandings.

Meets the Standards

The Word Family Trees strategy promotes interpreting word meaning (R.4), integrating ideas into visual representations (R.7), comparing and contrasting with other sources of knowledge (R.9), and mentoring the reading of complex literary and informational texts (R.10). In addition, the collaborative conversations develop expressing and defending thinking using visual displays (SL.1, SL.2, SL.4). Writing elements provide practice in summarizing and explaining (W.2) and drawing evidence from texts for analysis and reflection (W.9). Vocabulary development includes determining and clarifying key vocabulary (L.4), attention to word relationships (L.5), and acquiring domain-specific vocabulary (L.6).

References

Buehl, D. (1999). Word family trees: Heritage sheds insight into words' meaning and use. *WEAC News & Views, 35*(2), 14.

Templeton, S., Johnston, F.R., Bear, D.R., & Invernizzi, M.R. (2010). *Vocabulary their way: Word study with middle and secondary students*. Boston: Pearson.

Written Conversations

r u k? sry 4gt 2 cal u lst nyt

Can you decipher this message? Chances are, if you are a devoted texter, this is a quick read, which mandates an instant reply: "im gr8."

The Digital Age has updated the age-old practice of passing notes by combining modern equivalents of telegraphic brevity with a desire for immediate response, as demonstrated with our opening modern dialogue, "Are you okay? I'm sorry, I forgot to call you last night," and the reply, "I'm great." Computerized communication forms, such as text messaging, e-mail, chat rooms, blogging, and Twitter, have made it easier to carry on a written conversation over a distance, whether it is across a classroom or across continents. Classroom activities that capitalize on students' desire to talk to one another represent promising strategies for focused discussions around reading assignments. Daniels, Zemelman, and Steineke (2007) suggest planning written conversations, which engage students in shared writing with their classmates to pursue their thinking about classroom texts.

Written Conversations is a variation of dialogue journaling and can be used with fiction or informational texts. Unlike class discussions that feature one person talking while the rest of the students wait for a possible turn to add their comments, Written Conversations are silent, ongoing discussions that involve every student as a communicator in the entire process.

Using the Strategy

Written Conversations can be configured in a number of ways, depending on the nature of the material and the course objectives.

1 Students complete their reading of a passage from a textbook, article, chapter, or story. Inform students that they will be participants in a silent conversation about topics and ideas in their reading. Outline the ground rules for a Written Conversation:

• All talking during a Written Conversation must be in writing; no oral communication is permitted. If you want to say something, put it in writing.

• The "no oral communication" rule also applies to transition periods when Written Conversations are passed on to the next student.

• A Written Conversation is a Quick-Write (see the Quick-Writes strategy pages). In other words, the writing format is expected to be generally informal, as if students were chatting about the topic. Students need not be preoccupied with turning out clean, highly edited pieces. However, writing fluency practice is prized, so text-message shorthand is also not intended here. Students' writing needs to be readable as they quickly jot down what they are thinking. The rule is "just write!"

• A written entry must be focused on the task and the text; students are expected to avoid going off topic in their responses.

• All responses need to respect the comments and ideas of conversational partners. However, disagreeing with a viewpoint is a natural dynamic in many conversations, and students are encouraged to respectfully disagree and offer their own interpretations.

• Students are expected to fill their allotted writing time. When students inquire, "How much am I supposed to write?" underscore the expectation that they will write as much as they can until told to pass the paper. At this juncture, a conversation is forwarded to the next student, and the process continues.

• Finally, students' writing is personal. They are writing to their partners or classmates and are responding to what their fellow students are thinking, as well as offering their own comments.

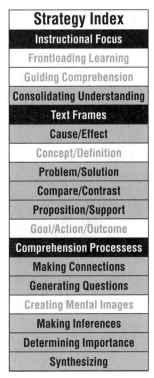

Strategy Index
Instructional Focus
Frontloading Learning
Guiding Comprehension
Consolidating Understanding
Text Frames
Cause/Effect
Concept/Definition
Problem/Solution
Compare/Contrast
Proposition/Support
Goal/Action/Outcome
Comprehension Processess
Making Connections
Generating Questions
Creating Mental Images
Making Inferences
Determining Importance
Synthesizing

2 Decide on an organization for the Written Conversation. For example, students can be assigned a partner, and their conversation will represent thoughts that pass back and forth between the two of them. Or students can work in groups of five and pass the paper to the left each time, until the conversation they started returns to them.

In addition, the format of the conversation can vary. Each student can begin by writing the initial entry on a sheet of paper or on a page in their class journals. These papers are then swapped, and partners write their thoughts in response to these first entries. The papers move back and forth for continued conversation. Another method is to use large sticky notes affixed to the text that students are responding to. One partner may be using yellow notes, and the other green. The text with the sticky-note comments is then passed between partners.

3 Provide a focus for the Written Conversation. Of course, students can be instructed to write about anything in the text that they want to talk about, but many will benefit from a prompt that offers some specific directions for targeting their thinking.

Possible writing prompts for literary fiction include the following:

- I made a connection to...
- I know the feeling...
- I love the way...
- I don't really understand...
- I can't believe...
- I realized that...
- I wonder why...
- I noticed that...
- I was surprised...
- I think...
- If I were...
- I'm not sure...

Possible writing prompts for informational texts include the following:

- I learned that...
- I was surprised to learn that...
- I already knew that...
- I was wrong to think...
- I wonder why...
- I still don't know...
- I found it interesting that...
- I thought it was especially important...
- I would tell someone...

- I found it confusing when...
- This helped me explain...

4 Decide on an appropriate amount of time for each individual written entry. A range of one to three minutes per round will provide students with just enough time to record some of their thoughts before passing the conversation on. Then, start the Written Conversations. Emphasize that these are simultaneous responses; all students are writing. When the allotted writing time has expired, say, "Pass." Provide students with a brief period to read their partner's response. Then, say, "Start," to cue students to comment on their partner's thoughts.

With partners, allow three or four exchanges, pausing each time to grant some reading time before continuing with the Written Conversation. With the Write Around variation, which expands the conversation to groups of five, every student responds to ideas initiated by four classmates. The fifth exchange lands the conversation back where it started, so the final entry features feedback from four classmates and allows each initiating student to write the final word on that series of comments.

5 After students have gone through all the exchanges, end the conversation on an oral note: "What would you like to talk about now with your partner or group?" For the first time, students can converse out loud about their thinking. You will likely notice that many of your students are eager to elaborate on their written thoughts and to follow up on some of their comments. Finally, ask partners to share some of their conversation with the entire class, and use this invitation to start a large-group discussion about the topic and ideas from the text.

Advantages

- Written Conversations provides students with valuable practice in verbalizing their thoughts about written texts.
- Students have an opportunity to comment on, question, and summarize what they are reading and learning.
- Students can listen in on the thinking of their classmates and add their own take on the material.
- Students are afforded a way to socialize as they learn, interacting with their peers as they discuss their reading.
- As technology becomes available to all students in the classroom, Written Conversations can be undertaken as electronic interchanges, both during class time and at home.

Meets the Standards

The Written Conversations strategy promotes careful reading and rereading of an author's message (R.1), discerning main ideas and summarizing (R.2), examining interrelationships of details or ideas (R.3), tracking the author's perspective and purpose (R.6), supporting argumentation (R.8), comparing and contrasting with other sources of knowledge (R.9), and mentoring the reading of complex literary and informational texts (R.10). In addition, the continuation of the conversations as group and whole-class discussions develops expressing and defending thinking (SL.1, SL.3, SL.4). Writing prompts can provide practice in using text-based evidence in supporting arguments (W.1), summarizing and explaining (W.2), drawing evidence from texts for analysis and reflection (W.9), and developing writing fluency (W.10). Vocabulary development includes attention to word relationships (L.5) and acquiring domain-specific vocabulary (L.6).

Reference

Daniels, H., Zemelman, S., & Steineke, N. (2007). *Content-area writing: Every teacher's guide*. Portsmouth, NH: Heinemann.

Reproducibles

The reproducibles are listed by the chapter or strategy pages where they are discussed in the book.

Fact Pyramid

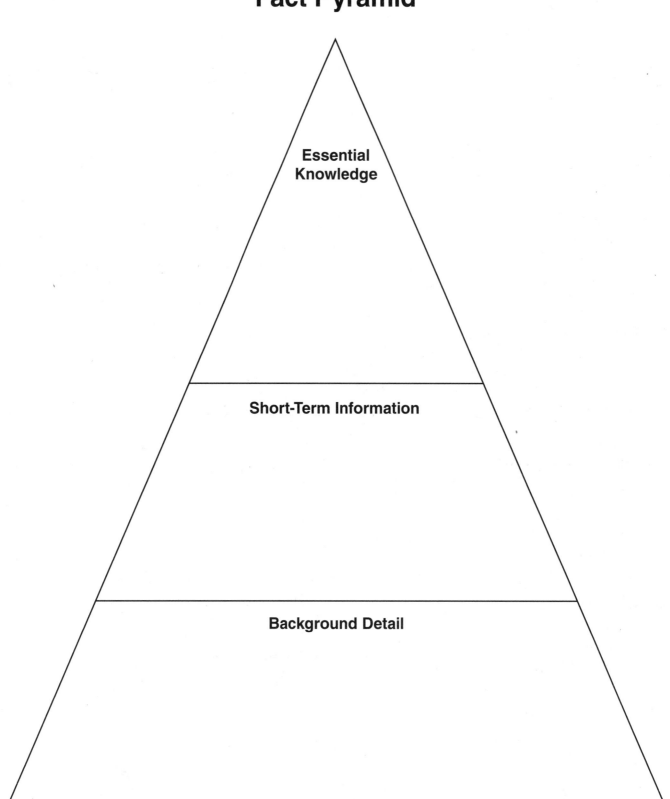

Note. Adapted from "Fact Pyramids," by D. Buehl, 1991, *New Perspectives: Reading Across the Curriculum, 7*(6), p. 2. Copyright © 1991 by Doug Buehl.

Analogy Chart

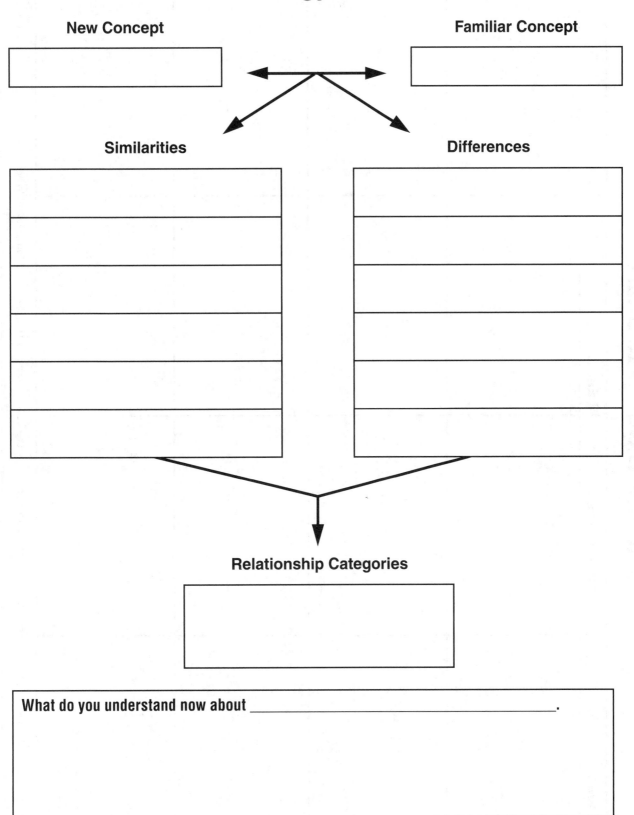

New Concept

Familiar Concept

Similarities

Differences

Relationship Categories

What do you understand now about _____.

Note. Adapted from "Analogy Graphic Organizer," by D. Buehl and D. Hein, 1990, *The Exchange*, *3*(2), p. 6. Copyright © 1990 by the International Reading Association.

Author Says/I Say Chart

I Wonder...	The Author Says...	I Say...	And So...

B/D/A Questioning Chart

What questions helped you work your understanding?

Before Reading	During Reading	After Reading

What do you understand now that you didn't understand before?

Alphabet Brainstorming Chart

A	B	C	D	E	F	G

H	I	J	K	L	M	N

O	P	Q	R	S	T	U

V	W	X	Y	Z		

Note. Adapted from *The Key to Know "PAINE" Know Gain,* by G. Ricci and C. Wahlgren, May 1998, paper presented at the 43rd annual convention of the International Reading Association, Orlando, FL.

Classroom Strategies for Interactive Learning (4th ed.) by Doug Buehl. Copyright © 2014 by the International Reading Association. May be copied for classroom use.

Reading With Attitude Chart

Quote	Character's Emotion	Author's Emotion	Reader's Emotion

Concept/Definition Map

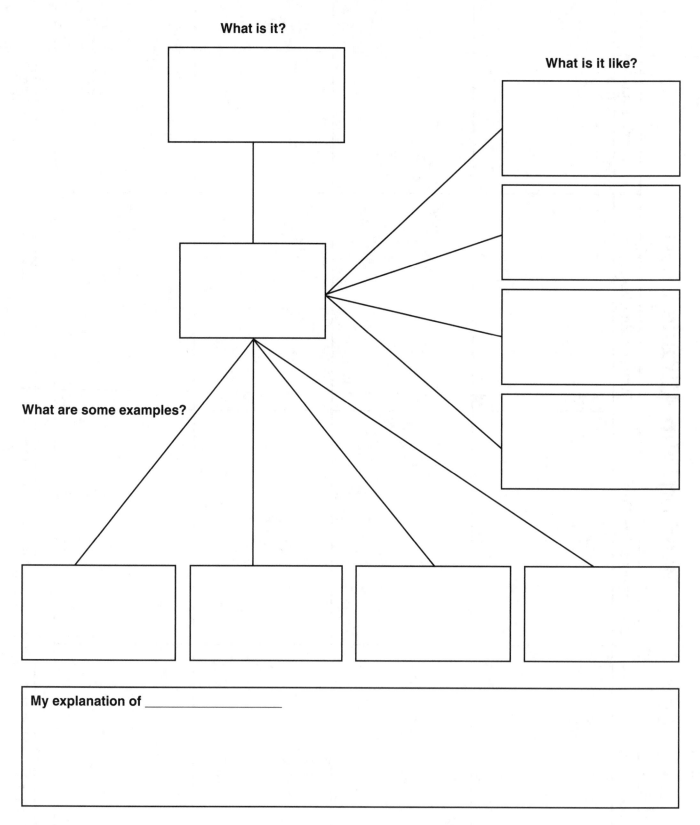

What is it?

What is it like?

What are some examples?

My explanation of _____

Frayer Model

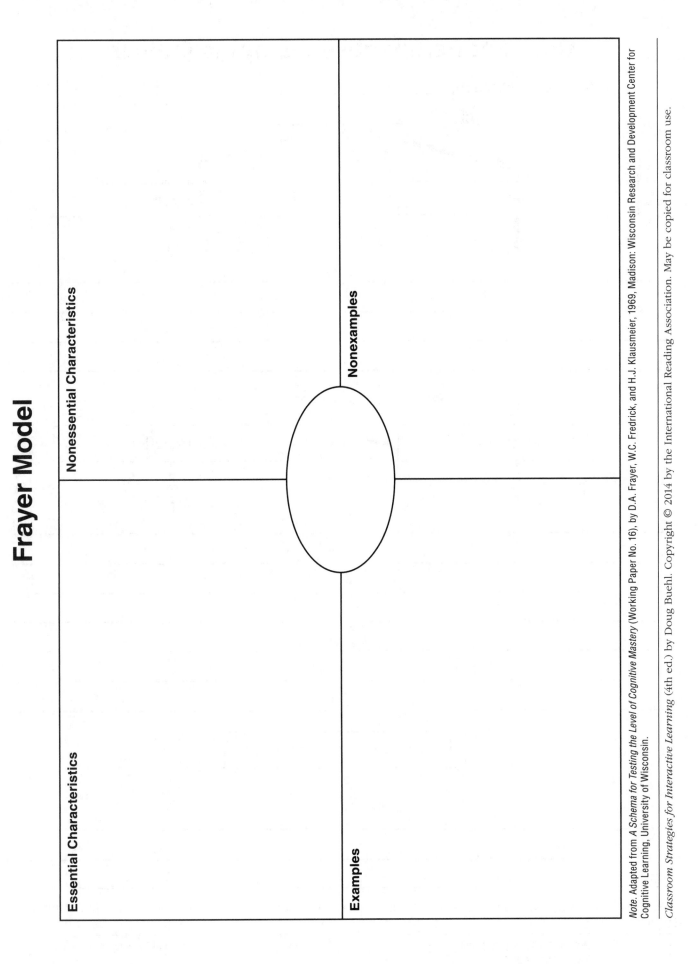

Essential Characteristics

Nonessential Characteristics

Examples

Nonexamples

Note. Adapted from *A Schema for Testing the Level of Cognitive Mastery* (Working Paper No. 16), by D.A. Frayer, W.C. Fredrick, and H.J. Klausmeier, 1969, Madison: Wisconsin Research and Development Center for Cognitive Learning, University of Wisconsin.

Classroom Strategies for Interactive Learning (4th ed.) by Doug Buehl. Copyright © 2014 by the International Reading Association. May be copied for classroom use.

Different Perspectives Graphic Outline

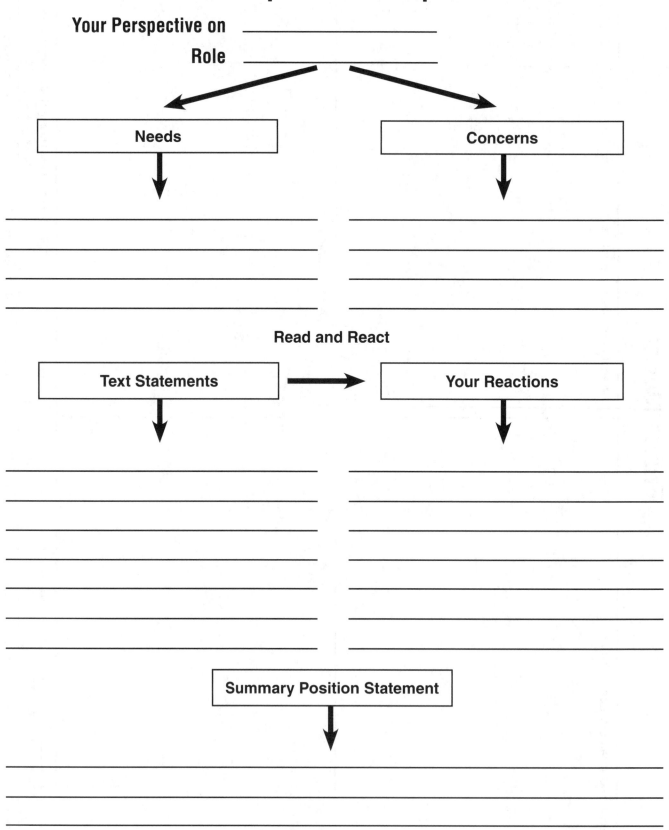

Your Perspective on _____

Role _____

| Needs | Concerns |

_____   _____
_____   _____
_____   _____
_____   _____

Read and React

| Text Statements | → | Your Reactions |

_____   _____
_____   _____
_____   _____
_____   _____
_____   _____
_____   _____

| Summary Position Statement |

_____
_____
_____

Discussion Web

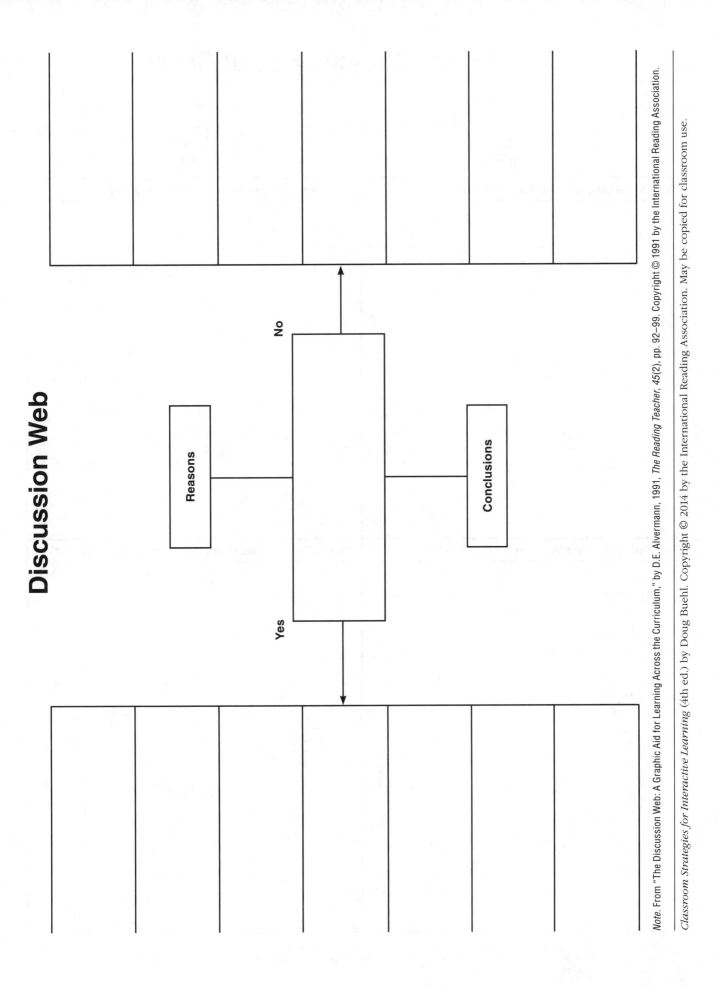

Reasons

No

Yes

Conclusions

Note. From "The Discussion Web: A Graphic Aid for Learning Across the Curriculum," by D.E. Alvermann, 1991, *The Reading Teacher, 45*(2), pp. 92–99. Copyright © 1991 by the International Reading Association.

Classroom Strategies for Interactive Learning (4th ed.) by Doug Buehl. Copyright © 2014 by the International Reading Association. May be copied for classroom use.

Thumbs Up! Thumbs Down! Chart

Topic: _____

Your Ideas/Arguments/Evidence For	Your Ideas/Arguments/Evidence Against
The Author's Ideas/Arguments/Evidence For	**The Author's Ideas/Arguments/Evidence Against**

Eyewitness Testimony Chart

I Was There (and can describe...)	The Author's Words ("The author wrote...")	My Version ("I saw, heard, felt, or experienced...")

First Impressions Chart

The Author's Words		My Impressions
First		
Then		
Finally		

Character Analysis Grid

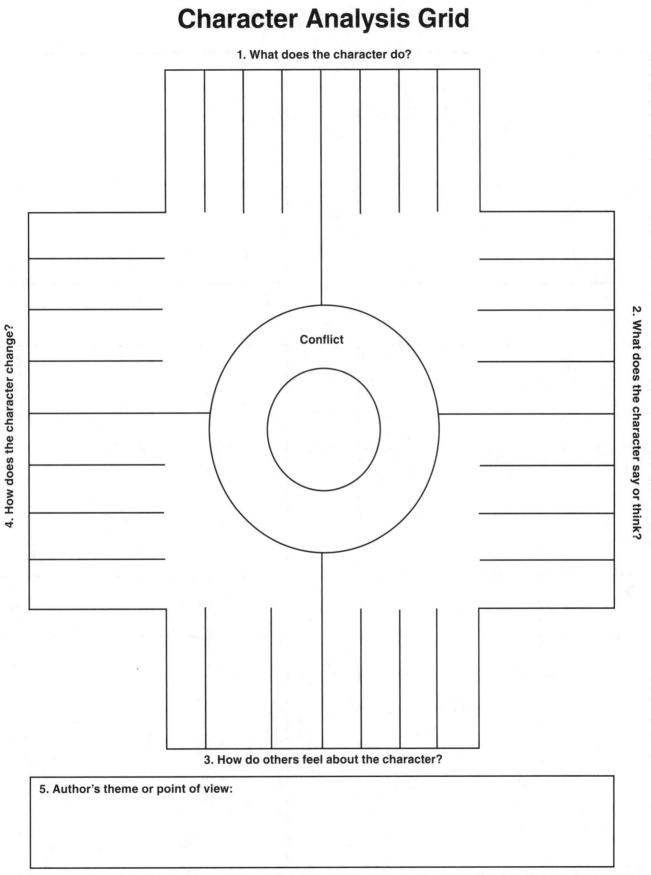

1. What does the character do?

2. What does the character say or think?

3. How do others feel about the character?

4. How does the character change?

Conflict

5. Author's theme or point of view:

DVD Scene Selection

1.

2.

3.

4.

5.

6.

Hands-On Reading Bookmark

Hands-On Reading Bookmark

1. **Size up the task...**
   a. to figure out what you will need to do.
   b. to determine what the final outcome should be.
   c. to inventory items or tools needed for the task.

2. **Clarify vocabulary...**
   a. to review terms you have previously learned.
   b. to identify and explain new terms.

3. **Scan the visuals...**
   a. to compare the illustrations with any physical items you will be using.
   b. to help imagine what you should be doing at each phase.
   c. to identify items or objects you will be handling.

4. **Look out for cautions...**
   a. to avoid common errors.
   b. to avoid harmful or dangerous mistakes.

5. **Read and apply...**
   a. to make sure each sentence makes sense.
   b. to clear up things you don't understand.
   c. to connect the directions to the illustrations.

6. **Collaborate...**
   a. to work out understandings with your partner.
   b. to reread and confirm your understandings.
   c. to complete each step of the task.

Hands-On Reading Bookmark

1. **Size up the task...**
   a. to figure out what you will need to do.
   b. to determine what the final outcome should be.
   c. to inventory items or tools needed for the task.

2. **Clarify vocabulary...**
   a. to review terms you have previously learned.
   b. to identify and explain new terms.

3. **Scan the visuals...**
   a. to compare the illustrations with any physical items you will be using.
   b. to help imagine what you should be doing at each phase.
   c. to identify items or objects you will be handling.

4. **Look out for cautions...**
   a. to avoid common errors.
   b. to avoid harmful or dangerous mistakes.

5. **Read and apply...**
   a. to make sure each sentence makes sense.
   b. to clear up things you don't understand.
   c. to connect the directions to the illustrations.

6. **Collaborate...**
   a. to work out understandings with your partner.
   b. to reread and confirm your understandings.
   c. to complete each step of the task.

History Change Frame

Group	What Problems Did They Face?	What Changes Affected These People?	What Did They Do to Solve Their Problems?

Note. Adapted from "A Frame of Mind for Reading History," by D. Buehl, 1992, *The Exchange, 5*(1), p. 5. Copyright © 1992 by Doug Buehl.

History Memory Bubbles

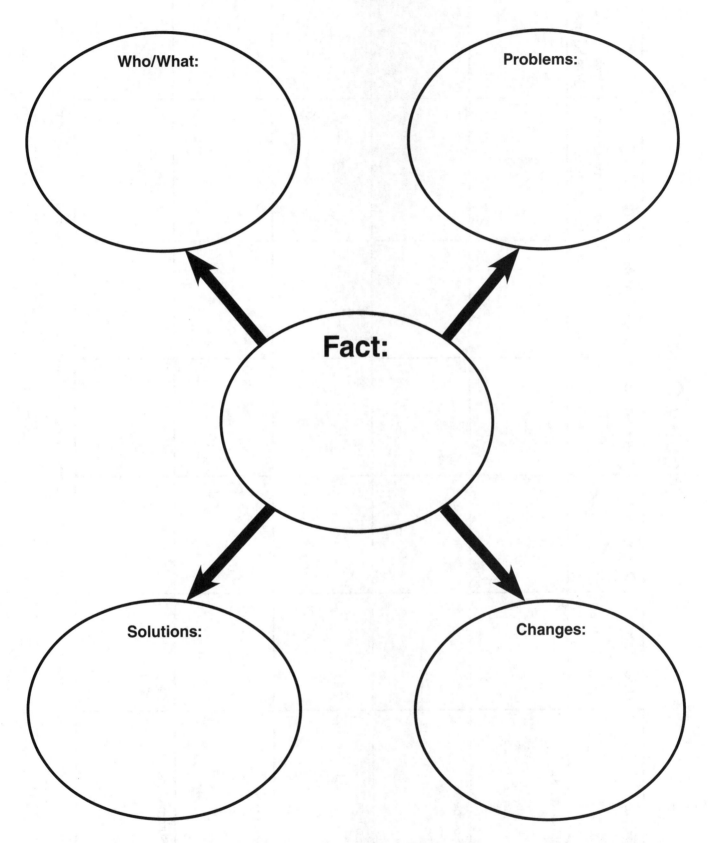

Who/What:

Problems:

Fact:

Solutions:

Changes:

Inquiry Chart

Topic:	Question 1:	Question 2:	Question 3:	Question 4:	Other Important Information	New Questions
What We Know						
Source 1:						
Source 2:						
Source 3:						
Summaries						

Note. Adapted from "Critical Reading/Thinking Across the Curriculum: Using I-Charts to Support Learning," by J.V. Hoffman, 1992, *Language Arts, 69*(2), pp. 121–127. Copyright © 1992 by the National Council of Teachers of English.

Knowledge/Question/Response Chart

Knowledge	Question	Response

Note. Adapted from *Strategies That Work: Teaching Comprehension for Understanding and Engagement* (2nd ed.), by S. Harvey and A. Goudvis, 2007, Portland, ME: Stenhouse. Copyright © 2007 by Stenhouse.

Confirming to Extending Grid

Confirming	Revising

Inquiring	Resolving

Extending

Math Reading Keys Bookmark

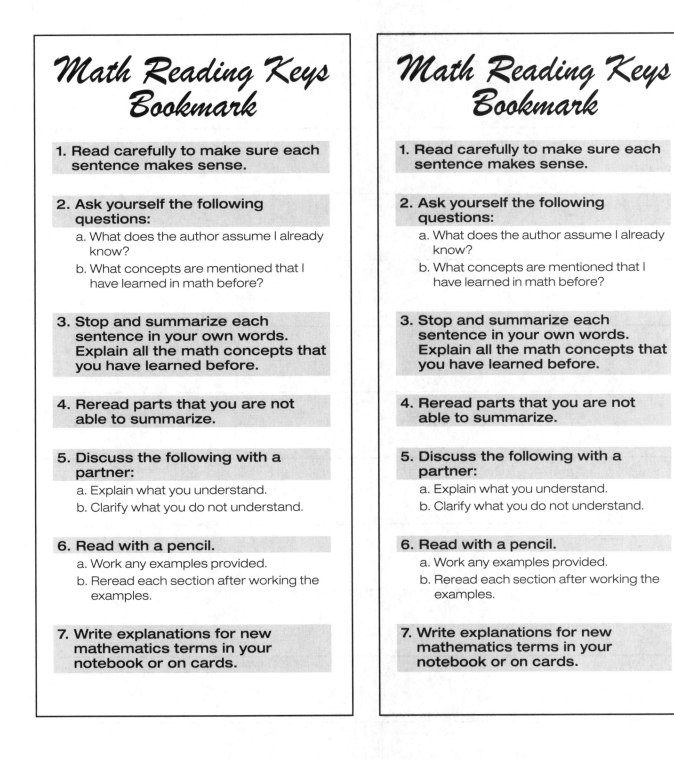

Math Reading Keys Bookmark

1. **Read carefully to make sure each sentence makes sense.**

2. **Ask yourself the following questions:**
   a. What does the author assume I already know?
   b. What concepts are mentioned that I have learned in math before?

3. **Stop and summarize each sentence in your own words. Explain all the math concepts that you have learned before.**

4. **Reread parts that you are not able to summarize.**

5. **Discuss the following with a partner:**
   a. Explain what you understand.
   b. Clarify what you do not understand.

6. **Read with a pencil.**
   a. Work any examples provided.
   b. Reread each section after working the examples.

7. **Write explanations for new mathematics terms in your notebook or on cards.**

Math Reading Keys Bookmark

1. **Read carefully to make sure each sentence makes sense.**

2. **Ask yourself the following questions:**
   a. What does the author assume I already know?
   b. What concepts are mentioned that I have learned in math before?

3. **Stop and summarize each sentence in your own words. Explain all the math concepts that you have learned before.**

4. **Reread parts that you are not able to summarize.**

5. **Discuss the following with a partner:**
   a. Explain what you understand.
   b. Clarify what you do not understand.

6. **Read with a pencil.**
   a. Work any examples provided.
   b. Reread each section after working the examples.

7. **Write explanations for new mathematics terms in your notebook or on cards.**

Note. Adapted from "Making Math Make Sense: Tactics Help Kids Understand Math Language," by D. Buehl, 1998, *WEAC News & Views, 34*(3), p. 17. Copyright © 1998 by Doug Buehl.

Review/New Chart

Review	New

Note. Developed from a strategy by Rita Crotty, Hempstead High School, Dubuque, IA.

Questioning the Author Bookmark

Questioning the Author Bookmark

- What is the author telling you?

- What does the author assume you already know?

- Why is the author telling you this?

- What is the point of the author's message?

- What does the author want you to understand?

- What does the author apparently think is most important?

- How does the author signal what is most important?

- How does this follow with what the author has told you before?

- How does what the author tells you connect with your previous knowledge or experience?

- What does the author say that you need to clarify?

- What can you do to clarify what the author says?

- Does the author explain why something is so?

Questioning the Author Bookmark

- What is the author telling you?

- What does the author assume you already know?

- Why is the author telling you this?

- What is the point of the author's message?

- What does the author want you to understand?

- What does the author apparently think is most important?

- How does the author signal what is most important?

- How does this follow with what the author has told you before?

- How does what the author tells you connect with your previous knowledge or experience?

- What does the author say that you need to clarify?

- What can you do to clarify what the author says?

- Does the author explain why something is so?

Note. Adapted from *Questioning the Author: An Approach for Enhancing Student Engagement With Text*, by I.L. Beck, M.G. McKeown, R.L. Hamilton, and L. Kucan, 1997, Newark, DE: International Reading Association. Copyright © 1997 by the International Reading Association.

RAFT Role Definition Chart

Personality: Who am I, and what are some aspects of my character?	Attitude: What are my feelings, beliefs, ideas, and/or concerns?	Information: What do I know that I need to share in my writing?

Note. Adapted from *Classroom Strategies for Interactive Learning* (3rd ed., p. 209), by D. Buehl, 2009, Newark, DE: International Reading Association. Copyright © 2009 by the International Reading Association.

Classroom Strategies for Interactive Learning (4th ed.) by Doug Buehl. Copyright © 2014 by the International Reading Association. May be copied for classroom use.

Science Connection Overview

What's familiar?

What topics are covered?

What are you wondering?

What will the author tell you?

Read and explain.

Note. Adapted from "The Connection Overview: A Strategy for Learning in Science," by D. Buehl, 1992, *WSRA Journal, 36*(2), p. 24. Copyright © 1992 by Doug Buehl.

Self-Questioning Chart

Level of Thinking	Focusing Question	Comprehension Statement
Creating	How has the author changed what I understand?	
Evaluating	What perspective or authority does the author bring to what he or she is telling me?	
Analyzing	How is this similar to (or different from) what I've heard or read before?	
Applying	How can I connect what the author is telling me to understand something better?	
Understanding	What does the author want me to understand?	
Remembering	What do I need to remember to make sense of this text?	

Story Map

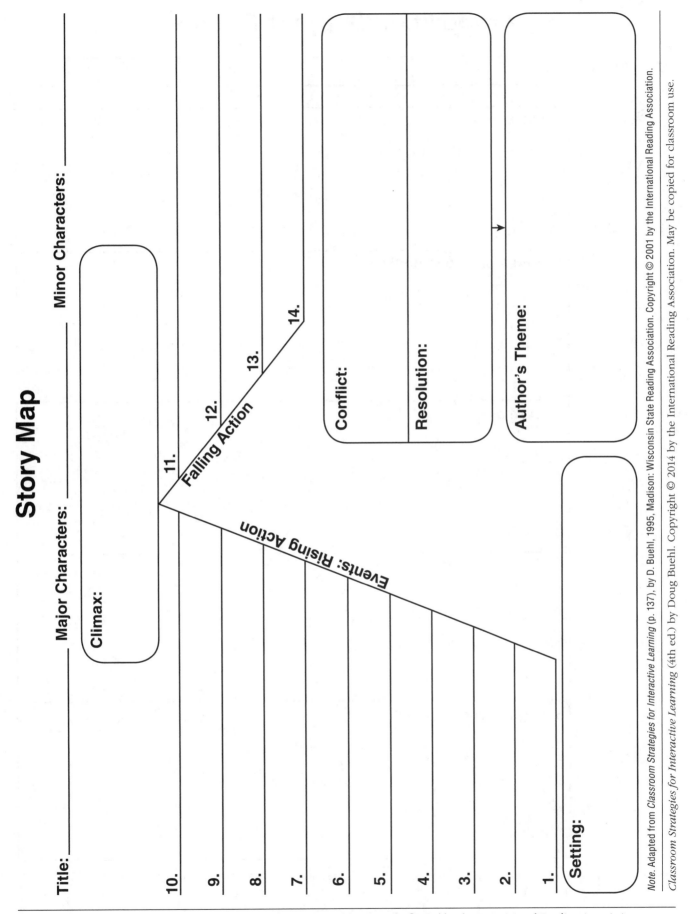

Title: _____

Major Characters: _____

Minor Characters: _____

Climax:

11. 12. 13. 14.

Falling Action

Events: Rising Action

10.
9.
8.
7.
6.
5.
4.
3.
2.
1.

Setting:

Conflict:

Resolution:

Author's Theme:

Proposition/Support Outline

Proposition:

Support:

1. Facts

2. Research and statistics

3. Examples

4. Expert authority

5. Logic and reasoning

Note. Adapted from "Outline Helps Students Analyze Credibility of Author's Premise," by D. Buehl, 1992, *WEAC News & Views, 28*(1), p. 8. Copyright © 1992 by Doug Buehl.

Vocabulary Overview Guide

Clue:

Explain:

Use:

Clue:

Explain:

Use:

Clue:

Explain:

Use:

Clue:

Explain:

Use:

Clue:

Explain:

Use:

Clue:

Explain:

Use:

Note. Adapted from "The Vocabulary Overview Guide: A Metacognitive Strategy to Improve Vocabulary Comprehension and Retention," by E.M. Carr, 1985, *Journal of Reading, 28*(8), pp. 684–689. Copyright © 1985 by the International Reading Association.

Word Family Tree

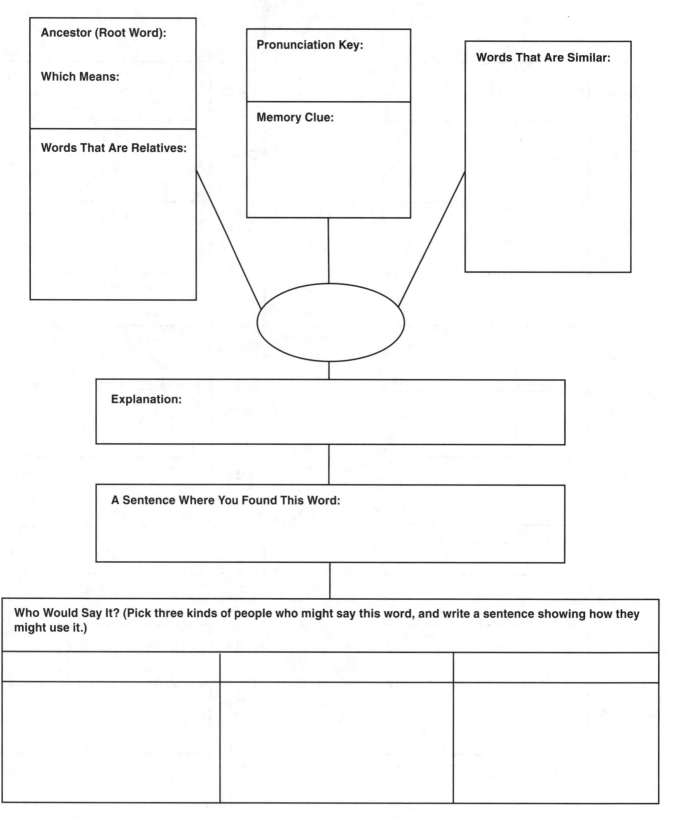